ST. ♥ DRAGON GIRL

VOLUME THREE

 Story & Art by **Natsumi Matsumoto**

ST. ♥ DRAGON GIRL CHARACTERS

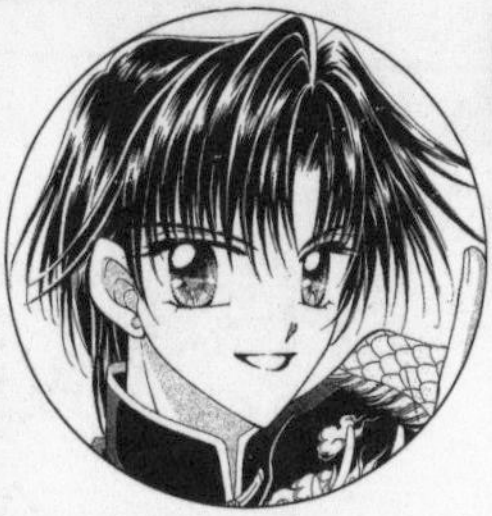

Ryuga Kou

Momoka's childhood friend and magic master.

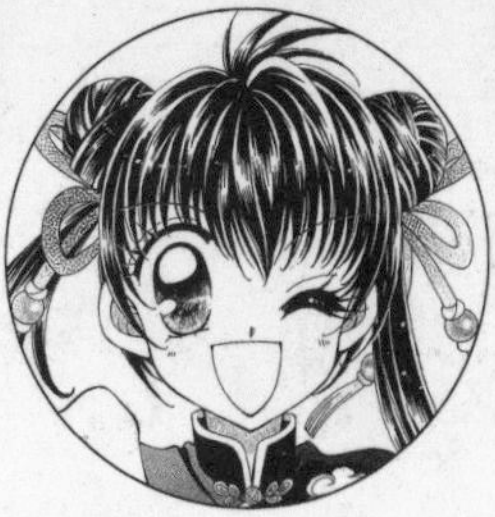

Momoka Sendou

She's possessed by a dragon spirit Ryuga called forth. When the seal on the dragon is broken, she becomes an invincible dragon girl.

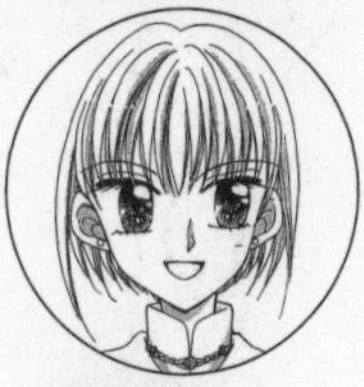

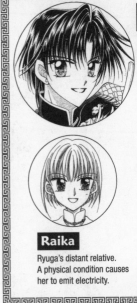

Raika

Ryuga's distant relative. A physical condition causes her to emit electricity.

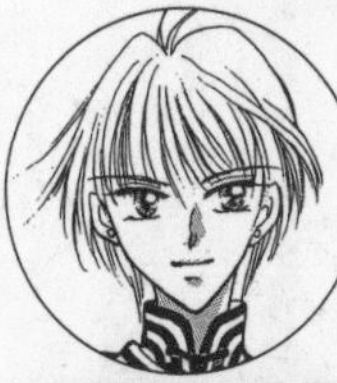

Kouryu Kou

Ryuga's relative. A genius of sorcery in the Kou clan.

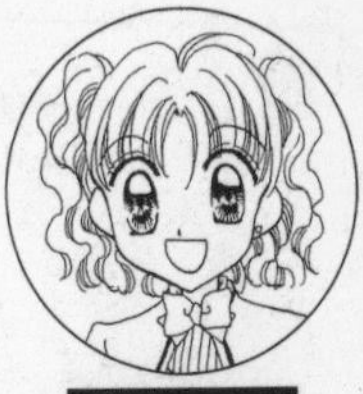

Shunran

Ryuga's cousin and Momoka's best friend. Has psychic abilites.

STORY THUS FAR

Momoka is a first-year student and a member of the kenpo club at Yokohama's Tourin Academy. When Momoka and Ryuga work together as a team to banish demons, they're invincible!

Momoka and Ryuga's relationship has been stormy....
First there was Kouryu who came from Hong Kong. He was after Momoka because of her dragon and tried to woo her. Then Raika came to Japan as an exchange student. She has a physical condition that makes her emit electrical energy when she gets excited. Momoka heard that Raika was Ryuga's fiancée and panicked. However, Raika had a personality such that Momoka couldn't hate her, and Momoka reluctantly agreed to help her get together with Ryuga. In the end, though, Raika realized how close Momoka and Ryuga were, so she finally gave up on him.

Ryuga always comes to Momoka's rescue, but she doesn't know how he really feels about her. What will happen next in their relationship...?

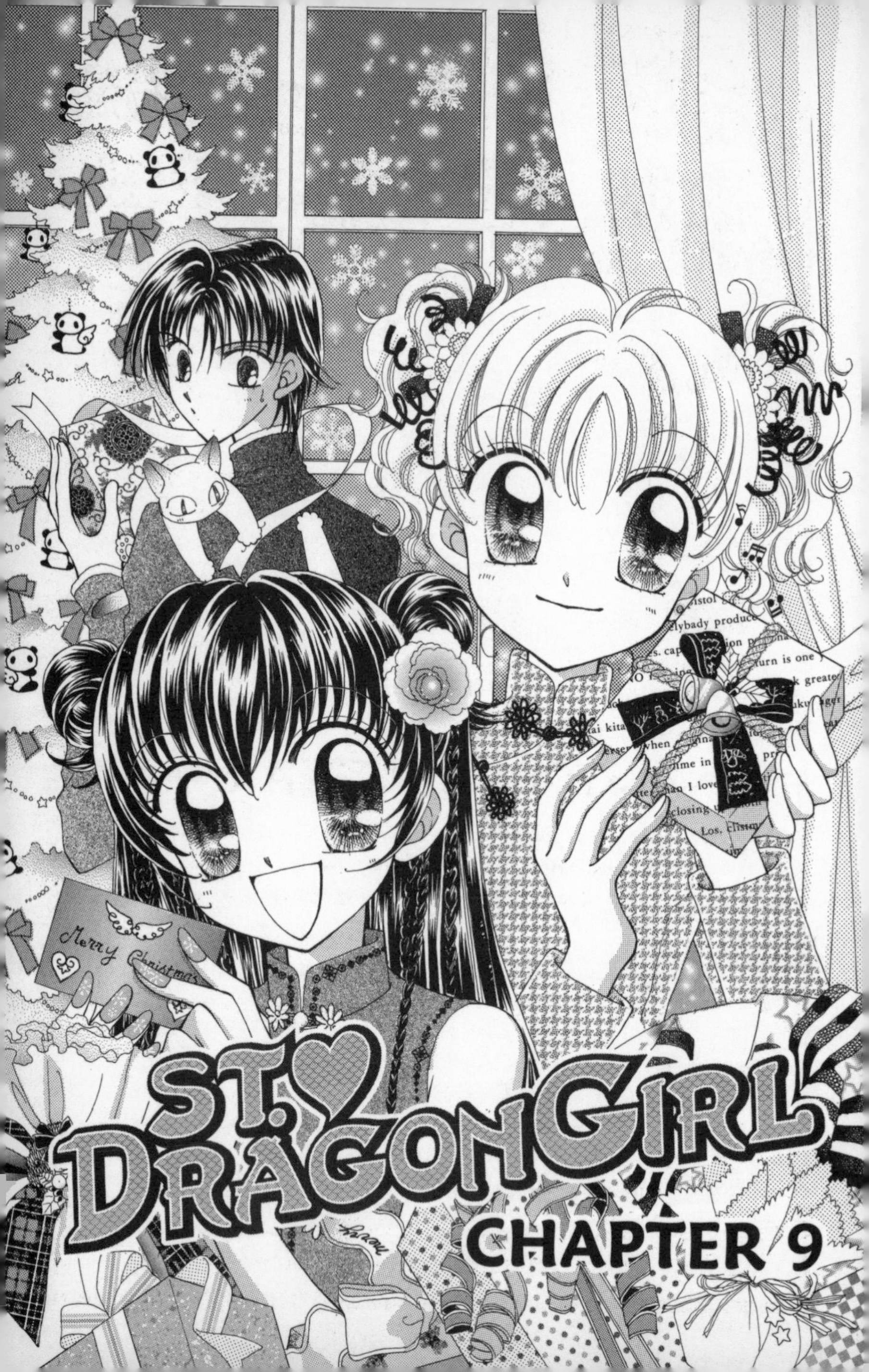
Merry Christmas
ST. DRAGON GIRL
CHAPTER 9

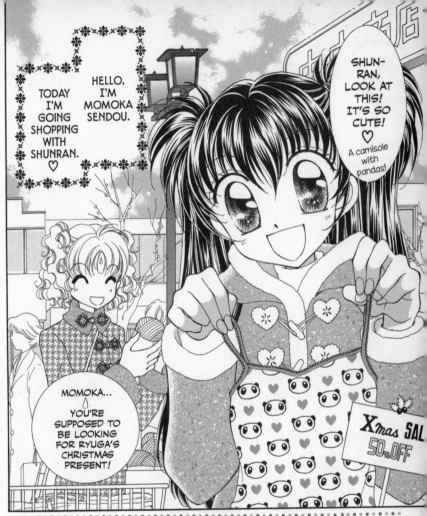

HELLO, I'M MOMOKA SENDOU.
TODAY I'M GOING SHOPPING WITH SHUNRAN. ♡
SHUN-RAN, LOOK AT THIS! IT'S SO CUTE! ♡
A camisole with pandas!
MOMOKA... YOU'RE SUPPOSED TO BE LOOKING FOR RYUGA'S CHRISTMAS PRESENT!
Xmas SAL
50% OFF

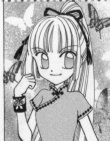

Ageha Inui

Born November 3.
Scorpio, Blood Type: B.
Kenpo Club Member.
Raised in Yokohama, she belongs to a family of martial artists (like Momoka's family).
She's Momoka's friend and rival.
She has lots of crushes and is attracted to older guys.

She hates to lose and has a strong-willed personality.
She's very popular with you readers.
She's on a straight path to love.
When she likes someone, she's the type to boldly go after that person. She tries her hardest to get a great boyfriend.
She has a gentle side, however, and encourages Momoka's love for Ryuga.

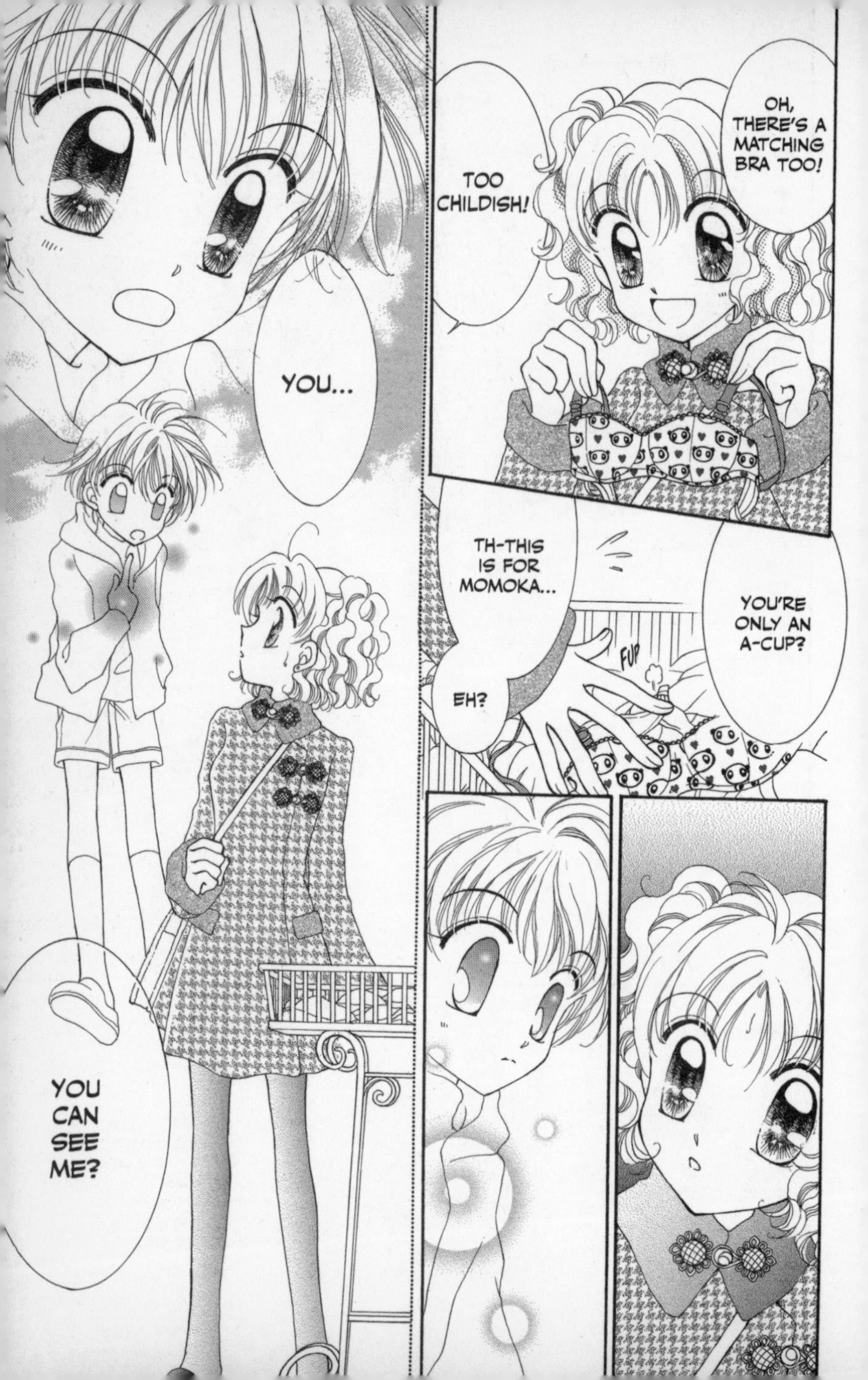
OH, THERE'S A MATCHING BRA TOO!
TOO CHILDISH!
YOU'RE ONLY AN A-CUP?
FUP
TH-THIS IS FOR MOMOKA...
EH?
YOU...
YOU CAN SEE ME?

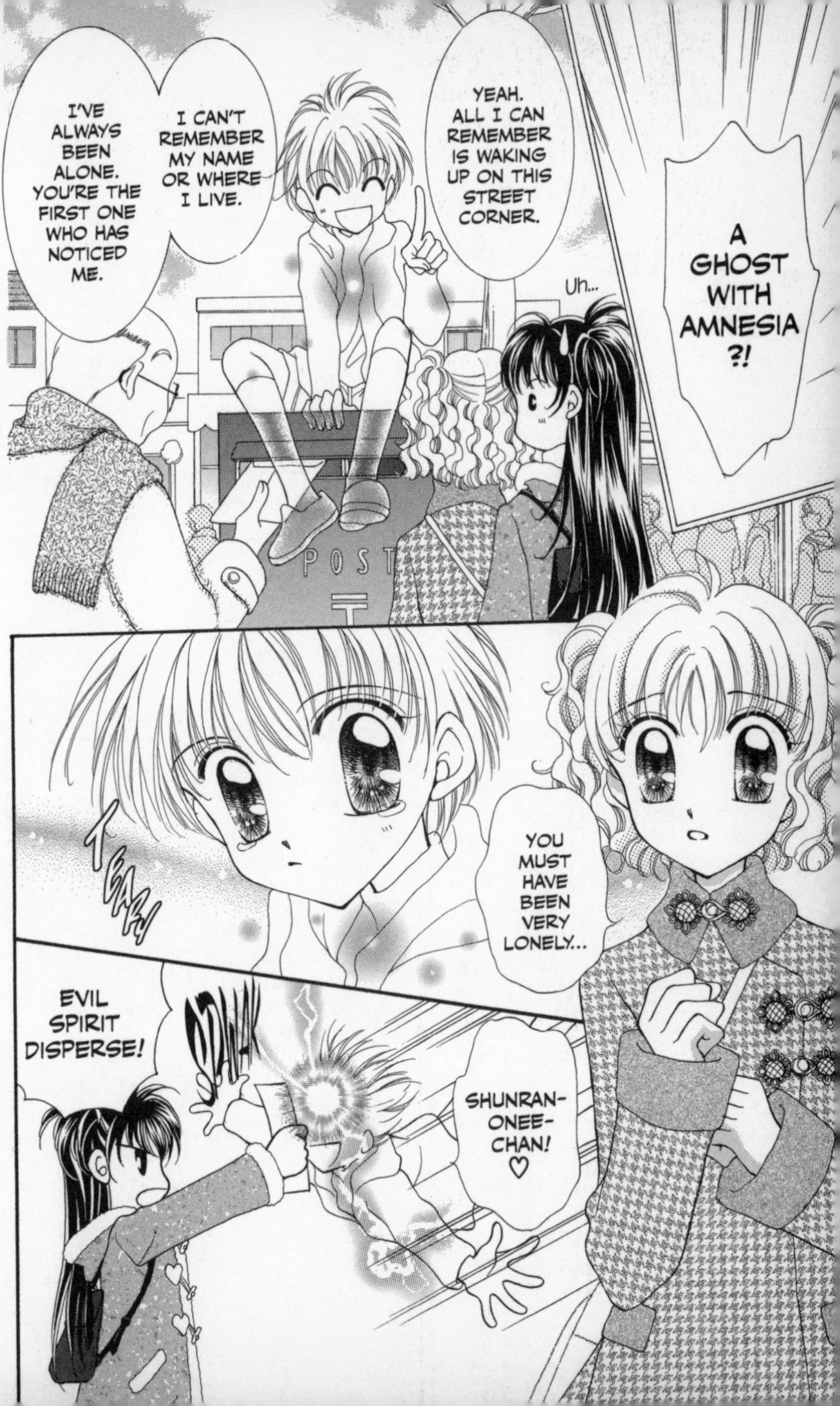

A GHOST WITH AMNESIA ?!
Uh...
YEAH. ALL I CAN REMEMBER IS WAKING UP ON THIS STREET CORNER.
I CAN'T REMEMBER MY NAME OR WHERE I LIVE.
I'VE ALWAYS BEEN ALONE. YOU'RE THE FIRST ONE WHO HAS NOTICED ME.
POST
YOU MUST HAVE BEEN VERY LONELY...
SHUNRAN-ONEE-CHAN! ♡
EVIL SPIRIT DISPERSE!

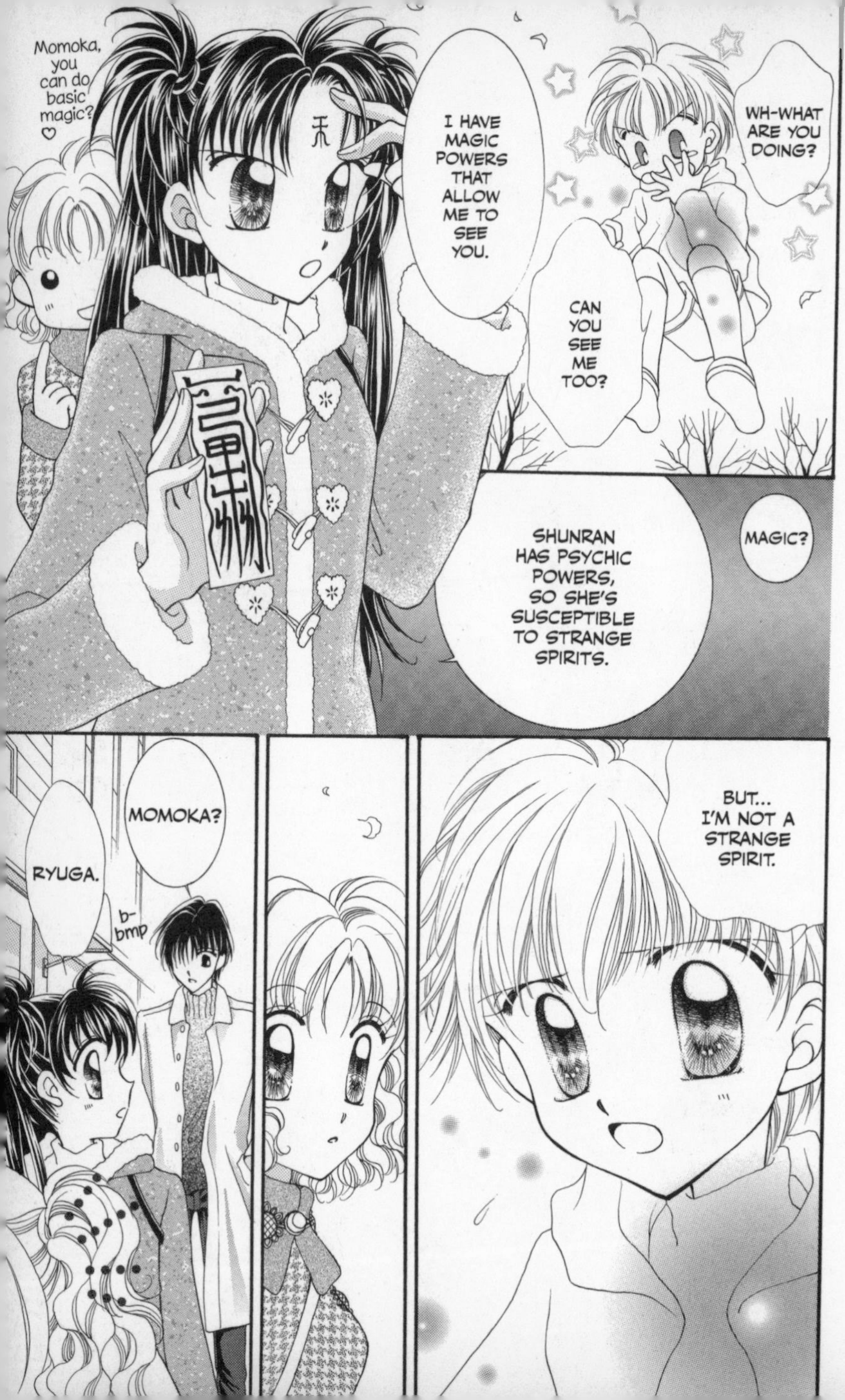
WH-WHAT ARE YOU DOING?
CAN YOU SEE ME TOO?
MAGIC?
SHUNRAN HAS PSYCHIC POWERS, SO SHE'S SUSCEPTIBLE TO STRANGE SPIRITS.
I HAVE MAGIC POWERS THAT ALLOW ME TO SEE YOU.
Momoka, you can do basic magic? ♡
BUT... I'M NOT A STRANGE SPIRIT.
MOMOKA?
RYUGA.
b-bmp

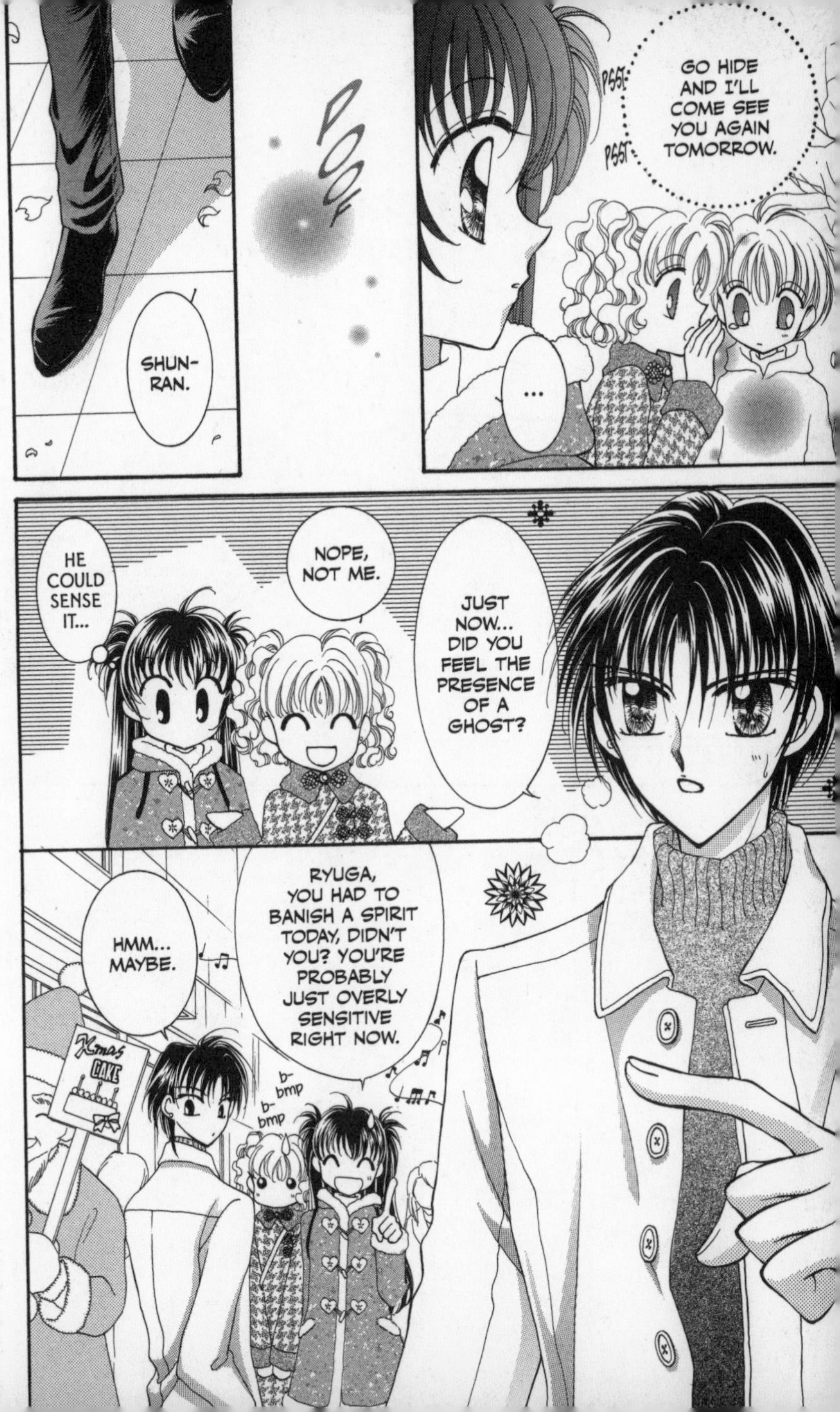
GO HIDE AND I'LL COME SEE YOU AGAIN TOMORROW.
PSST
PSST
...
SHUN-RAN.
JUST NOW... DID YOU FEEL THE PRESENCE OF A GHOST?
NOPE, NOT ME.
HE COULD SENSE IT...
RYUGA, YOU HAD TO BANISH A SPIRIT TODAY, DIDN'T YOU? YOU'RE PROBABLY JUST OVERLY SENSITIVE RIGHT NOW.
HMM... MAYBE.
Xmas CAKE
b-bmp
b-bmp

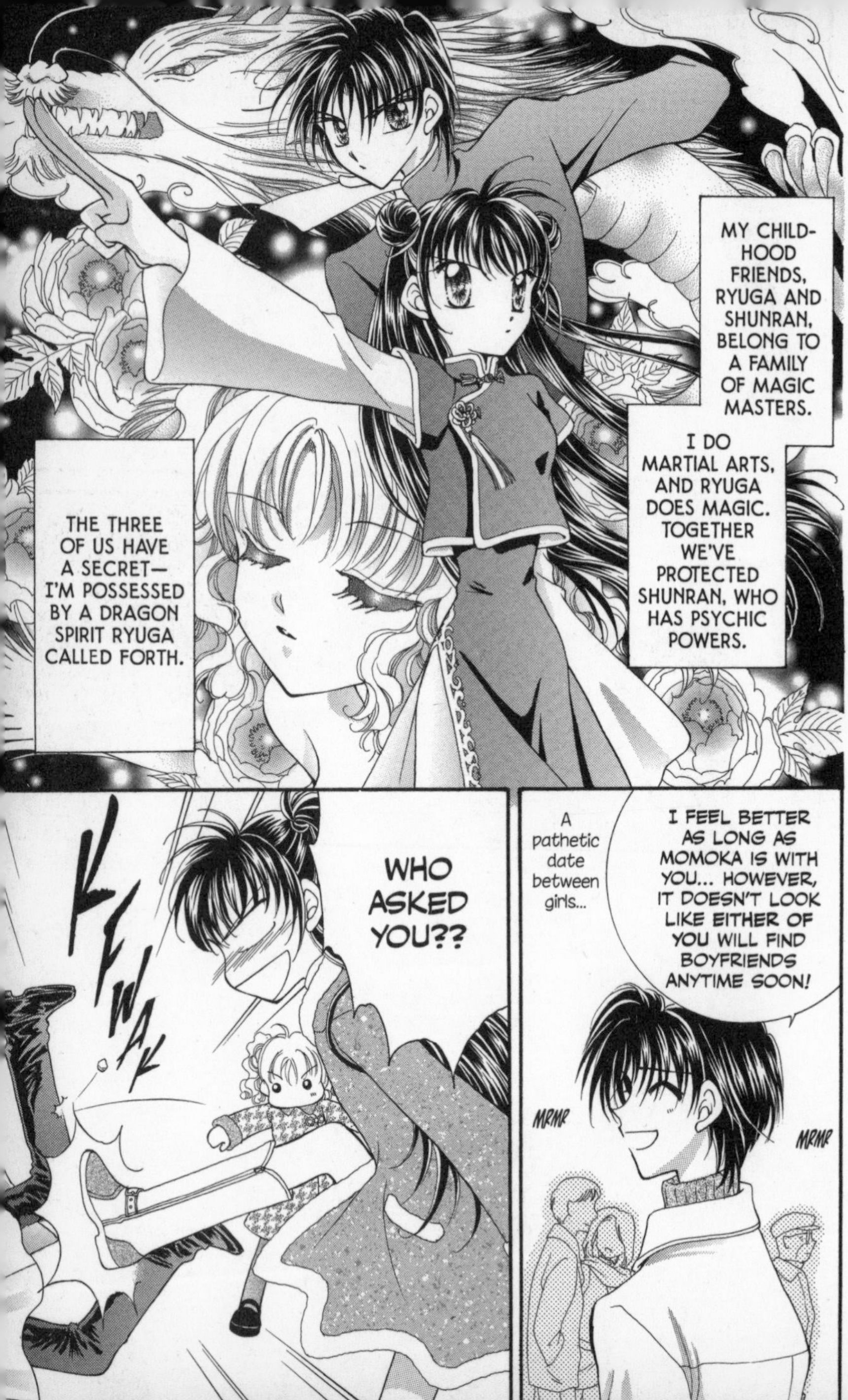
MY CHILDHOOD FRIENDS, RYUGA AND SHUNRAN, BELONG TO A FAMILY OF MAGIC MASTERS.
I DO MARTIAL ARTS, AND RYUGA DOES MAGIC. TOGETHER WE'VE PROTECTED SHUNRAN, WHO HAS PSYCHIC POWERS.
THE THREE OF US HAVE A SECRET—I'M POSSESSED BY A DRAGON SPIRIT RYUGA CALLED FORTH.
I FEEL BETTER AS LONG AS MOMOKA IS WITH YOU... HOWEVER, IT DOESN'T LOOK LIKE EITHER OF YOU WILL FIND BOYFRIENDS ANYTIME SOON!
A pathetic date between girls...
MRMR
MRMR
WHO ASKED YOU??
KFWAK

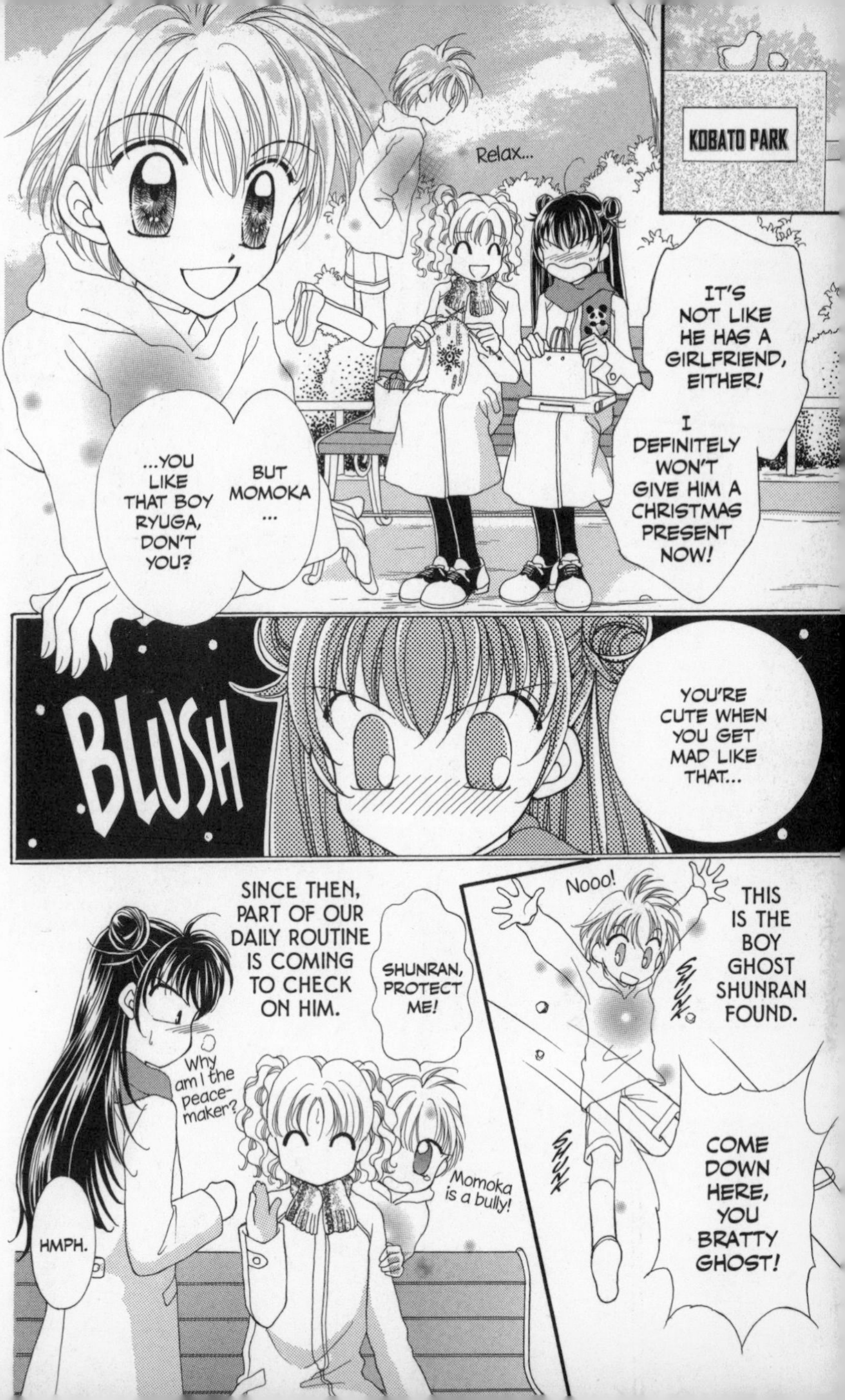
KOBATO PARK
IT'S NOT LIKE HE HAS A GIRLFRIEND, EITHER!
I DEFINITELY WON'T GIVE HIM A CHRISTMAS PRESENT NOW!
Relax...
BUT MOMOKA...
...YOU LIKE THAT BOY RYUGA, DON'T YOU?
YOU'RE CUTE WHEN YOU GET MAD LIKE THAT...
BLUSH
THIS IS THE BOY GHOST SHUNRAN FOUND.
Nooo!
SHUNK
COME DOWN HERE, YOU BRATTY GHOST!
SHUNK
SINCE THEN, PART OF OUR DAILY ROUTINE IS COMING TO CHECK ON HIM.
SHUNRAN, PROTECT ME!
Why am I the peace-maker?
Momoka is a bully!
HMPH.

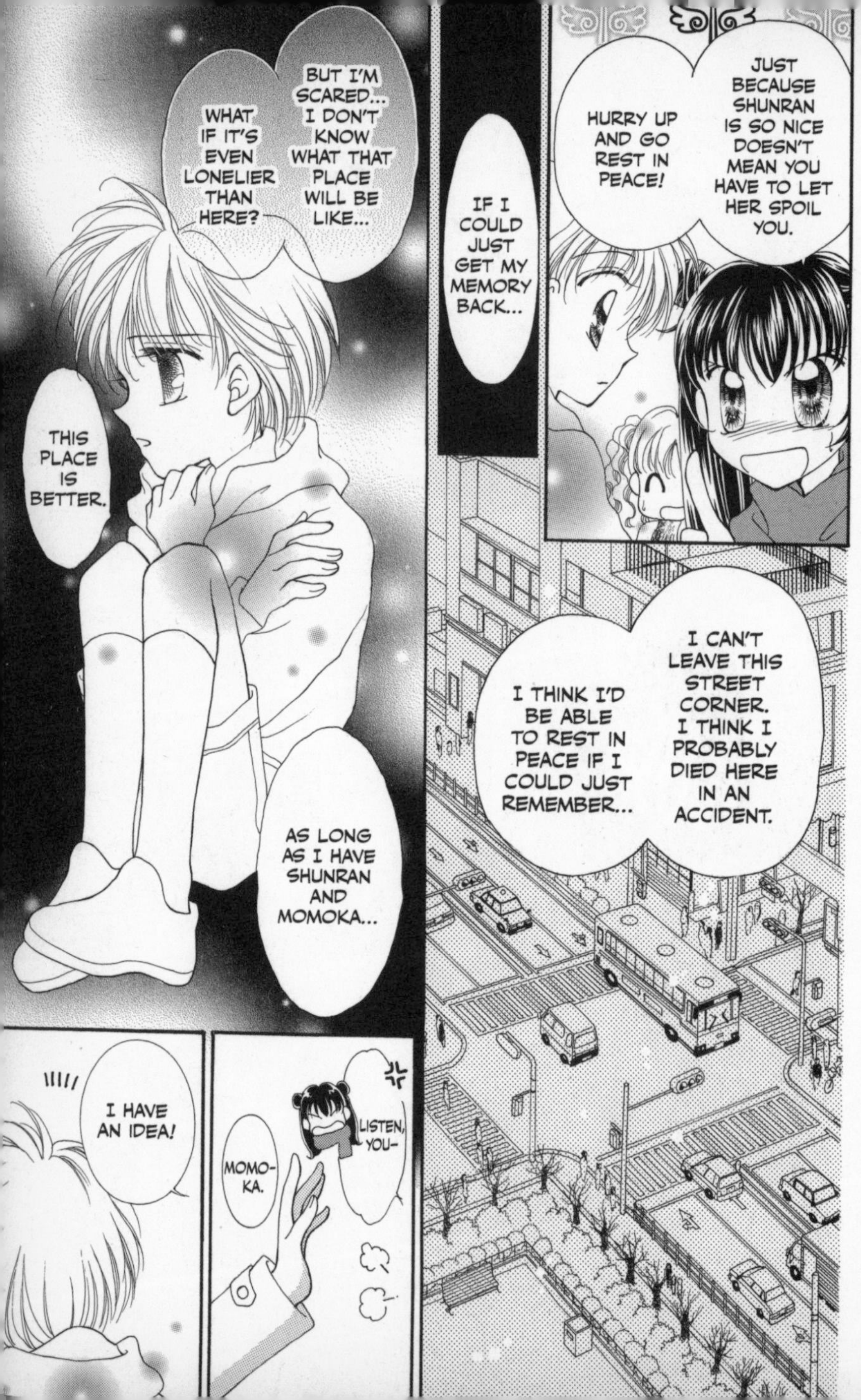
JUST BECAUSE SHUNRAN IS SO NICE DOESN'T MEAN YOU HAVE TO LET HER SPOIL YOU.
HURRY UP AND GO REST IN PEACE!
IF I COULD JUST GET MY MEMORY BACK...
I CAN'T LEAVE THIS STREET CORNER. I THINK I PROBABLY DIED HERE IN AN ACCIDENT.
I THINK I'D BE ABLE TO REST IN PEACE IF I COULD JUST REMEMBER...
BUT I'M SCARED... I DON'T KNOW WHAT THAT PLACE WILL BE LIKE...
WHAT IF IT'S EVEN LONELIER THAN HERE?
THIS PLACE IS BETTER.
AS LONG AS I HAVE SHUNRAN AND MOMOKA...
LISTEN, YOU-
MOMO-KA.
I HAVE AN IDEA!

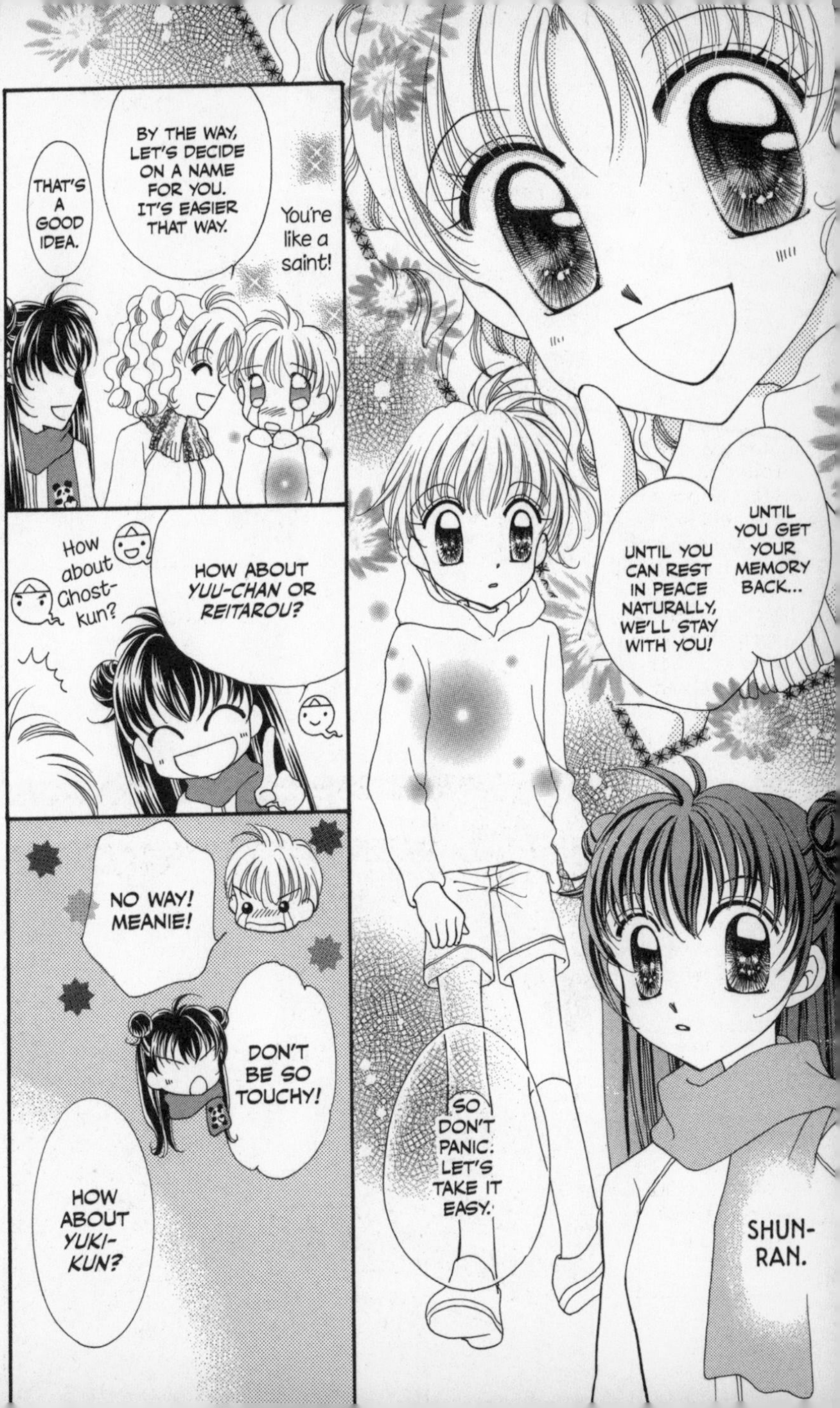
UNTIL YOU GET YOUR MEMORY BACK...
UNTIL YOU CAN REST IN PEACE NATURALLY, WE'LL STAY WITH YOU!
SO DON'T PANIC. LET'S TAKE IT EASY.
SHUN-RAN.
You're like a saint!
BY THE WAY, LET'S DECIDE ON A NAME FOR YOU. IT'S EASIER THAT WAY.
THAT'S A GOOD IDEA.
HOW ABOUT *YUU-CHAN* OR *REITAROU?*
How about Ghost-kun?
NO WAY! MEANIE!
DON'T BE SO TOUCHY!
HOW ABOUT *YUKI-KUN?*

1

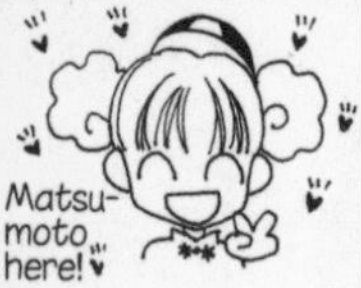

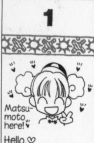

Matsu-moto here!

Hello.♡

This is the third volume of *St.♥Dragon Girl*. I didn't think it would be out so soon, so I was really surprised. But I'm really happy too!

In this volume, I feel that the story was very solid and it really provided structure for the series. In June 2001, *St.♥Dragon Girl* became a monthly manga in *Ribon* magazine.

It's a little hectic now that I have monthly deadlines, (*Eeek!*) but I'm having a lot of fun doing it.

I've also been able to do furoku, which I had been longing to do for many years, so I'm super-happy! I'll try even harder to make *St.♥Dragon Girl* a fun manga.

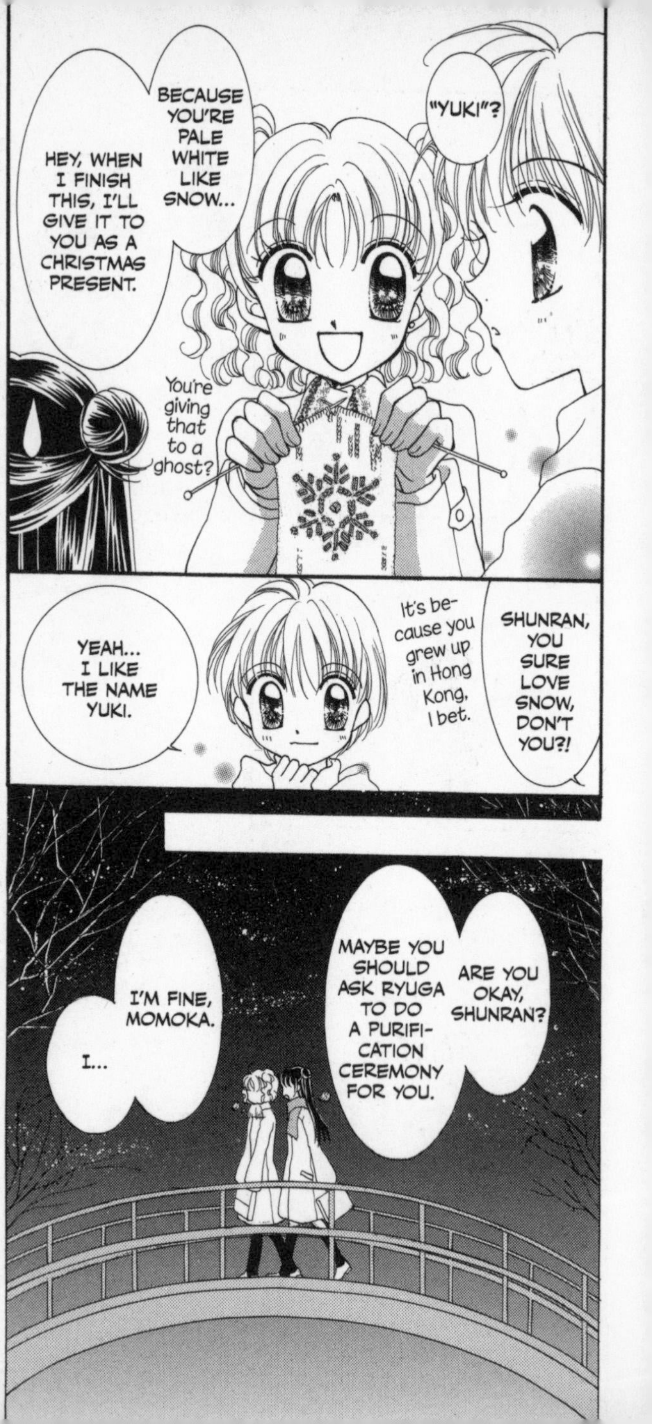
"YUKI"?
BECAUSE YOU'RE PALE WHITE LIKE SNOW...
HEY, WHEN I FINISH THIS, I'LL GIVE IT TO YOU AS A CHRISTMAS PRESENT.
You're giving that to a ghost?
SHUNRAN, YOU SURE LOVE SNOW, DON'T YOU?!
It's be-cause you grew up in Hong Kong, I bet.
YEAH... I LIKE THE NAME YUKI.
ARE YOU OKAY, SHUNRAN?
MAYBE YOU SHOULD ASK RYUGA TO DO A PURIFI-CATION CEREMONY FOR YOU.
I'M FINE, MOMOKA.
I...

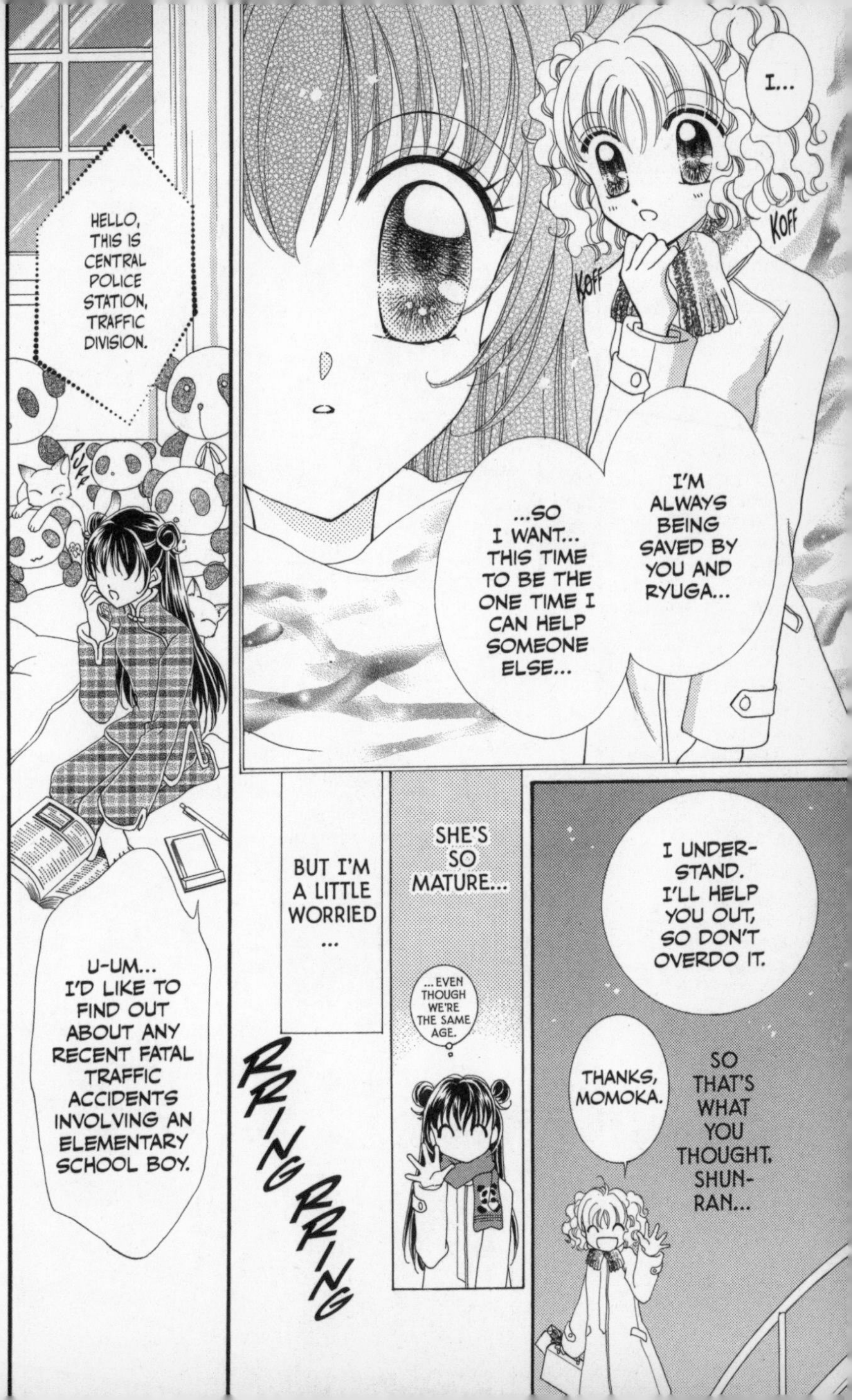
I...
KOFF
KOFF
I'M ALWAYS BEING SAVED BY YOU AND RYUGA...
...SO I WANT... THIS TIME TO BE THE ONE TIME I CAN HELP SOMEONE ELSE...
I UNDER-STAND. I'LL HELP YOU OUT, SO DON'T OVERDO IT.
SO THAT'S WHAT YOU THOUGHT. SHUN-RAN...
THANKS, MOMOKA.
SHE'S SO MATURE...
...EVEN THOUGH WE'RE THE SAME AGE.
BUT I'M A LITTLE WORRIED ...
RRING RRING
HELLO, THIS IS CENTRAL POLICE STATION, TRAFFIC DIVISION.
PUFF
U-UM... I'D LIKE TO FIND OUT ABOUT ANY RECENT FATAL TRAFFIC ACCIDENTS INVOLVING AN ELEMENTARY SCHOOL BOY.

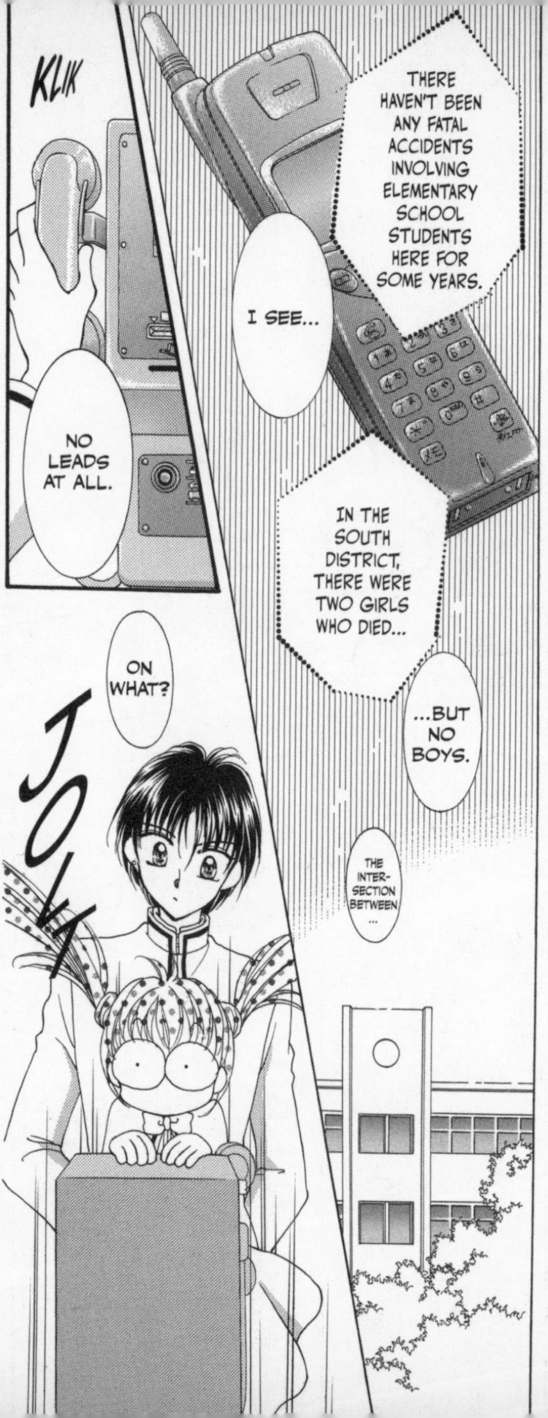
THERE HAVEN'T BEEN ANY FATAL ACCIDENTS INVOLVING ELEMENTARY SCHOOL STUDENTS HERE FOR SOME YEARS.
I SEE...
KLIK
NO LEADS AT ALL.
IN THE SOUTH DISTRICT, THERE WERE TWO GIRLS WHO DIED...
...BUT NO BOYS.
THE INTER-SECTION BETWEEN...
ON WHAT?

2

Even though this volume came out in August in Japan, it's a Christmas story... Ha ha...

Chapter 9 first appeared in the December issue of *Ribon Original* magazine.

This story holds a very special place in my heart.

It's because Yuki-kun's character is based on a true story involving the son of an acquaintance of mine. A long time ago, when he was in sixth grade, I tutored him at home. But around New Year's last year he died in a motorcycle accident. On the way home from work one night, a younger friend of his didn't have a full-face helmet, so he told him it was dangerous and gave him his own full-face helmet. Unfortunately, he was the one who ended up in an accident. He was a cheerful, cheeky boy...

It was hard not to like him. I thought the least I could do was make his story have a happy ending in my manga, so I wrote this. I used the same name as his, Yuki-kun (although the kanji is different).

I'd be happy if everyone realizes, even a little bit, what this boy was like.

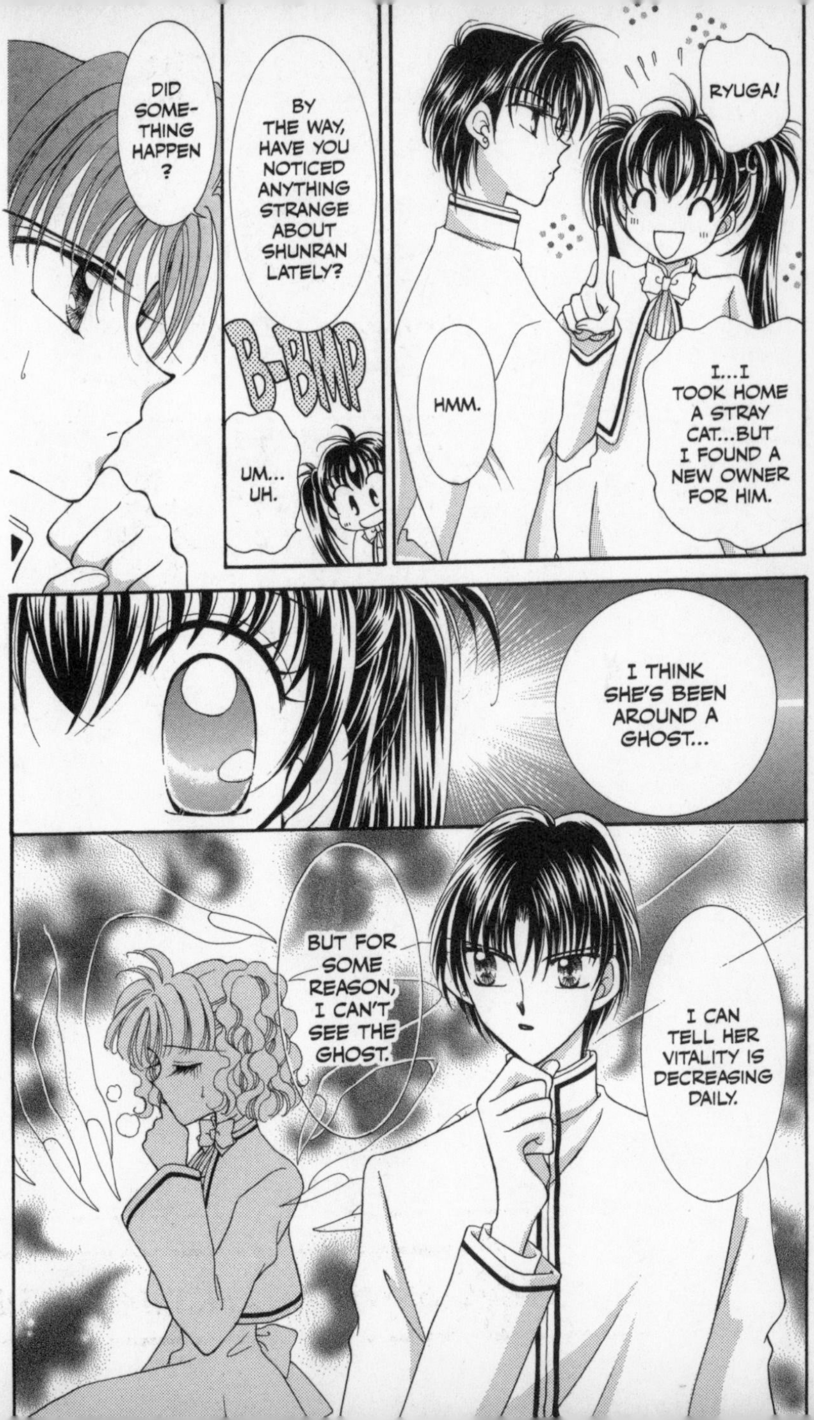
RYUGA!
I...I TOOK HOME A STRAY CAT...BUT I FOUND A NEW OWNER FOR HIM.
HMM.
BY THE WAY, HAVE YOU NOTICED ANYTHING STRANGE ABOUT SHUNRAN LATELY?
B-BMP
UM... UH.
DID SOME-THING HAPPEN?
I THINK SHE'S BEEN AROUND A GHOST...
I CAN TELL HER VITALITY IS DECREASING DAILY.
BUT FOR SOME REASON, I CAN'T SEE THE GHOST.

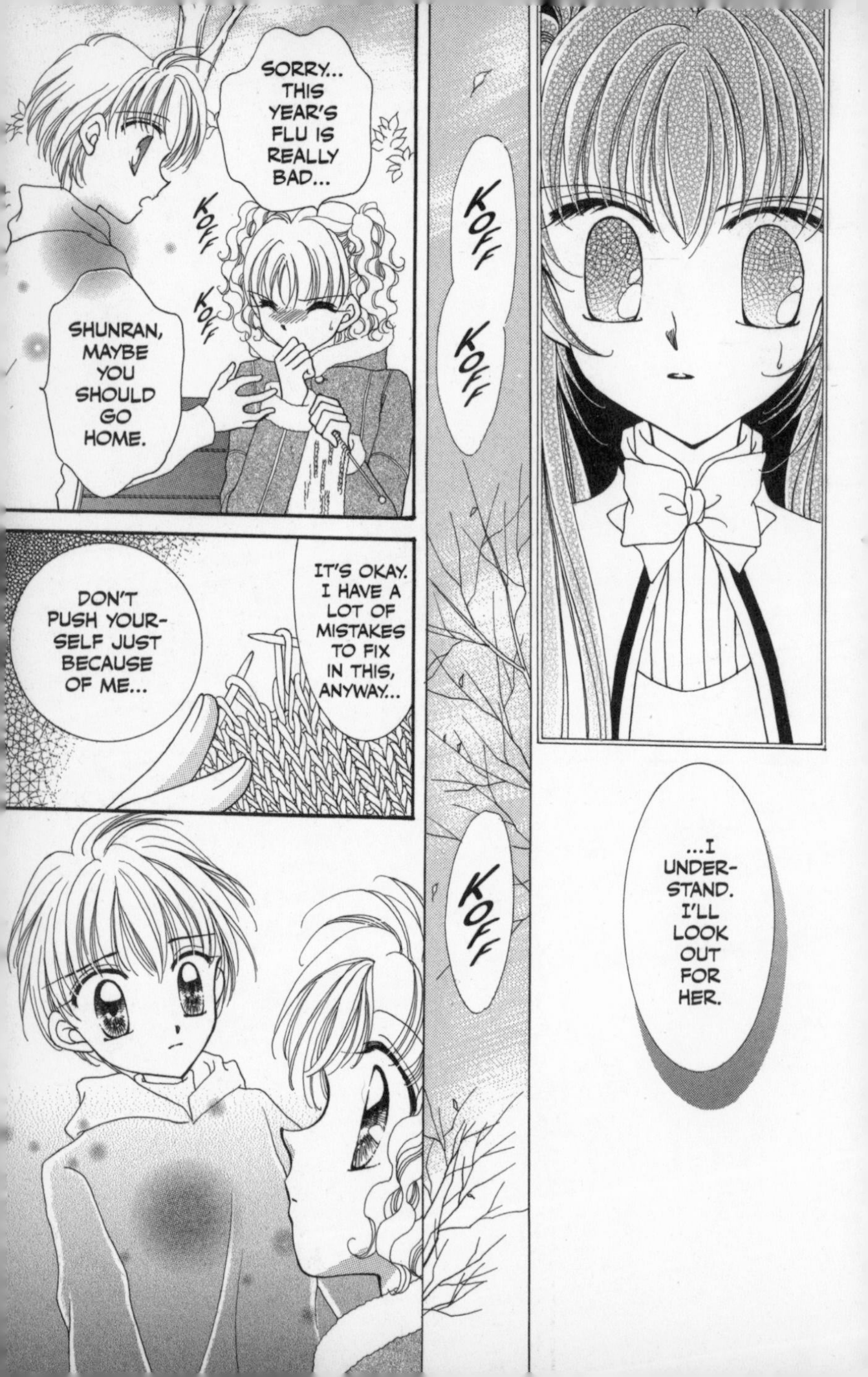
KOFF
KOFF
...I UNDERSTAND. I'LL LOOK OUT FOR HER.
KOFF
SORRY... THIS YEAR'S FLU IS REALLY BAD...
KOFF
KOFF
SHUNRAN, MAYBE YOU SHOULD GO HOME.
IT'S OKAY. I HAVE A LOT OF MISTAKES TO FIX IN THIS, ANYWAY...
DON'T PUSH YOURSELF JUST BECAUSE OF ME...

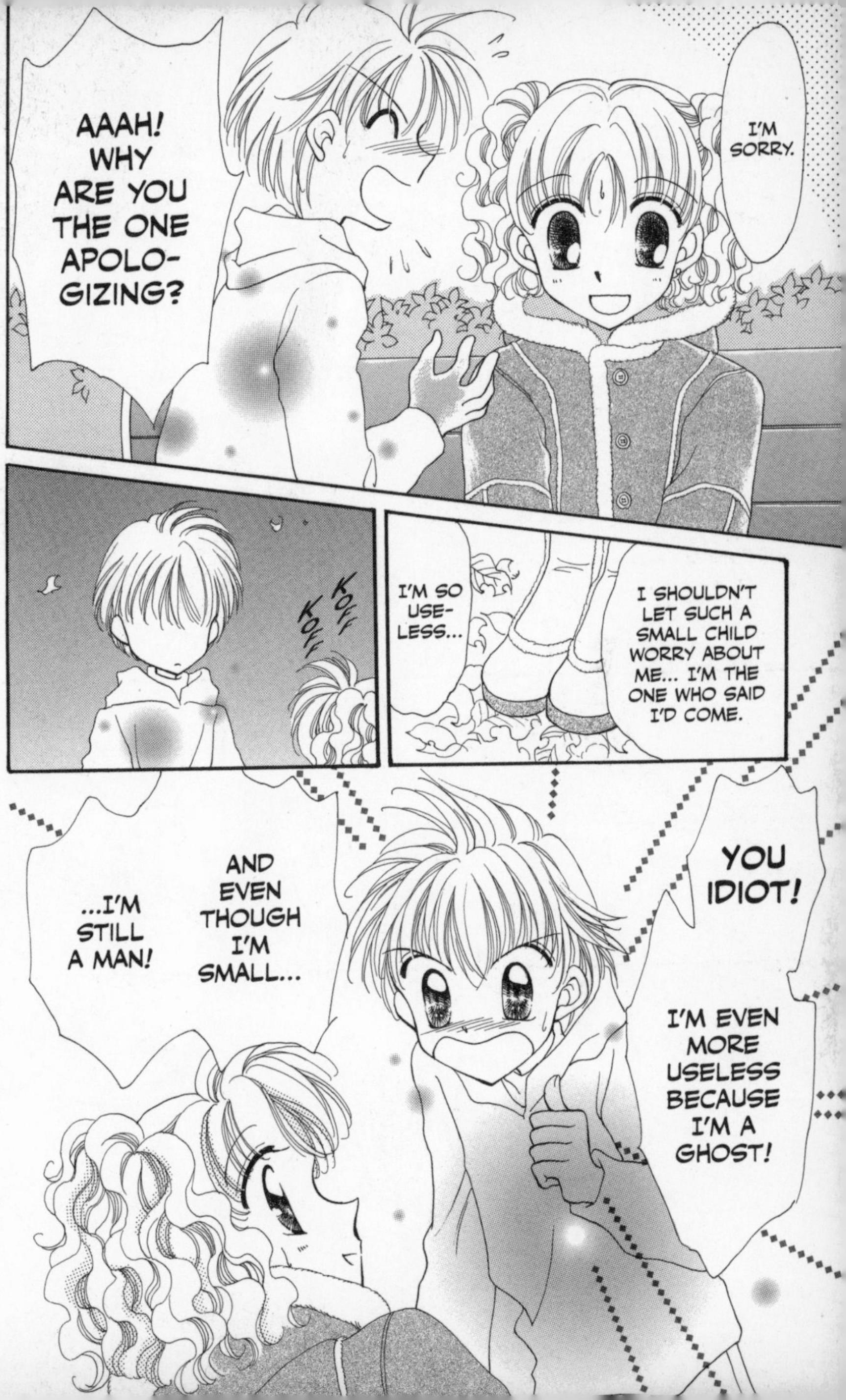
I'M SORRY.
AAAH! WHY ARE YOU THE ONE APOLOGIZING?
I SHOULDN'T LET SUCH A SMALL CHILD WORRY ABOUT ME... I'M THE ONE WHO SAID I'D COME.
I'M SO USELESS...
KOFF KOFF
YOU IDIOT!
I'M EVEN MORE USELESS BECAUSE I'M A GHOST!
AND EVEN THOUGH I'M SMALL...
...I'M STILL A MAN!

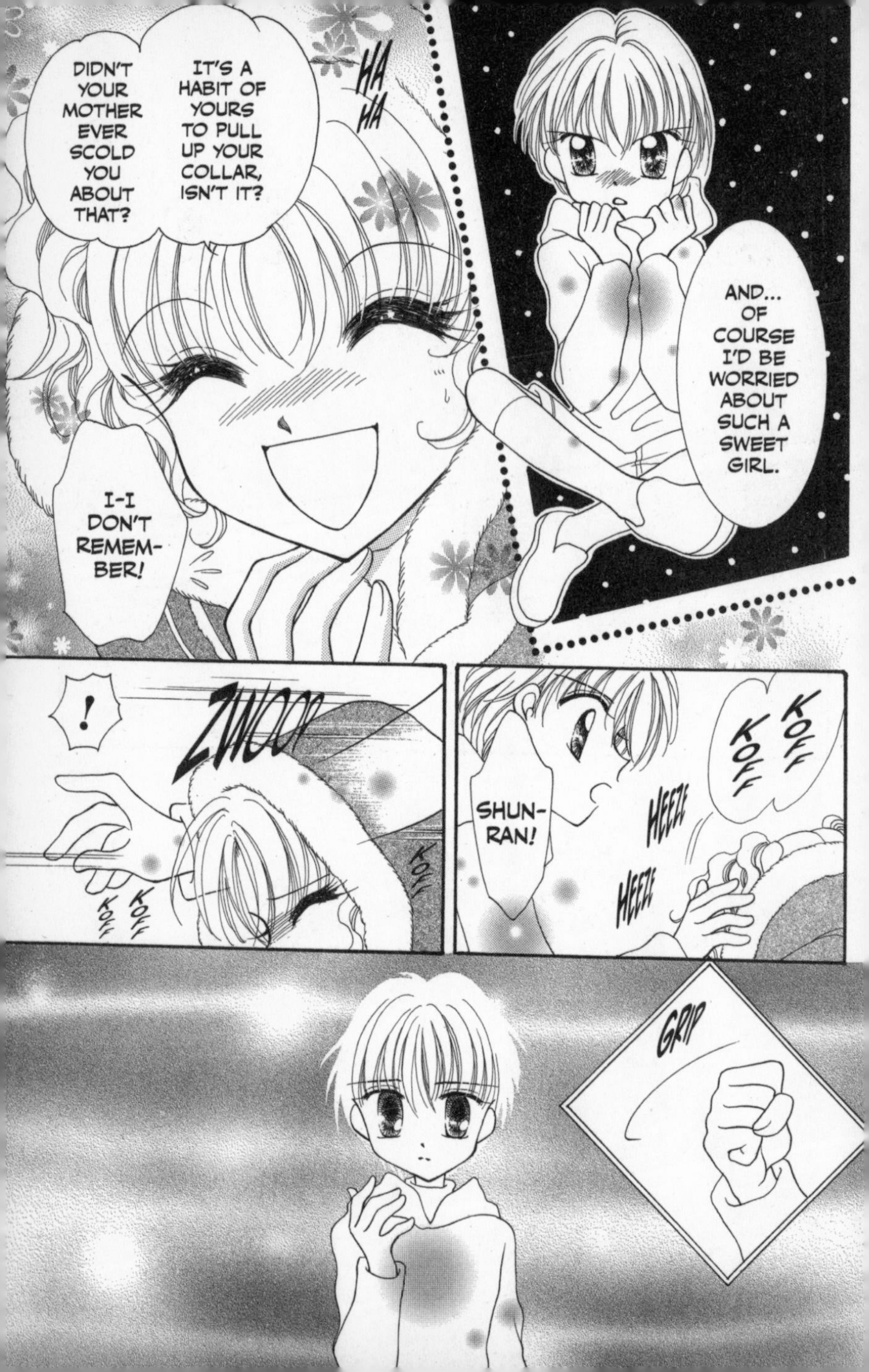
AND... OF COURSE I'D BE WORRIED ABOUT SUCH A SWEET GIRL.
HA HA
IT'S A HABIT OF YOURS TO PULL UP YOUR COLLAR, ISN'T IT?
DIDN'T YOUR MOTHER EVER SCOLD YOU ABOUT THAT?
I-I DON'T REMEMBER!
KOFF KOFF
SHUN-RAN!
HEEZE
HEEZE
ZWOOP
!
KOFF
KOFF KOFF
GRIP

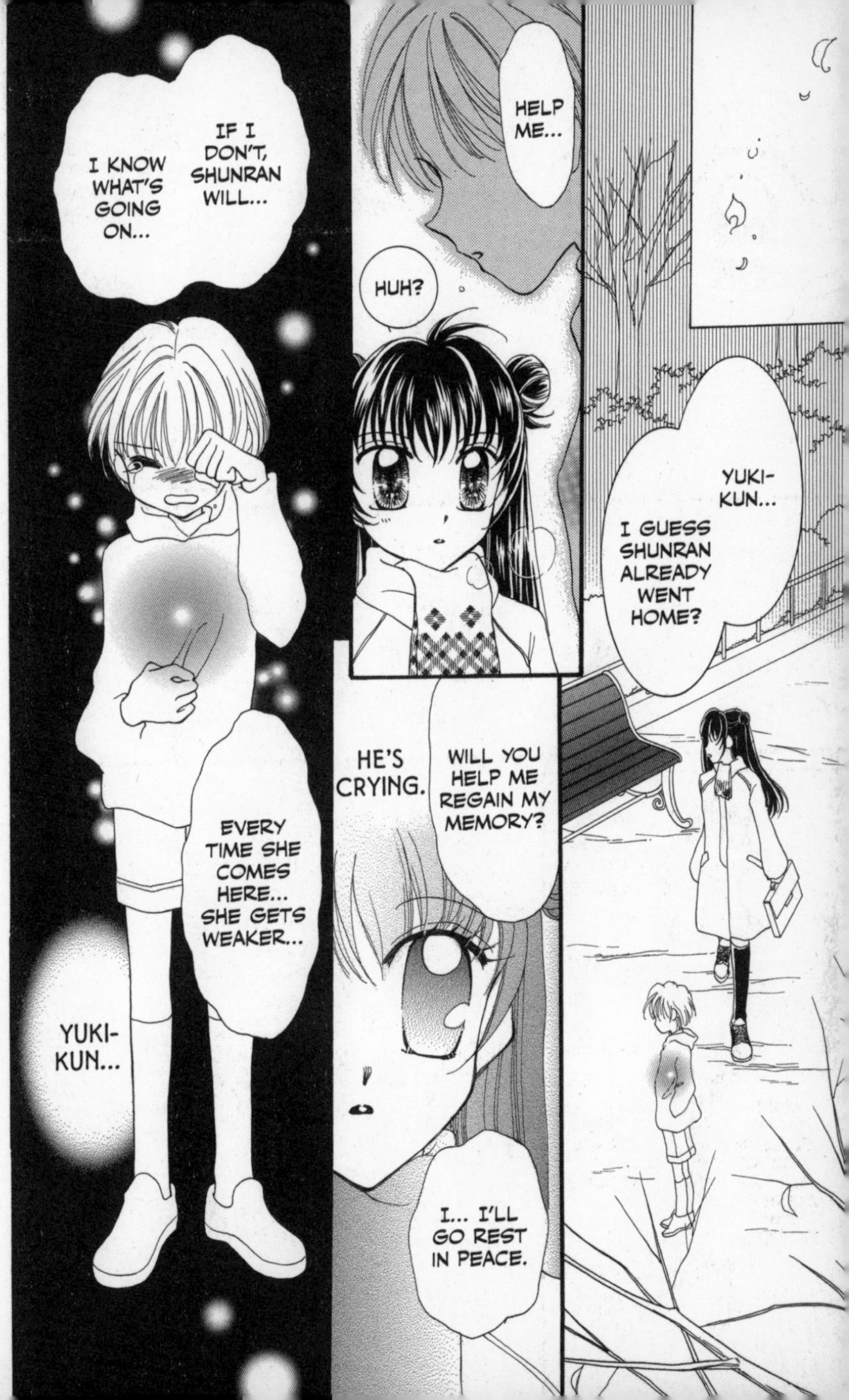
YUKI-KUN...
I GUESS SHUNRAN ALREADY WENT HOME?
HELP ME...
HUH?
WILL YOU HELP ME REGAIN MY MEMORY?
HE'S CRYING.
I... I'LL GO REST IN PEACE.
IF I DON'T, SHUNRAN WILL...
I KNOW WHAT'S GOING ON...
EVERY TIME SHE COMES HERE... SHE GETS WEAKER...
YUKI-KUN...

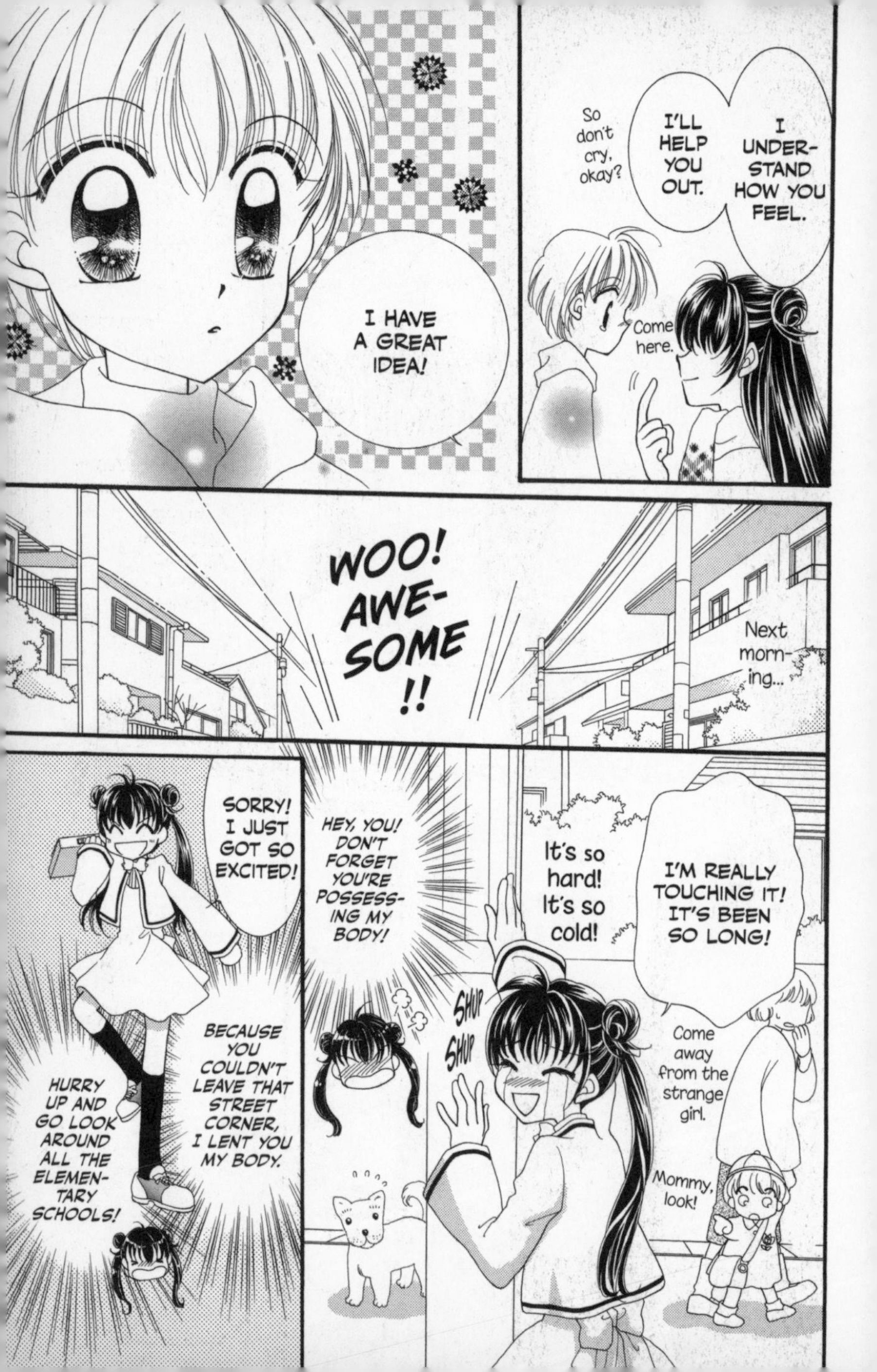
I UNDERSTAND HOW YOU FEEL.
I'LL HELP YOU OUT.
So don't cry, okay?
Come here.
I HAVE A GREAT IDEA!
Next morning...
WOO! AWESOME!!
I'M REALLY TOUCHING IT! IT'S BEEN SO LONG!
It's so hard! It's so cold!
Come away from the strange girl.
Mommy, look!
SHUP SHUP
HEY, YOU! DON'T FORGET YOU'RE POSSESSING MY BODY!
SORRY! I JUST GOT SO EXCITED!
BECAUSE YOU COULDN'T LEAVE THAT STREET CORNER, I LENT YOU MY BODY.
HURRY UP AND GO LOOK AROUND ALL THE ELEMENTARY SCHOOLS!

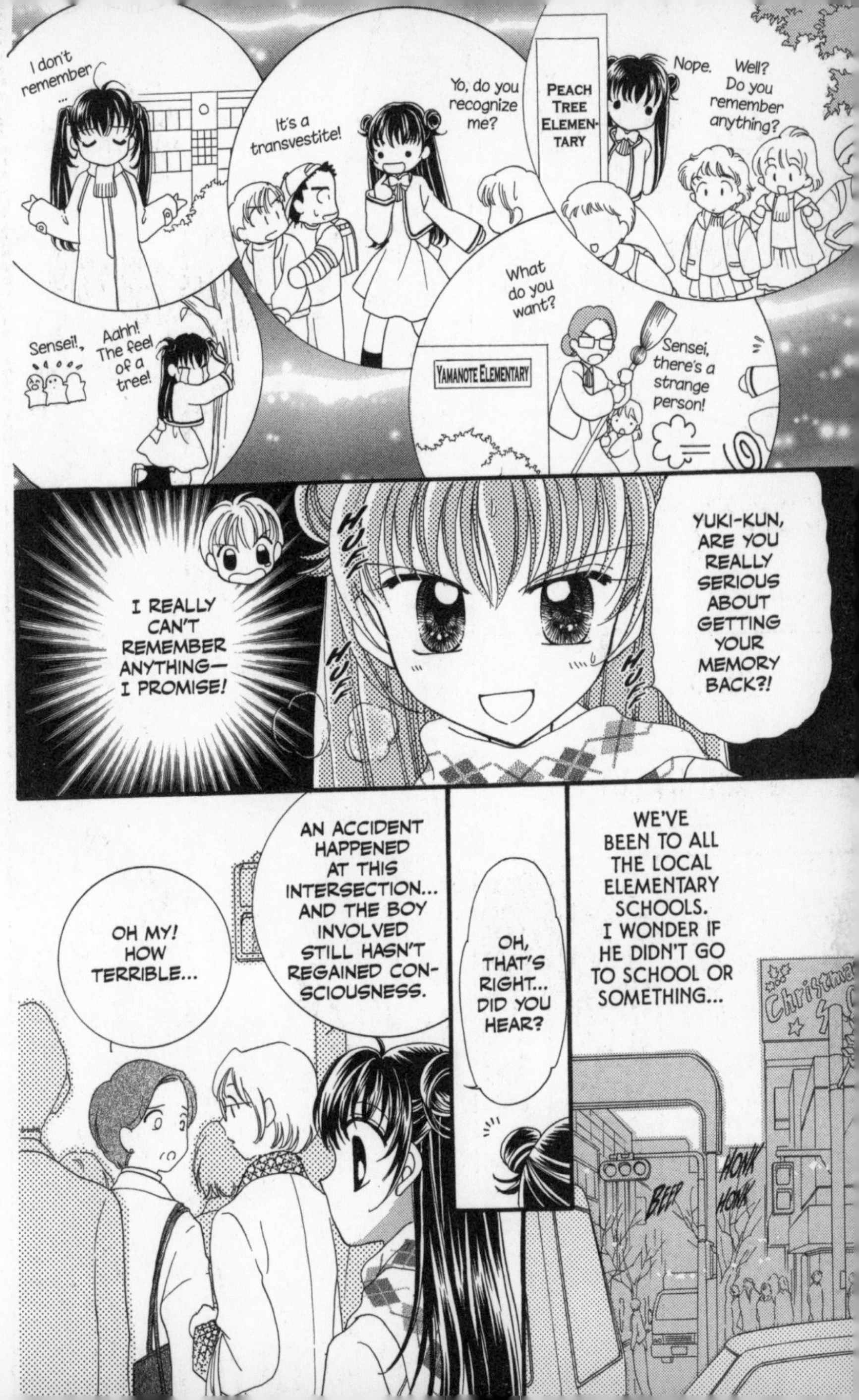
Well? Do you remember anything?
Nope.
PEACH TREE ELEMENTARY
Yo, do you recognize me?
It's a transvestite!
I don't remember ...
What do you want?
Sensei, there's a strange person!
YAMANOTE ELEMENTARY
Aahh! The feel of a tree!
Sensei!,
YUKI-KUN, ARE YOU REALLY SERIOUS ABOUT GETTING YOUR MEMORY BACK?!
I REALLY CAN'T REMEMBER ANYTHING— I PROMISE!
WE'VE BEEN TO ALL THE LOCAL ELEMENTARY SCHOOLS. I WONDER IF HE DIDN'T GO TO SCHOOL OR SOMETHING...
OH, THAT'S RIGHT... DID YOU HEAR?
AN ACCIDENT HAPPENED AT THIS INTERSECTION... AND THE BOY INVOLVED STILL HASN'T REGAINED CONSCIOUSNESS.
OH MY! HOW TERRIBLE...
HONK HONK
BEEP

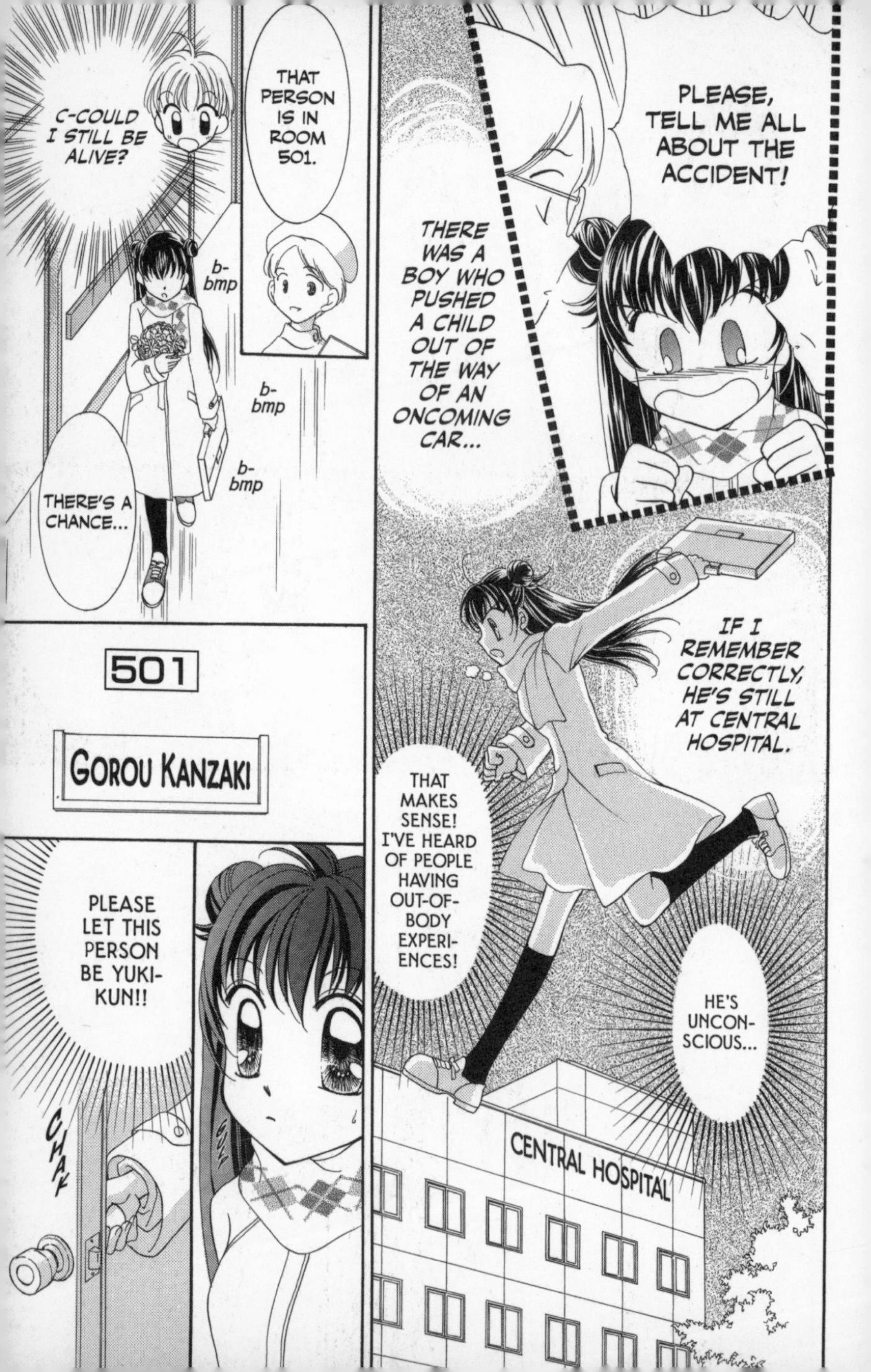
PLEASE, TELL ME ALL ABOUT THE ACCIDENT!
THERE WAS A BOY WHO PUSHED A CHILD OUT OF THE WAY OF AN ONCOMING CAR...
IF I REMEMBER CORRECTLY, HE'S STILL AT CENTRAL HOSPITAL.
HE'S UNCON-SCIOUS...
THAT MAKES SENSE! I'VE HEARD OF PEOPLE HAVING OUT-OF-BODY EXPERI-ENCES!
CENTRAL HOSPITAL
THAT PERSON IS IN ROOM 501.
C-COULD I STILL BE ALIVE?
b-bmp
b-bmp
b-bmp
THERE'S A CHANCE...
501
GOROU KANZAKI
PLEASE LET THIS PERSON BE YUKI-KUN!!
CHAK

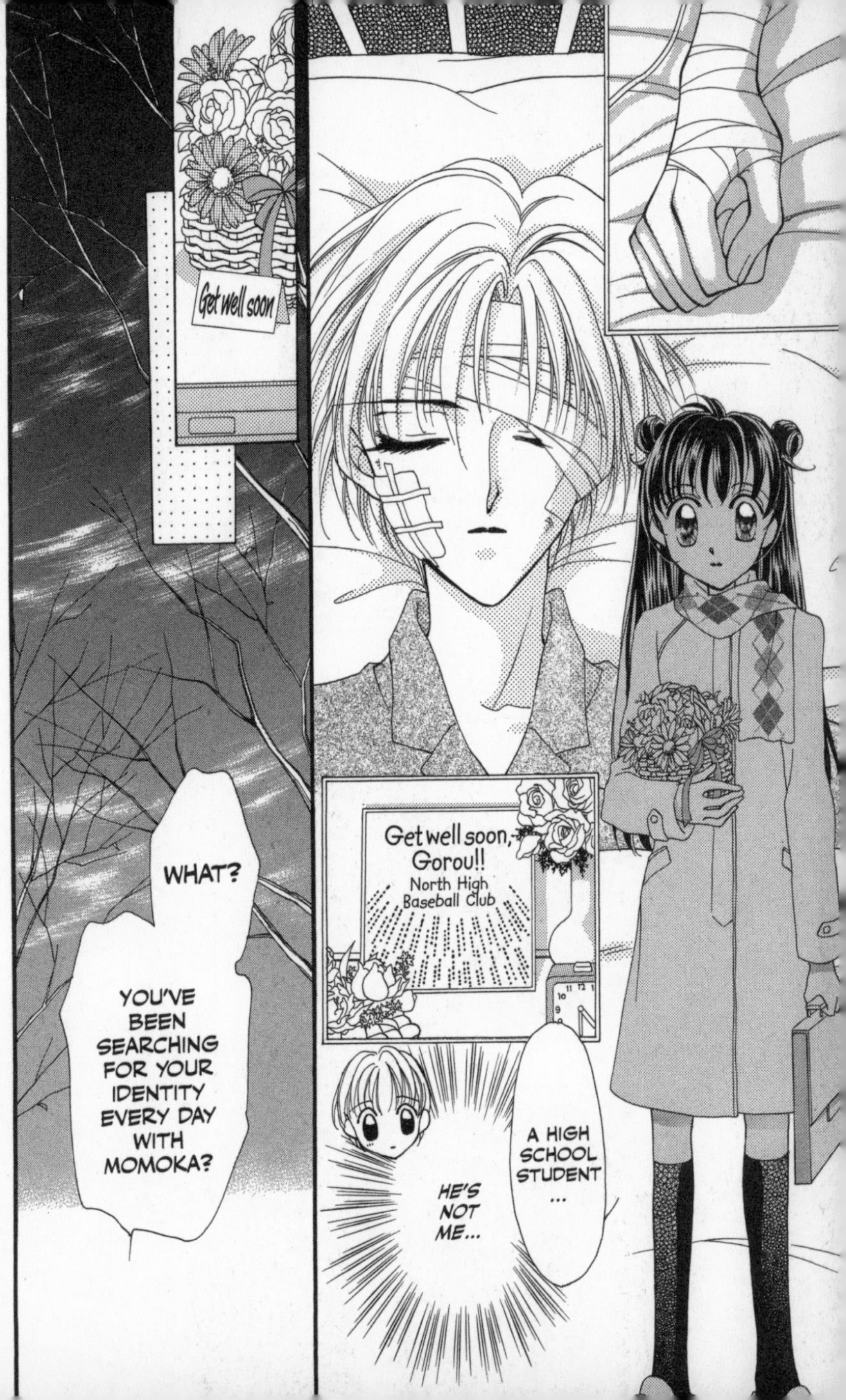
Get well soon, Gorou!!
North High Baseball Club
A HIGH SCHOOL STUDENT ...
HE'S NOT ME...
Get well soon
WHAT?
YOU'VE BEEN SEARCHING FOR YOUR IDENTITY EVERY DAY WITH MOMOKA?

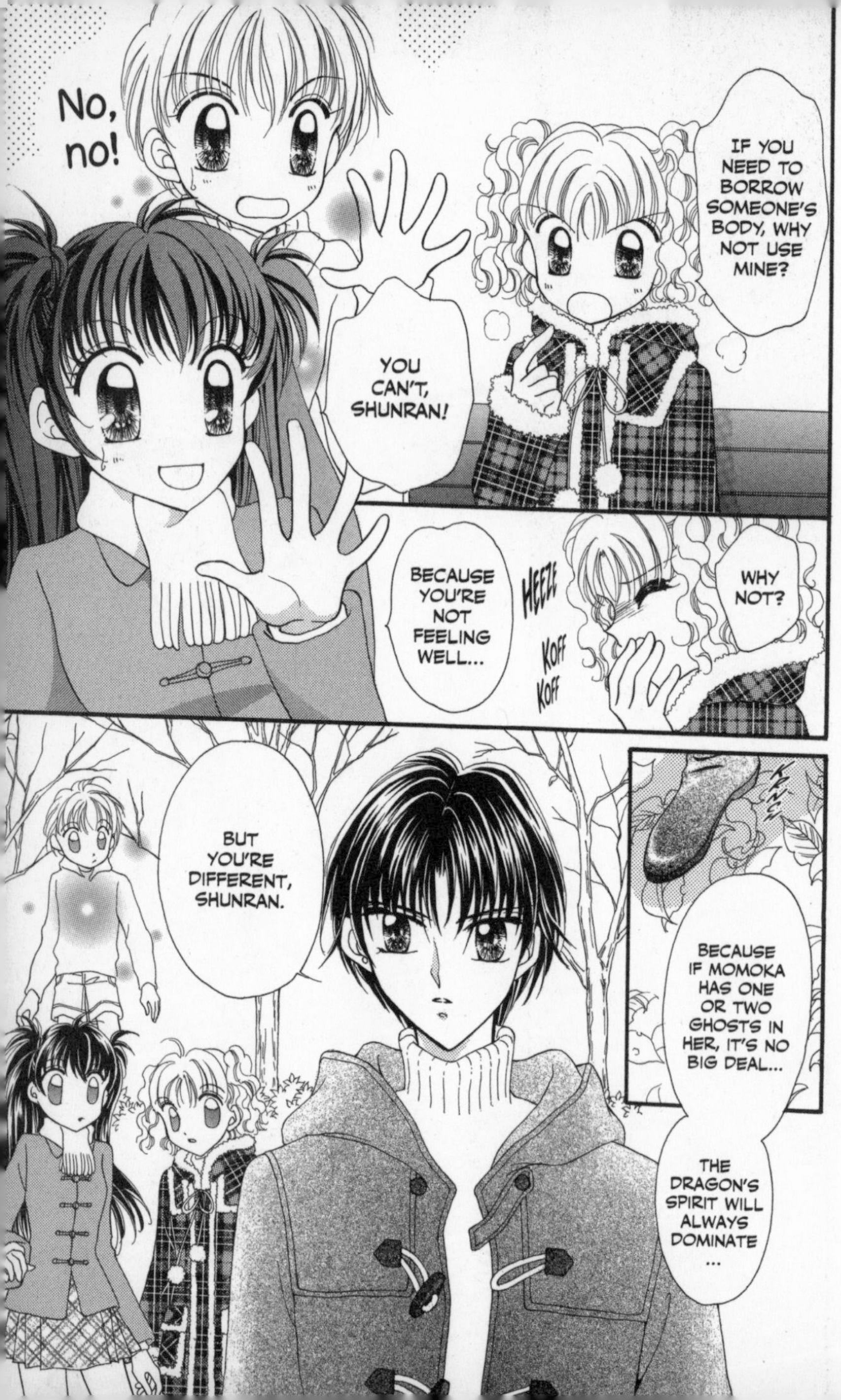
IF YOU NEED TO BORROW SOMEONE'S BODY, WHY NOT USE MINE?
YOU CAN'T, SHUNRAN!
No, no!
WHY NOT?
HEEZE
KOFF KOFF
BECAUSE YOU'RE NOT FEELING WELL...
KRNCH
BECAUSE IF MOMOKA HAS ONE OR TWO GHOSTS IN HER, IT'S NO BIG DEAL...
THE DRAGON'S SPIRIT WILL ALWAYS DOMINATE ...
BUT YOU'RE DIFFERENT, SHUNRAN.

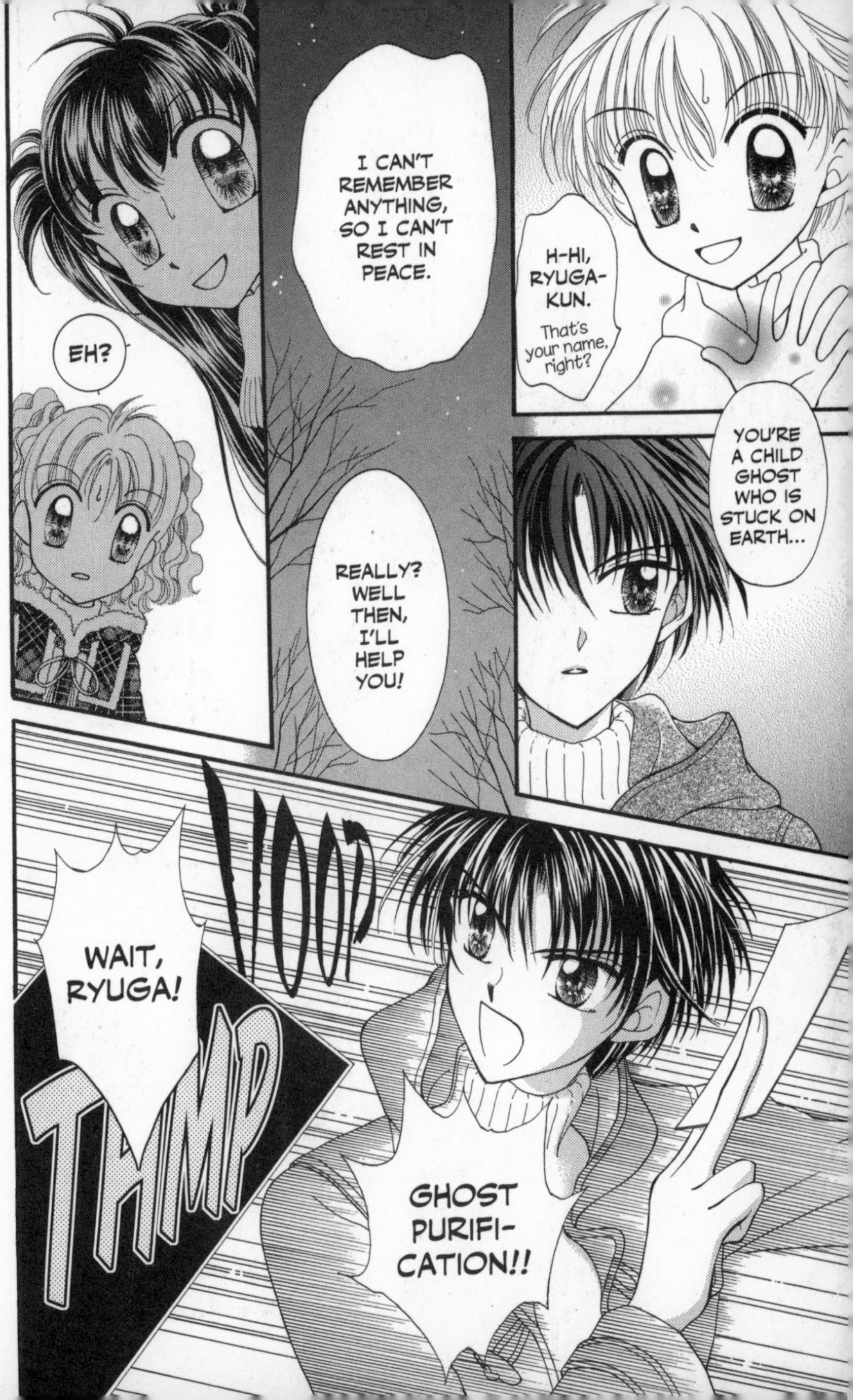
H-HI, RYUGA-KUN.
That's your name, right?
YOU'RE A CHILD GHOST WHO IS STUCK ON EARTH...
I CAN'T REMEMBER ANYTHING, SO I CAN'T REST IN PEACE.
REALLY? WELL THEN, I'LL HELP YOU!
EH?
GHOST PURIFICATION!!
WAIT, RYUGA!

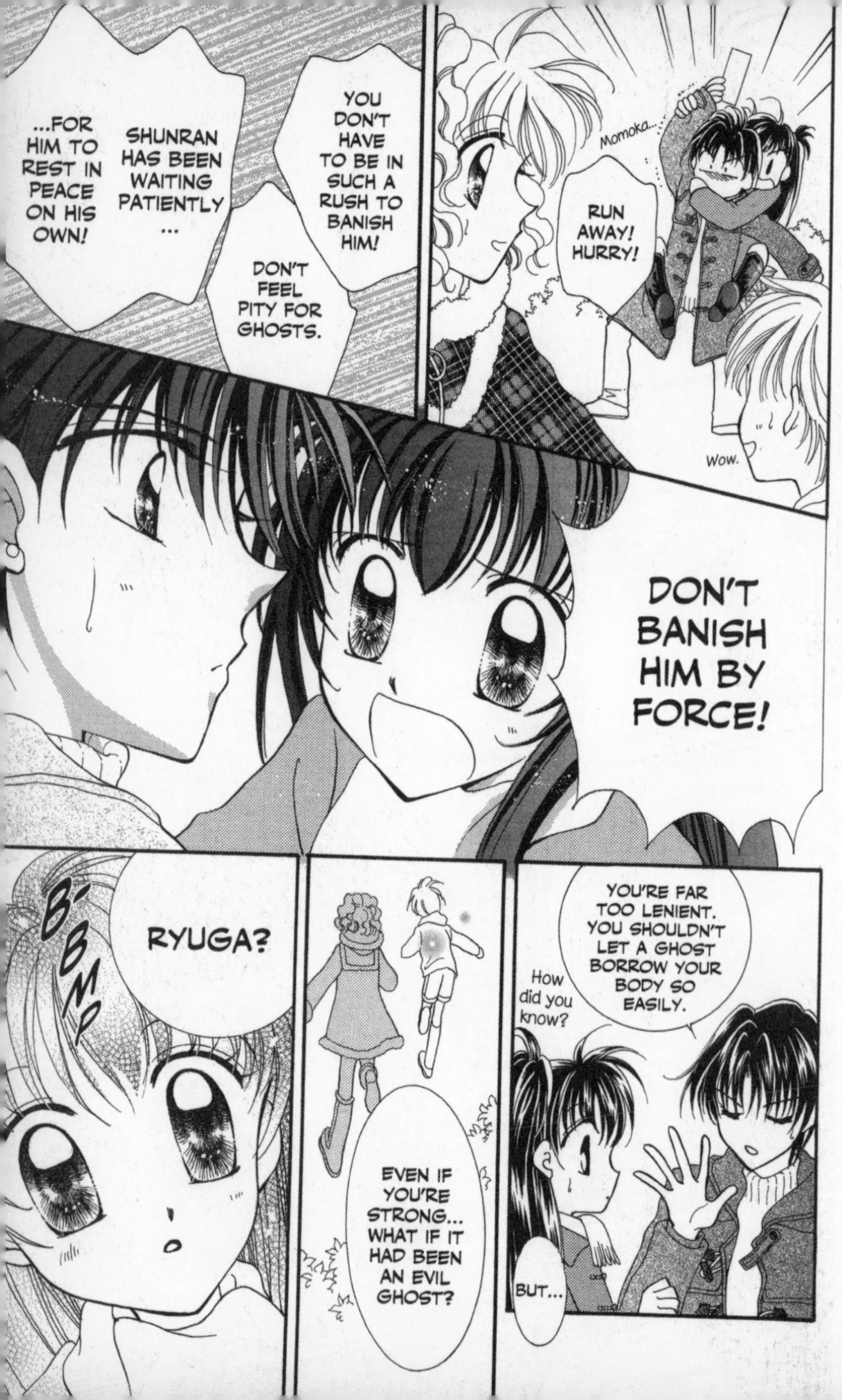
Momoka...
RUN AWAY! HURRY!
Wow.
YOU DON'T HAVE TO BE IN SUCH A RUSH TO BANISH HIM!
DON'T FEEL PITY FOR GHOSTS.
SHUNRAN HAS BEEN WAITING PATIENTLY...
...FOR HIM TO REST IN PEACE ON HIS OWN!
DON'T BANISH HIM BY FORCE!
YOU'RE FAR TOO LENIENT. YOU SHOULDN'T LET A GHOST BORROW YOUR BODY SO EASILY.
How did you know?
BUT...
EVEN IF YOU'RE STRONG... WHAT IF IT HAD BEEN AN EVIL GHOST?
RYUGA?
B-BMP

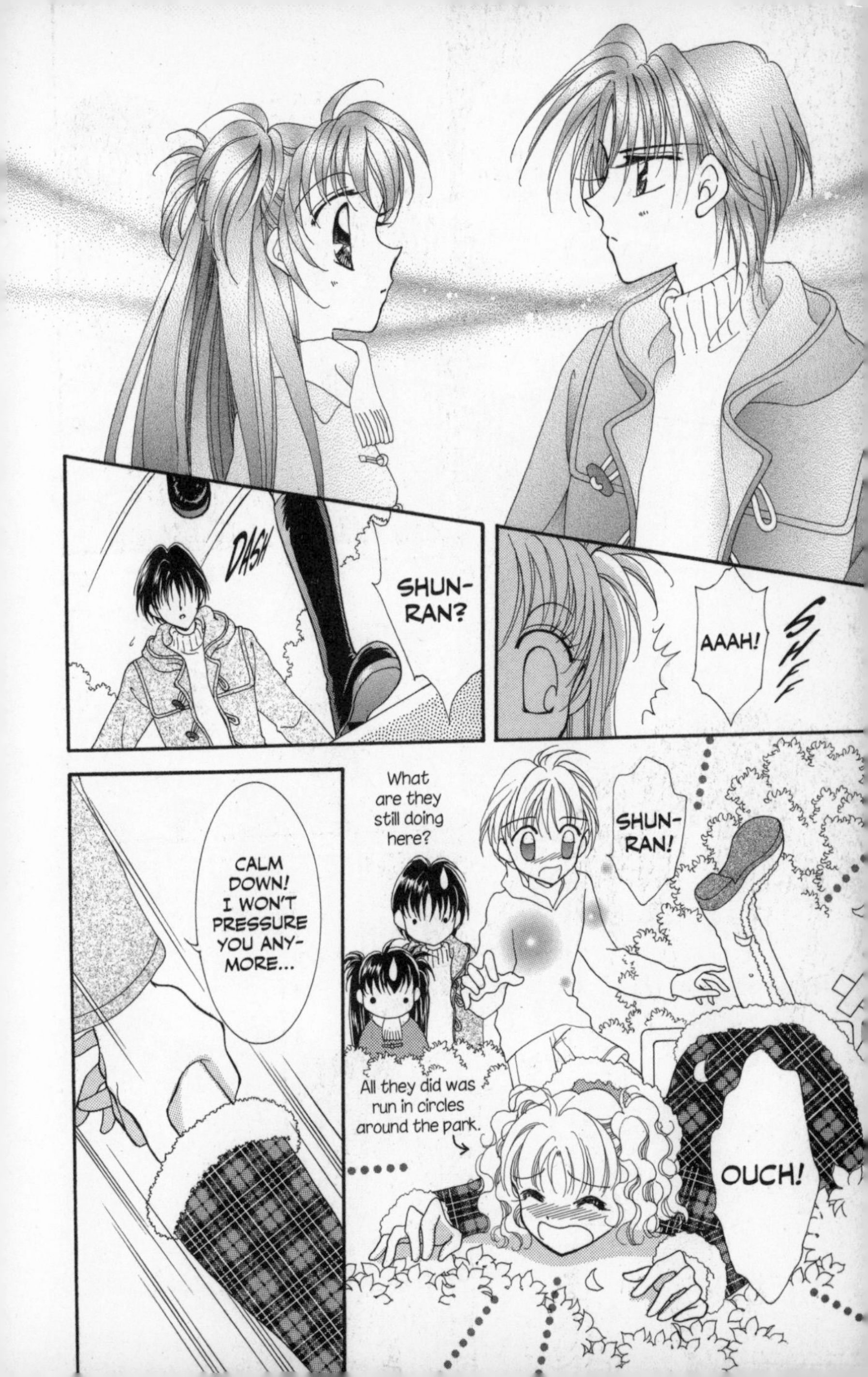
AAAH!
SHFF
SHUN-RAN?
DASH
SHUN-RAN!
What are they still doing here?
All they did was run in circles around the park.
OUCH!
CALM DOWN! I WON'T PRESSURE YOU ANYMORE...

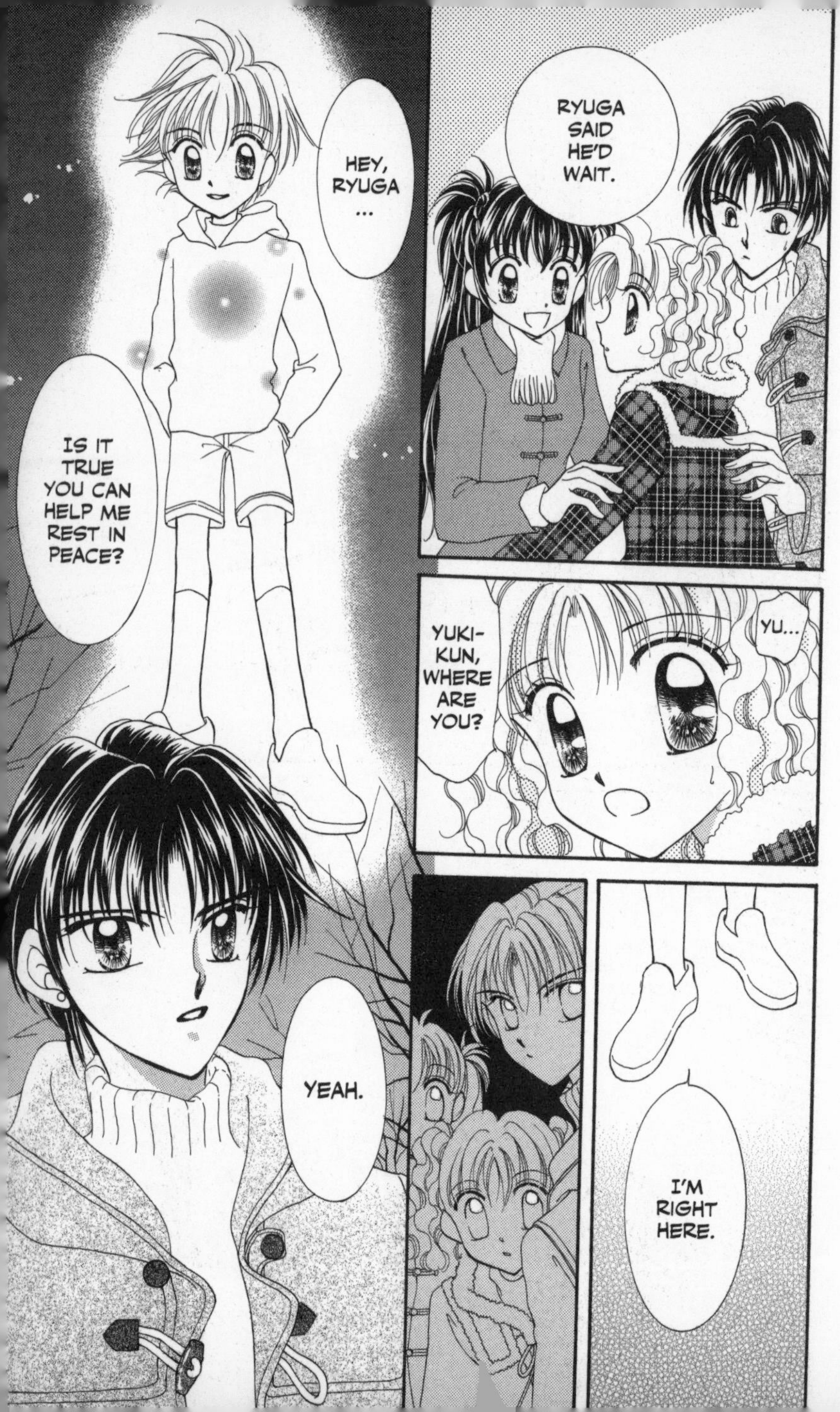
RYUGA SAID HE'D WAIT.
YU...
YUKI-KUN, WHERE ARE YOU?
I'M RIGHT HERE.
HEY, RYUGA ...
IS IT TRUE YOU CAN HELP ME REST IN PEACE?
YEAH.

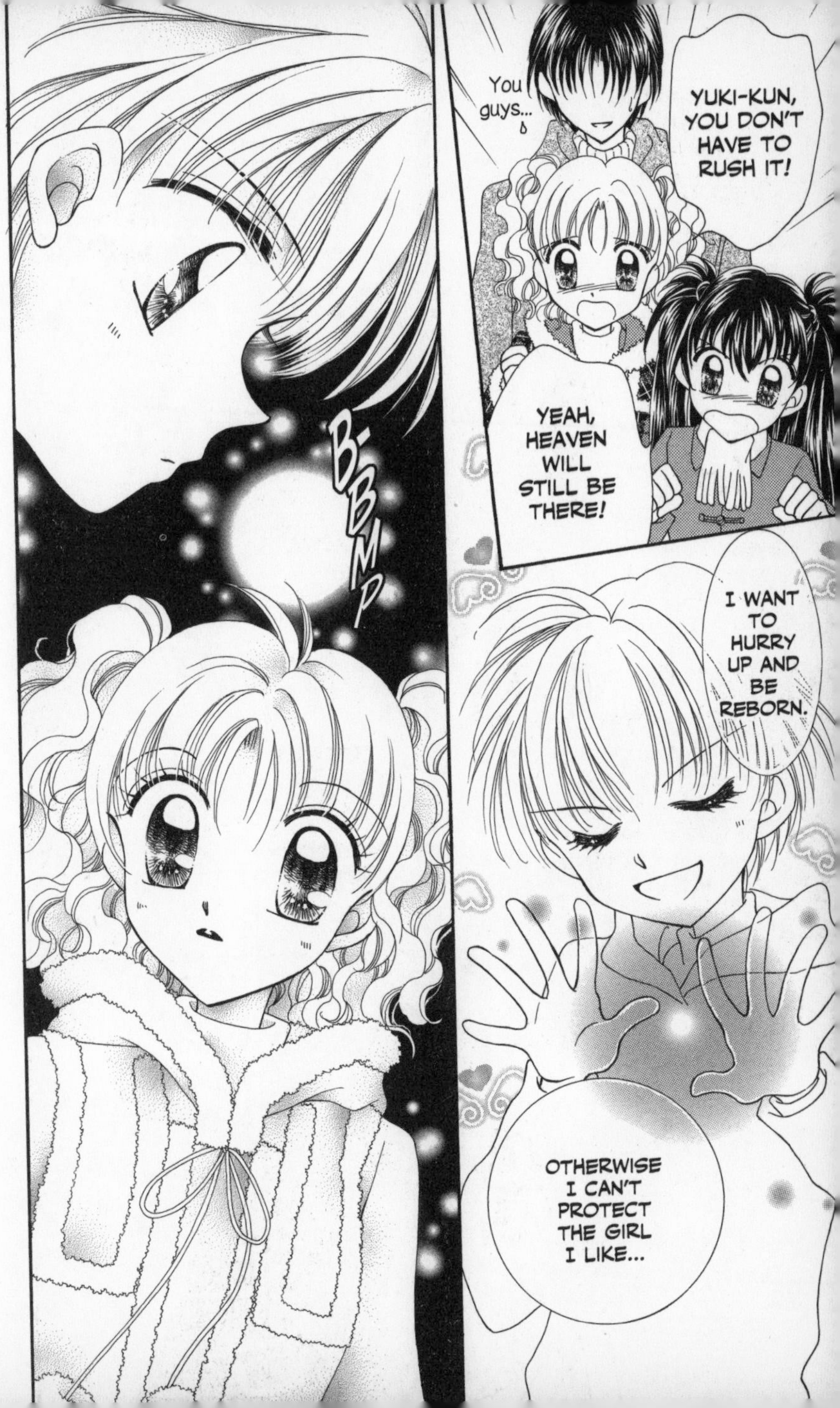
YUKI-KUN, YOU DON'T HAVE TO RUSH IT!
You guys...
YEAH, HEAVEN WILL STILL BE THERE!
I WANT TO HURRY UP AND BE REBORN.
OTHERWISE I CAN'T PROTECT THE GIRL I LIKE...
B-BMP

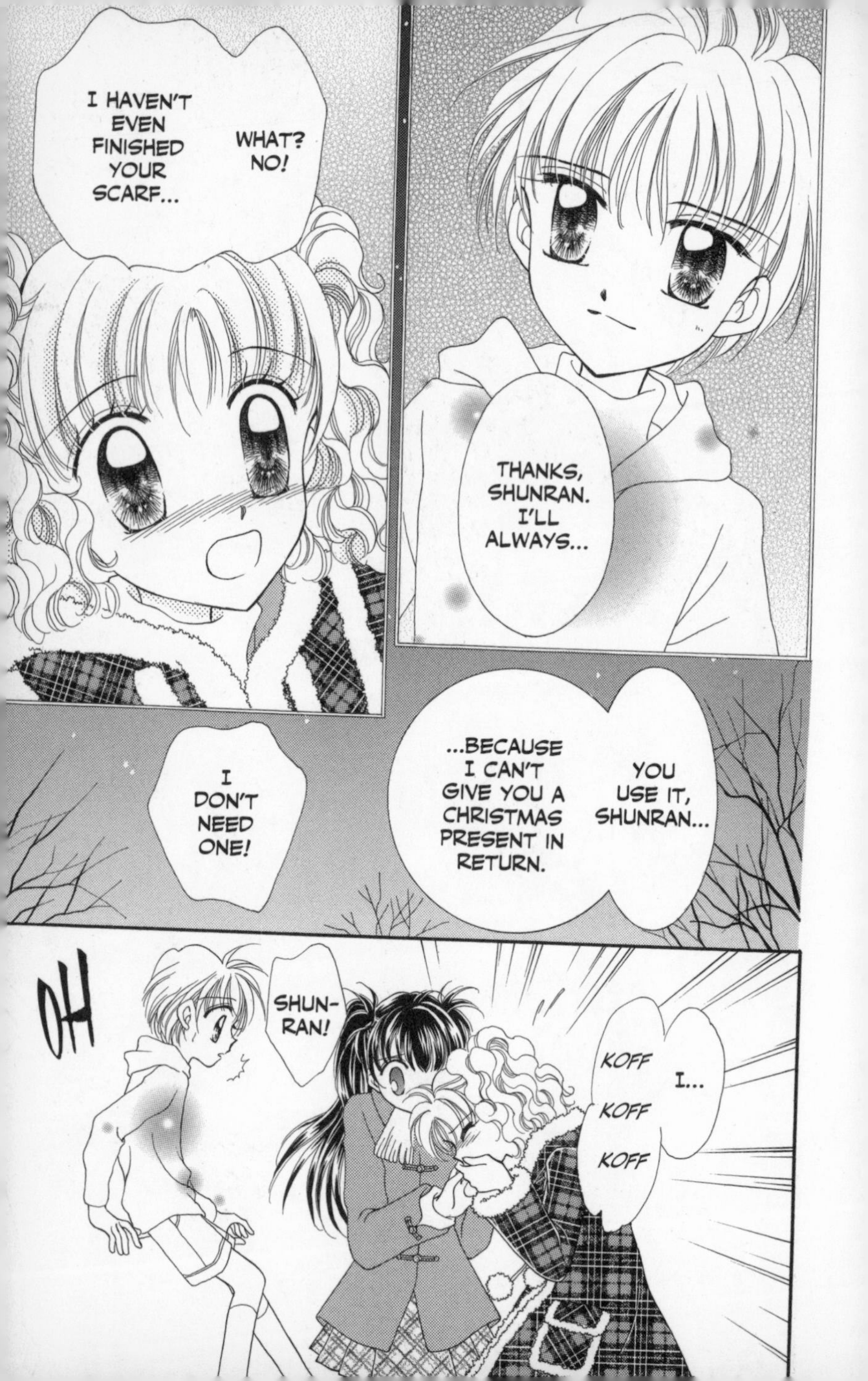
THANKS, SHUNRAN. I'LL ALWAYS...
WHAT? NO!
I HAVEN'T EVEN FINISHED YOUR SCARF...
YOU USE IT, SHUNRAN...
...BECAUSE I CAN'T GIVE YOU A CHRISTMAS PRESENT IN RETURN.
I DON'T NEED ONE!
I...
KOFF KOFF KOFF
SHUN-RAN!

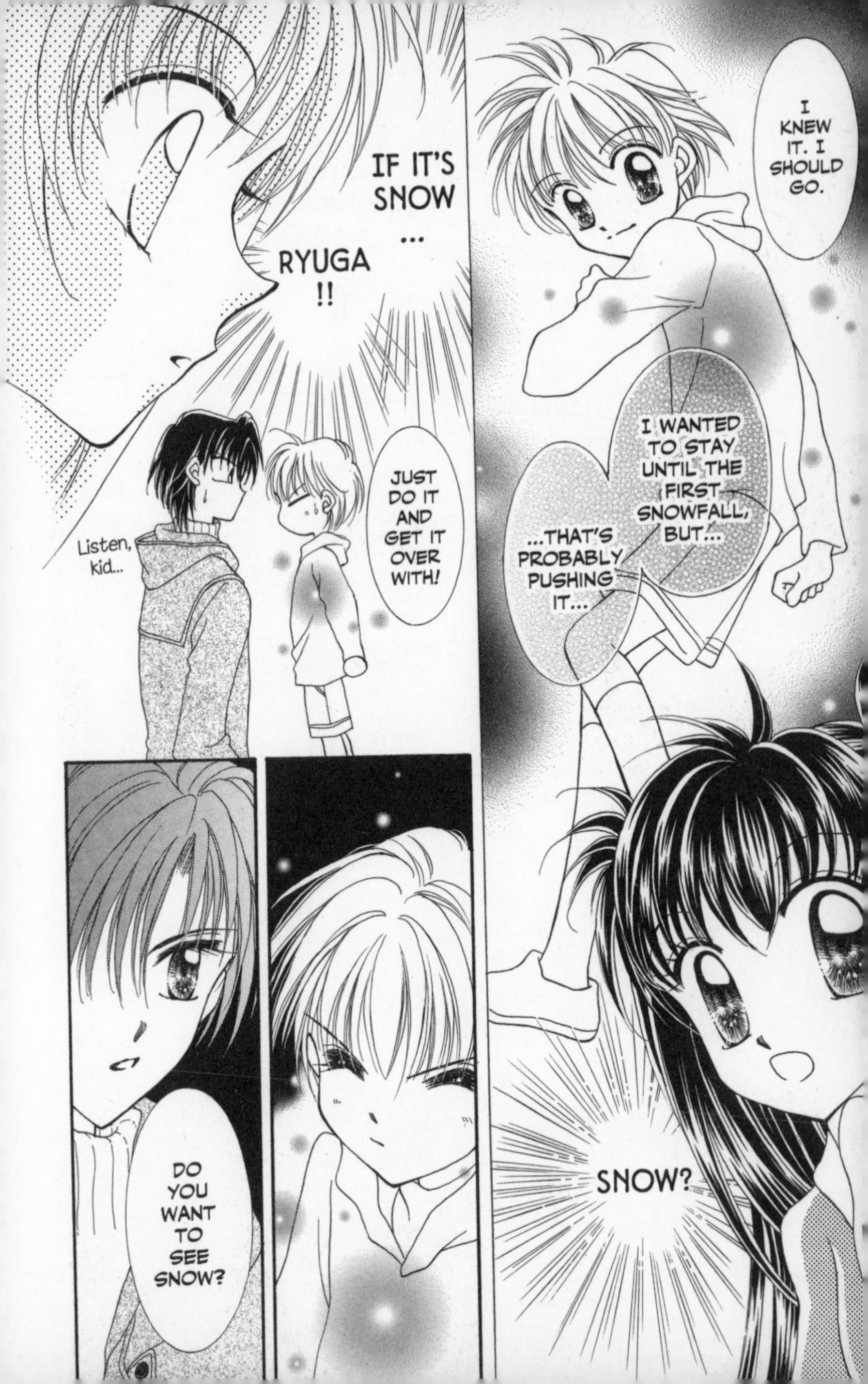
I KNEW IT. I SHOULD GO.
I WANTED TO STAY UNTIL THE FIRST SNOWFALL, BUT...
...THAT'S PROBABLY PUSHING IT...
SNOW?
IF IT'S SNOW ...
RYUGA !!
JUST DO IT AND GET IT OVER WITH!
Listen, kid...
DO YOU WANT TO SEE SNOW?

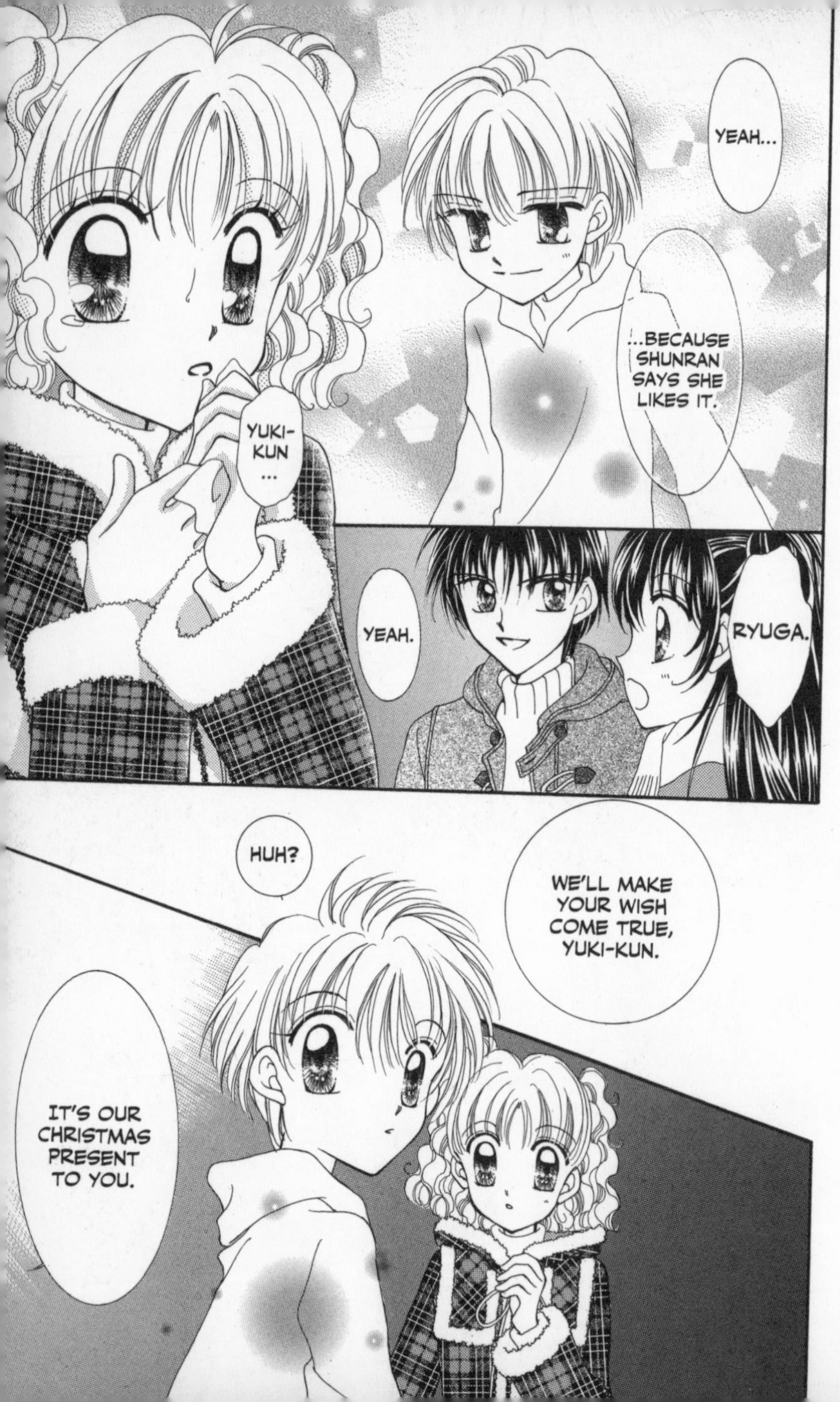
YEAH...
...BECAUSE SHUNRAN SAYS SHE LIKES IT.
RYUGA.
YEAH.
YUKI-KUN ...
WE'LL MAKE YOUR WISH COME TRUE, YUKI-KUN.
HUH?
IT'S OUR CHRISTMAS PRESENT TO YOU.

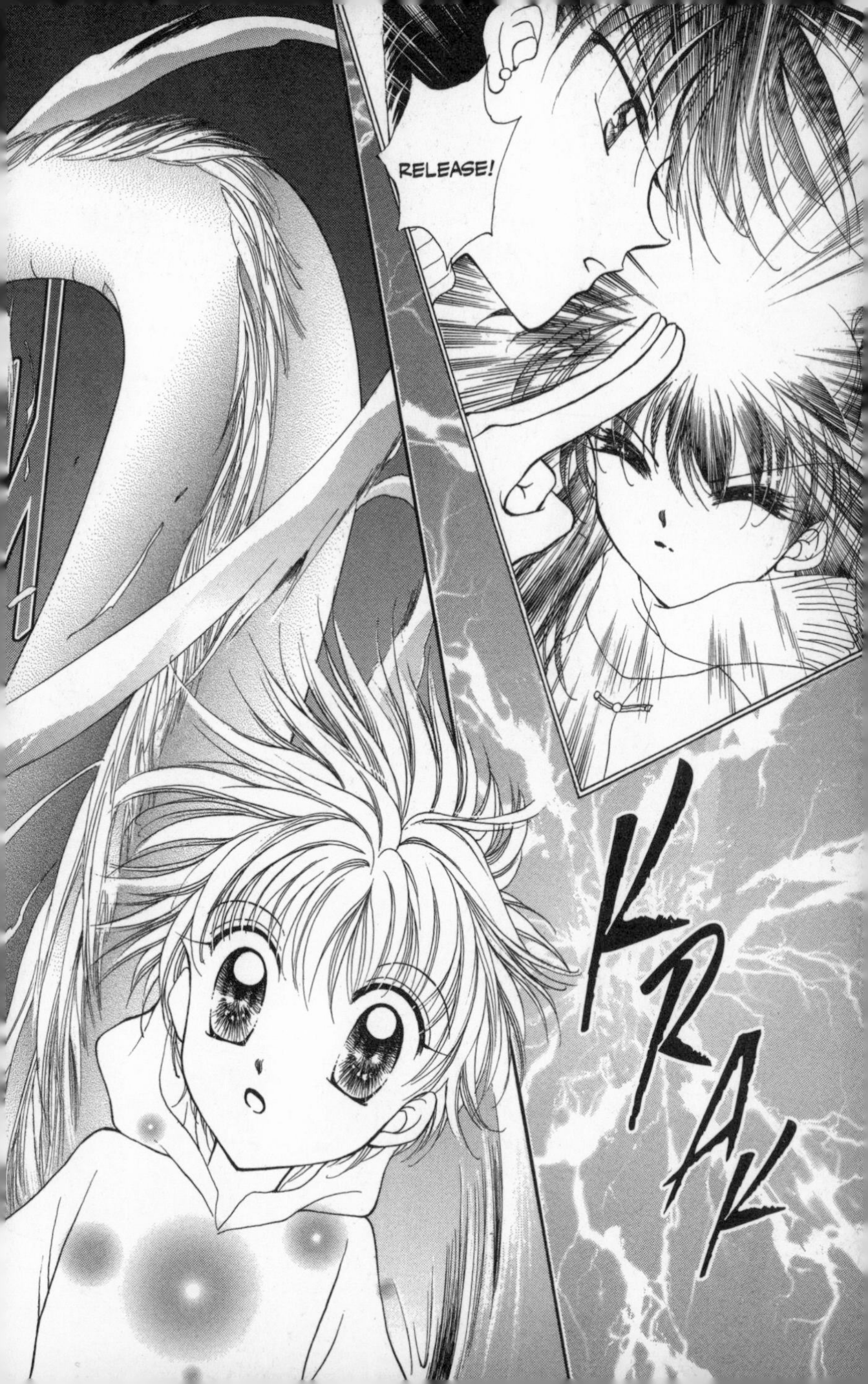
RELEASE!
KRAK

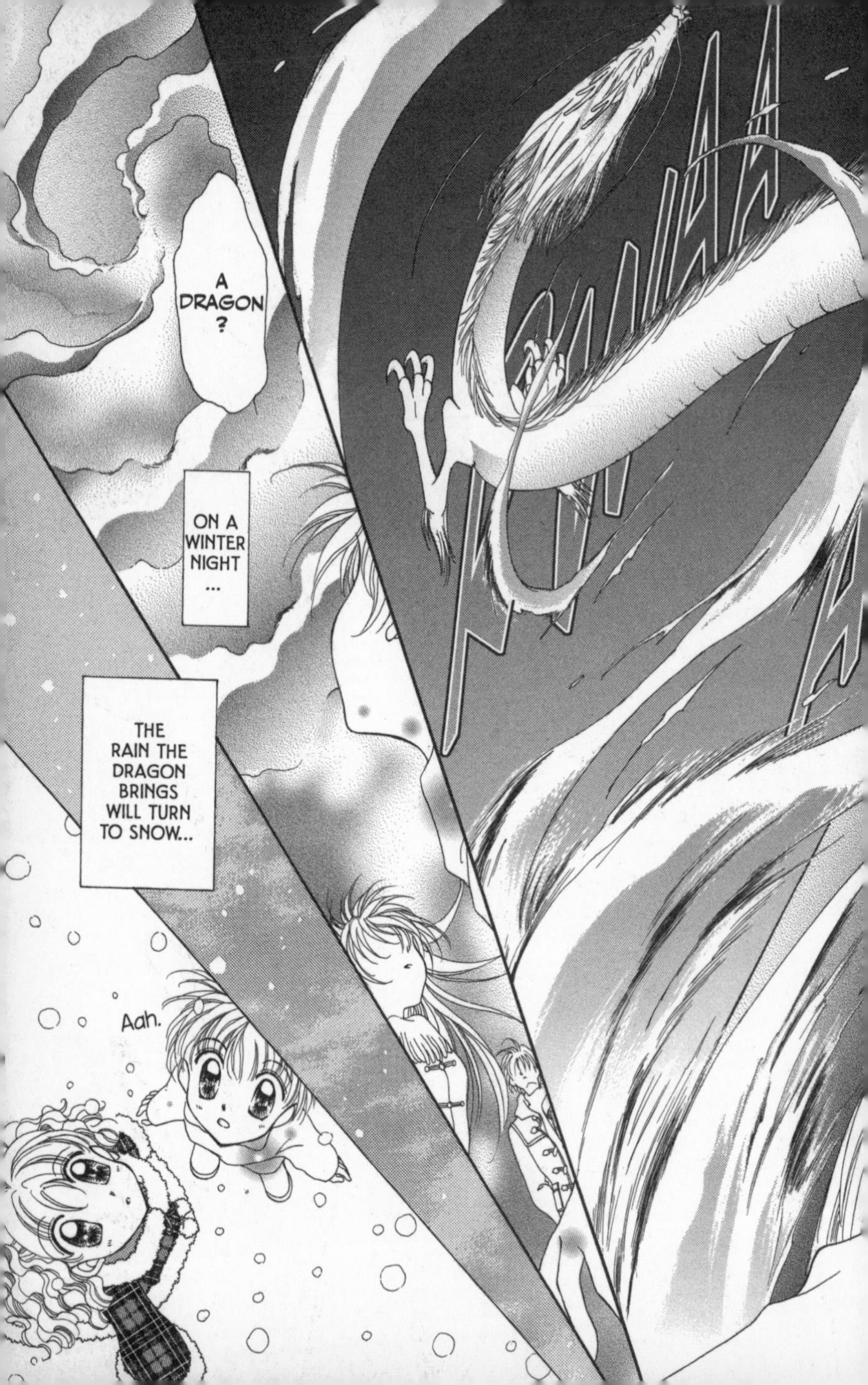
A DRAGON?
ON A WINTER NIGHT...
THE RAIN THE DRAGON BRINGS WILL TURN TO SNOW...
Aah.

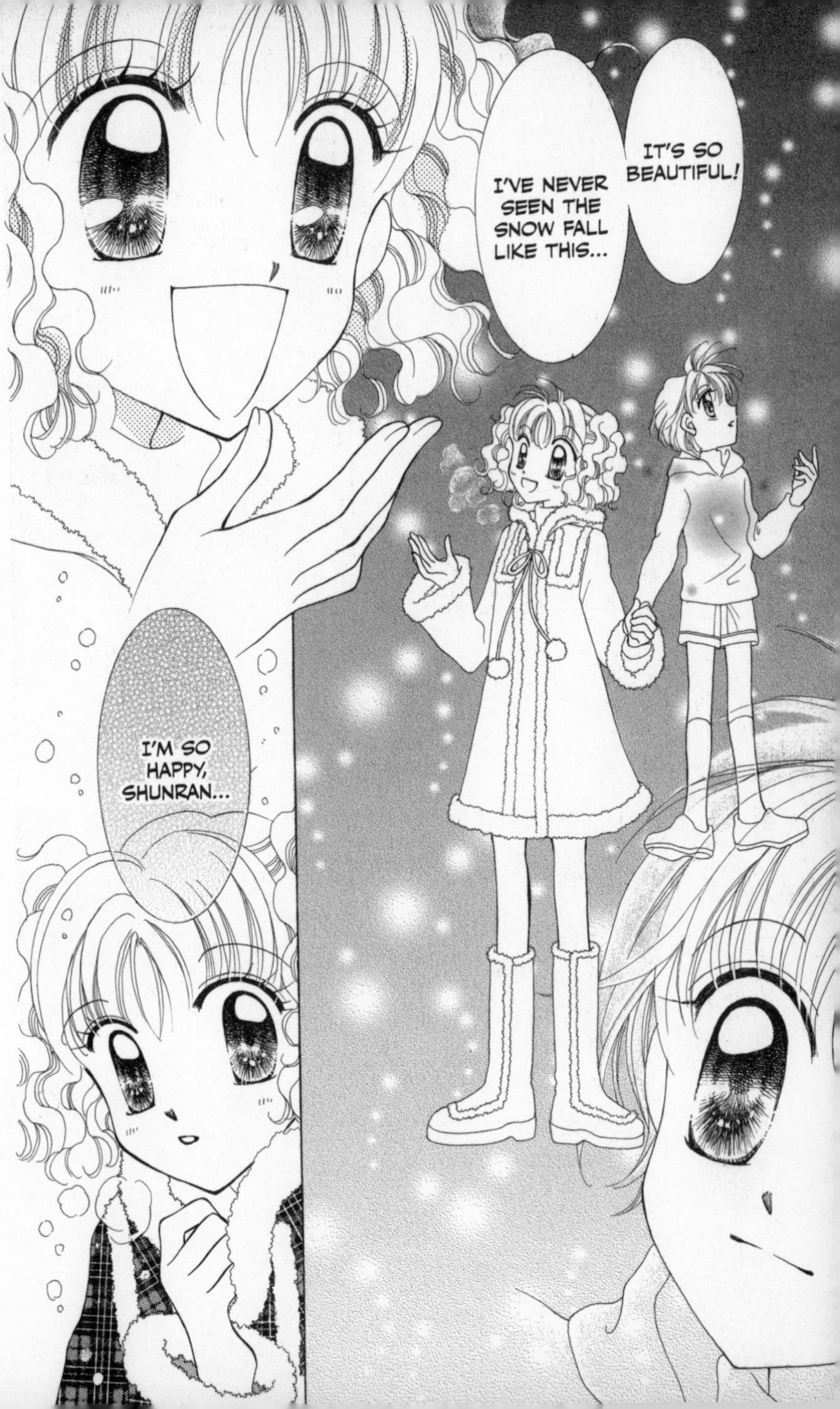
IT'S SO BEAUTIFUL!
I'VE NEVER SEEN THE SNOW FALL LIKE THIS...
I'M SO HAPPY, SHUNRAN...

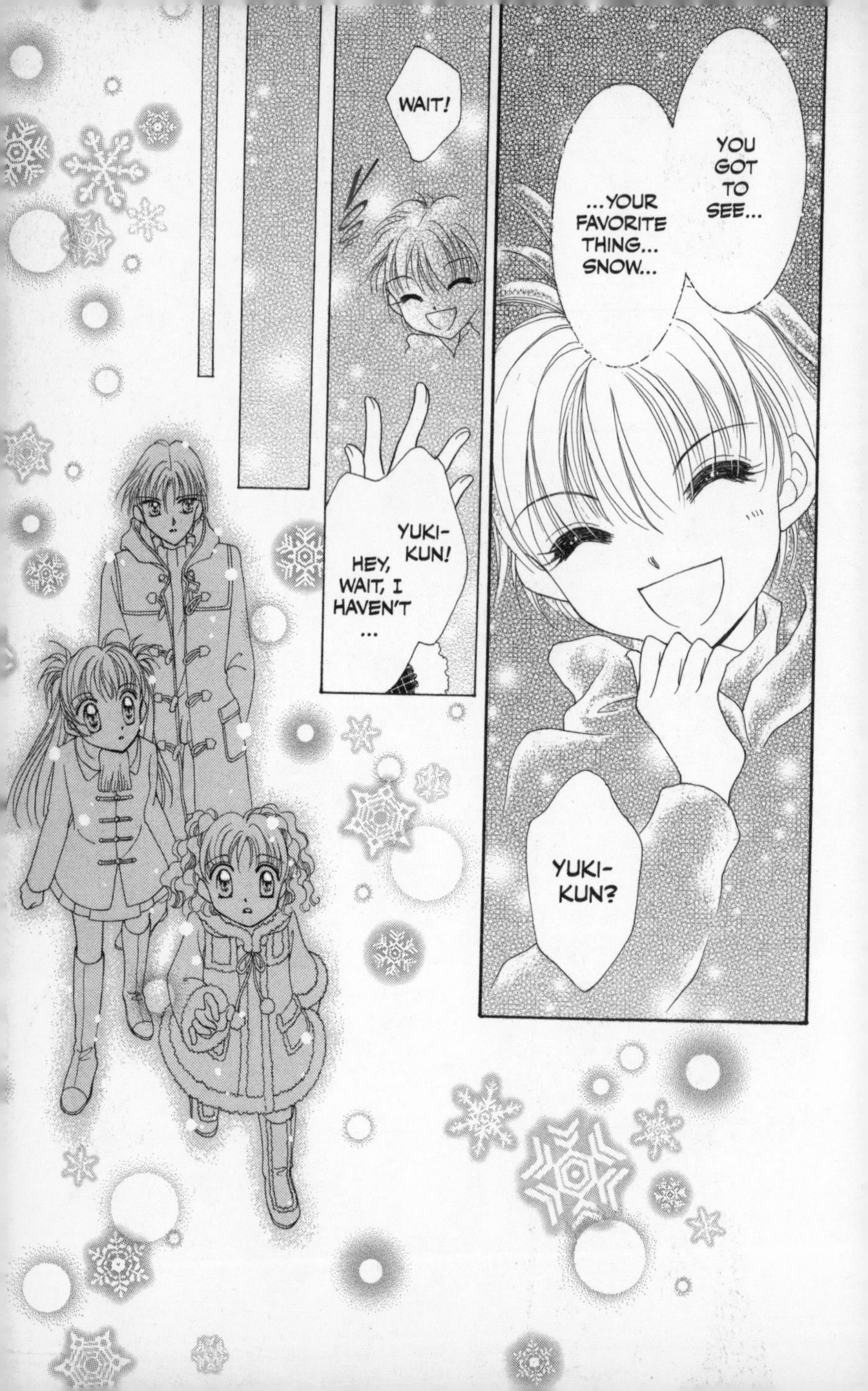
YOU GOT TO SEE...
...YOUR FAVORITE THING... SNOW...
YUKI-KUN?
WAIT!
YUKI-KUN!
HEY, WAIT, I HAVEN'T ...

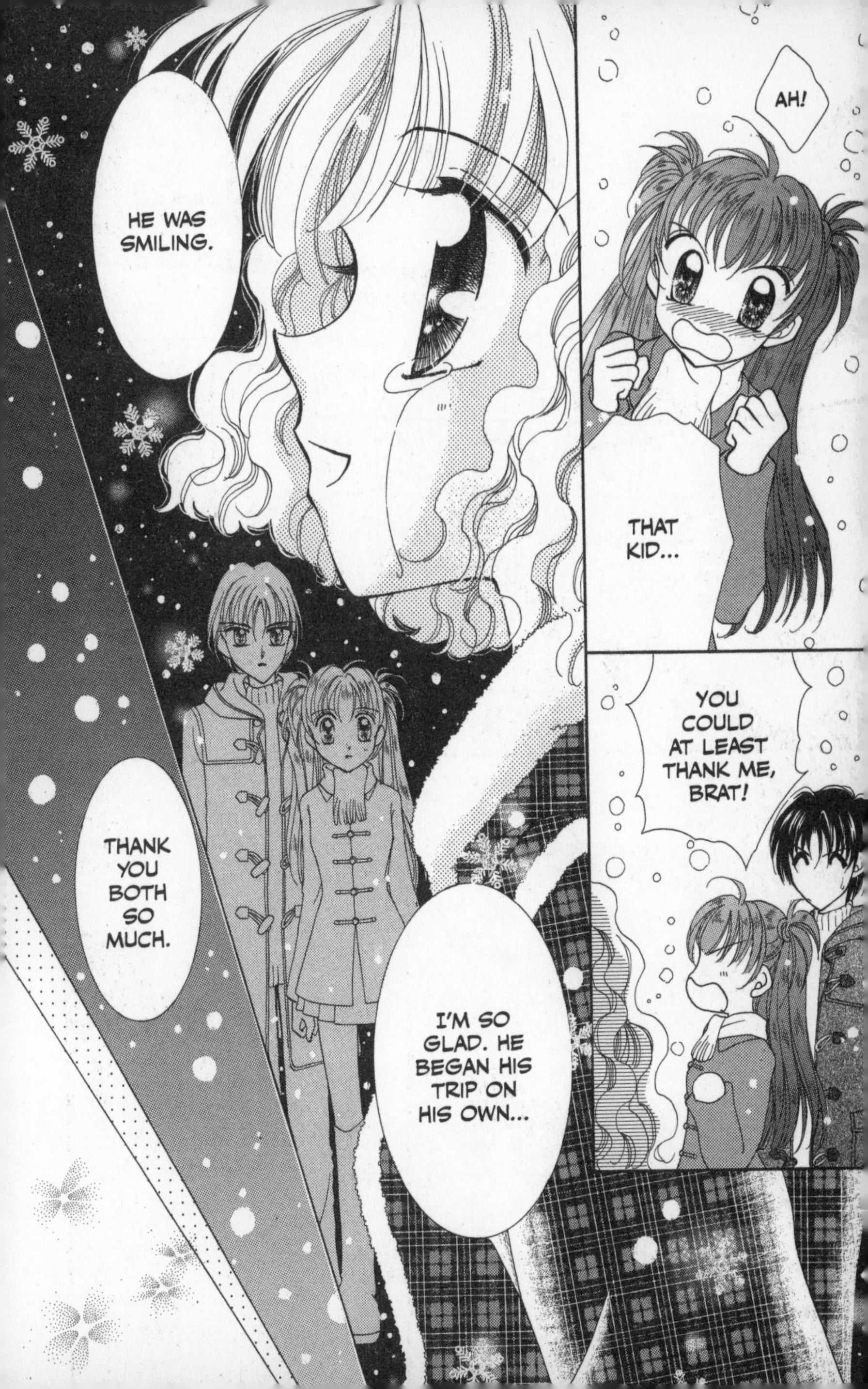
AH!
THAT KID...
YOU COULD AT LEAST THANK ME, BRAT!
HE WAS SMILING.
THANK YOU BOTH SO MUCH.
I'M SO GLAD. HE BEGAN HIS TRIP ON HIS OWN...

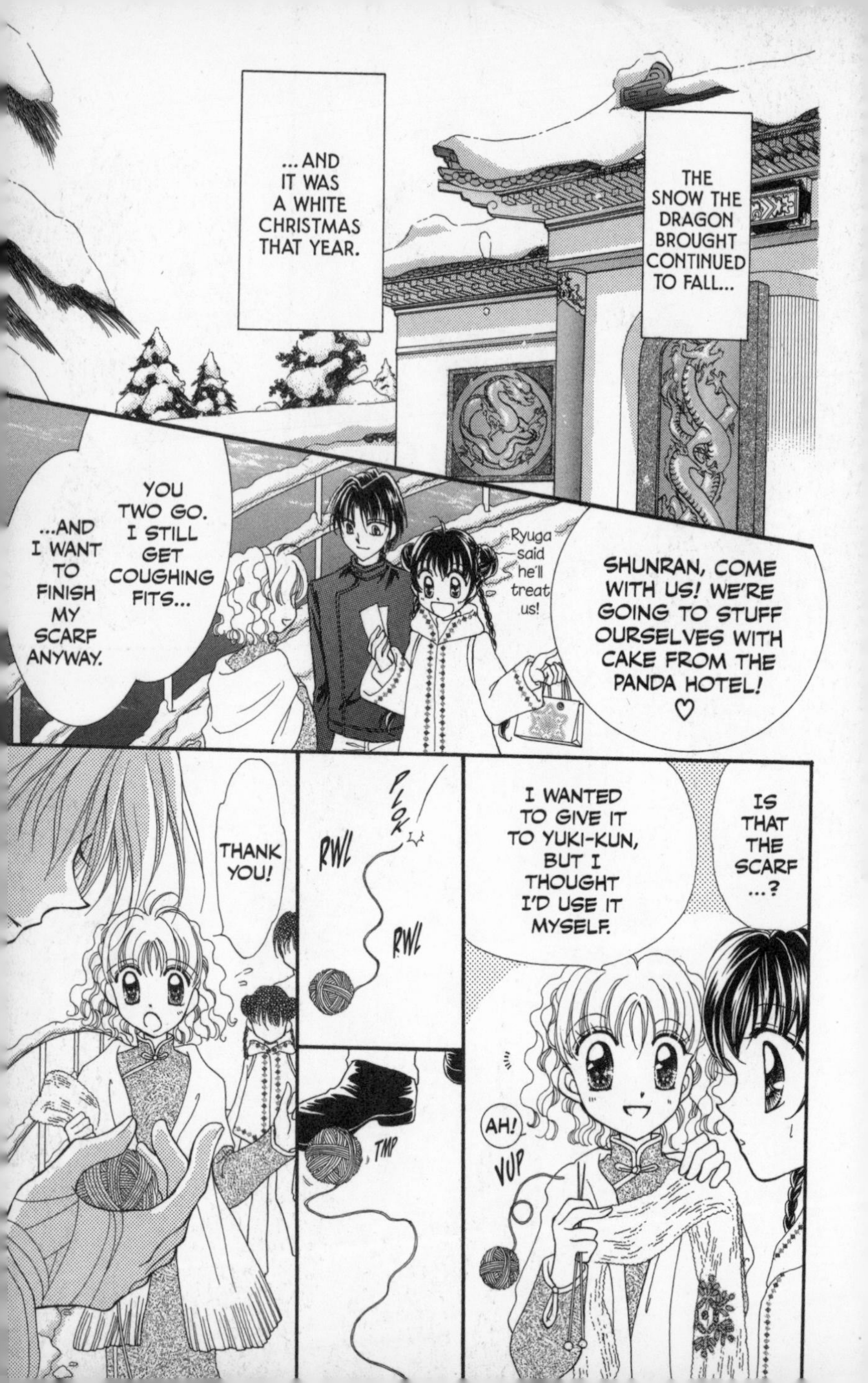
THE SNOW THE DRAGON BROUGHT CONTINUED TO FALL...
...AND IT WAS A WHITE CHRISTMAS THAT YEAR.
SHUNRAN, COME WITH US! WE'RE GOING TO STUFF OURSELVES WITH CAKE FROM THE PANDA HOTEL! ♡
Ryuga said he'll treat us!
YOU TWO GO. I STILL GET COUGHING FITS...
...AND I WANT TO FINISH MY SCARF ANYWAY.
IS THAT THE SCARF ...?
I WANTED TO GIVE IT TO YUKI-KUN, BUT I THOUGHT I'D USE IT MYSELF.
AH!
VUP
PLOK
RWL
RWL
TMP
THANK YOU!

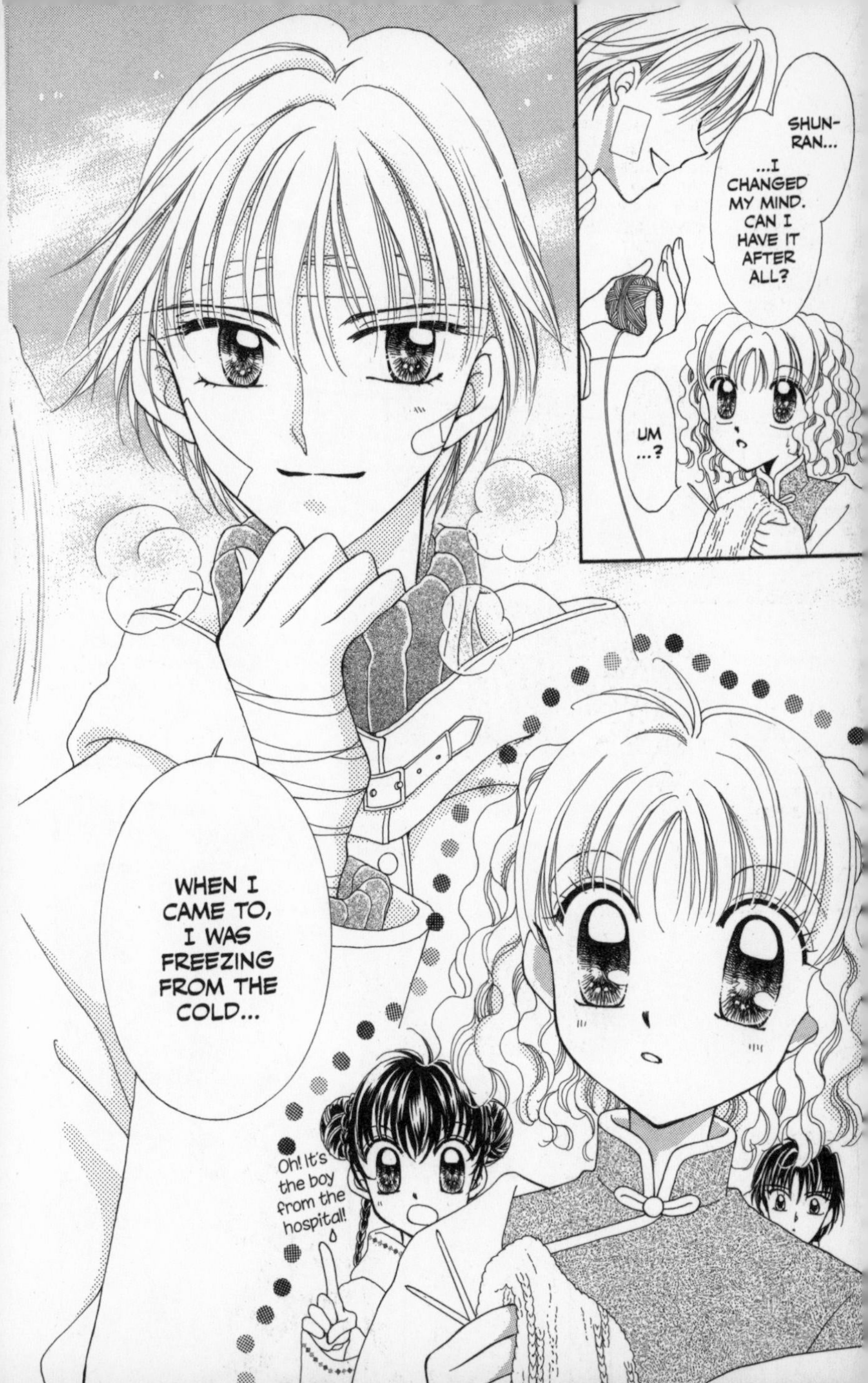
SHUN-RAN...
...I CHANGED MY MIND. CAN I HAVE IT AFTER ALL?
UM ...?
WHEN I CAME TO, I WAS FREEZING FROM THE COLD...
Oh! It's the boy from the hospital!

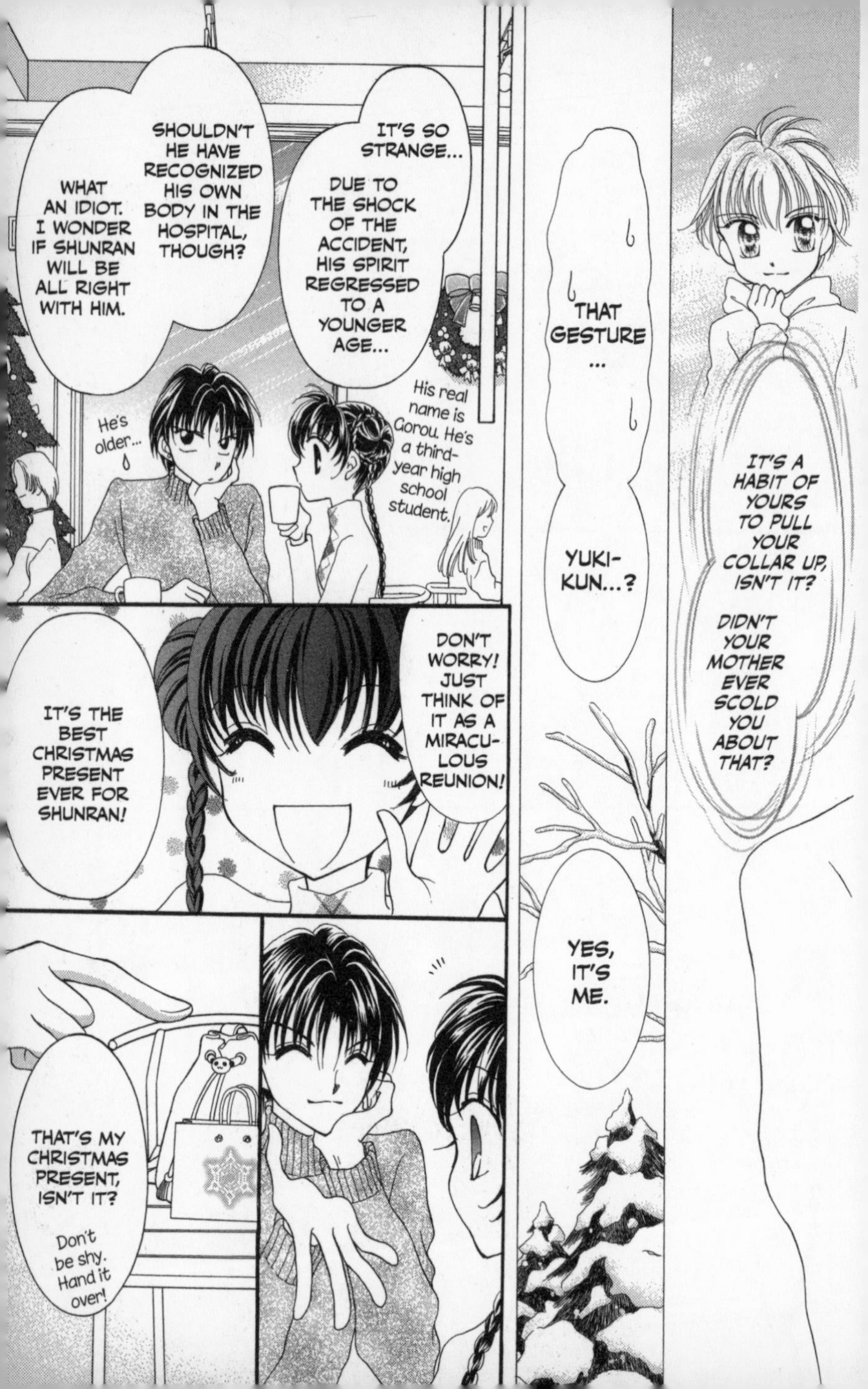
IT'S A HABIT OF YOURS TO PULL YOUR COLLAR UP, ISN'T IT?
DIDN'T YOUR MOTHER EVER SCOLD YOU ABOUT THAT?
THAT GESTURE...
YUKI-KUN...?
YES, IT'S ME.
IT'S SO STRANGE...
DUE TO THE SHOCK OF THE ACCIDENT, HIS SPIRIT REGRESSED TO A YOUNGER AGE...
SHOULDN'T HE HAVE RECOGNIZED HIS OWN BODY IN THE HOSPITAL, THOUGH?
WHAT AN IDIOT. I WONDER IF SHUNRAN WILL BE ALL RIGHT WITH HIM.
His real name is Gorou. He's a third-year high school student.
He's older...
DON'T WORRY! JUST THINK OF IT AS A MIRACULOUS REUNION!
IT'S THE BEST CHRISTMAS PRESENT EVER FOR SHUNRAN!
THAT'S MY CHRISTMAS PRESENT, ISN'T IT?
Don't be shy. Hand it over!

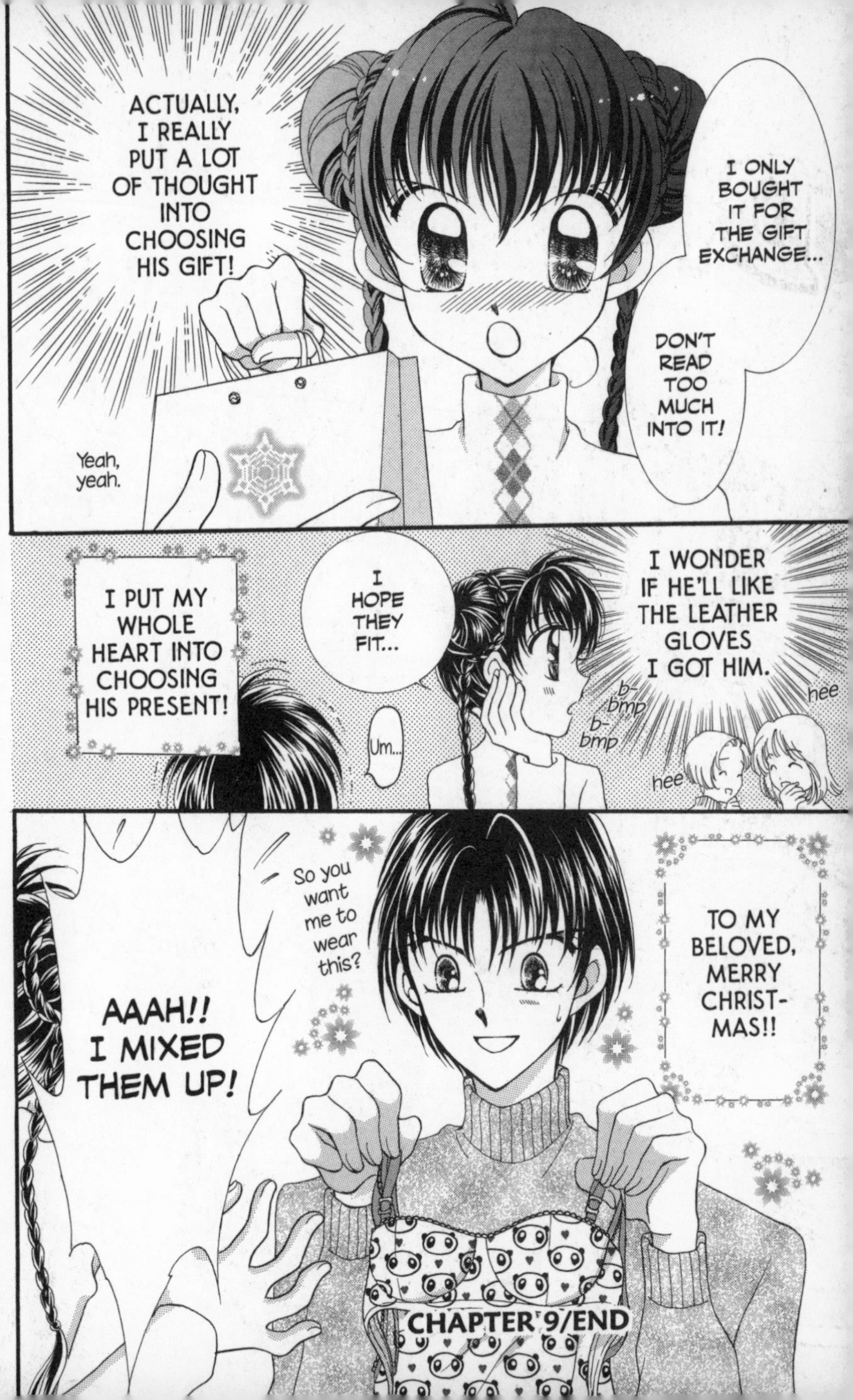

I ONLY BOUGHT IT FOR THE GIFT EXCHANGE...
DON'T READ TOO MUCH INTO IT!
ACTUALLY, I REALLY PUT A LOT OF THOUGHT INTO CHOOSING HIS GIFT!
Yeah, yeah.
I WONDER IF HE'LL LIKE THE LEATHER GLOVES I GOT HIM.
hee
hee
b-bmp
b-bmp
I HOPE THEY FIT...
Um...
I PUT MY WHOLE HEART INTO CHOOSING HIS PRESENT!
TO MY BELOVED, MERRY CHRIST-MAS!!
So you want me to wear this?
AAAH!! I MIXED THEM UP!
CHAPTER 9/END

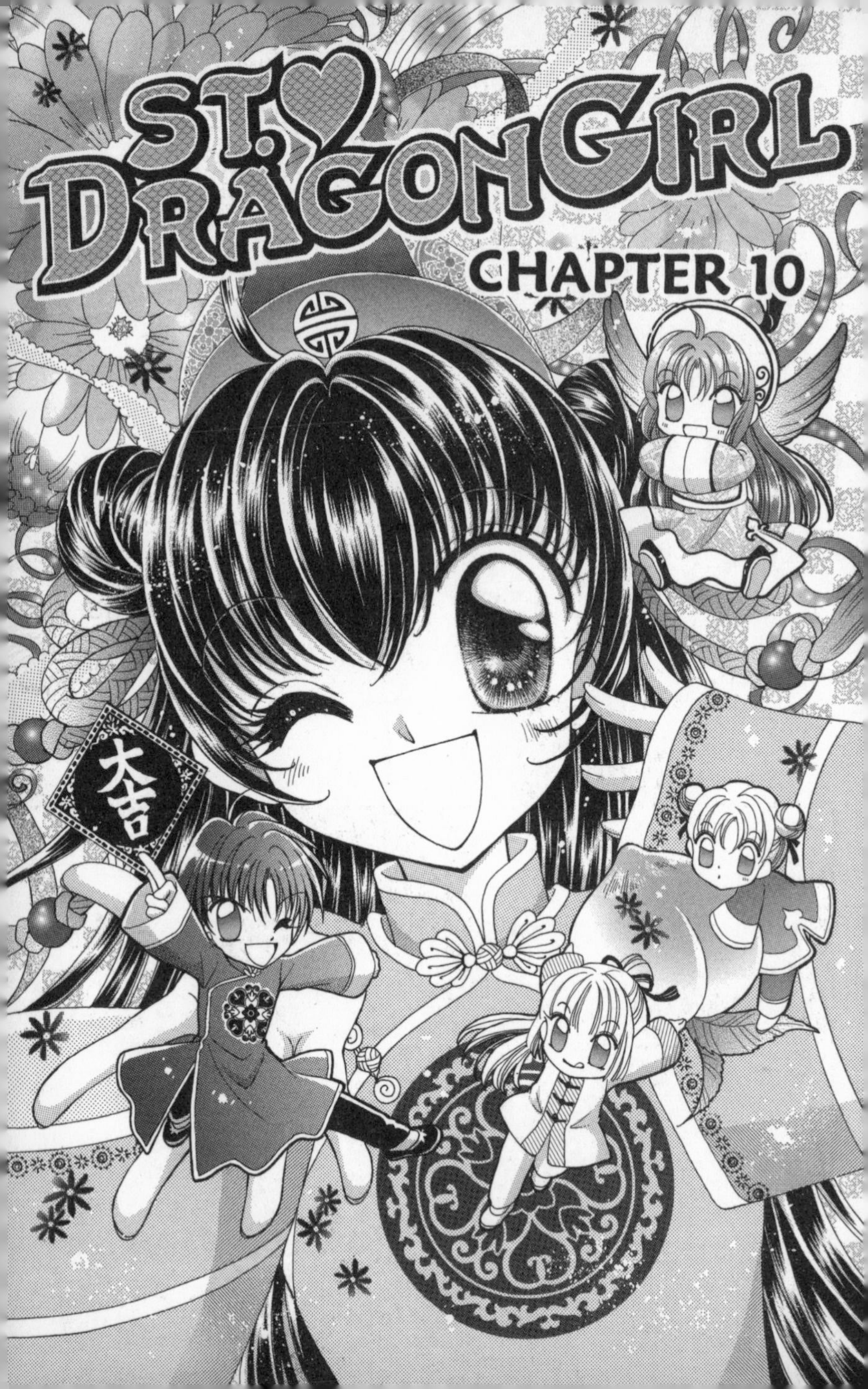
ST. DRAGON GIRL
CHAPTER 10
大吉

Suzaku.

It's the divine beast that protects the south; the scarlet bird that governs fire.

THERE WAS ANOTHER SMALL FIRE IN THE SOUTH...

THEY'RE INVESTIGATING THE SOURCE OF THE FIRE.

Shueisha Newspaper   December 30 (S

Another Suspected Arson!!

Kenpo Dojo

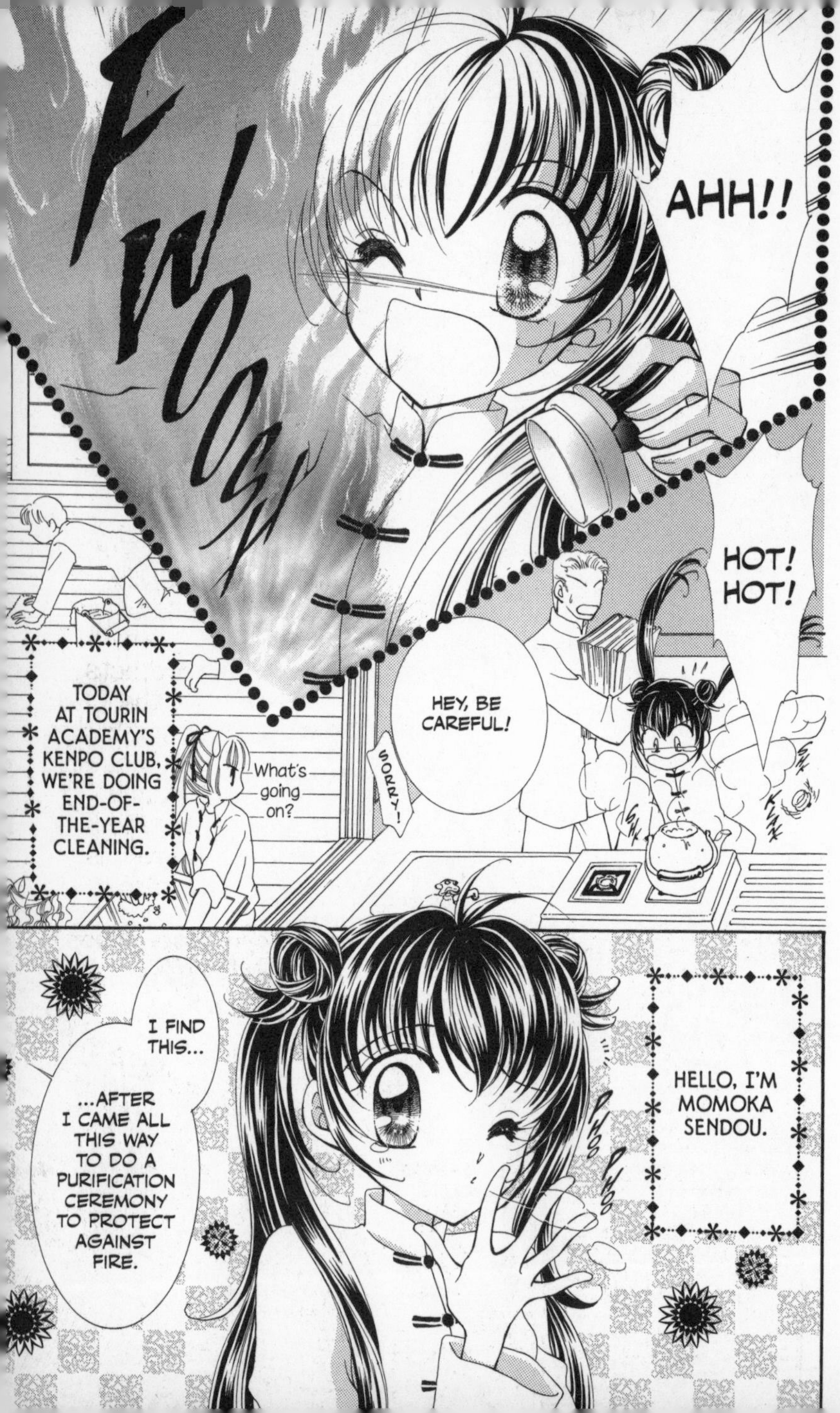
FWOOSH
AHH!!
HOT! HOT!
HEY, BE CAREFUL!
SORRY!
What's going on?
TODAY AT TOURIN ACADEMY'S KENPO CLUB, WE'RE DOING END-OF-THE-YEAR CLEANING.
HELLO, I'M MOMOKA SENDOU.
I FIND THIS...
...AFTER I CAME ALL THIS WAY TO DO A PURIFICATION CEREMONY TO PROTECT AGAINST FIRE.

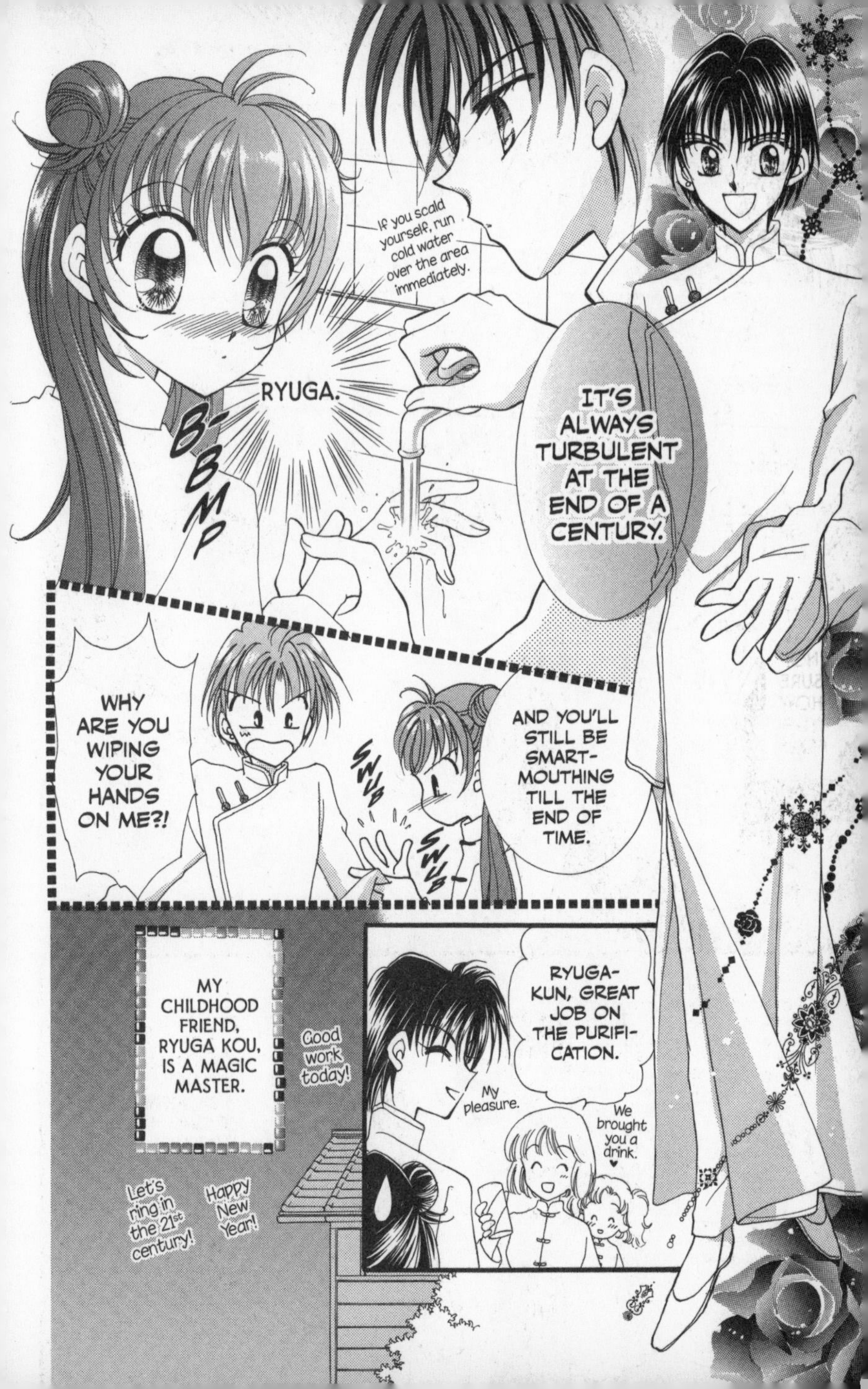

If you scald yourself, run cold water over the area immediately.
RYUGA.
B-BMP
IT'S ALWAYS TURBULENT AT THE END OF A CENTURY.
AND YOU'LL STILL BE SMART-MOUTHING TILL THE END OF TIME.
SWUB SWUB
WHY ARE YOU WIPING YOUR HANDS ON ME?!
RYUGA-KUN, GREAT JOB ON THE PURIFI-CATION.
My pleasure.
We brought you a drink.
MY CHILDHOOD FRIEND, RYUGA KOU, IS A MAGIC MASTER.
Good work today!
Happy New Year!
Let's ring in the 21st century!

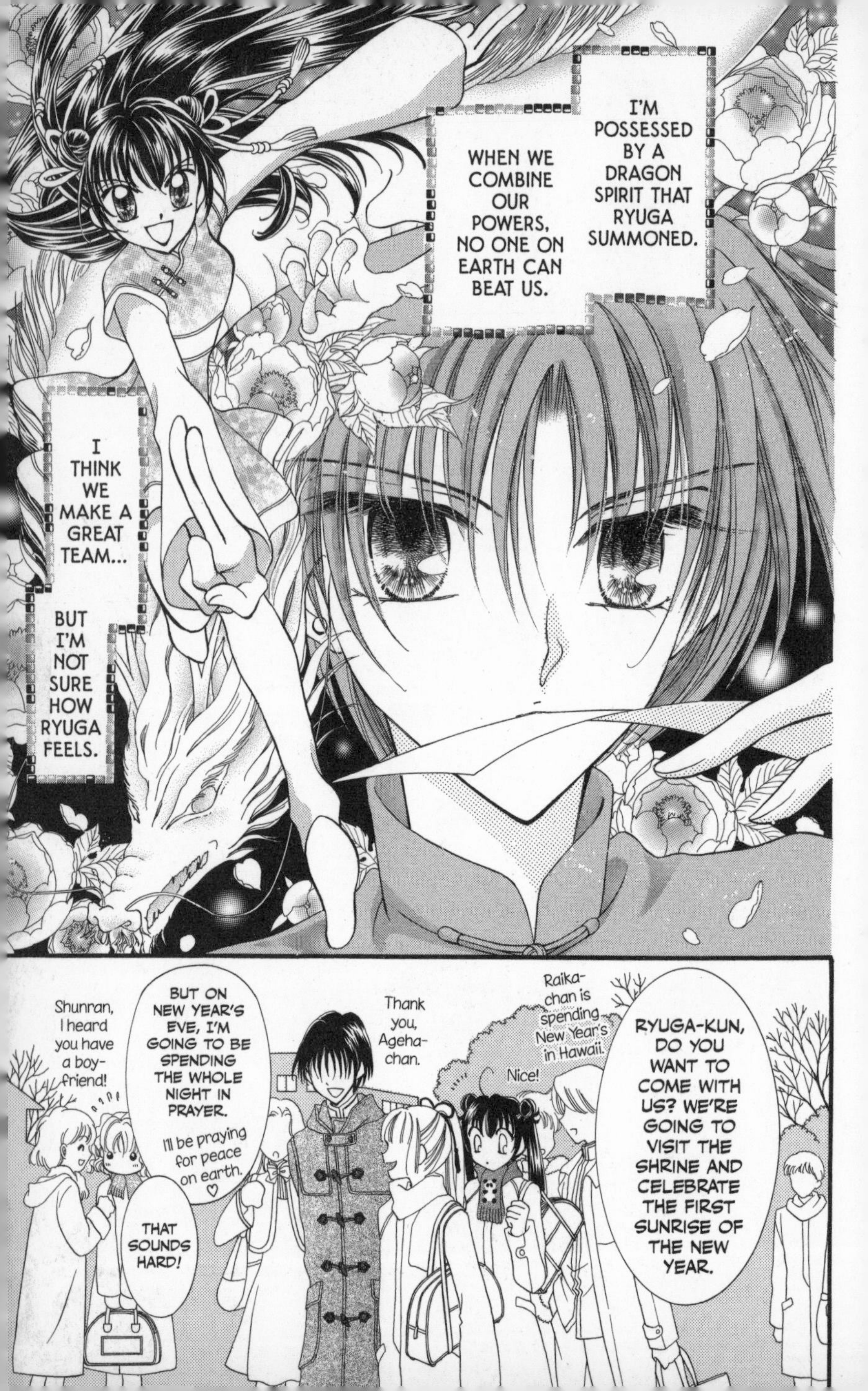
I'M POSSESSED BY A DRAGON SPIRIT THAT RYUGA SUMMONED.
WHEN WE COMBINE OUR POWERS, NO ONE ON EARTH CAN BEAT US.
I THINK WE MAKE A GREAT TEAM...
BUT I'M NOT SURE HOW RYUGA FEELS.
RYUGA-KUN, DO YOU WANT TO COME WITH US? WE'RE GOING TO VISIT THE SHRINE AND CELEBRATE THE FIRST SUNRISE OF THE NEW YEAR.
Raika-chan is spending New Year's in Hawaii.
Nice!
Thank you, Ageha-chan.
BUT ON NEW YEAR'S EVE, I'M GOING TO BE SPENDING THE WHOLE NIGHT IN PRAYER.
I'll be praying for peace on earth. ♡
Shunran, I heard you have a boy-friend!
THAT SOUNDS HARD!

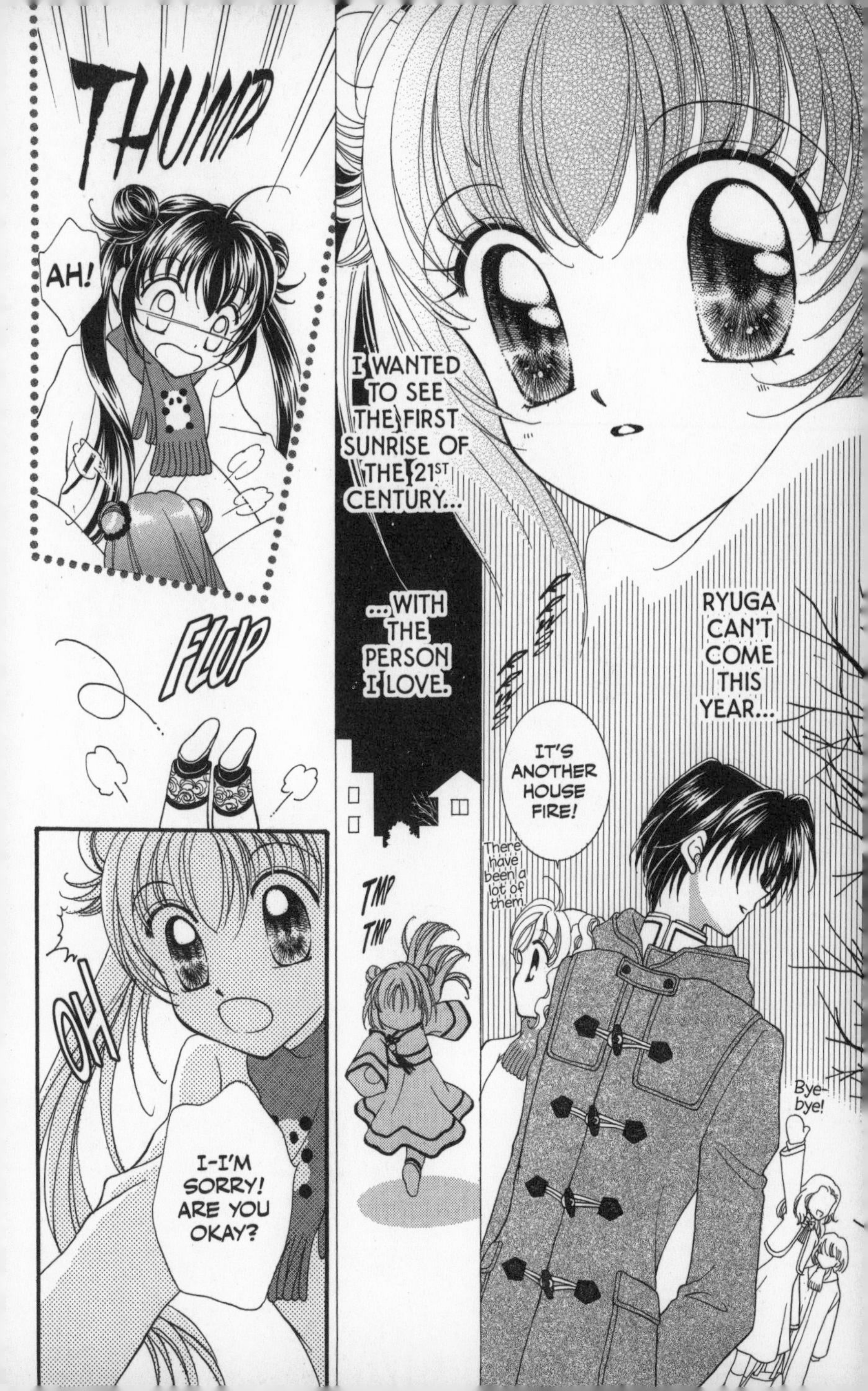
I WANTED TO SEE THE FIRST SUNRISE OF THE 21ST CENTURY...
...WITH THE PERSON I LOVE.
RYUGA CAN'T COME THIS YEAR...
IT'S ANOTHER HOUSE FIRE!
There have been a lot of them.
Bye-bye!
TMP TMP
THUMP
AH!
FLUP
OH
I-I'M SORRY! ARE YOU OKAY?

3

This story about Suzaku appeared in the February issue of *Ribon.*

There were a lot of letters saying how cute Suzaku is. ♥

I really like this character a lot, so I'd like her to appear again sometime. I also had requests to see the human versions of Byakko, Seiryuu, and Genbu. I'd love to draw Byakko, but I can't even imagine what Genbu's human form would look like! But maybe I'll challenge myself someday.

This story was printed in red ink in the magazine, and it fit Suzaku's story so perfectly. I was thrilled. ♡

Finally, if only 2001 had been the year of the bird, it would have been even more perfect! (laugh) But it was the year of the snake.

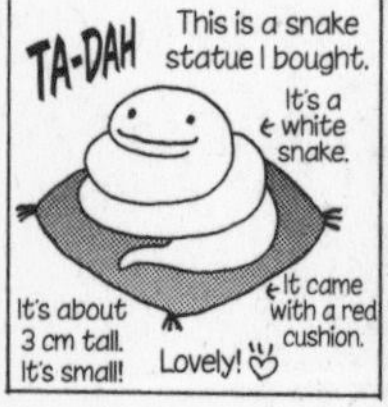
TA-DAH
This is a snake statue I bought.
It's a white snake.
It came with a red cushion.
It's about 3 cm tall. It's small!
Lovely! ♡

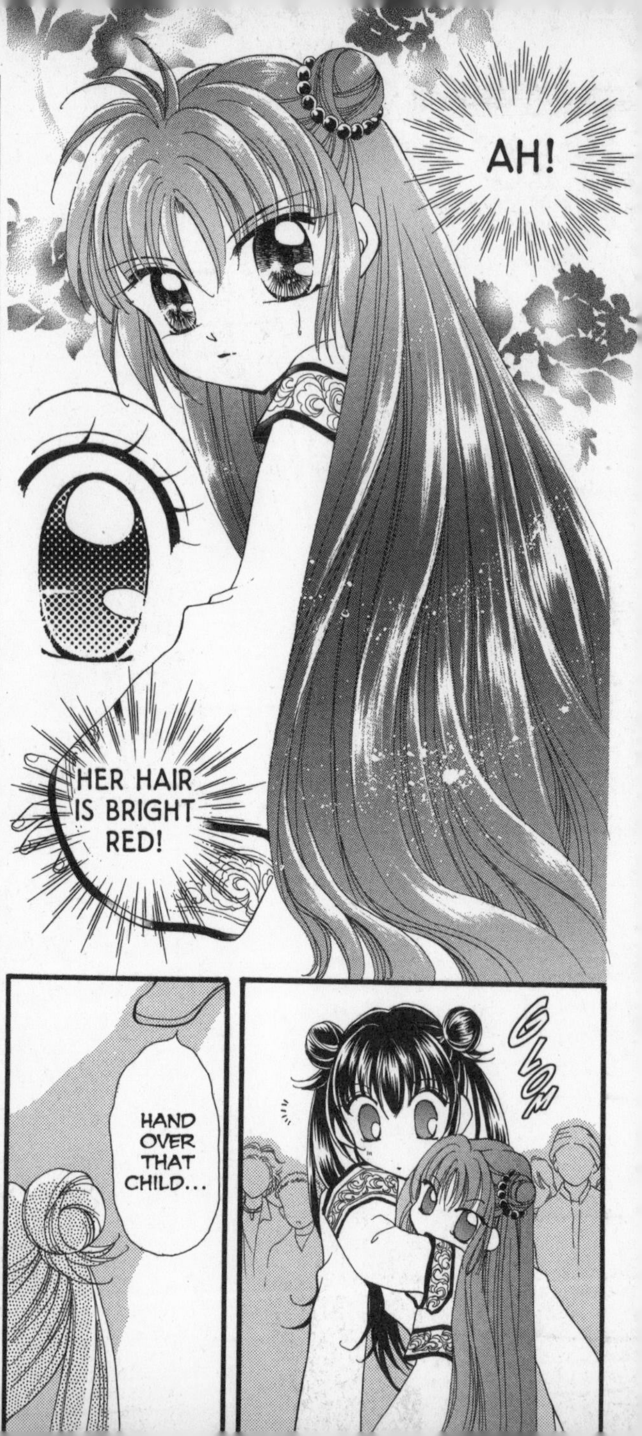
AH!
HER HAIR IS BRIGHT RED!
GLOM
HAND OVER THAT CHILD...

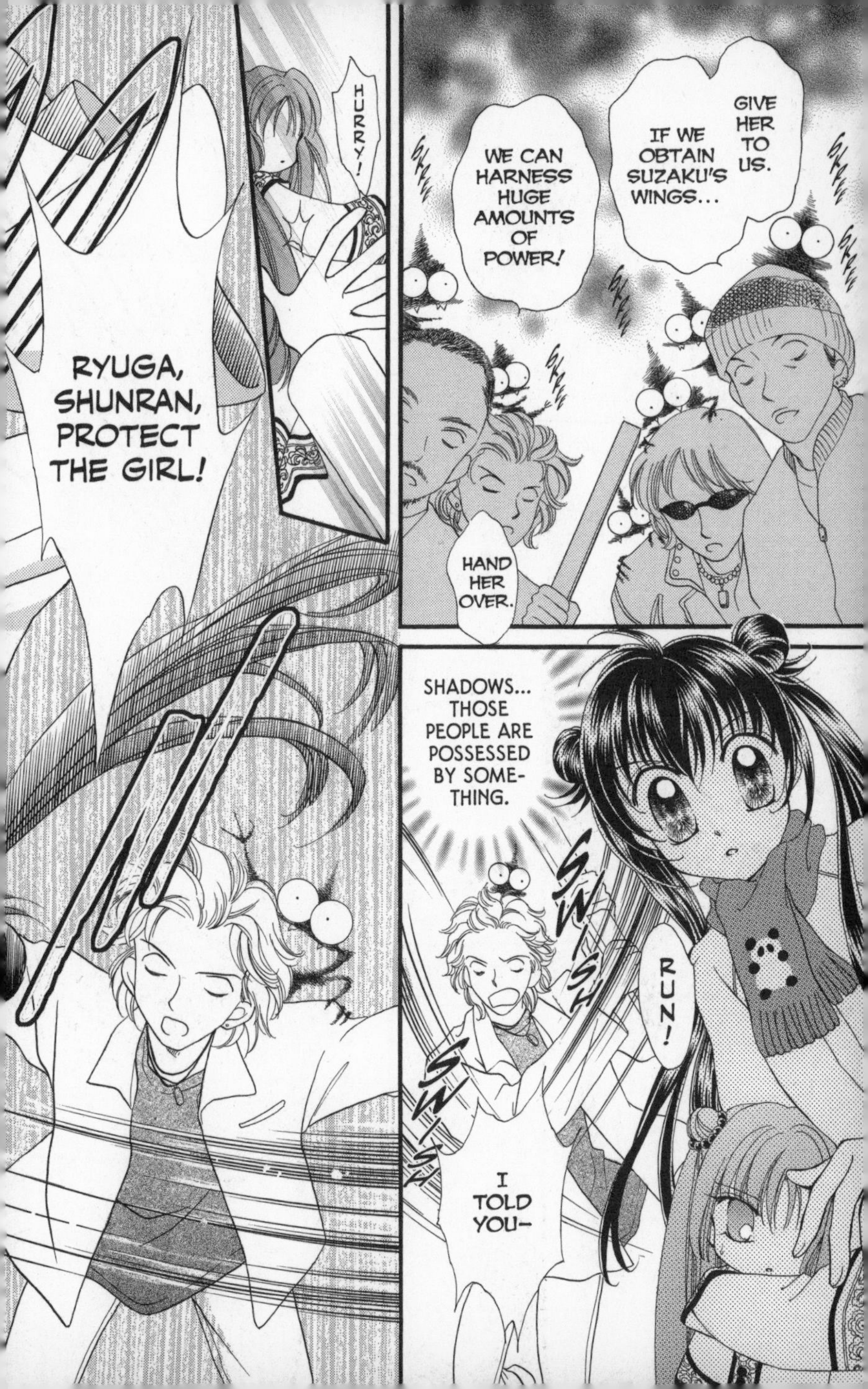
GIVE HER TO US.
IF WE OBTAIN SUZAKU'S WINGS...
WE CAN HARNESS HUGE AMOUNTS OF POWER!
HAND HER OVER.
SHADOWS... THOSE PEOPLE ARE POSSESSED BY SOME-THING.
RUN!
SWISH
SWISH
I TOLD YOU-
HURRY!
RYUGA, SHUNRAN, PROTECT THE GIRL!

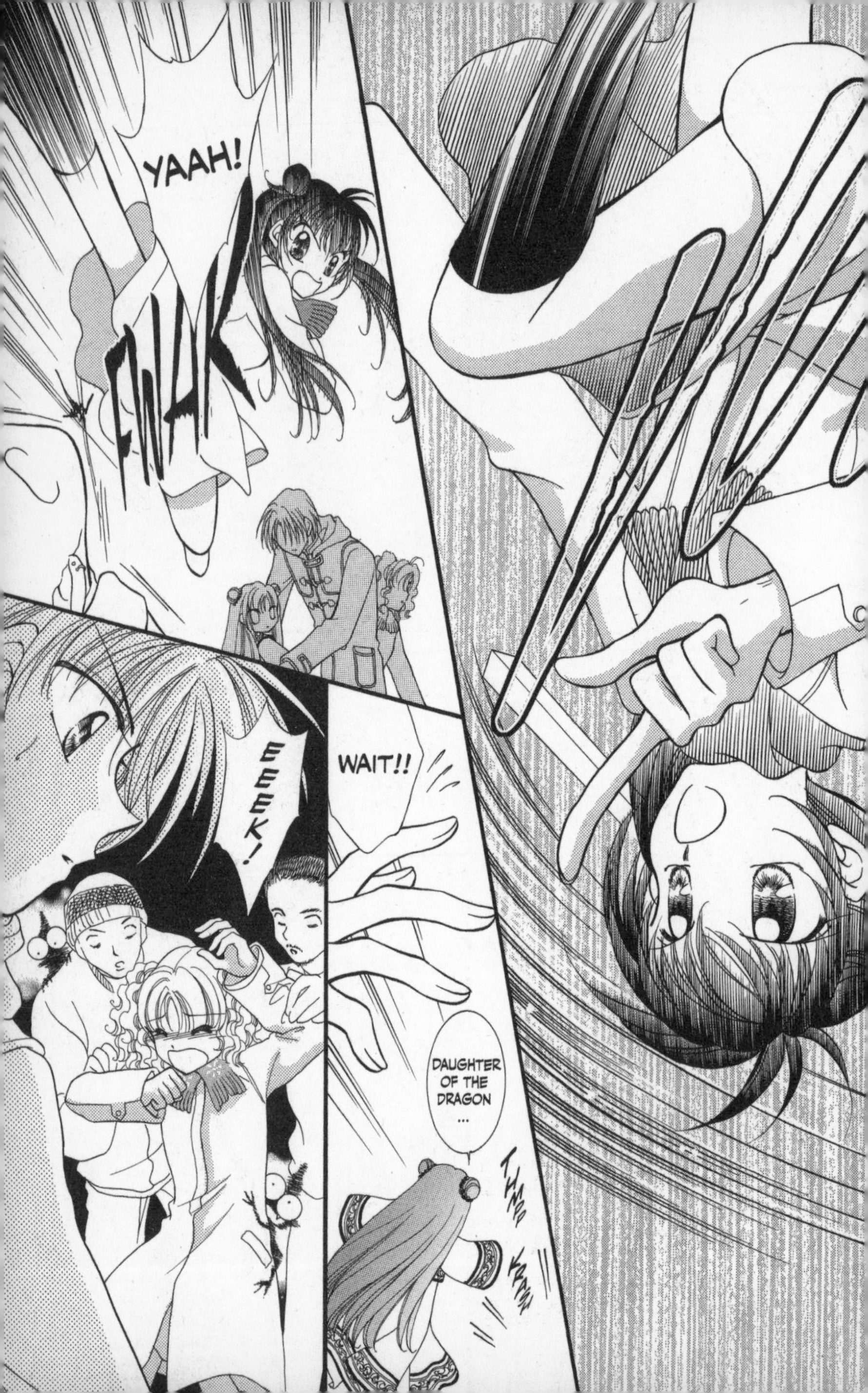
YAAH!
FWAK
WAIT!!
DAUGHTER OF THE DRAGON ...
EEEEK!

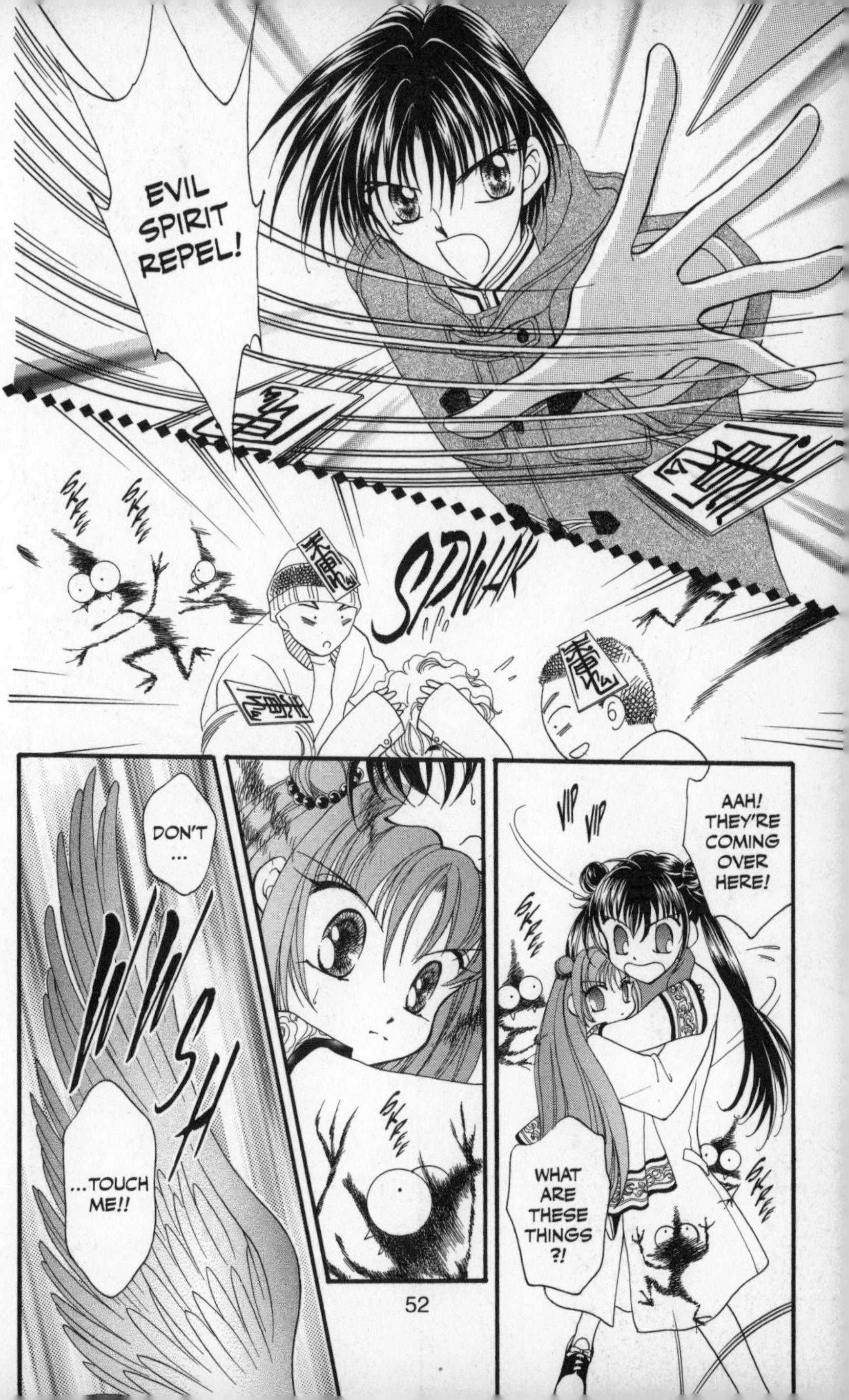
EVIL SPIRIT REPEL!
SKREE
SKREE
SPWAK
VIP VIP
AAH! THEY'RE COMING OVER HERE!
WHAT ARE THESE THINGS?!
DON'T ...
...TOUCH ME!!

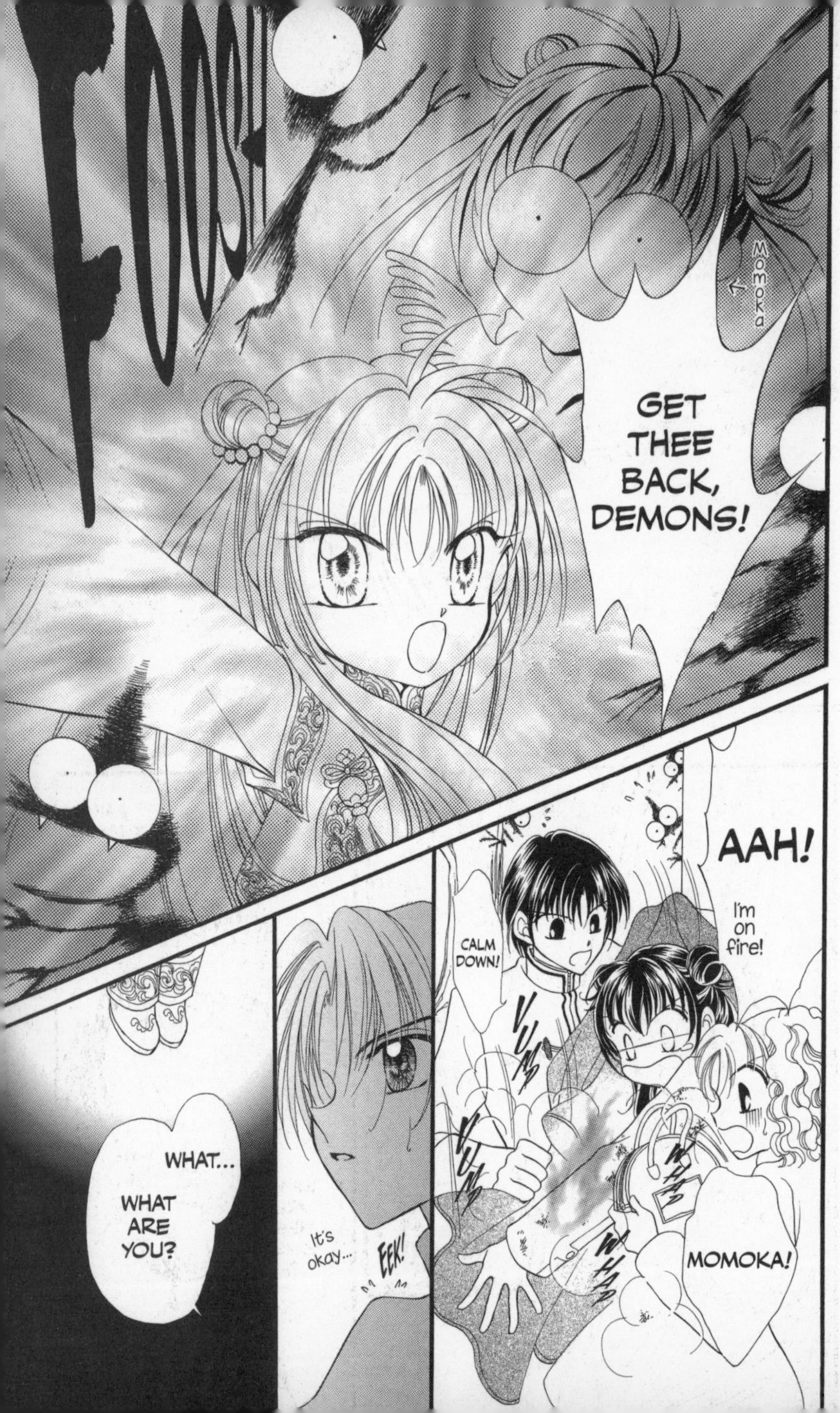
← Momoka
GET THEE BACK, DEMONS!
FOOSH!
AAH!
I'm on fire!
CALM DOWN!
VUM
VUM
WHAM
WHAM
MOMOKA!
EEK!
It's okay...
WHAT...
WHAT ARE YOU?

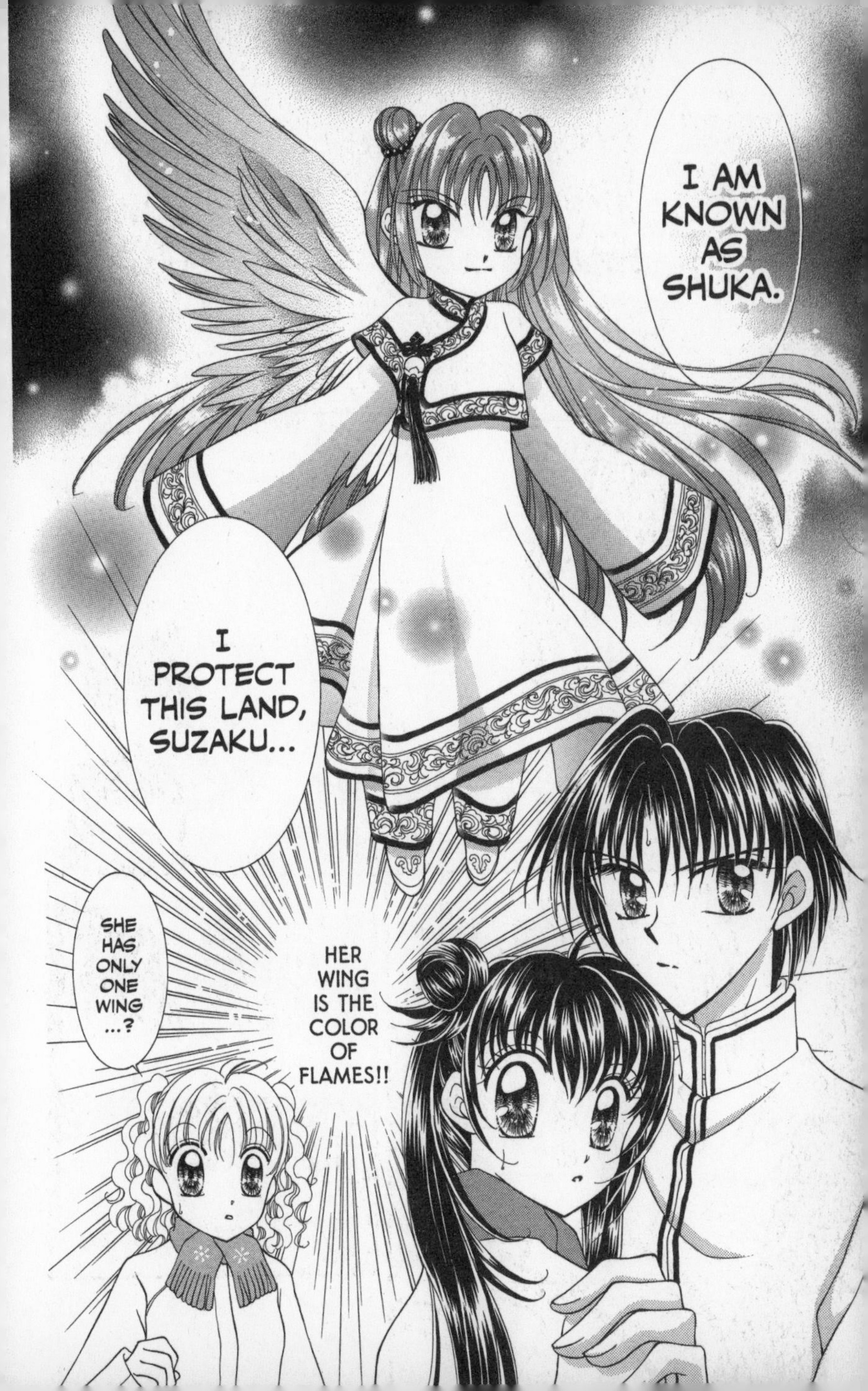
I AM KNOWN AS SHUKA.
I PROTECT THIS LAND, SUZAKU...
HER WING IS THE COLOR OF FLAMES!!
SHE HAS ONLY ONE WING ...?

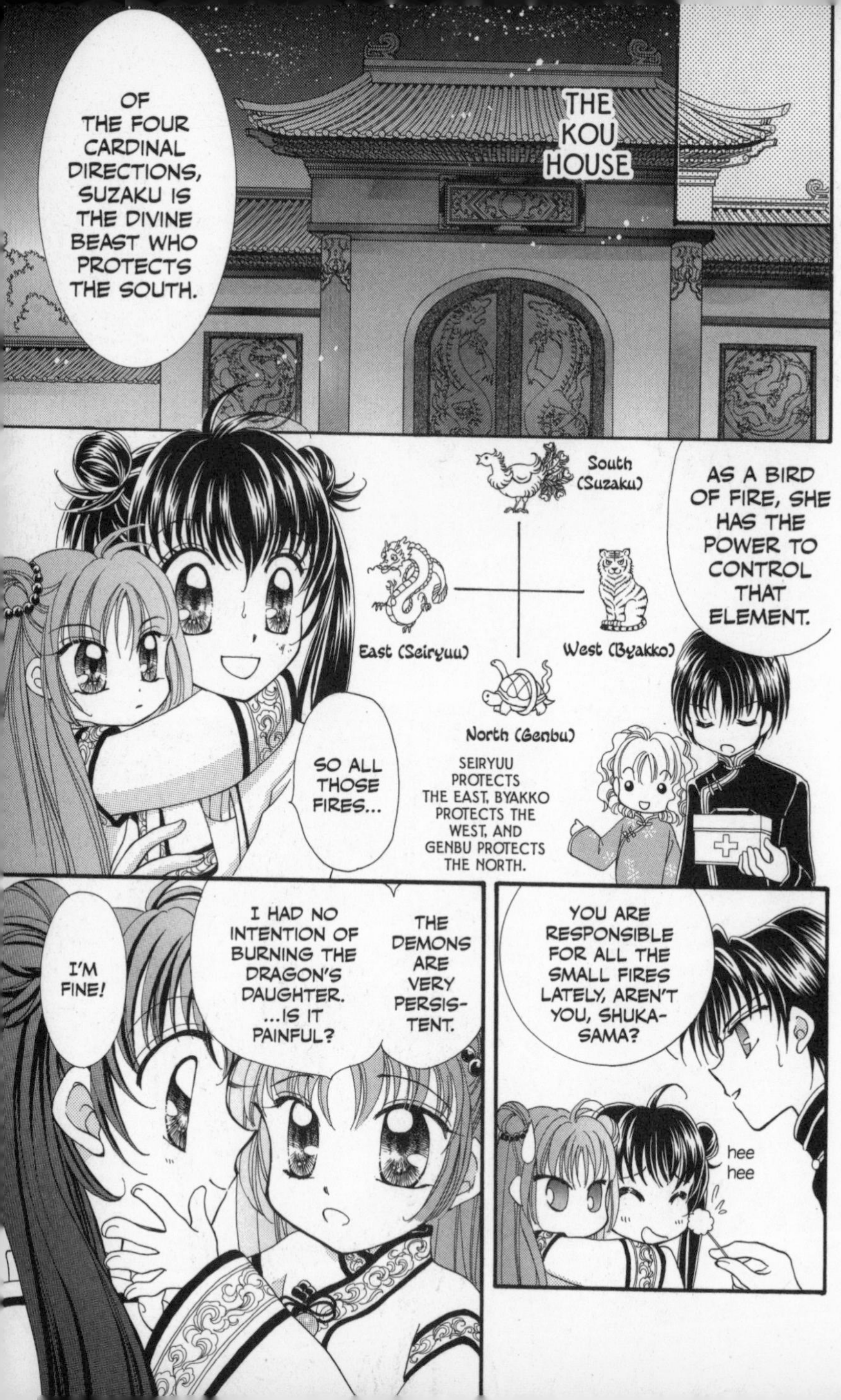
THE KOU HOUSE
OF THE FOUR CARDINAL DIRECTIONS, SUZAKU IS THE DIVINE BEAST WHO PROTECTS THE SOUTH.
AS A BIRD OF FIRE, SHE HAS THE POWER TO CONTROL THAT ELEMENT.
South (Suzaku)
West (Byakko)
East (Seiryuu)
North (Genbu)
SEIRYUU PROTECTS THE EAST, BYAKKO PROTECTS THE WEST, AND GENBU PROTECTS THE NORTH.
SO ALL THOSE FIRES...
YOU ARE RESPONSIBLE FOR ALL THE SMALL FIRES LATELY, AREN'T YOU, SHUKA-SAMA?
hee hee
THE DEMONS ARE VERY PERSIS-TENT.
I HAD NO INTENTION OF BURNING THE DRAGON'S DAUGHTER. ...IS IT PAINFUL?
I'M FINE!

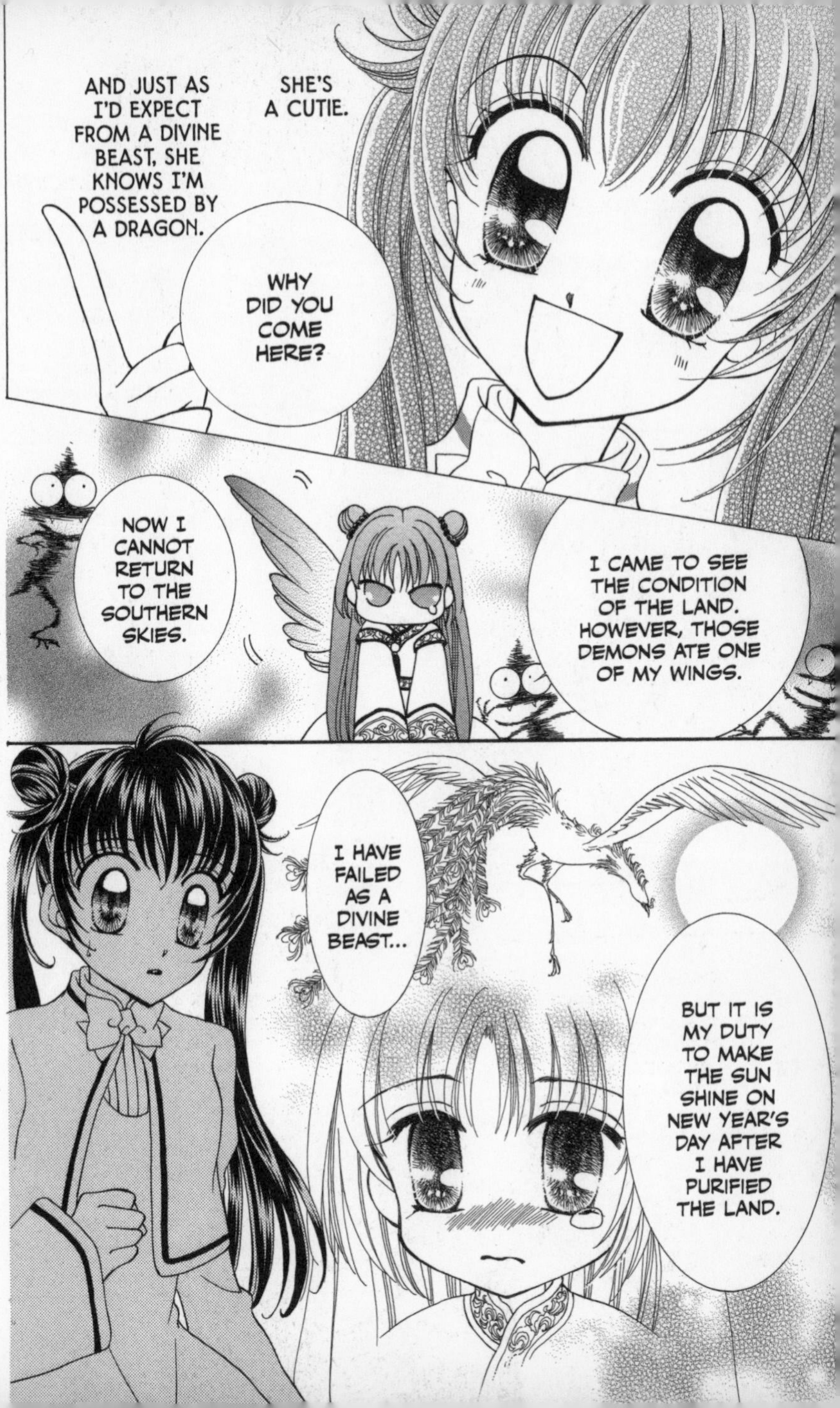
SHE'S A CUTIE.
AND JUST AS I'D EXPECT FROM A DIVINE BEAST, SHE KNOWS I'M POSSESSED BY A DRAGON.
WHY DID YOU COME HERE?
I CAME TO SEE THE CONDITION OF THE LAND. HOWEVER, THOSE DEMONS ATE ONE OF MY WINGS.
NOW I CANNOT RETURN TO THE SOUTHERN SKIES.
I HAVE FAILED AS A DIVINE BEAST...
BUT IT IS MY DUTY TO MAKE THE SUN SHINE ON NEW YEAR'S DAY AFTER I HAVE PURIFIED THE LAND.

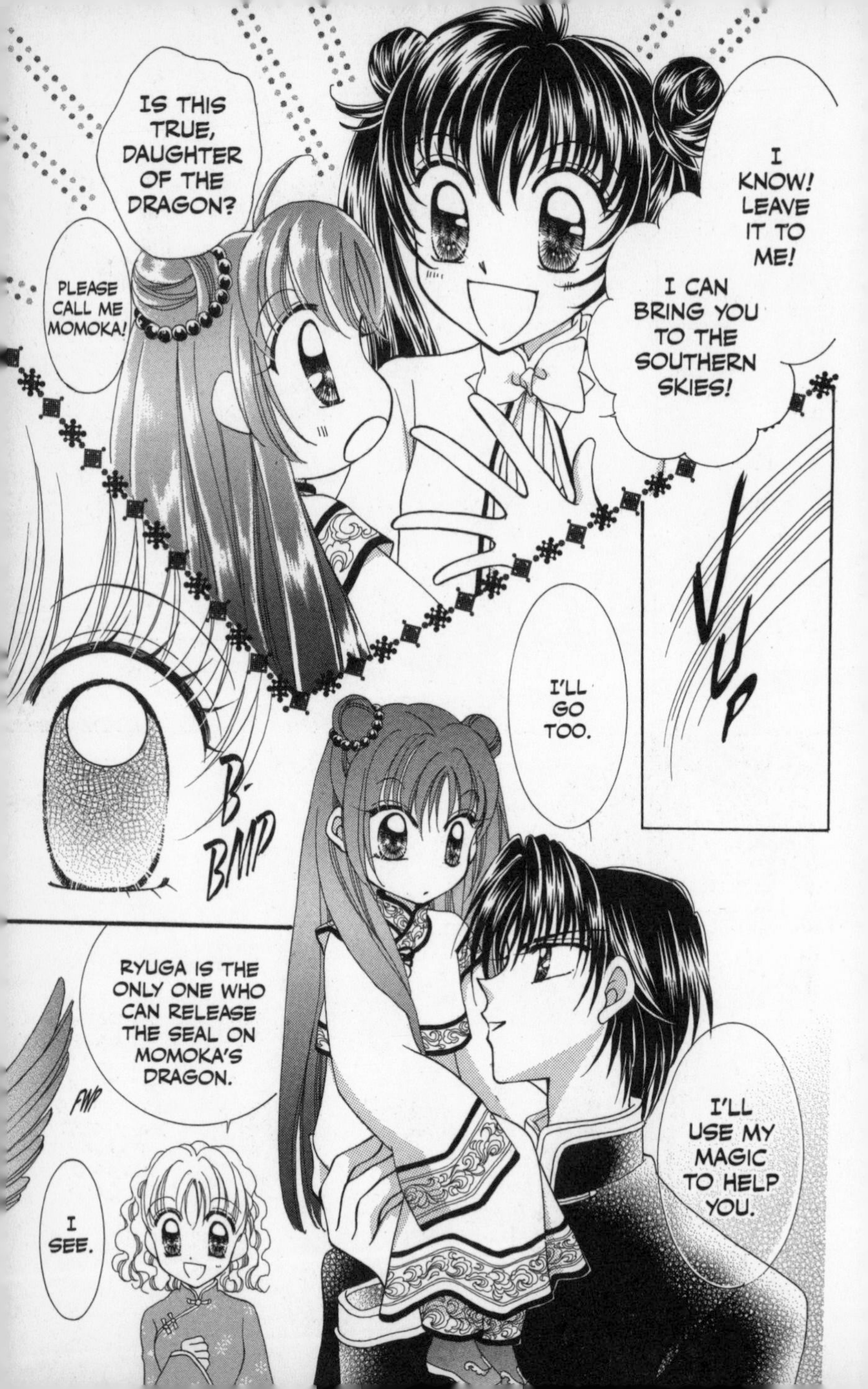
I KNOW! LEAVE IT TO ME!
I CAN BRING YOU TO THE SOUTHERN SKIES!
IS THIS TRUE, DAUGHTER OF THE DRAGON?
PLEASE CALL ME MOMOKA!
JUMP
I'LL GO TOO.
B-BMP
I'LL USE MY MAGIC TO HELP YOU.
RYUGA IS THE ONLY ONE WHO CAN RELEASE THE SEAL ON MOMOKA'S DRAGON.
FWP
I SEE.

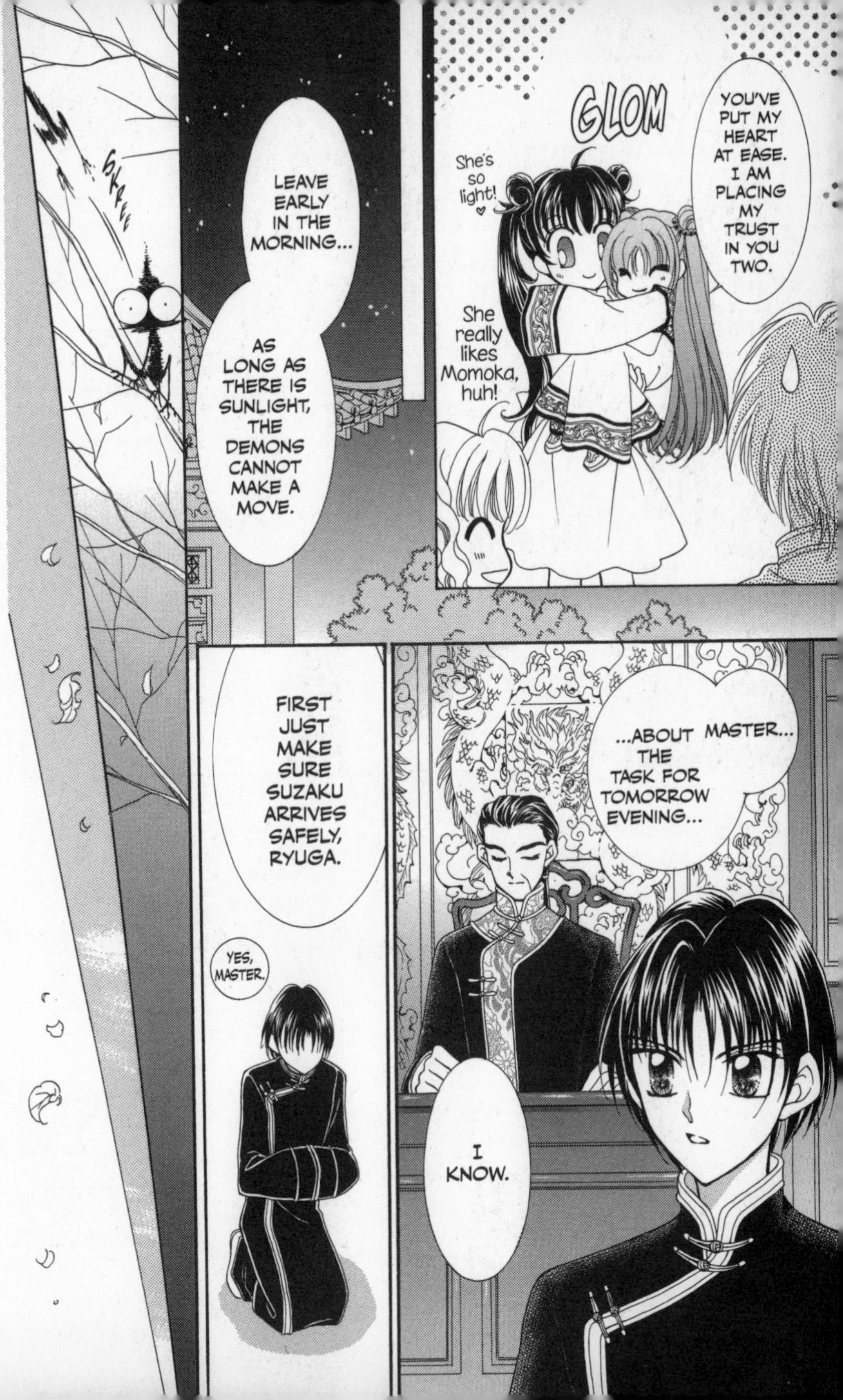
GLOM
YOU'VE PUT MY HEART AT EASE. I AM PLACING MY TRUST IN YOU TWO.
She's so light! ♡
She really likes Momoka, huh!
LEAVE EARLY IN THE MORNING...
AS LONG AS THERE IS SUNLIGHT, THE DEMONS CANNOT MAKE A MOVE.
MASTER...
...ABOUT THE TASK FOR TOMORROW EVENING...
I KNOW.
FIRST JUST MAKE SURE SUZAKU ARRIVES SAFELY, RYUGA.
YES, MASTER.
SKREEE

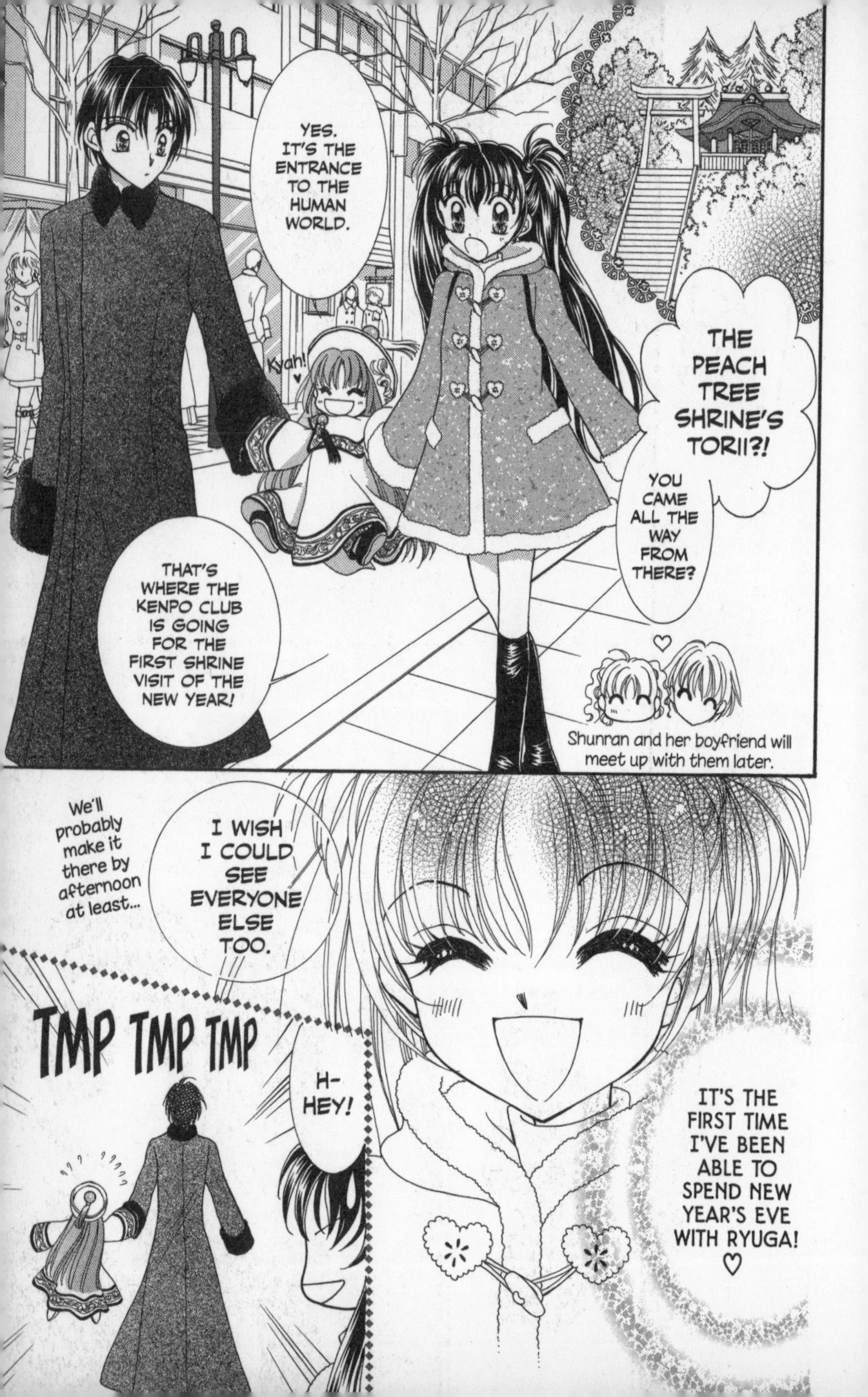
YES. IT'S THE ENTRANCE TO THE HUMAN WORLD.
THE PEACH TREE SHRINE'S TORII?!
YOU CAME ALL THE WAY FROM THERE?
Kyah! ♥
THAT'S WHERE THE KENPO CLUB IS GOING FOR THE FIRST SHRINE VISIT OF THE NEW YEAR!
Shunran and her boyfriend will meet up with them later.
IT'S THE FIRST TIME I'VE BEEN ABLE TO SPEND NEW YEAR'S EVE WITH RYUGA! ♡
I WISH I COULD SEE EVERYONE ELSE TOO.
We'll probably make it there by afternoon at least...
H-HEY!
TMP TMP TMP

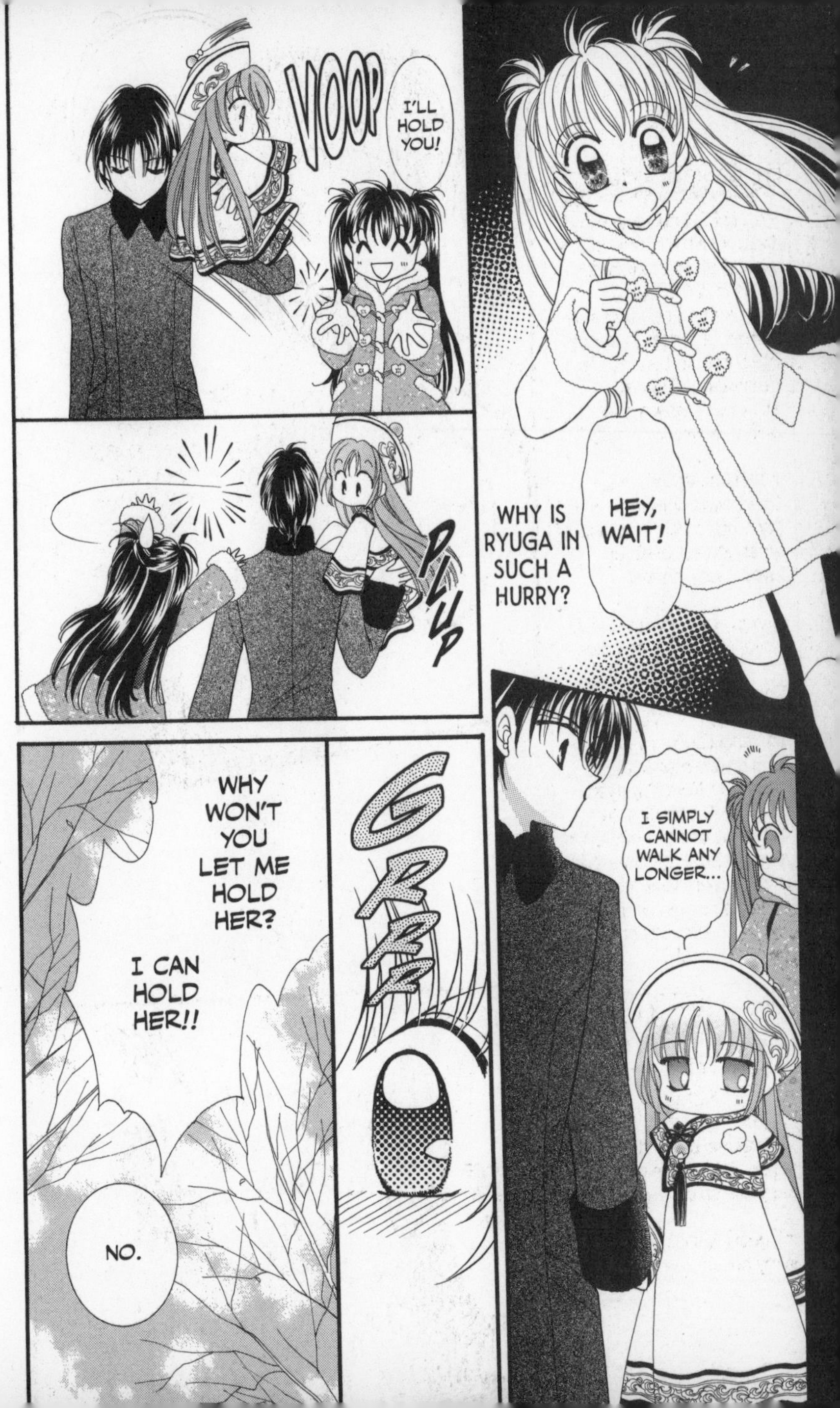
HEY, WAIT!
WHY IS RYUGA IN SUCH A HURRY?
I SIMPLY CANNOT WALK ANY LONGER...
VOOP
I'LL HOLD YOU!
PLUP
GRRR
WHY WON'T YOU LET ME HOLD HER?
I CAN HOLD HER!!
NO.

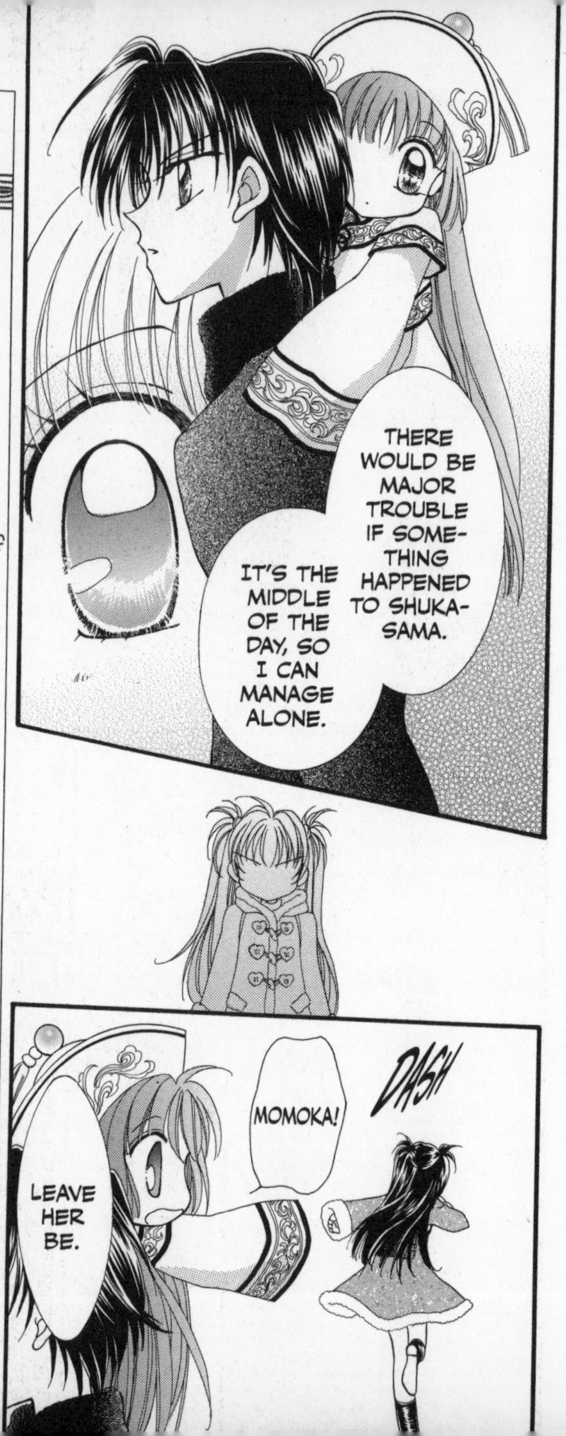
THERE WOULD BE MAJOR TROUBLE IF SOMETHING HAPPENED TO SHUKA-SAMA.
IT'S THE MIDDLE OF THE DAY, SO I CAN MANAGE ALONE.
DASH
MOMOKA!
LEAVE HER BE.

4

The thing I had the most trouble with in this story was Shuka's costume. She's a divine beast, so I wanted to make her gorgeous. I designed her costume to be a cross between a Chinese empress's gown and a bridal gown.

In letters from fans, there was someone who sent me a color version of when Shuka levels up (?). I was really happy.

It was really pretty, so I have it saved in my files.

Show me some more!

For the February issue there was a special item—an MD/CD player with an illustration of Momoka and pandas on it. It was the first time such a large item was made, so I was really surprised. Thanks Ribon Editorial Department!

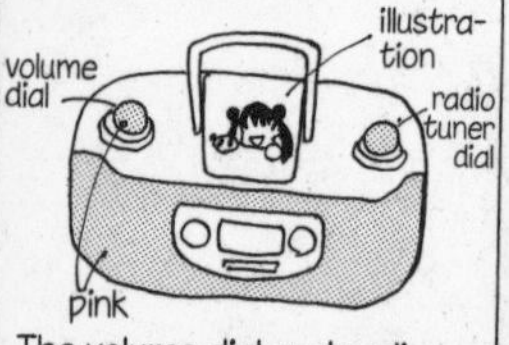
illustration
volume dial
radio tuner dial
pink

The volume dial and radio tuner dial look like peaches—they are so cute!

It's getting a lot of use in my house!

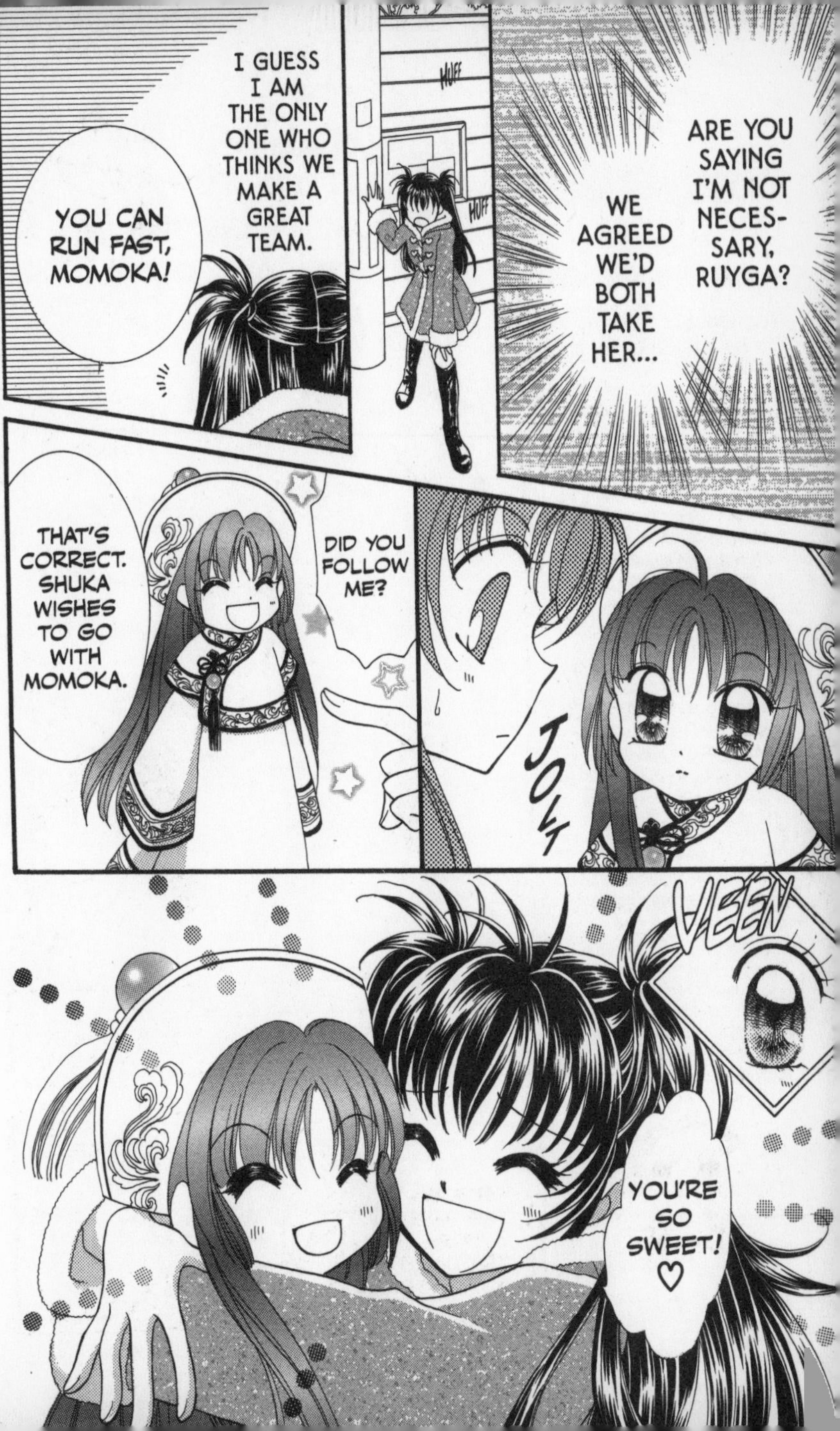
ARE YOU SAYING I'M NOT NECES-SARY, RUYGA?
WE AGREED WE'D BOTH TAKE HER...
HUFF
HUFF
I GUESS I AM THE ONLY ONE WHO THINKS WE MAKE A GREAT TEAM.
YOU CAN RUN FAST, MOMOKA!
JOLT
DID YOU FOLLOW ME?
THAT'S CORRECT. SHUKA WISHES TO GO WITH MOMOKA.
VEEN
YOU'RE SO SWEET! ♡

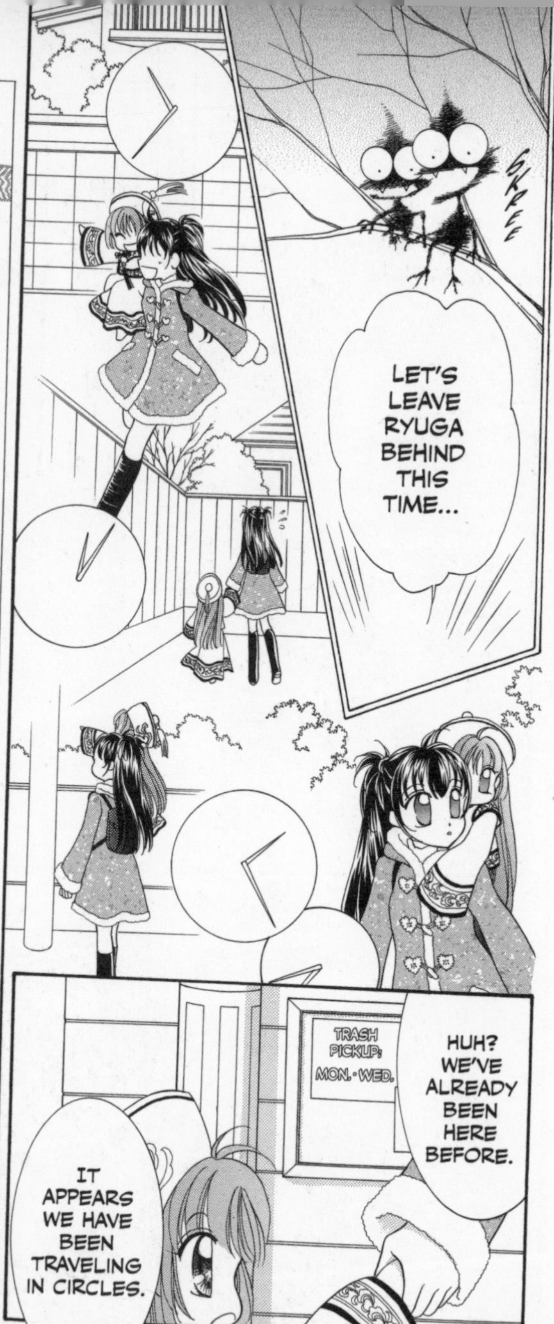
SKREE
LET'S LEAVE RYUGA BEHIND THIS TIME...
TRASH PICKUP: MON.・WED.
HUH? WE'VE ALREADY BEEN HERE BEFORE.
IT APPEARS WE HAVE BEEN TRAVELING IN CIRCLES.

5

I really love Shinto and Buddhist temples. I like to walk around the grounds even when it's not New Year's. The quiet atmosphere is really calming. Wow, that made me sound like an old lady! Eh, leave me alone!

Speaking of Shinto temples, what about omikuji? Is that right? It reminds me of my trip to Hong Kong. A lot of people sent me translations of the fortune I drew from the temple there, which I had featured in the bonus story of *St.♥Dragon Girl*. I couldn't read it because it was in Chinese (even though I had some understanding of the kanji)!

According to the translation, it said: Your recent efforts will be wasted, but come spring you will have a change in fortune for the better and will become busier. However, don't lose your original determination.

In the spring, *St.♥Dragon Girl* was serialized and every day was busy.

It was exactly right! I understand. I won't forget my determination, and I'll keep trying my best. Thanks to everyone who translated my fortune.

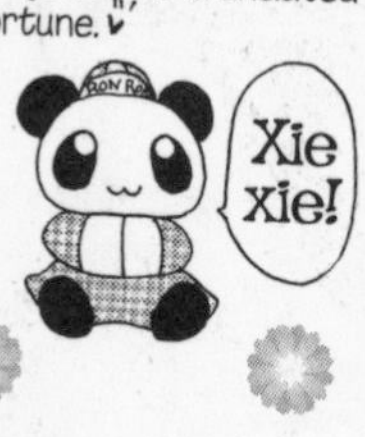
Xie xie!

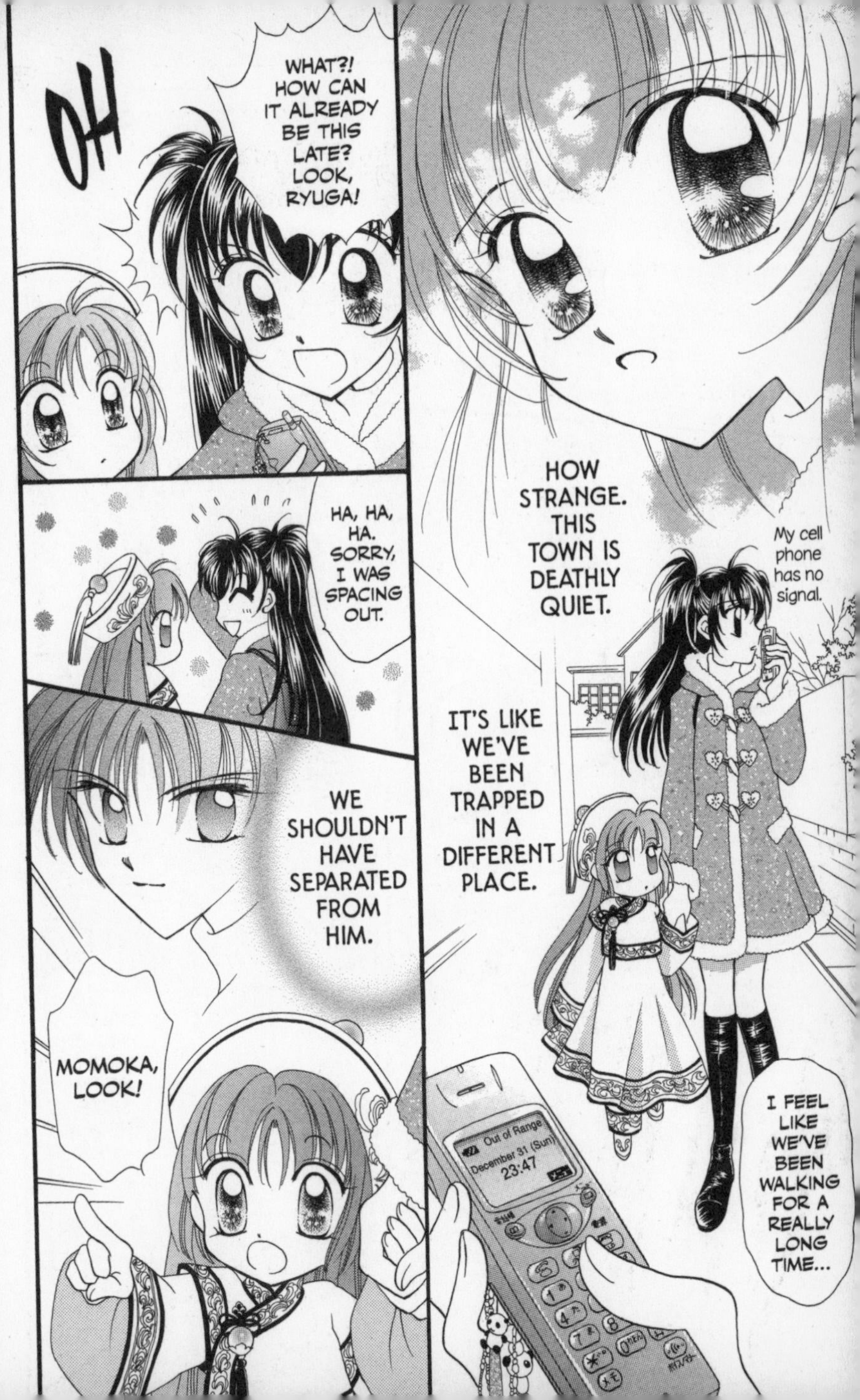
HOW STRANGE. THIS TOWN IS DEATHLY QUIET.
IT'S LIKE WE'VE BEEN TRAPPED IN A DIFFERENT PLACE.
My cell phone has no signal.
Out of Range
December 31 (Sun)
23:47
I FEEL LIKE WE'VE BEEN WALKING FOR A REALLY LONG TIME...
OH
WHAT?! HOW CAN IT ALREADY BE THIS LATE? LOOK, RYUGA!
HA, HA, HA. SORRY, I WAS SPACING OUT.
WE SHOULDN'T HAVE SEPARATED FROM HIM.
MOMOKA, LOOK!

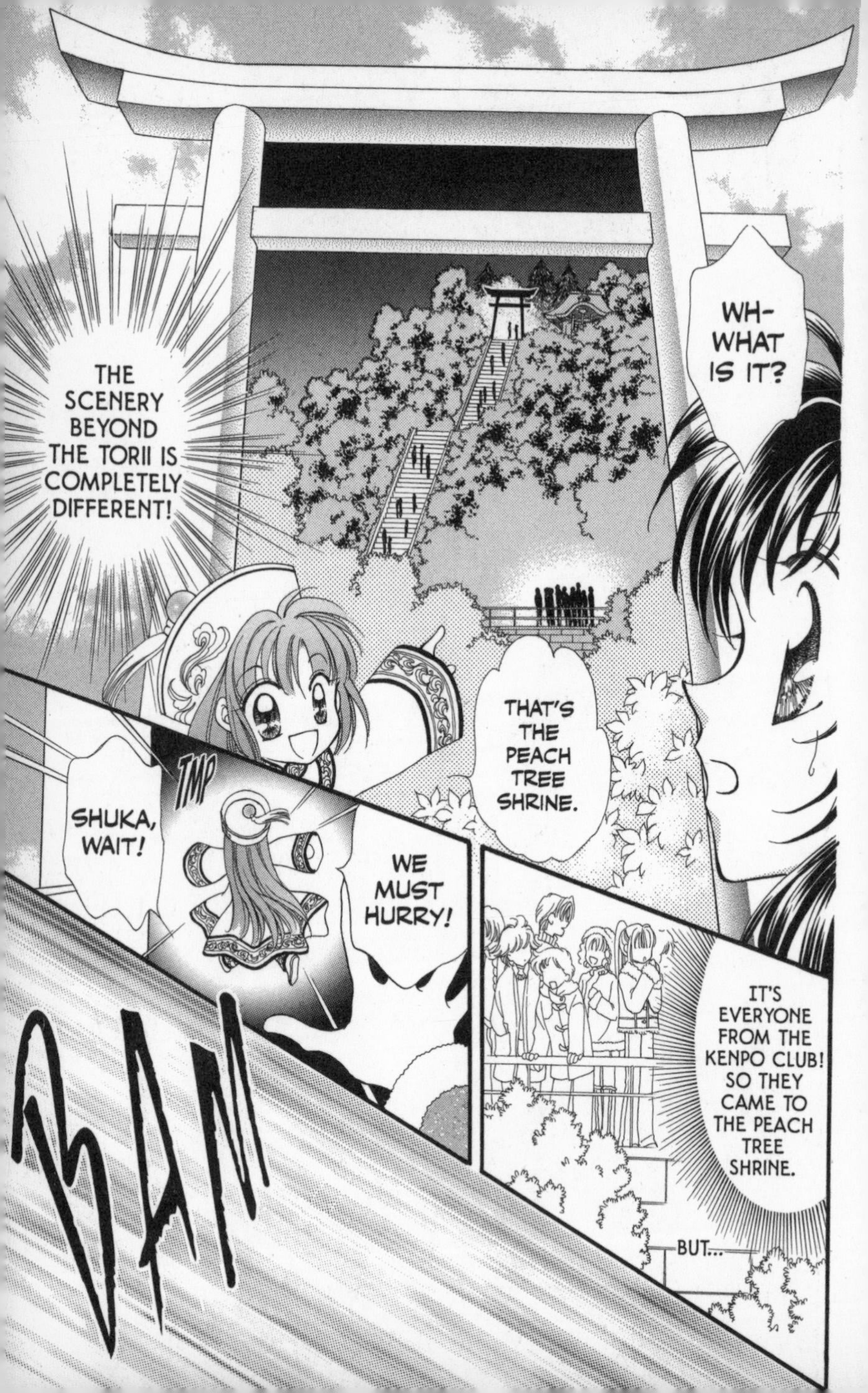
WH-WHAT IS IT?
THE SCENERY BEYOND THE TORII IS COMPLETELY DIFFERENT!
THAT'S THE PEACH TREE SHRINE.
IT'S EVERYONE FROM THE KENPO CLUB! SO THEY CAME TO THE PEACH TREE SHRINE.
BUT...
WE MUST HURRY!
TMP
SHUKA, WAIT!
BAM

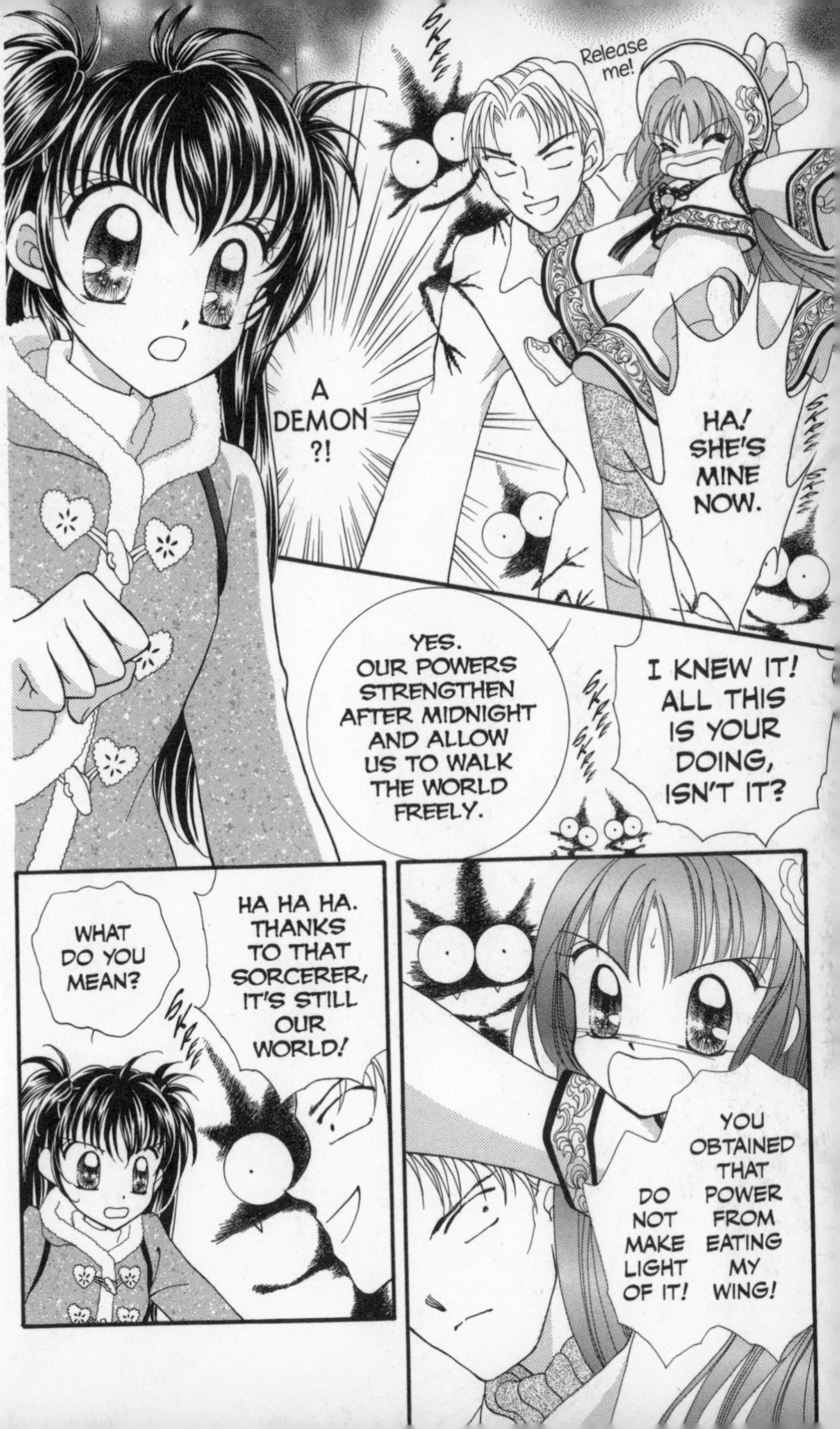
Release me!
A DEMON ?!
HA! SHE'S MINE NOW.
I KNEW IT! ALL THIS IS YOUR DOING, ISN'T IT?
YES. OUR POWERS STRENGTHEN AFTER MIDNIGHT AND ALLOW US TO WALK THE WORLD FREELY.
YOU OBTAINED THAT POWER FROM EATING MY WING!
DO NOT MAKE LIGHT OF IT!
WHAT DO YOU MEAN?
HA HA HA. THANKS TO THAT SORCERER, IT'S STILL OUR WORLD!

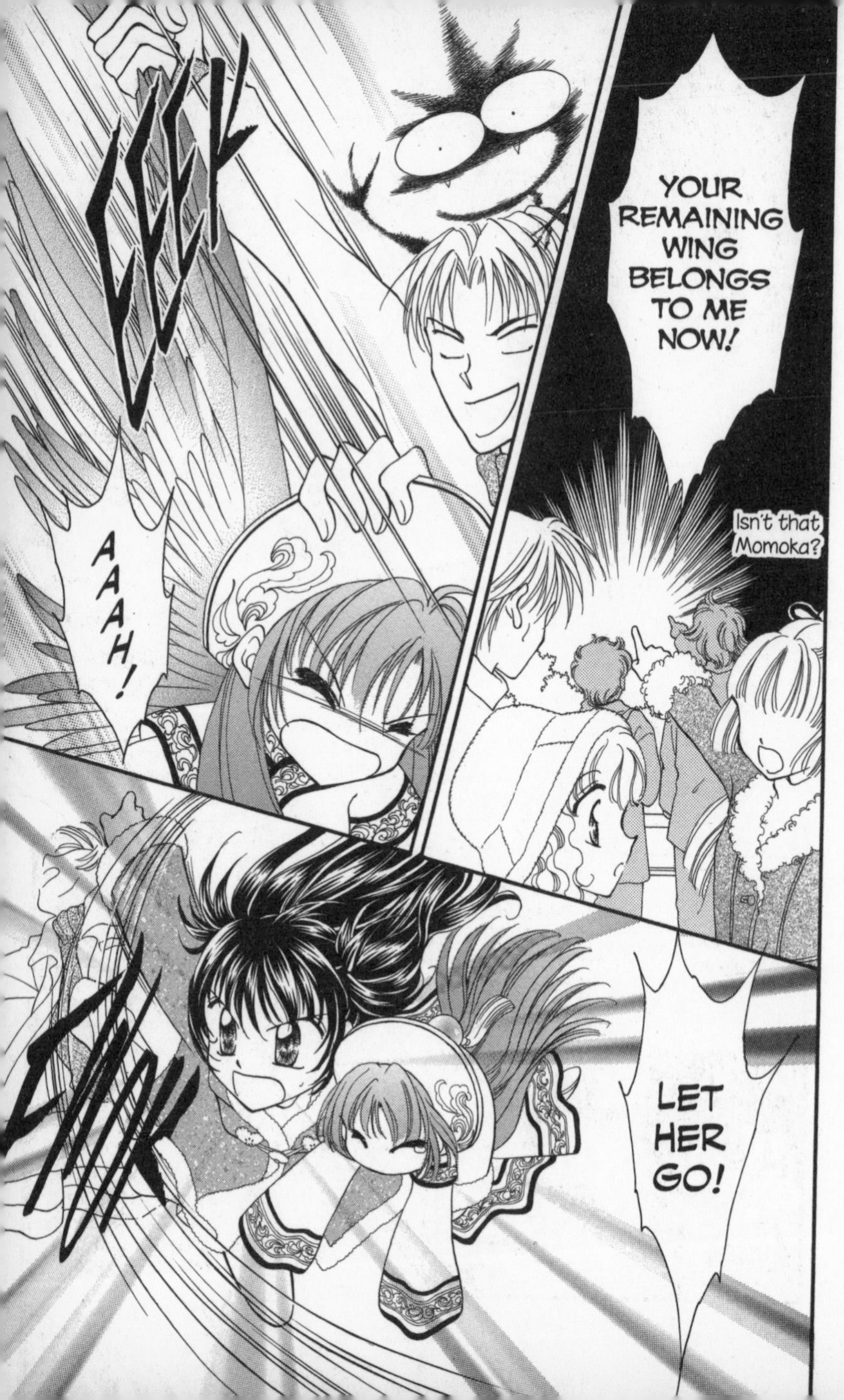
YOUR REMAINING WING BELONGS TO ME NOW!
Isn't that Momoka?
EEEK
AAAAH!
LET HER GO!
CHNK

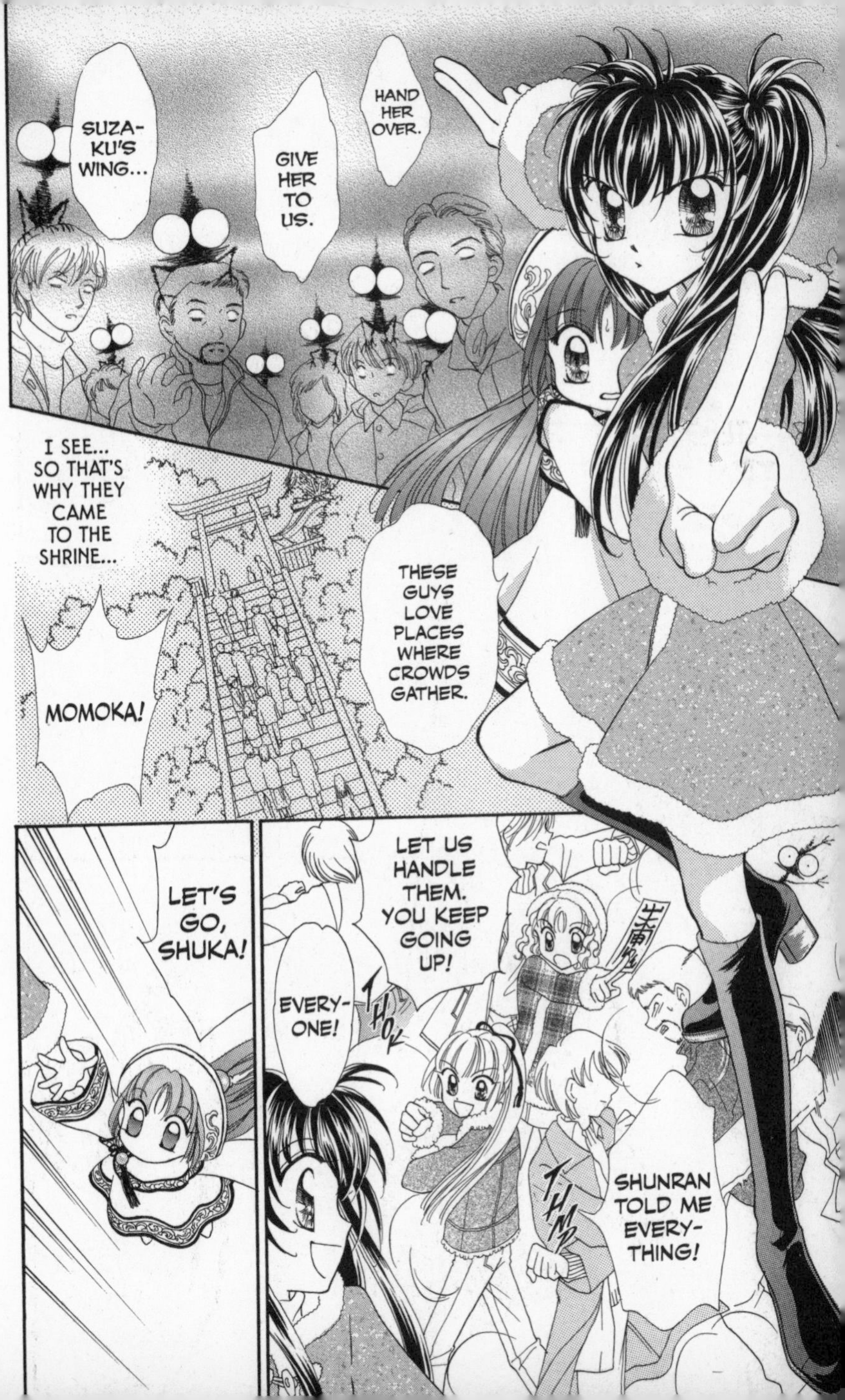
HAND HER OVER.
GIVE HER TO US.
SUZA-KU'S WING...
THESE GUYS LOVE PLACES WHERE CROWDS GATHER.
I SEE... SO THAT'S WHY THEY CAME TO THE SHRINE...
MOMOKA!
LET US HANDLE THEM. YOU KEEP GOING UP!
THOK
EVERY-ONE!
SHUNRAN TOLD ME EVERY-THING!
THMP
LET'S GO, SHUKA!

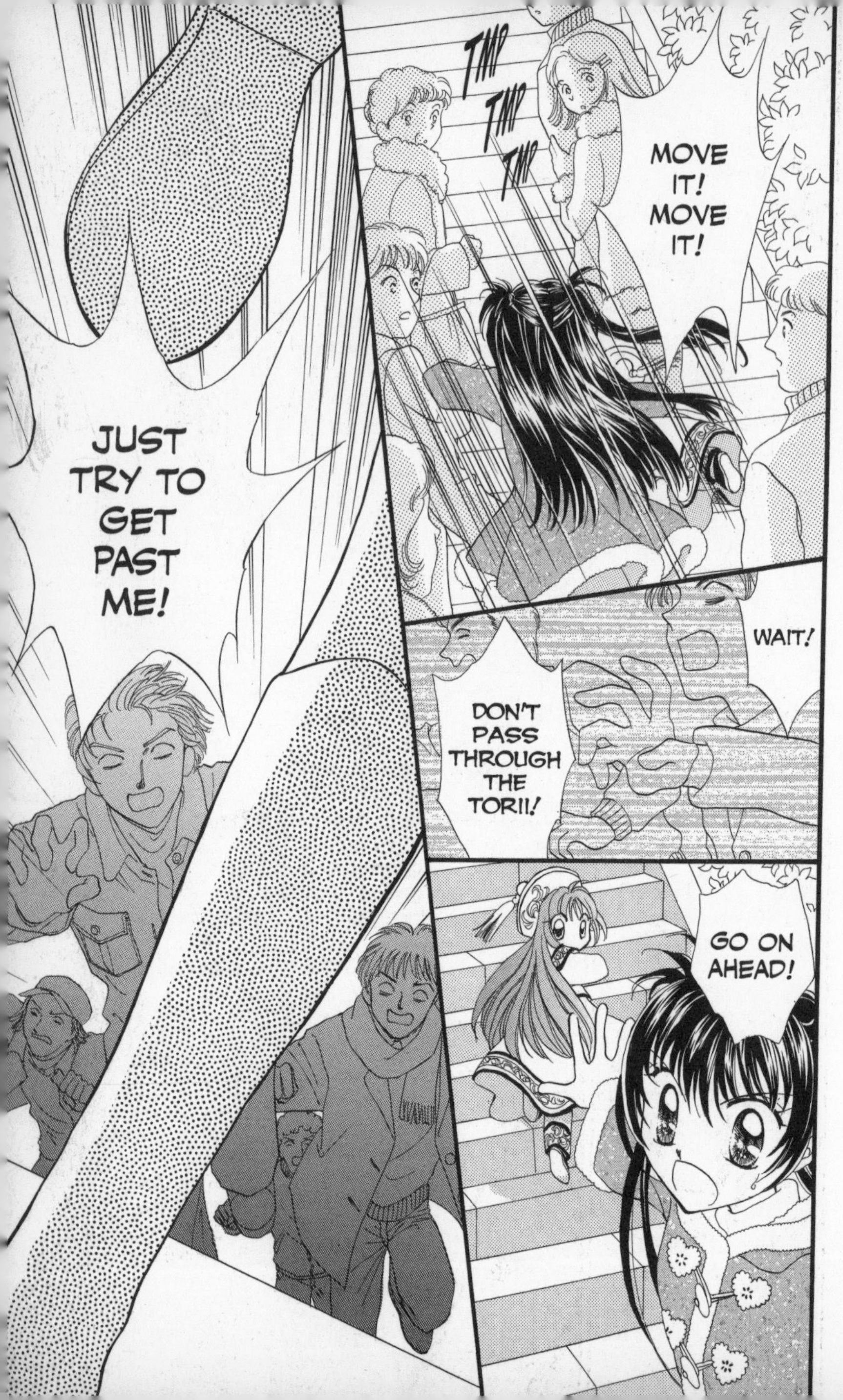
MOVE IT! MOVE IT!
TMP TMP TMP
WAIT!
DON'T PASS THROUGH THE TORII!
GO ON AHEAD!
JUST TRY TO GET PAST ME!

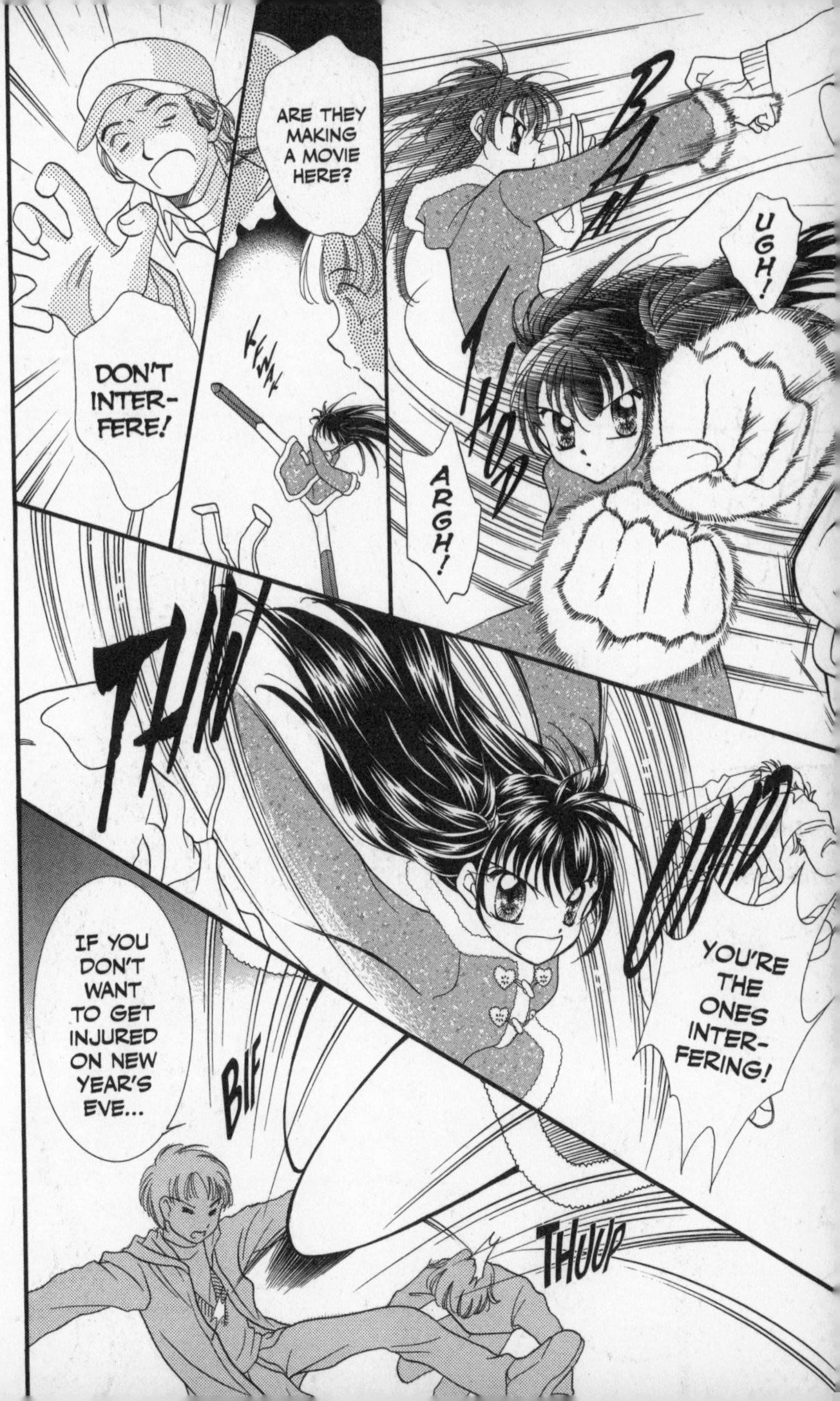
BAM
UGH!
ARGH!
ARE THEY MAKING A MOVIE HERE?
DON'T INTER-FERE!
YOU'RE THE ONES INTER-FERING!
BIF
THUUP
IF YOU DON'T WANT TO GET INJURED ON NEW YEAR'S EVE...

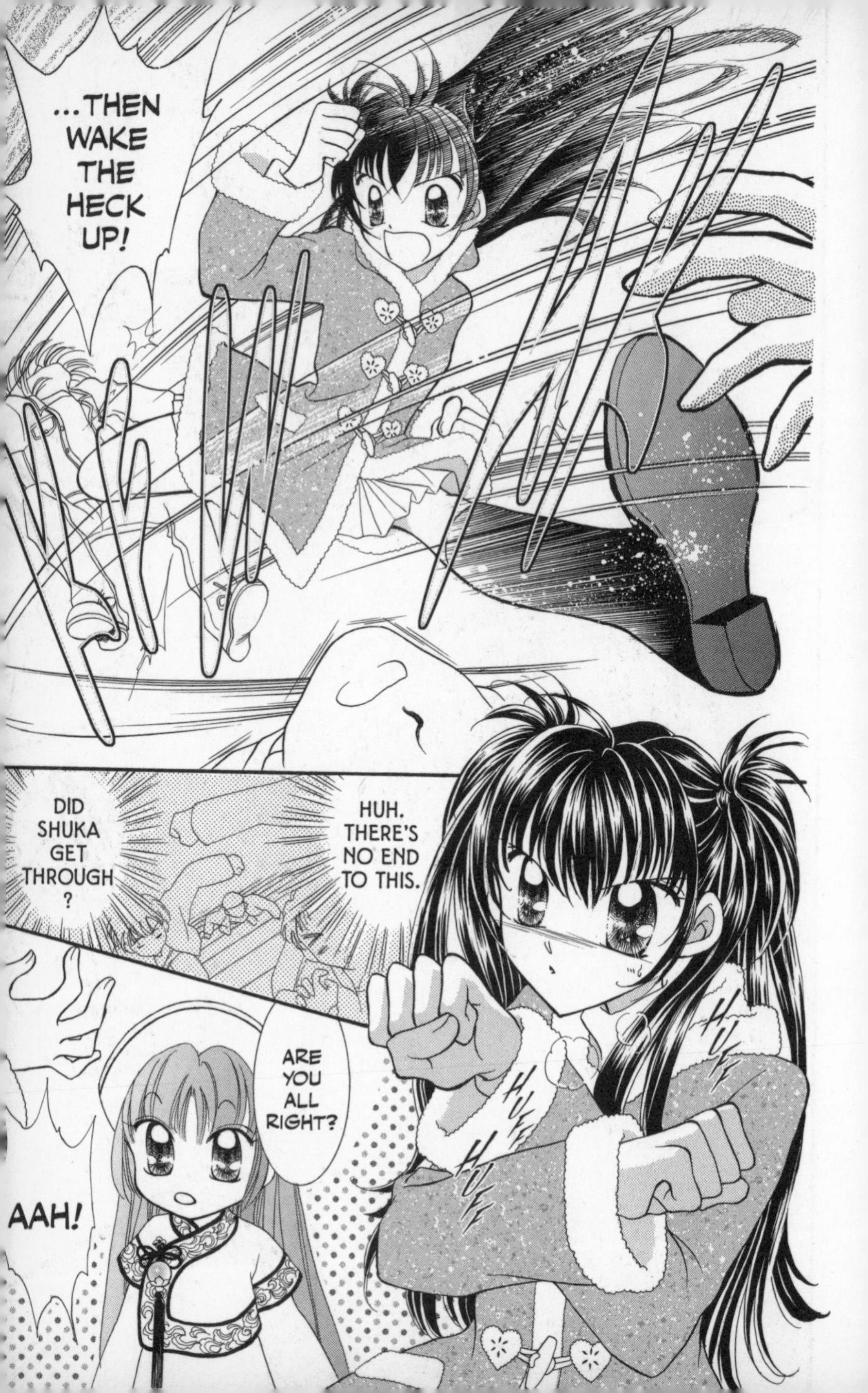
...THEN WAKE THE HECK UP!
HUH. THERE'S NO END TO THIS.
DID SHUKA GET THROUGH?
HUFF HUFF HUFF
ARE YOU ALL RIGHT?
AAH!

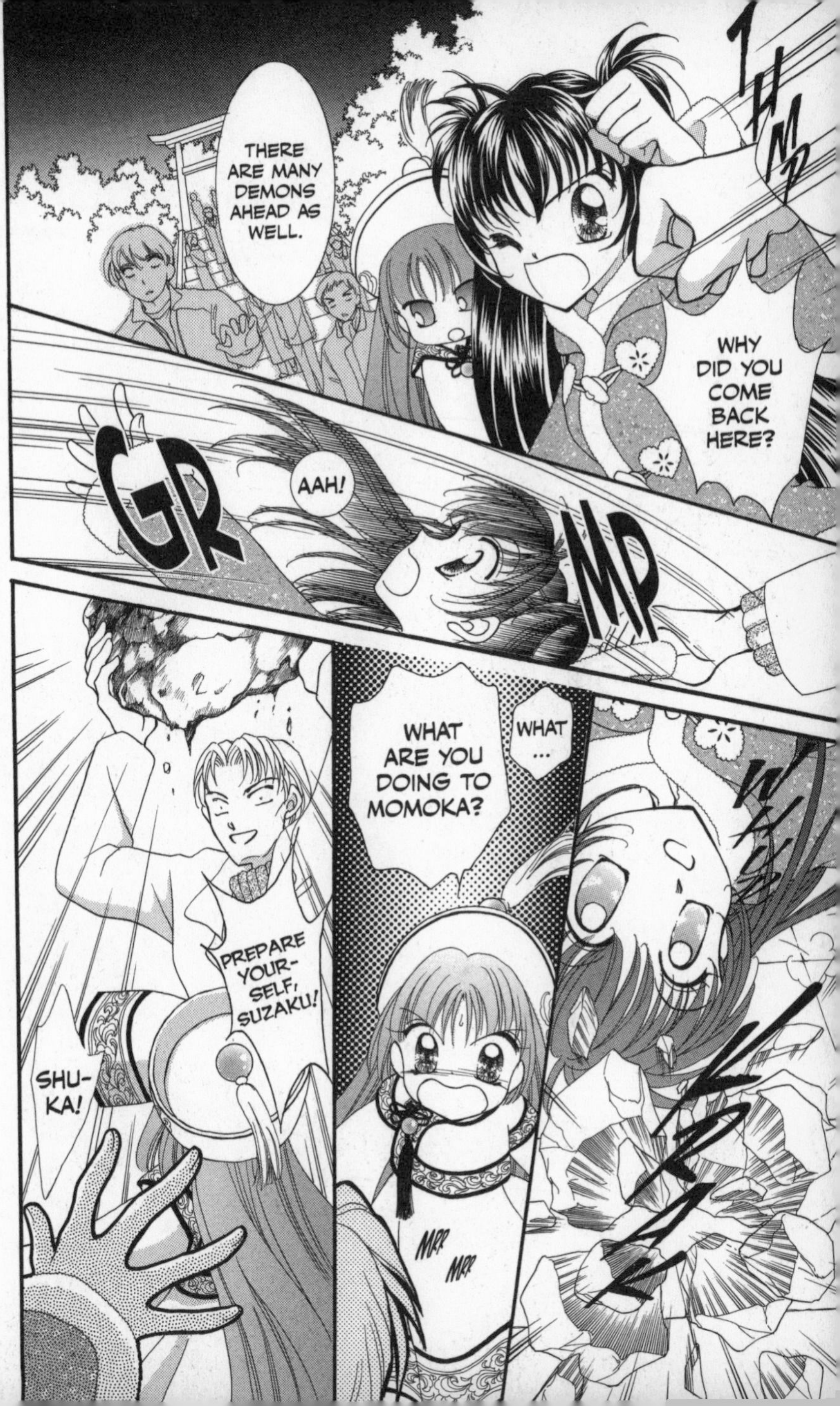
HMP
WHY DID YOU COME BACK HERE?
THERE ARE MANY DEMONS AHEAD AS WELL.
GR
AAH!
MP
WHAT ...
WHAT ARE YOU DOING TO MOMOKA?
MRR
MRR
PREPARE YOURSELF, SUZAKU!
SHU-KA!

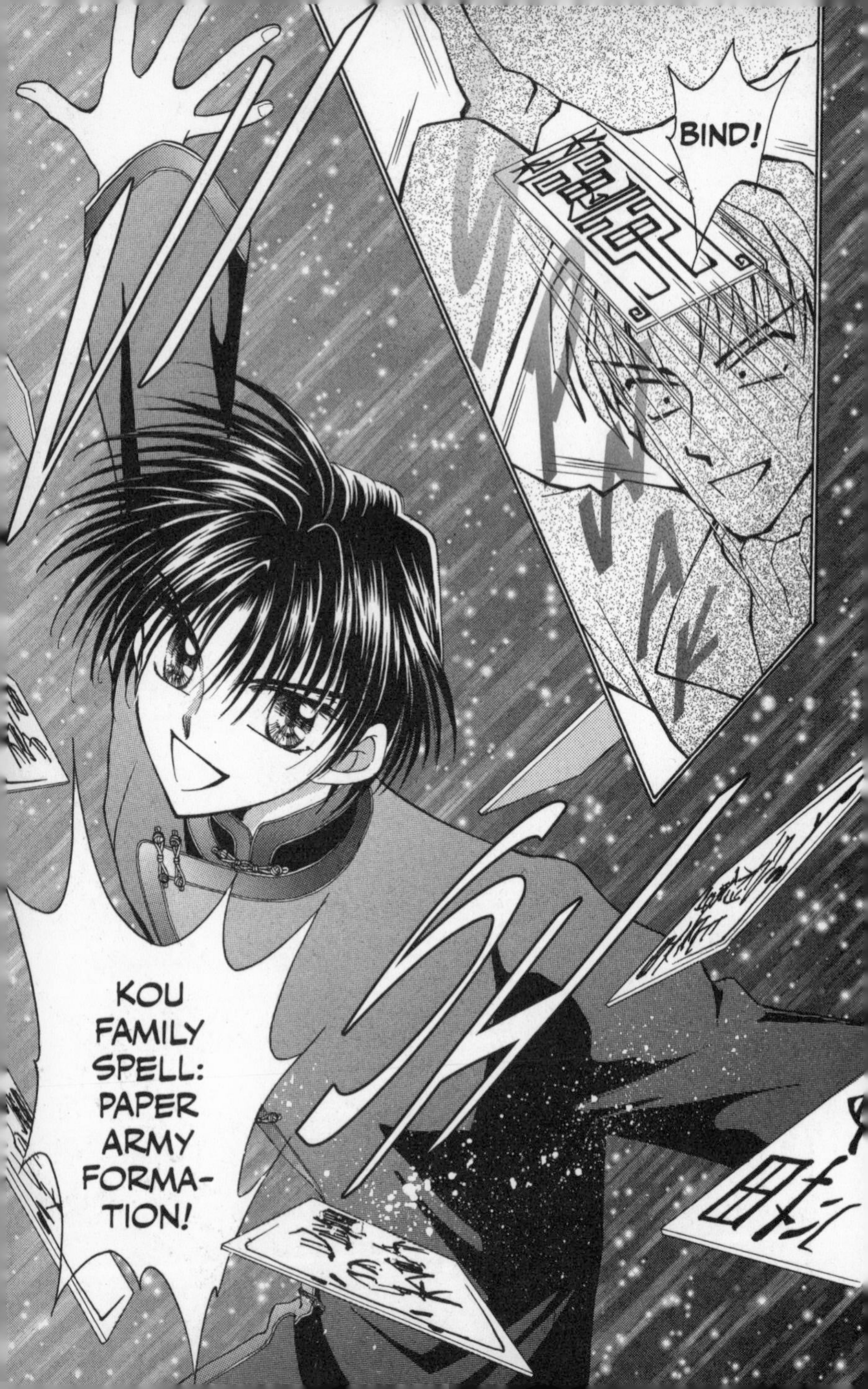
BIND!
KOU FAMILY SPELL: PAPER ARMY FORMATION!

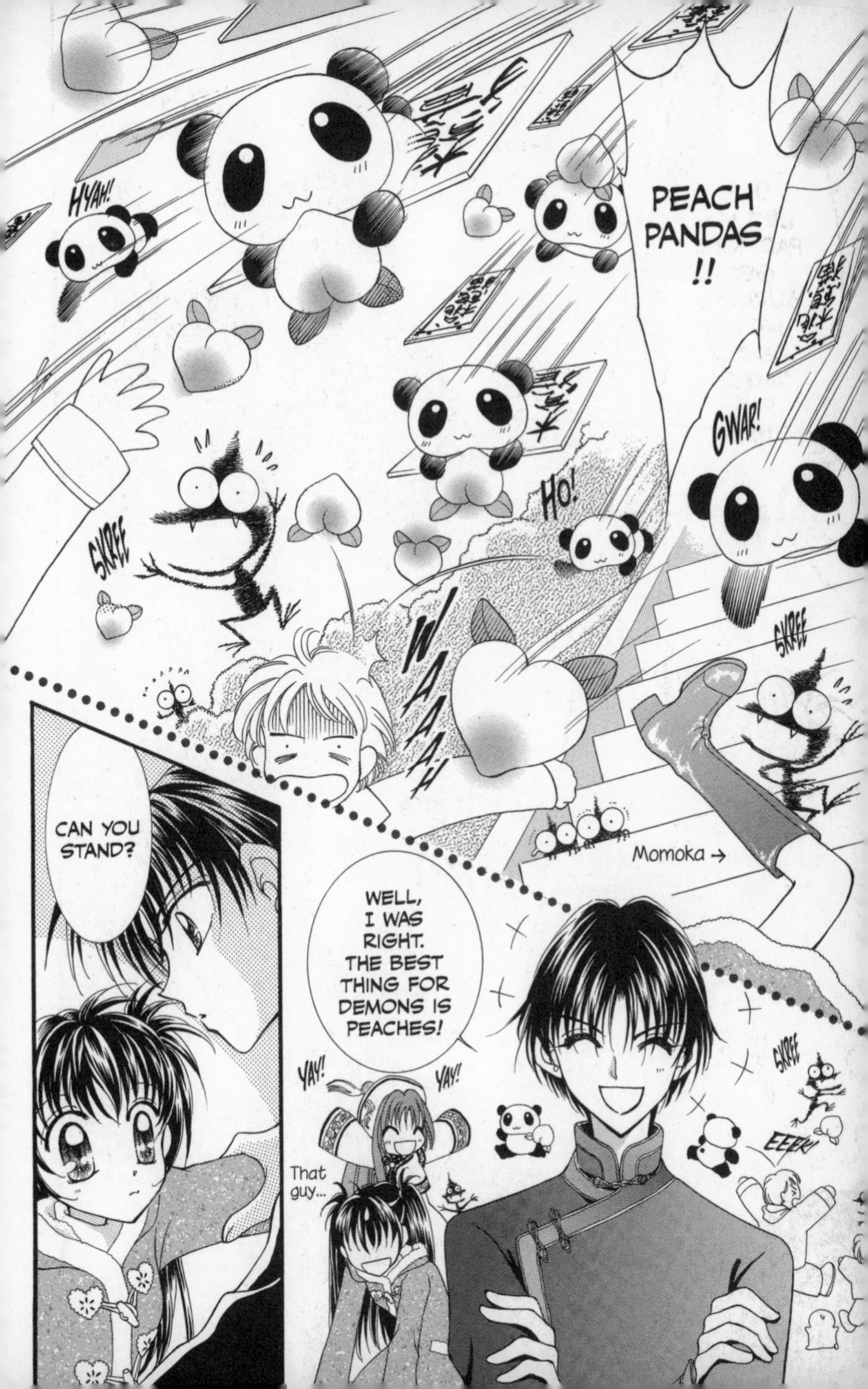
PEACH PANDAS !!
HYAH!
GWAR!
HO!
SKREE
WAAAAAH
SKREE
Momoka →
WELL, I WAS RIGHT. THE BEST THING FOR DEMONS IS PEACHES!
YAY!
YAY!
SKREE
EEEK!
That guy...
CAN YOU STAND?

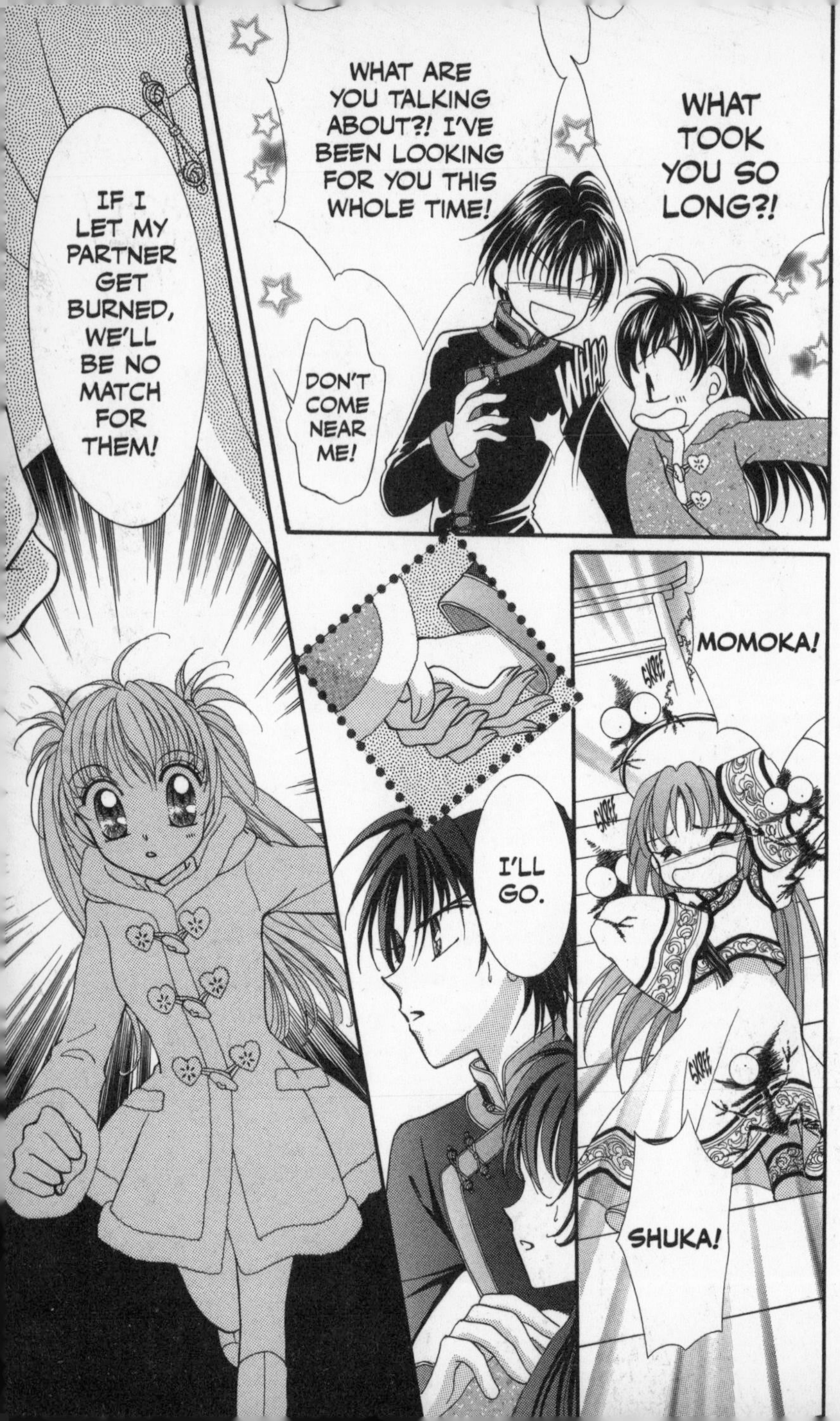
WHAT TOOK YOU SO LONG?!
WHAT ARE YOU TALKING ABOUT?! I'VE BEEN LOOKING FOR YOU THIS WHOLE TIME!
WHAP
DON'T COME NEAR ME!
MOMOKA!
SKREE
SKREE
SKREE
SHUKA!
I'LL GO.
IF I LET MY PARTNER GET BURNED, WE'LL BE NO MATCH FOR THEM!

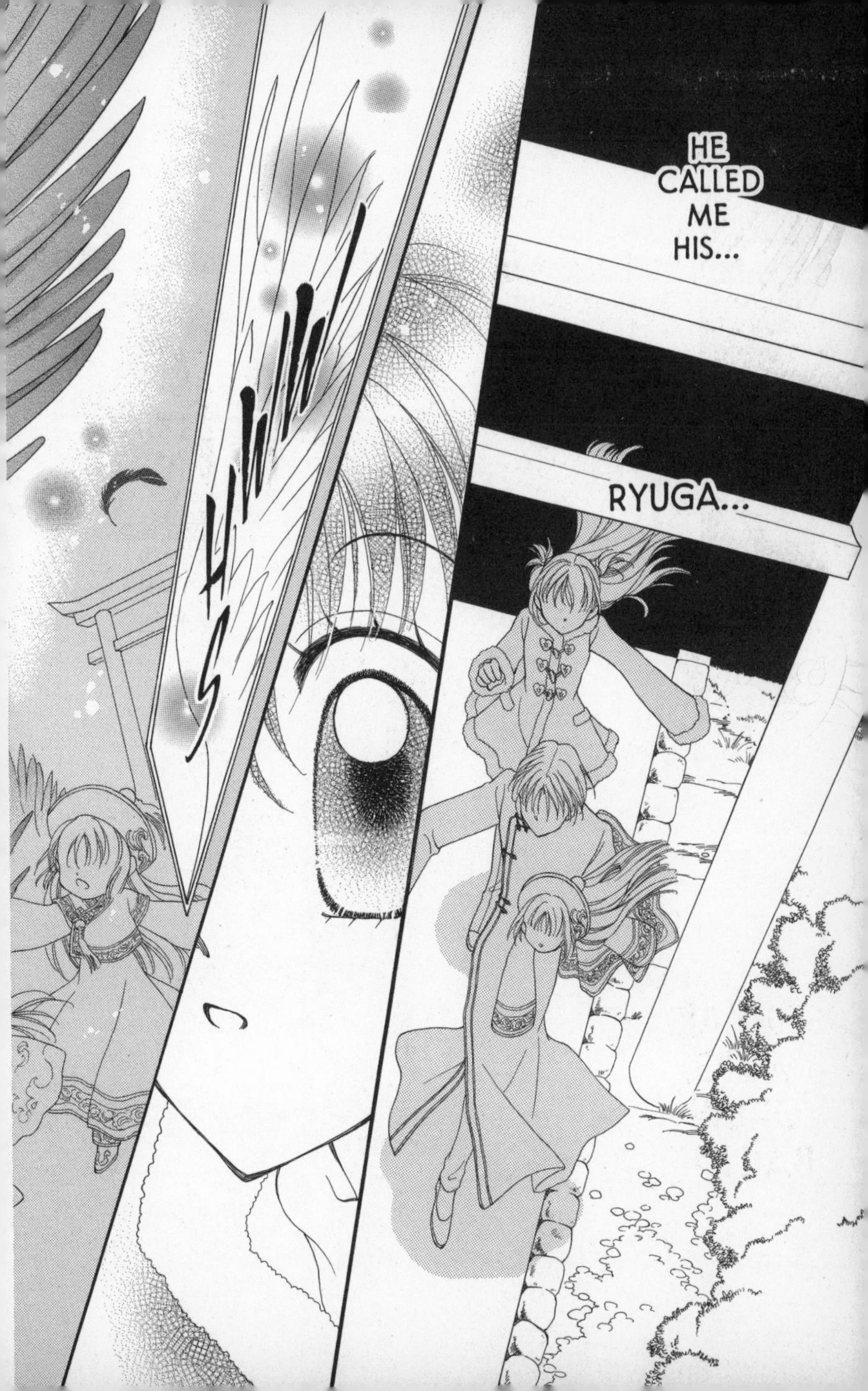
HE CALLED ME HIS...
RYUGA...

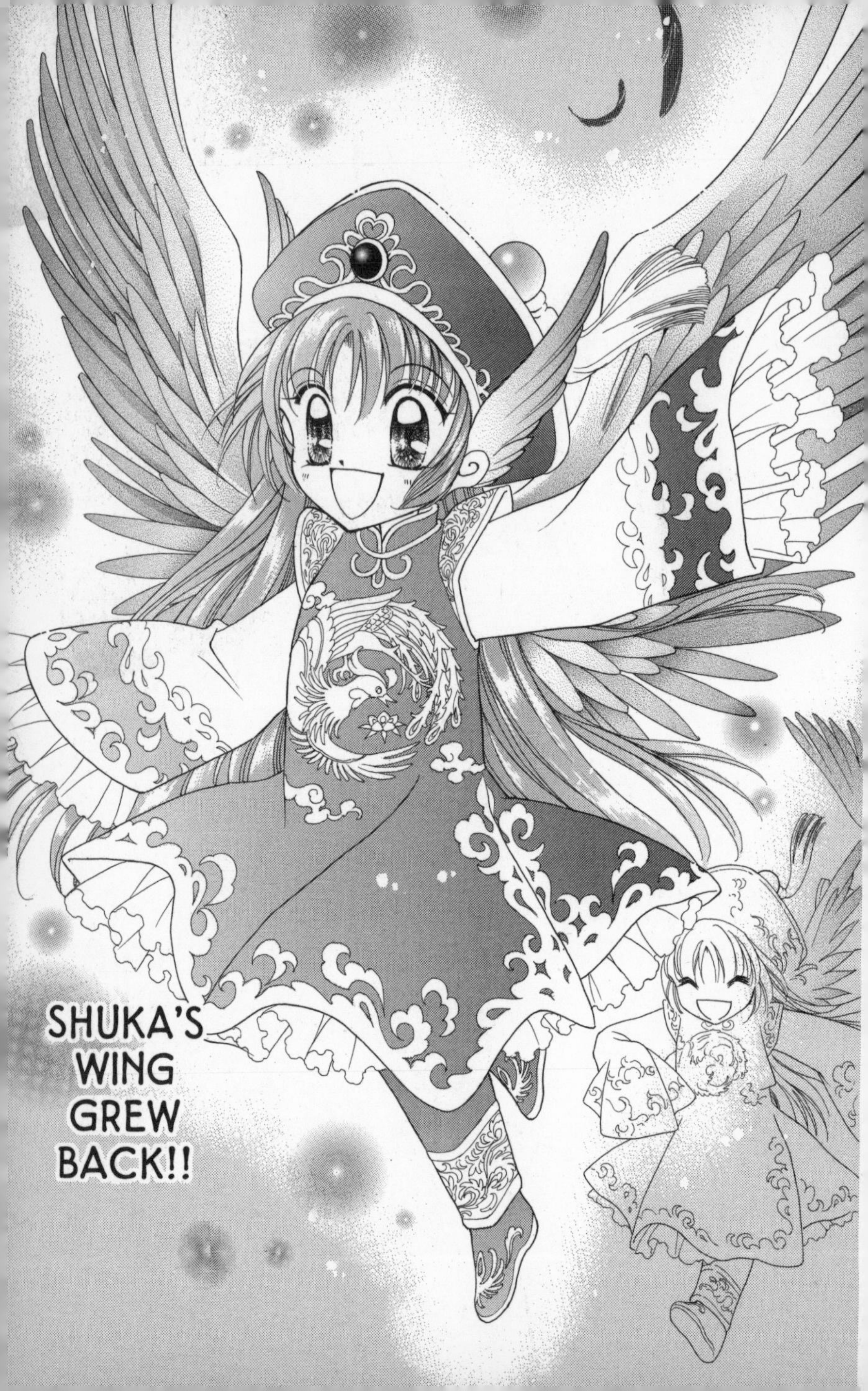
SHUKA'S WING GREW BACK!!

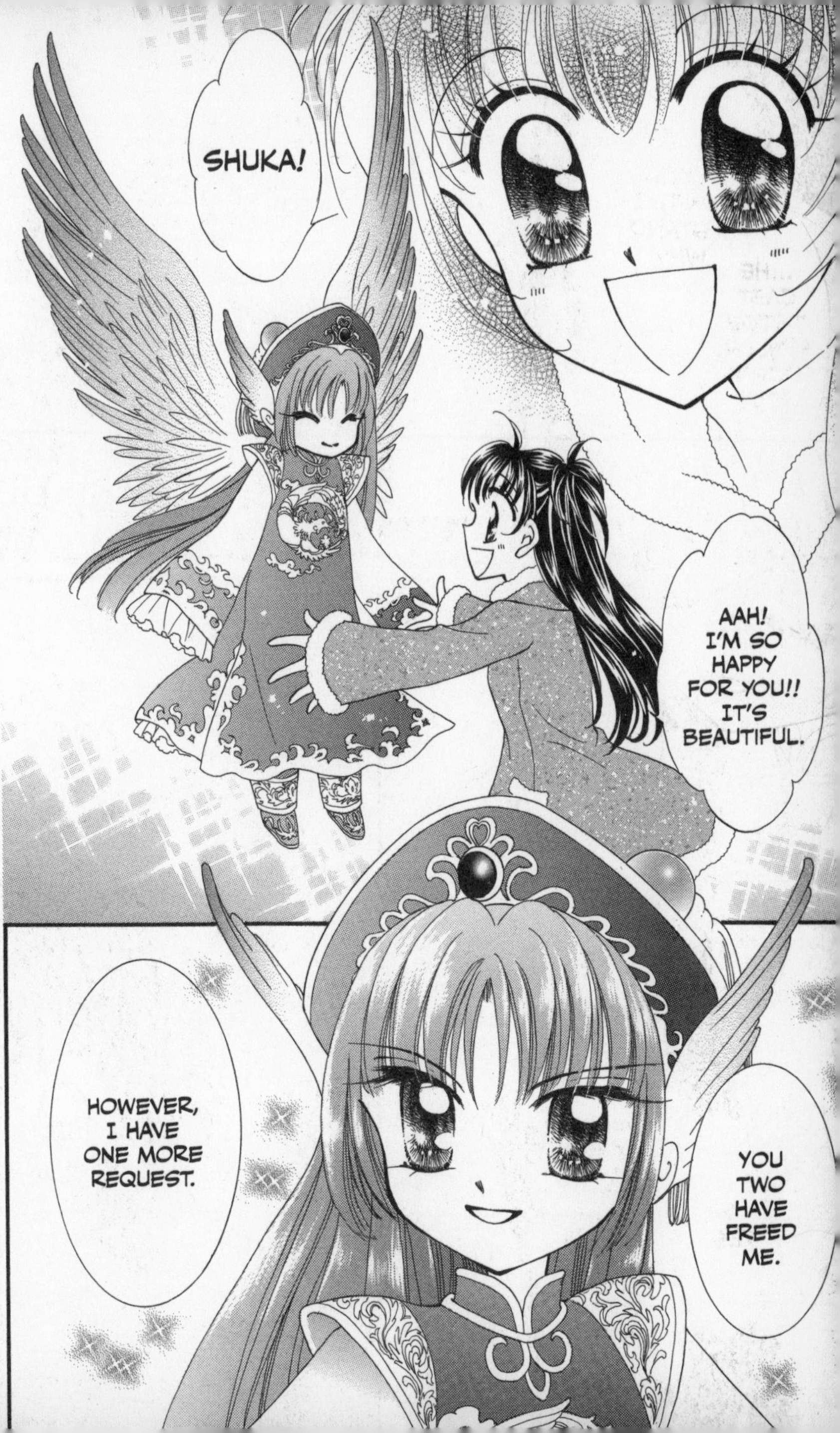
SHUKA!
AAH! I'M SO HAPPY FOR YOU!! IT'S BEAUTIFUL.
YOU TWO HAVE FREED ME.
HOWEVER, I HAVE ONE MORE REQUEST.

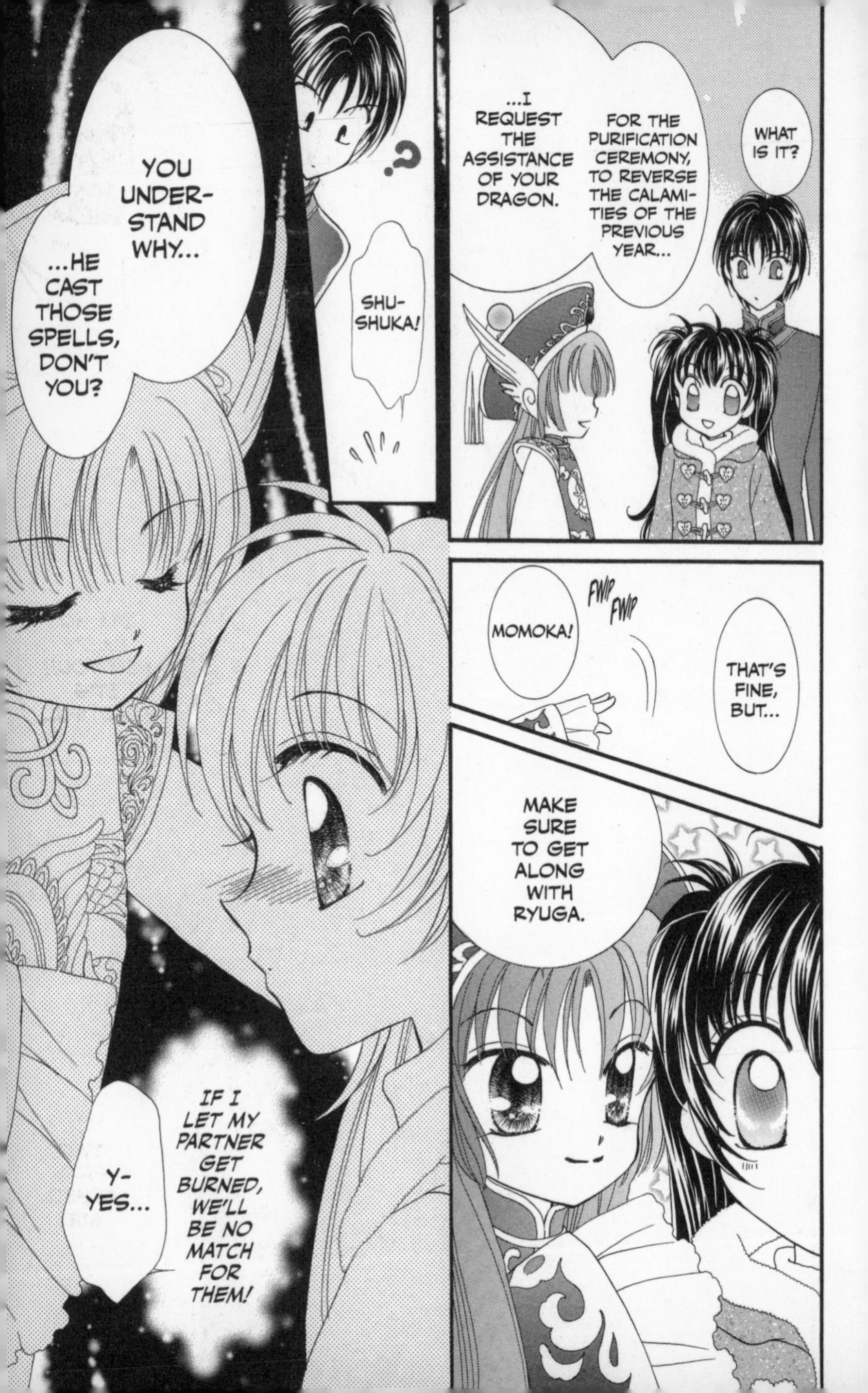
WHAT IS IT?
FOR THE PURIFICATION CEREMONY, TO REVERSE THE CALAMITIES OF THE PREVIOUS YEAR...
...I REQUEST THE ASSISTANCE OF YOUR DRAGON.
THAT'S FINE, BUT...
FWIP FWIP
MOMOKA!
MAKE SURE TO GET ALONG WITH RYUGA.
SHU-SHUKA!
YOU UNDER-STAND WHY...
...HE CAST THOSE SPELLS, DON'T YOU?
IF I LET MY PARTNER GET BURNED, WE'LL BE NO MATCH FOR THEM!
Y-YES...

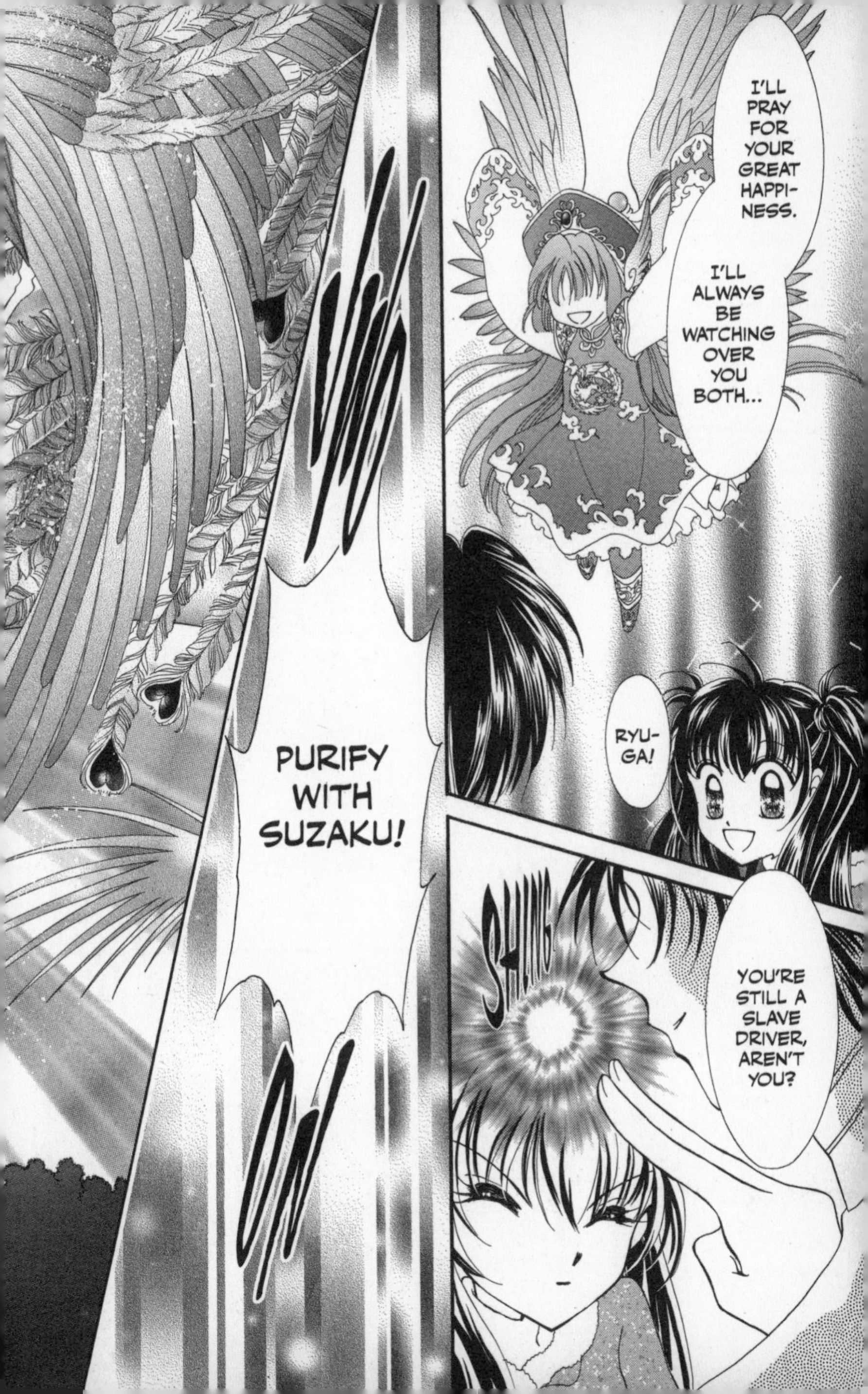
I'LL PRAY FOR YOUR GREAT HAPPI-NESS.
I'LL ALWAYS BE WATCHING OVER YOU BOTH...
RYU-GA!
SHING
YOU'RE STILL A SLAVE DRIVER, AREN'T YOU?
PURIFY WITH SUZAKU!

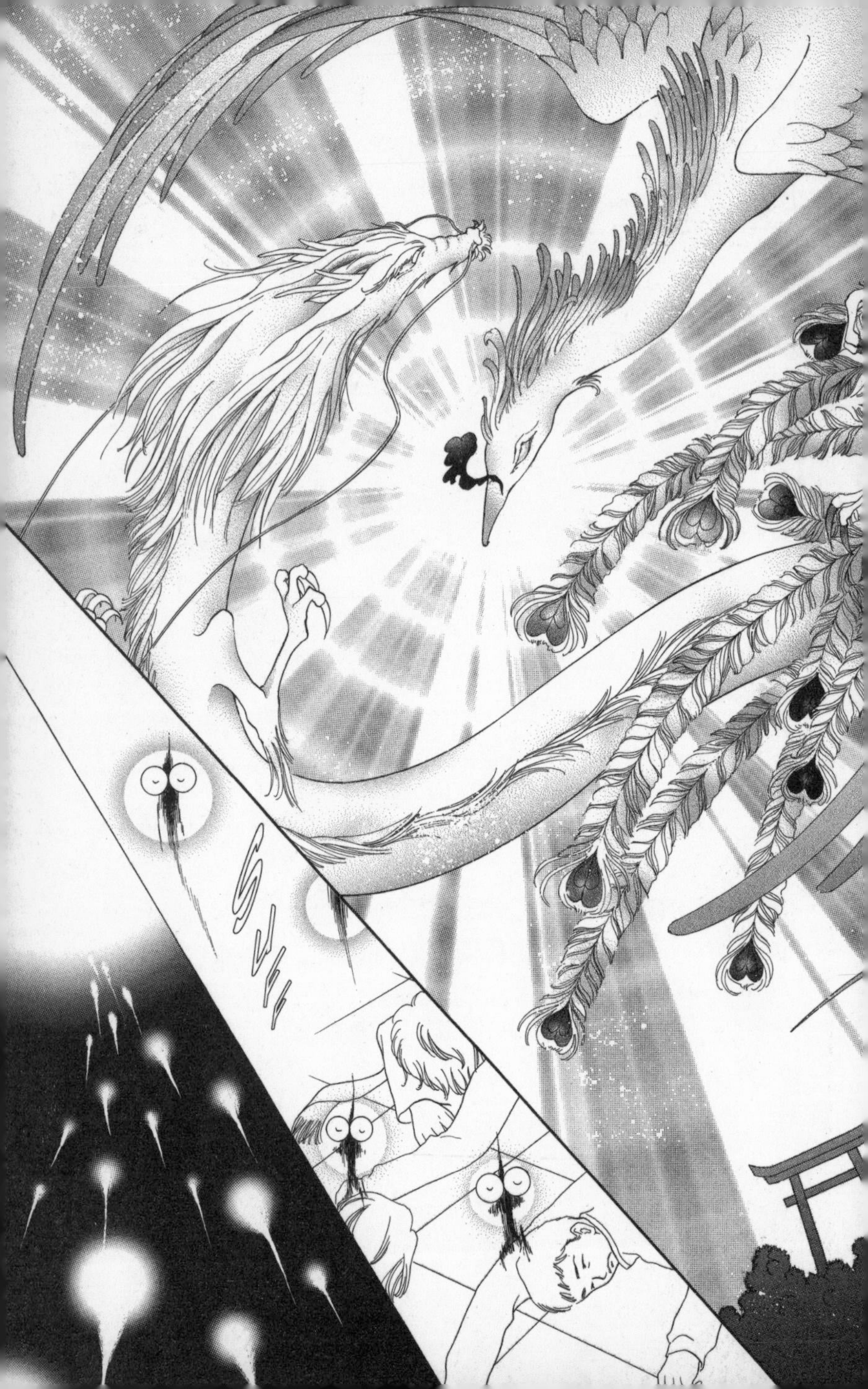

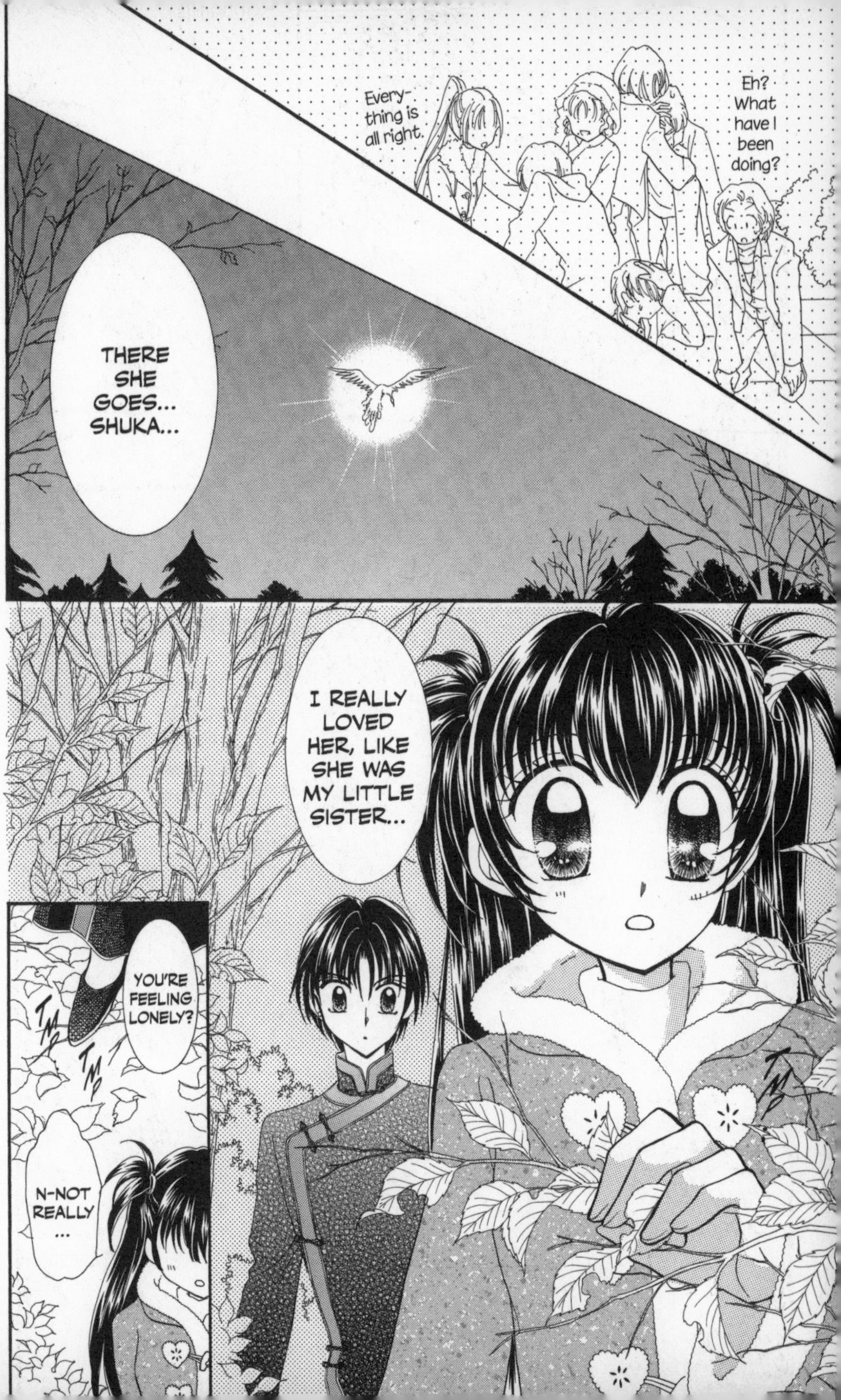
Eh? What have I been doing?
Every-thing is all right.
THERE SHE GOES... SHUKA...
I REALLY LOVED HER, LIKE SHE WAS MY LITTLE SISTER...
TMP
YOU'RE FEELING LONELY?
TMP
TMP
N-NOT REALLY ...

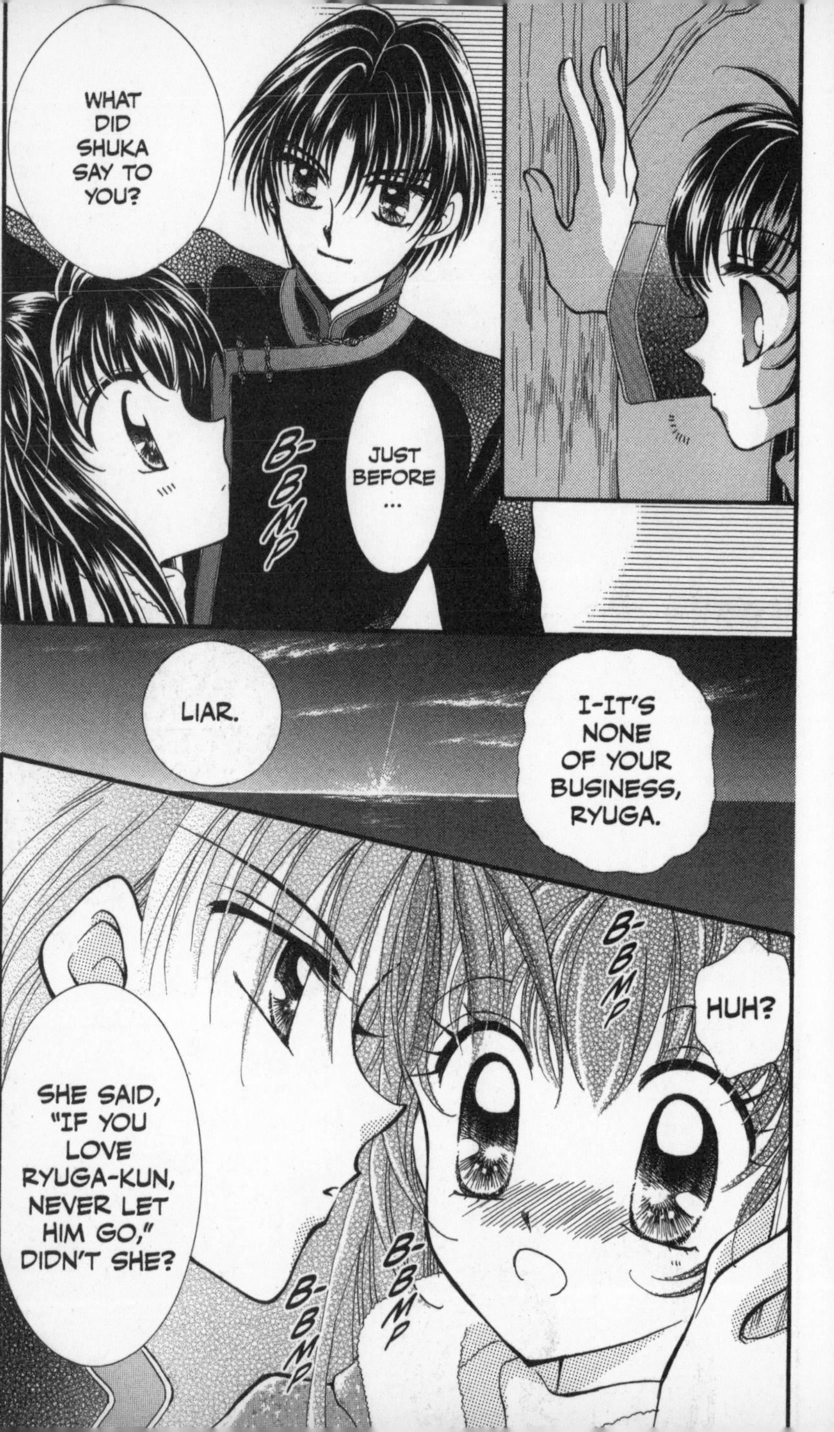
WHAT DID SHUKA SAY TO YOU?
B-BMP
JUST BEFORE ...
I-IT'S NONE OF YOUR BUSINESS, RYUGA.
LIAR.
B-BMP
HUH?
SHE SAID, "IF YOU LOVE RYUGA-KUN, NEVER LET HIM GO," DIDN'T SHE?
B-BMP
B-BMP

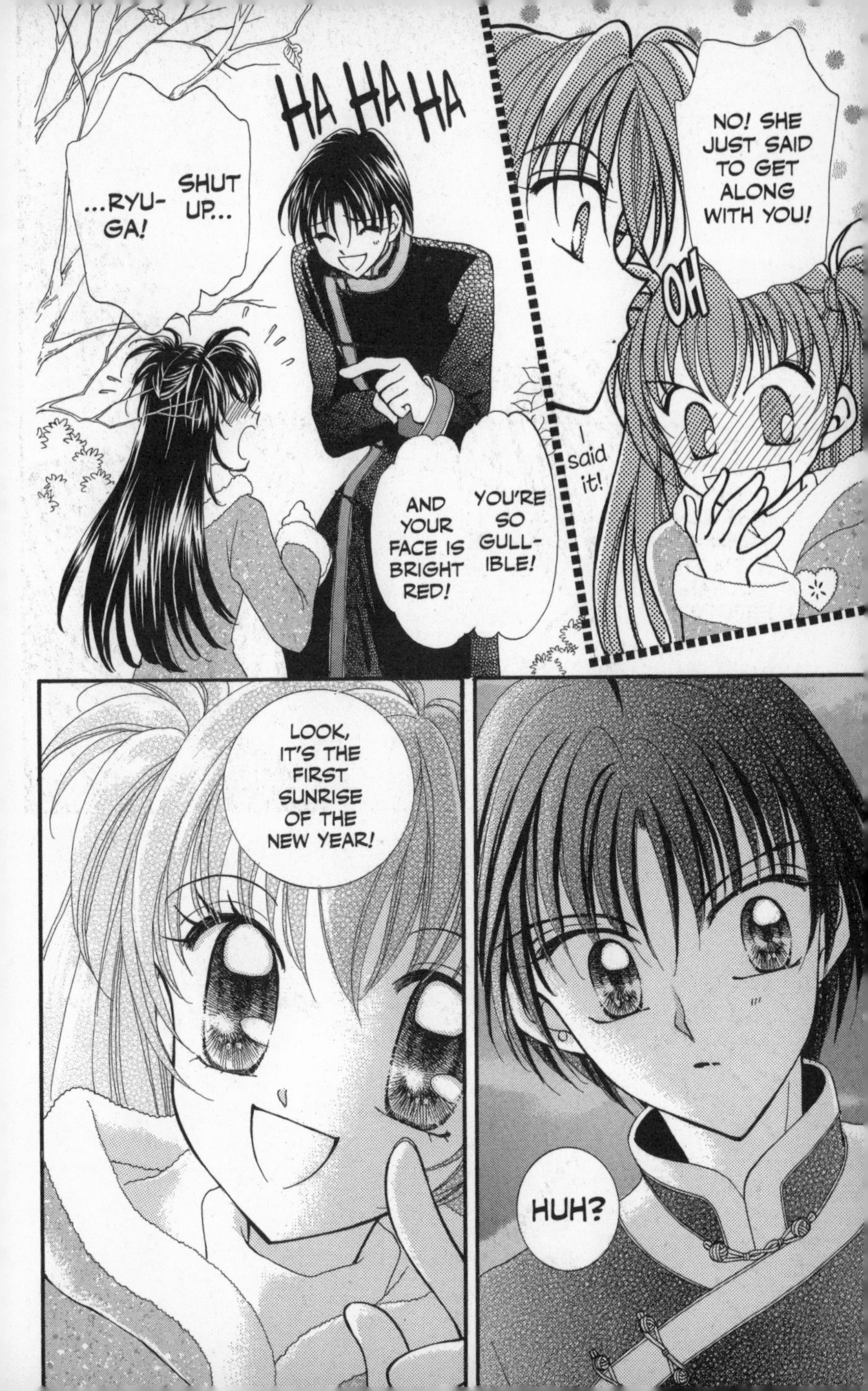
NO! SHE JUST SAID TO GET ALONG WITH YOU!
OH
I said it!
HA HA HA
SHUT UP... ...RYU-GA!
YOU'RE SO GULLIBLE! AND YOUR FACE IS BRIGHT RED!
HUH?
LOOK, IT'S THE FIRST SUNRISE OF THE NEW YEAR!

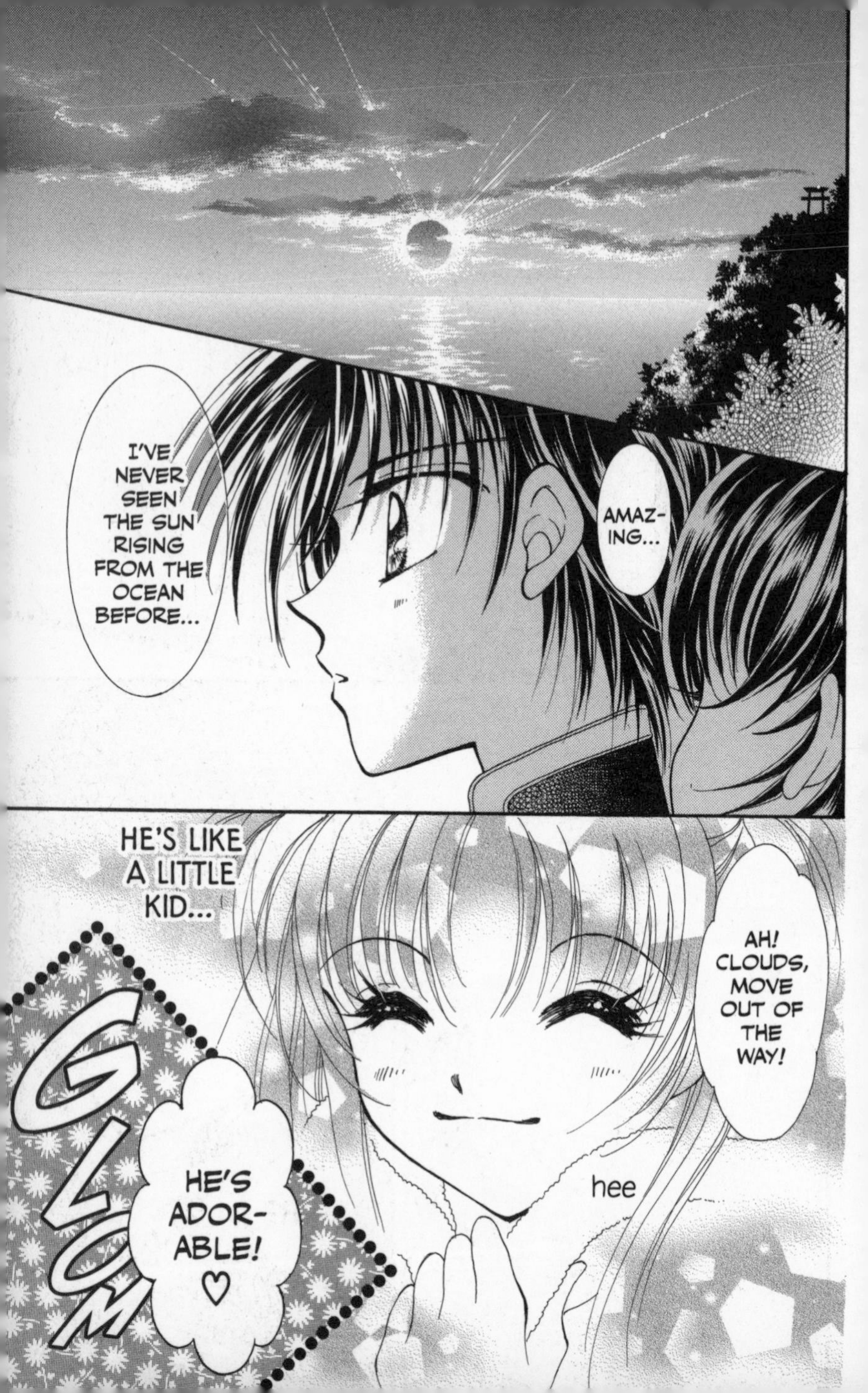
AMAZ-ING...
I'VE NEVER SEEN THE SUN RISING FROM THE OCEAN BEFORE...
AH! CLOUDS, MOVE OUT OF THE WAY!
HE'S LIKE A LITTLE KID...
hee
HE'S ADOR-ABLE! ♡
GLOW

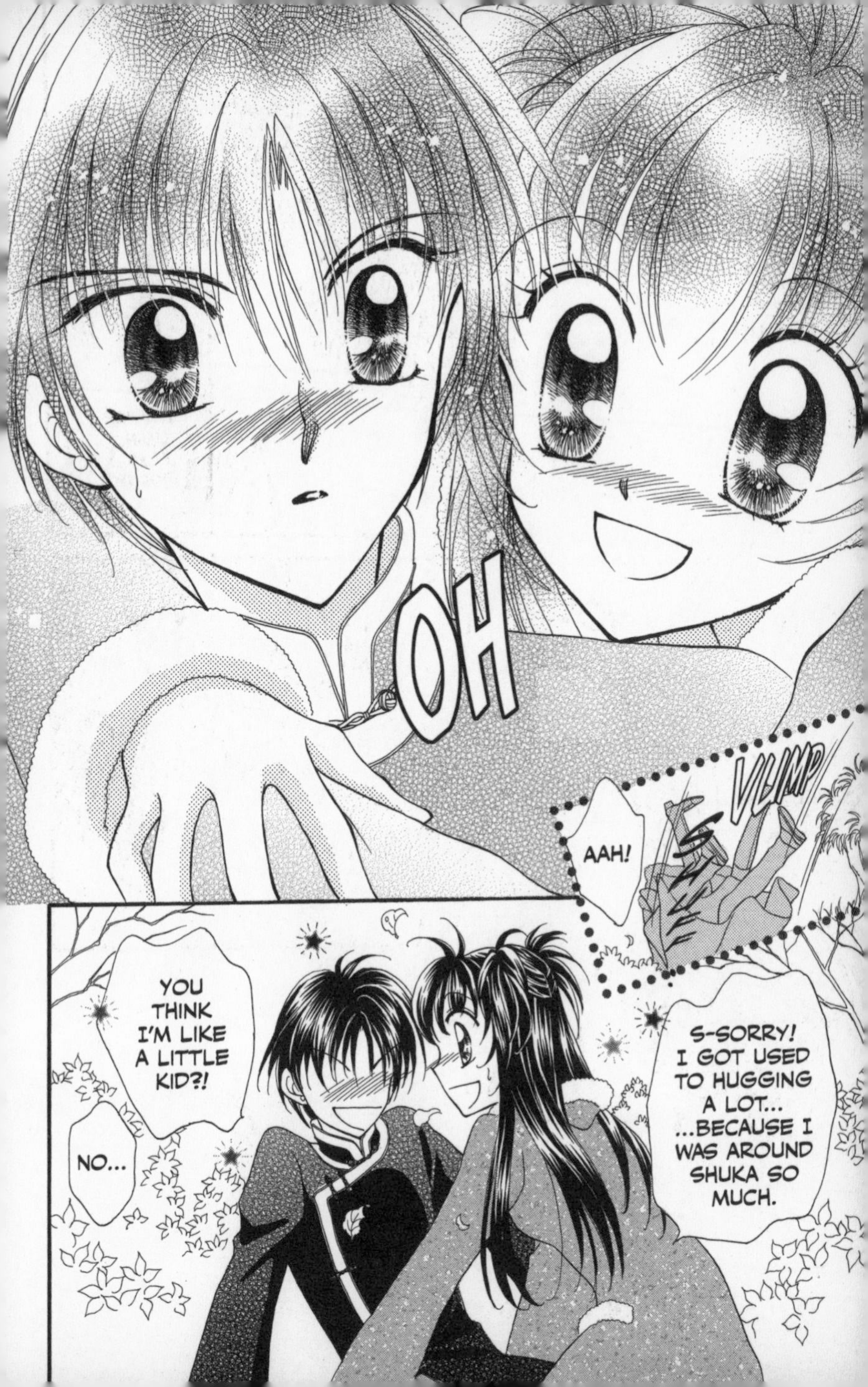
OH
VLUMP
AAH!
S-SORRY! I GOT USED TO HUGGING A LOT... ...BECAUSE I WAS AROUND SHUKA SO MUCH.
YOU THINK I'M LIKE A LITTLE KID?!
NO...

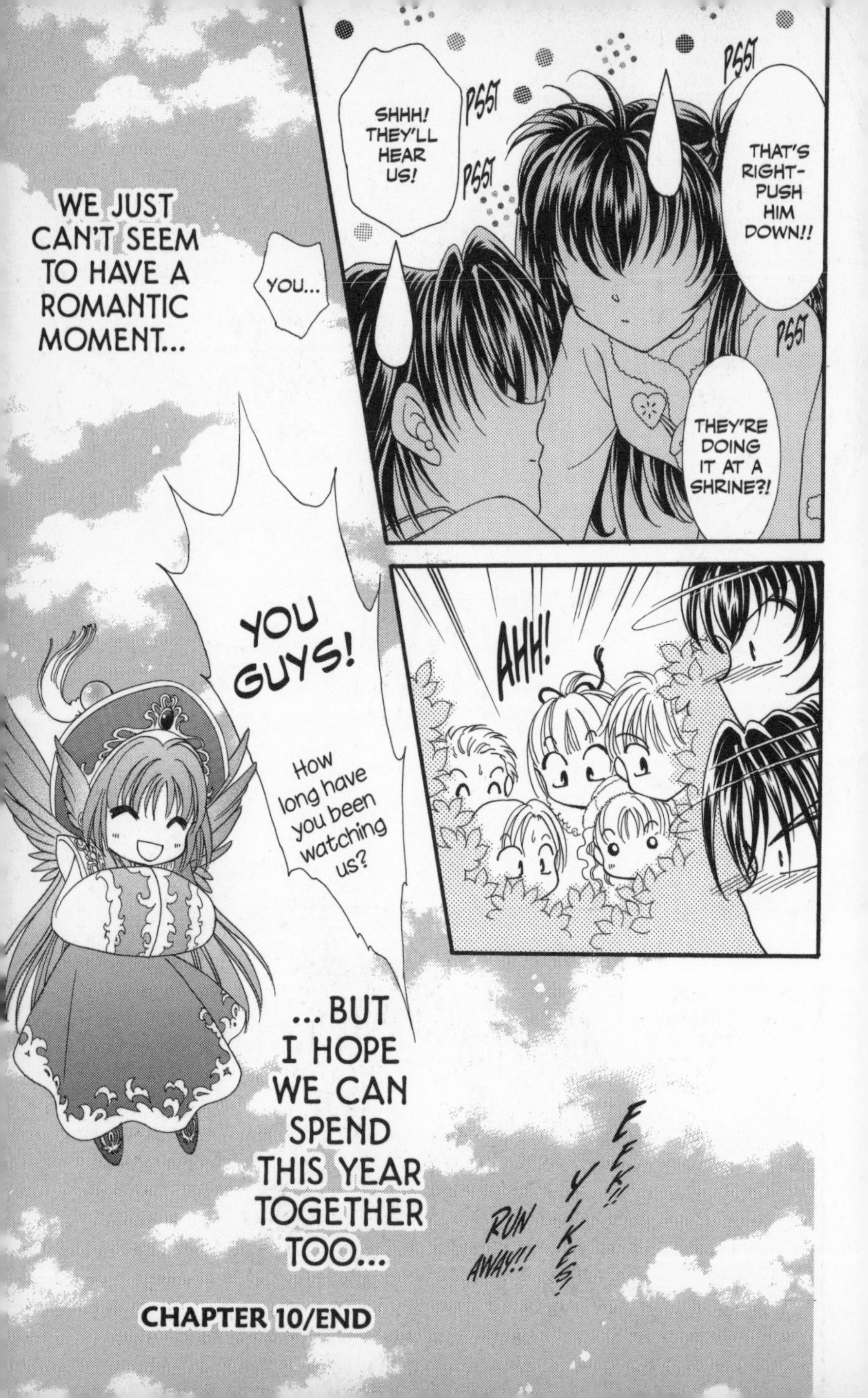
PSST
THAT'S RIGHT-PUSH HIM DOWN!!
PSST
SHHH! THEY'LL HEAR US!
PSST
PSST
THEY'RE DOING IT AT A SHRINE?!
YOU...
WE JUST CAN'T SEEM TO HAVE A ROMANTIC MOMENT...
AHH!
YOU GUYS!
How long have you been watching us?
...BUT I HOPE WE CAN SPEND THIS YEAR TOGETHER TOO...
EEK!!
YIKES!
RUN AWAY!!
CHAPTER 10/END

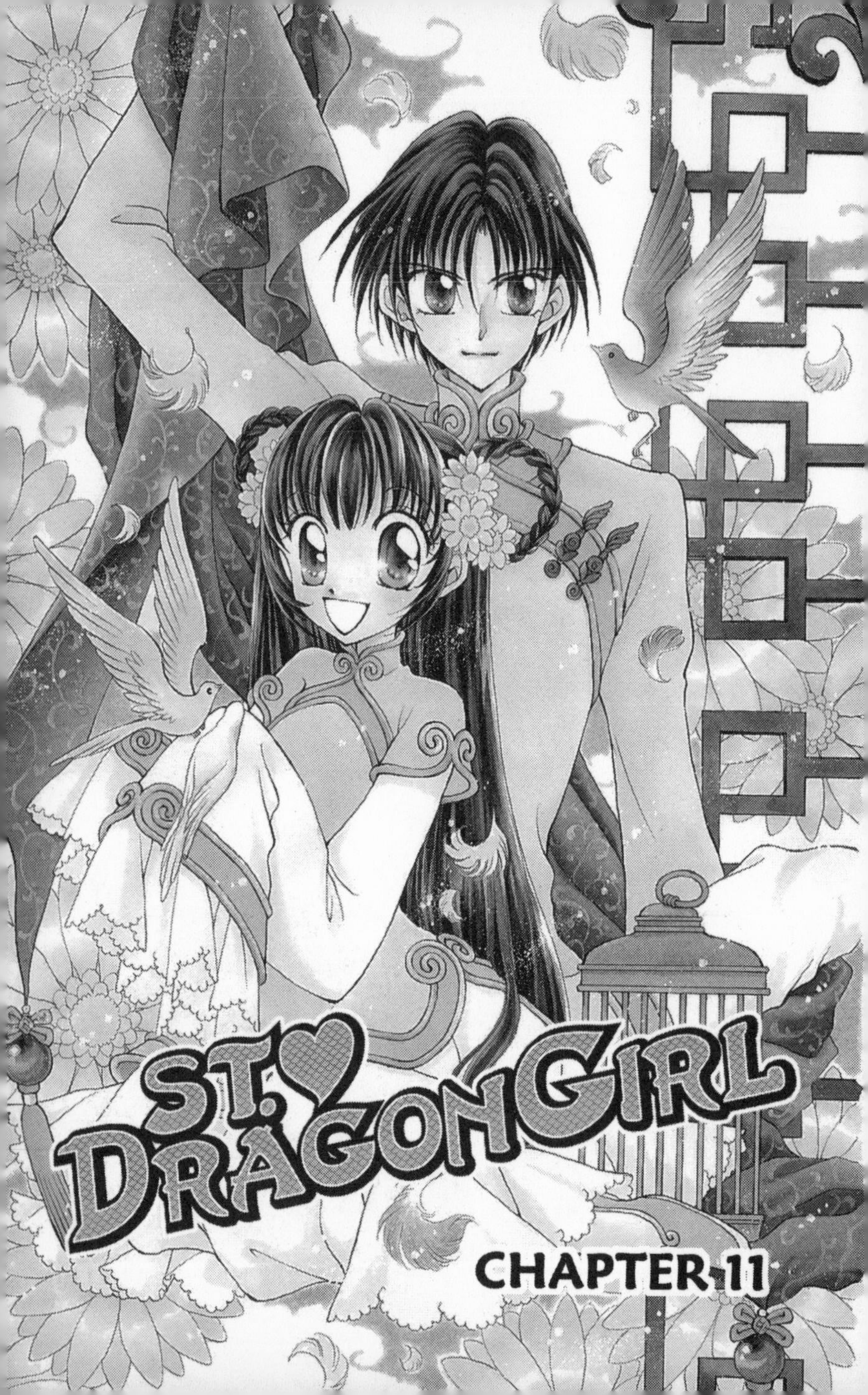
ST. DRAGON GIRL
CHAPTER 11

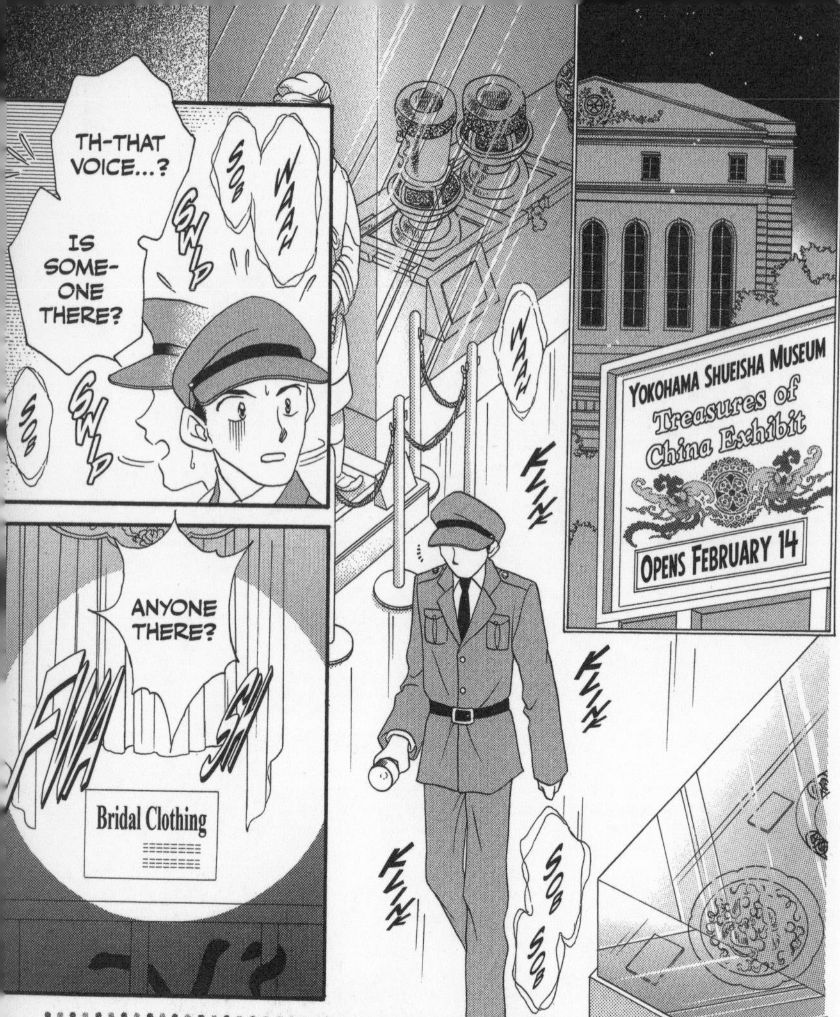
YOKOHAMA SHUEISHA MUSEUM
Treasures of China Exhibit
OPENS FEBRUARY 14
KLINK
KLINK
WAAH
SOB SOB
KLINK
WAAH
SOB
SWIP
TH-THAT VOICE...?
IS SOME-ONE THERE?
SWIP
SOB
ANYONE THERE?
SH
FWA
Bridal Clothing

Kouryu Kou

Born November 14.
Zodiac Sign: Scorpio. Blood Type: A
Residence: Hong Kong.
He is the eldest son of the main Kou family. Since childhood he has displayed a natural gift for sorcery. He first summoned a dragon when he was ten. He's a charismatic magic master. (laugh) He has one younger brother.

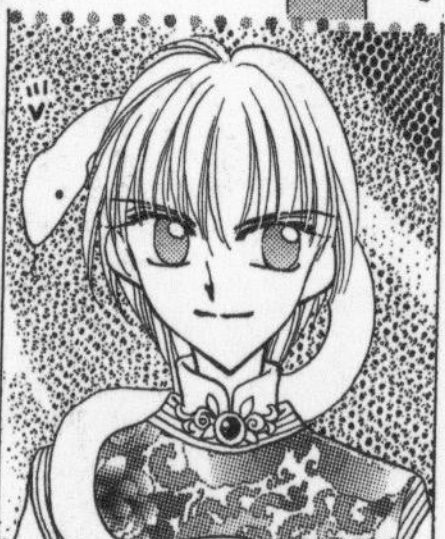

He'll use whatever means necessary in order to get what he wants.
He has a pushy, pompous personality. Apparenty he's as persistent as a snake (according to Shunran). His goal is to get Momoka, who is possessed by a dragon spirit, and take control of the Kou family.
He's two years older than Momoka and the others, but his outfits are flashy. Not only that, but they have become flashier and flashier! Why is that...? The readers either love him or hate him.

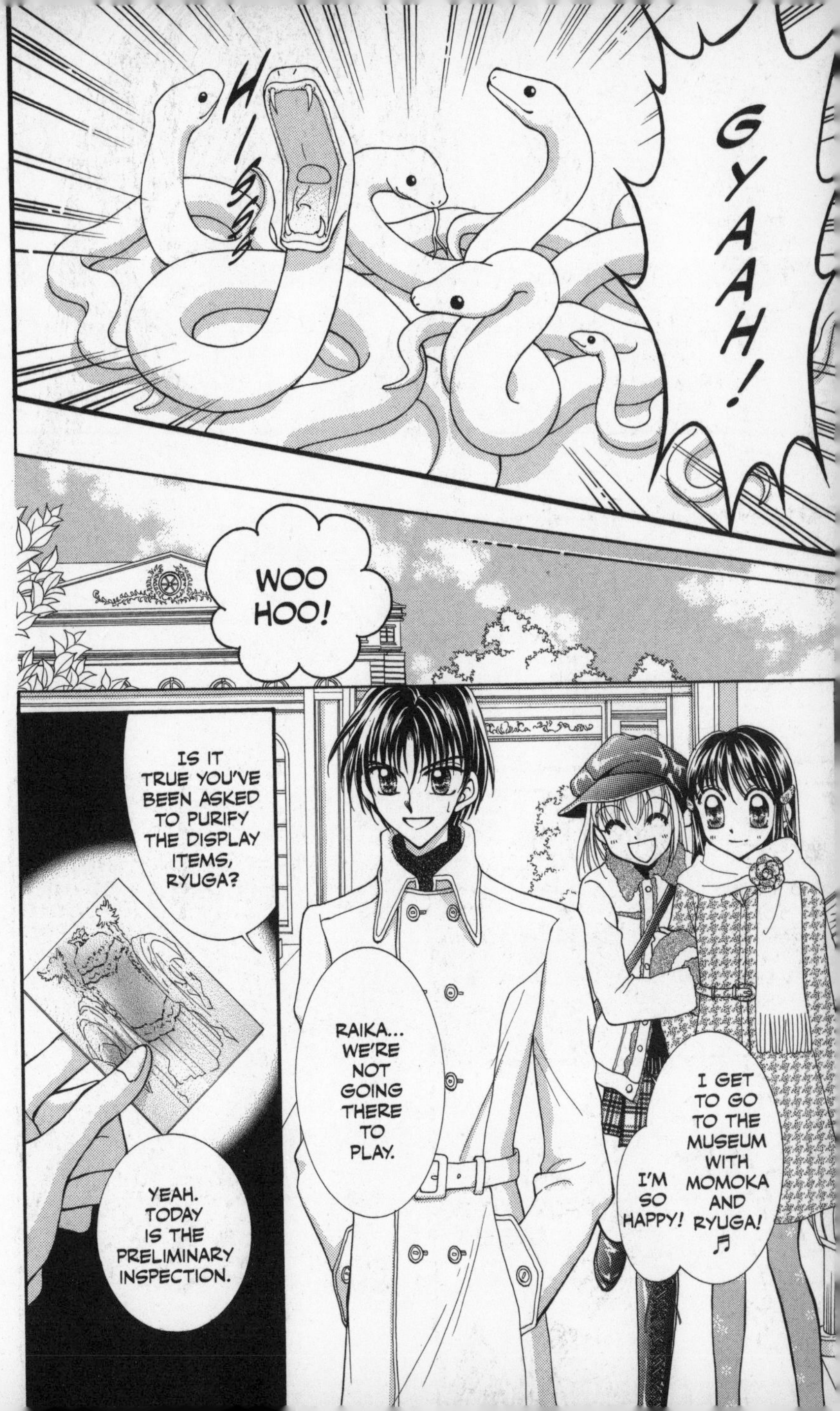
GYAAH!
HISS
WOO HOO!
I GET TO GO TO THE MUSEUM WITH MOMOKA AND RYUGA! ♬
I'M SO HAPPY!
RAIKA... WE'RE NOT GOING THERE TO PLAY.
IS IT TRUE YOU'VE BEEN ASKED TO PURIFY THE DISPLAY ITEMS, RYUGA?
YEAH. TODAY IS THE PRELIMINARY INSPECTION.

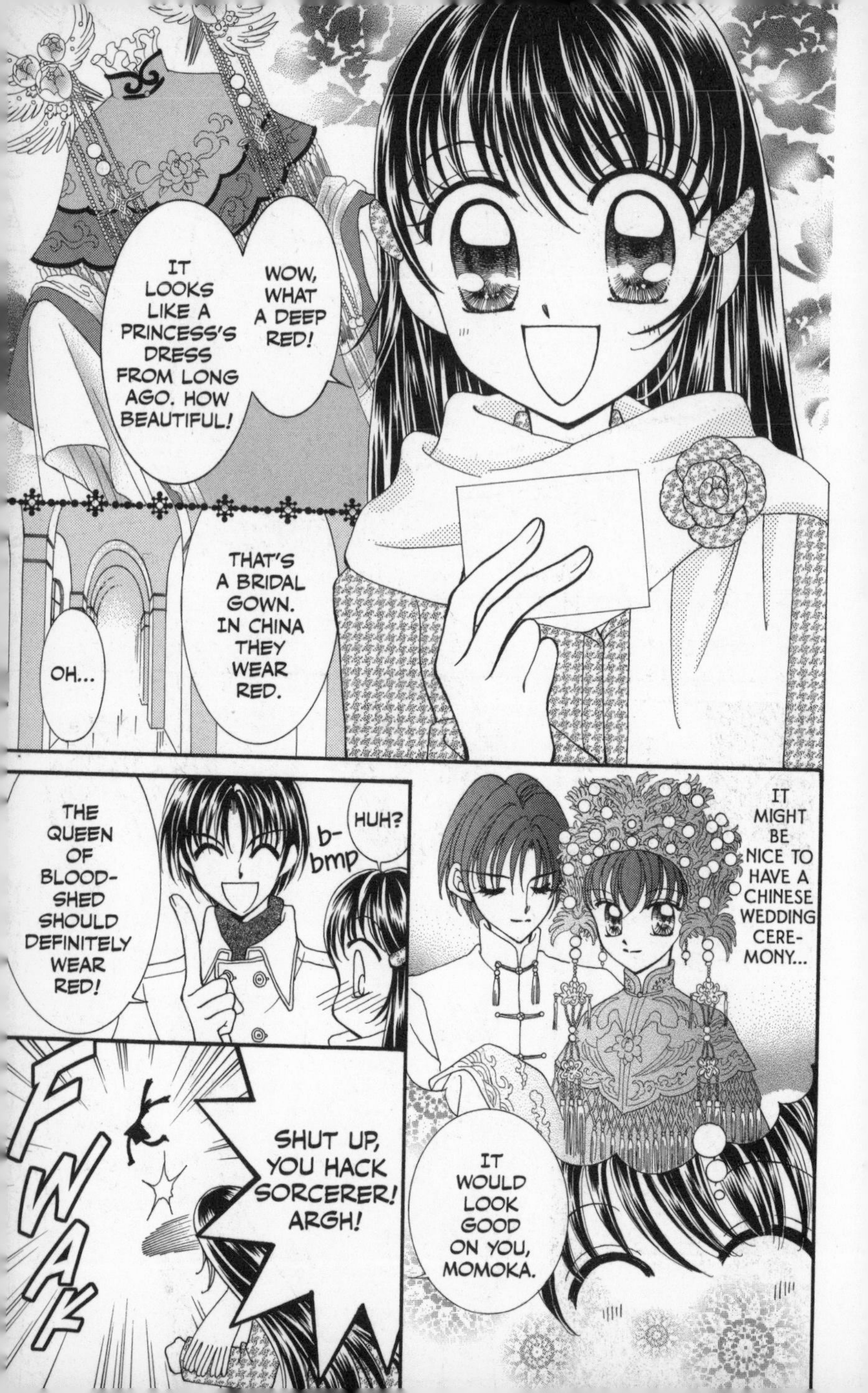
WOW, WHAT A DEEP RED!
IT LOOKS LIKE A PRINCESS'S DRESS FROM LONG AGO. HOW BEAUTIFUL!
THAT'S A BRIDAL GOWN. IN CHINA THEY WEAR RED.
OH...
IT MIGHT BE NICE TO HAVE A CHINESE WEDDING CERE-MONY...
IT WOULD LOOK GOOD ON YOU, MOMOKA.
HUH?
b-bmp
THE QUEEN OF BLOOD-SHED SHOULD DEFINITELY WEAR RED!
SHUT UP, YOU HACK SORCERER! ARGH!
FWAK

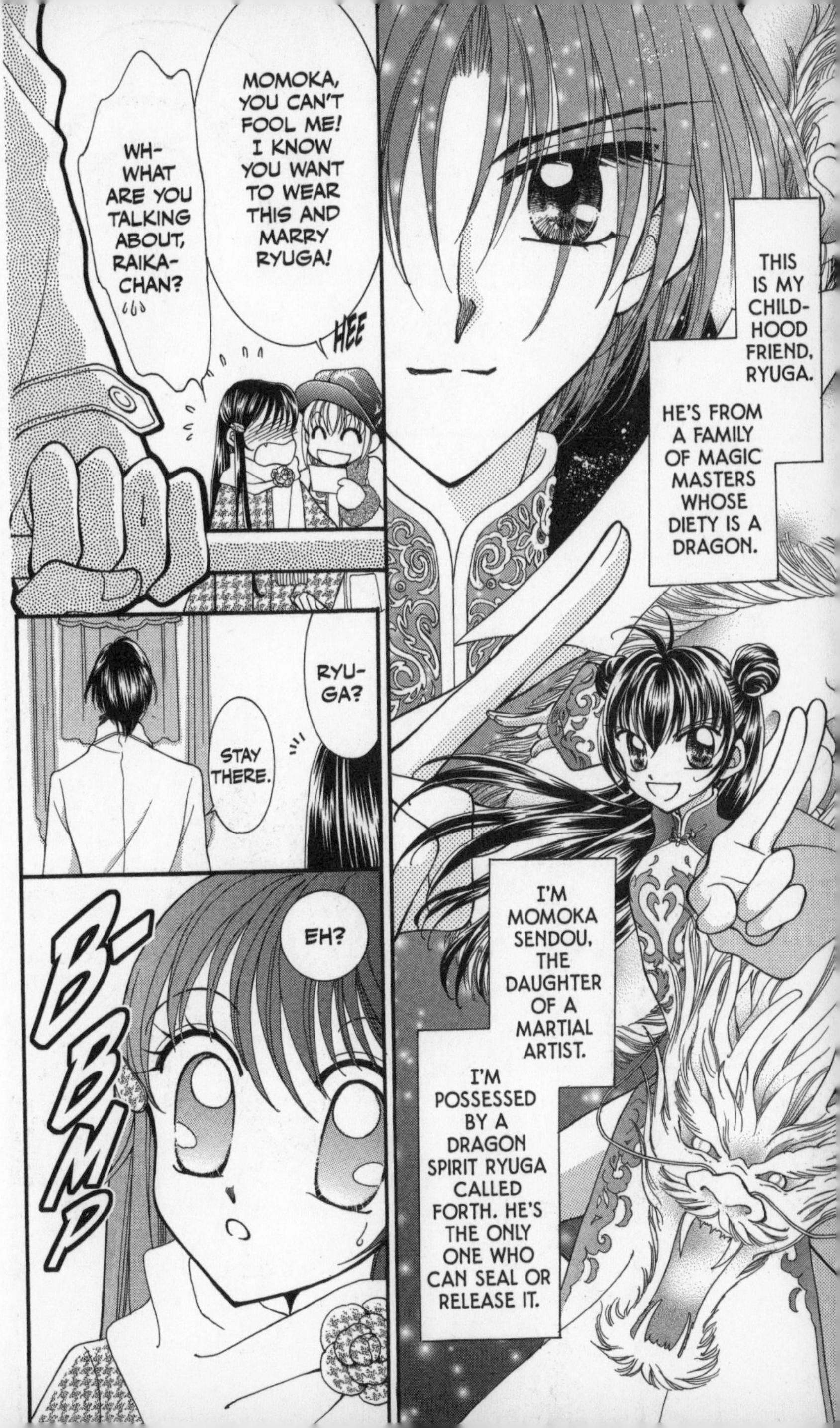
THIS IS MY CHILDHOOD FRIEND, RYUGA.
HE'S FROM A FAMILY OF MAGIC MASTERS WHOSE DIETY IS A DRAGON.
I'M MOMOKA SENDOU, THE DAUGHTER OF A MARTIAL ARTIST.
I'M POSSESSED BY A DRAGON SPIRIT RYUGA CALLED FORTH. HE'S THE ONLY ONE WHO CAN SEAL OR RELEASE IT.
MOMOKA, YOU CAN'T FOOL ME! I KNOW YOU WANT TO WEAR THIS AND MARRY RYUGA!
HEE
WH-WHAT ARE YOU TALKING ABOUT, RAIKA-CHAN?
RYU-GA?
STAY THERE.
EH?
B-BMP

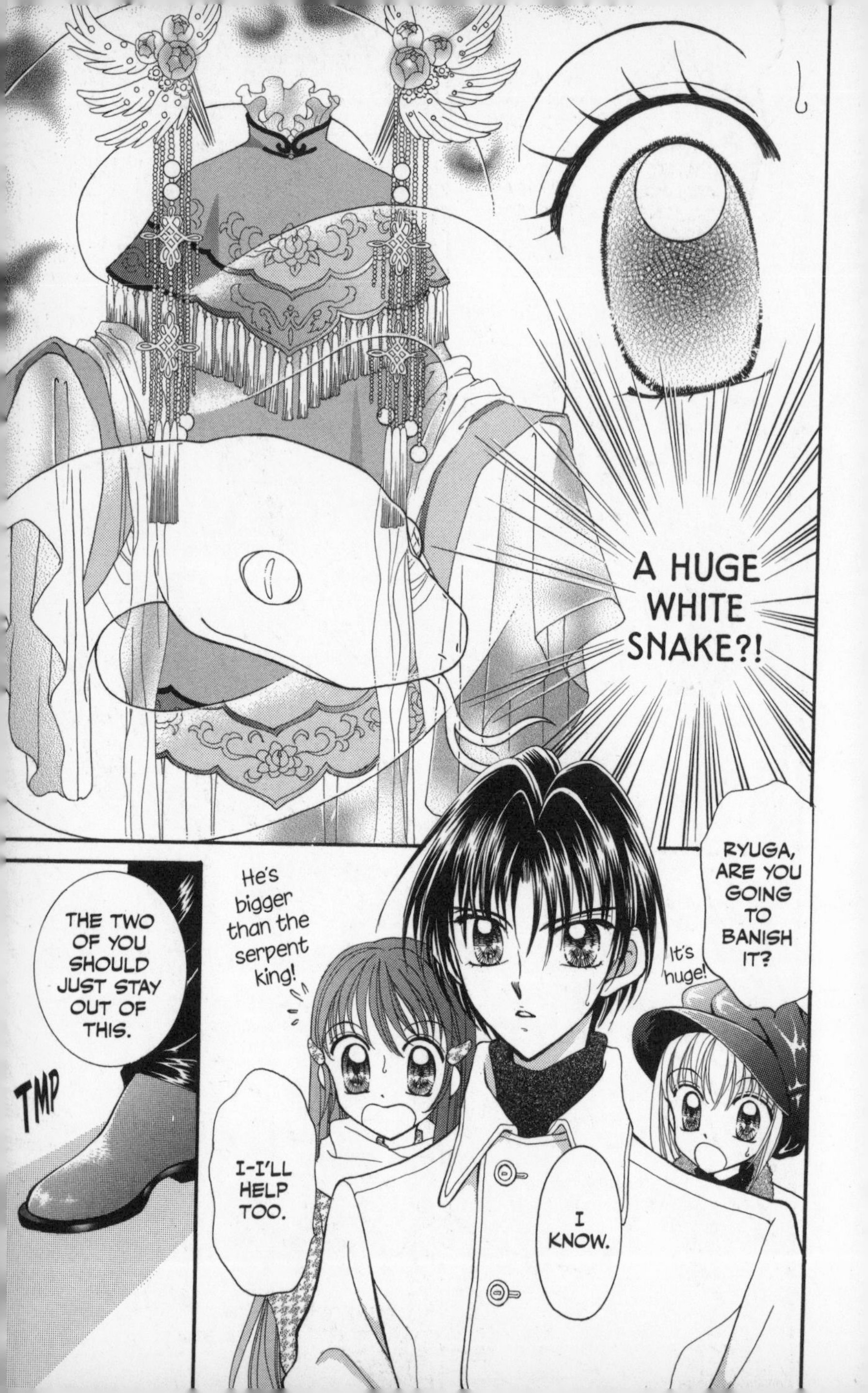
A HUGE WHITE SNAKE?!
RYUGA, ARE YOU GOING TO BANISH IT?
It's huge!
He's bigger than the serpent king!
I KNOW.
I-I'LL HELP TOO.
THE TWO OF YOU SHOULD JUST STAY OUT OF THIS.
TMP

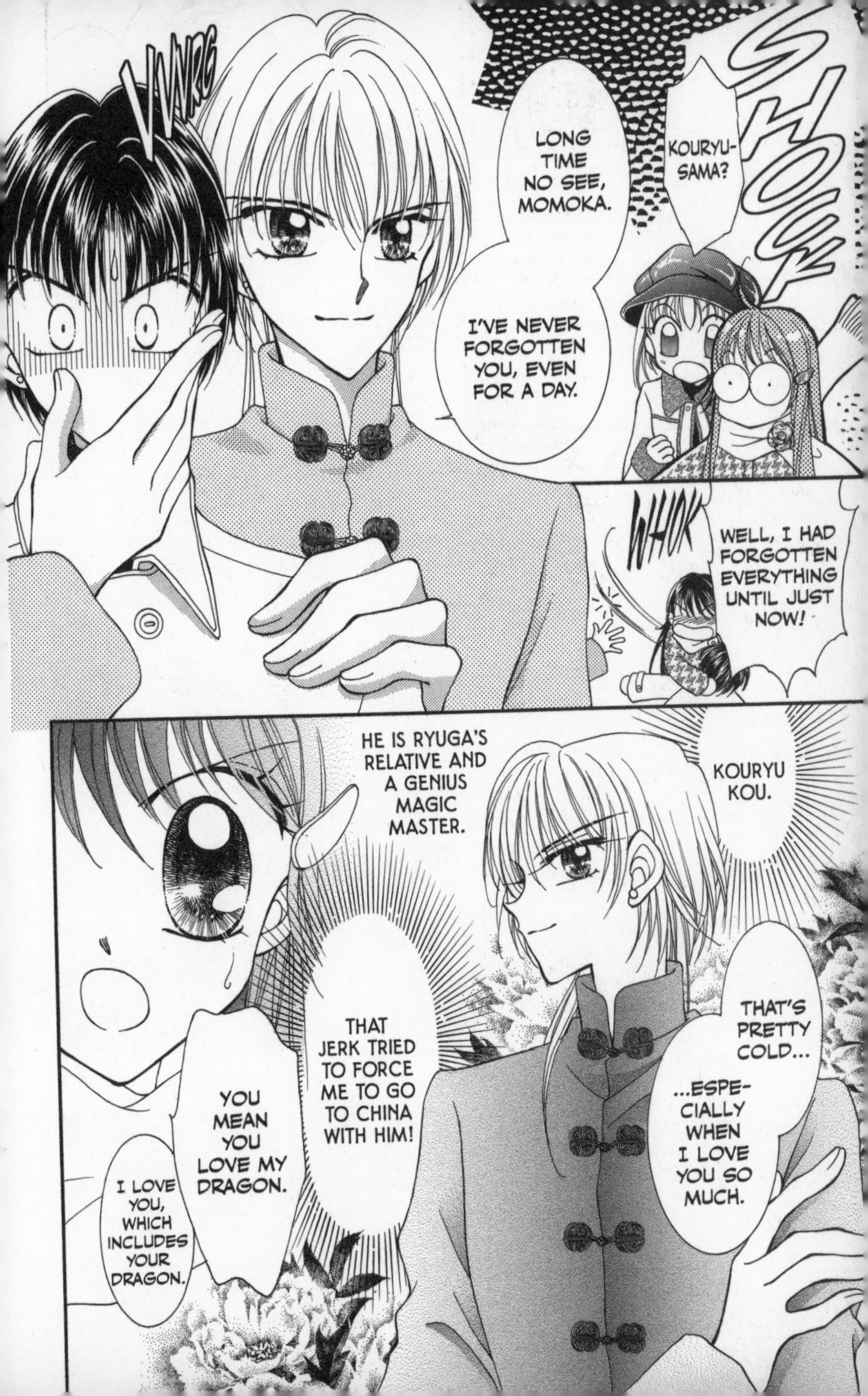
SHOOW
KOURYU-SAMA?
LONG TIME NO SEE, MOMOKA.
VVVRG
I'VE NEVER FORGOTTEN YOU, EVEN FOR A DAY.
WHOK
WELL, I HAD FORGOTTEN EVERYTHING UNTIL JUST NOW!
KOURYU KOU.
HE IS RYUGA'S RELATIVE AND A GENIUS MAGIC MASTER.
THAT'S PRETTY COLD...
...ESPE-CIALLY WHEN I LOVE YOU SO MUCH.
THAT JERK TRIED TO FORCE ME TO GO TO CHINA WITH HIM!
YOU MEAN YOU LOVE MY DRAGON.
I LOVE YOU, WHICH INCLUDES YOUR DRAGON.

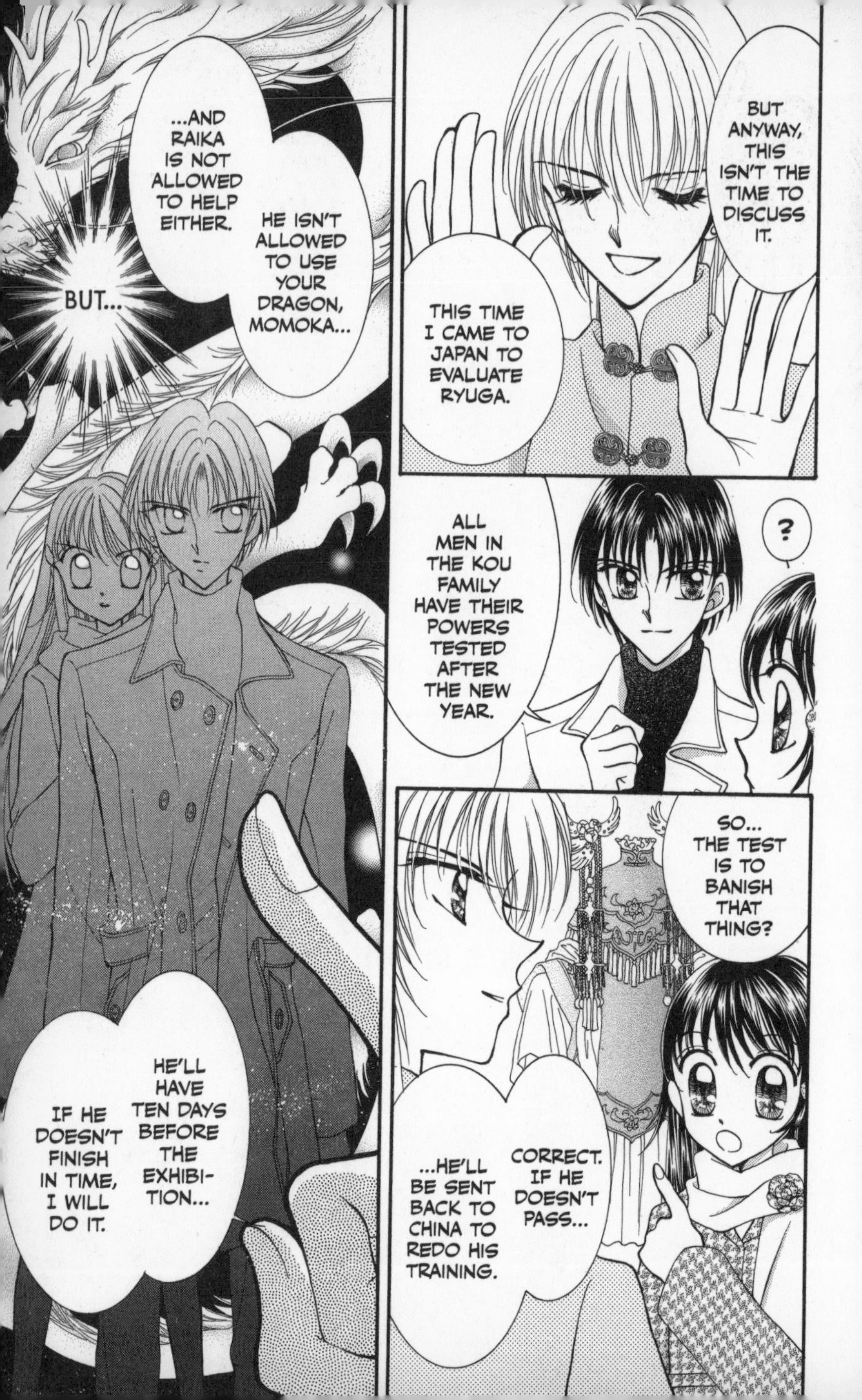
BUT ANYWAY, THIS ISN'T THE TIME TO DISCUSS IT.
THIS TIME I CAME TO JAPAN TO EVALUATE RYUGA.
?
ALL MEN IN THE KOU FAMILY HAVE THEIR POWERS TESTED AFTER THE NEW YEAR.
SO... THE TEST IS TO BANISH THAT THING?
CORRECT. IF HE DOESN'T PASS...
...HE'LL BE SENT BACK TO CHINA TO REDO HIS TRAINING.
HE ISN'T ALLOWED TO USE YOUR DRAGON, MOMOKA...
...AND RAIKA IS NOT ALLOWED TO HELP EITHER.
BUT...
HE'LL HAVE TEN DAYS BEFORE THE EXHIBITION...
IF HE DOESN'T FINISH IN TIME, I WILL DO IT.

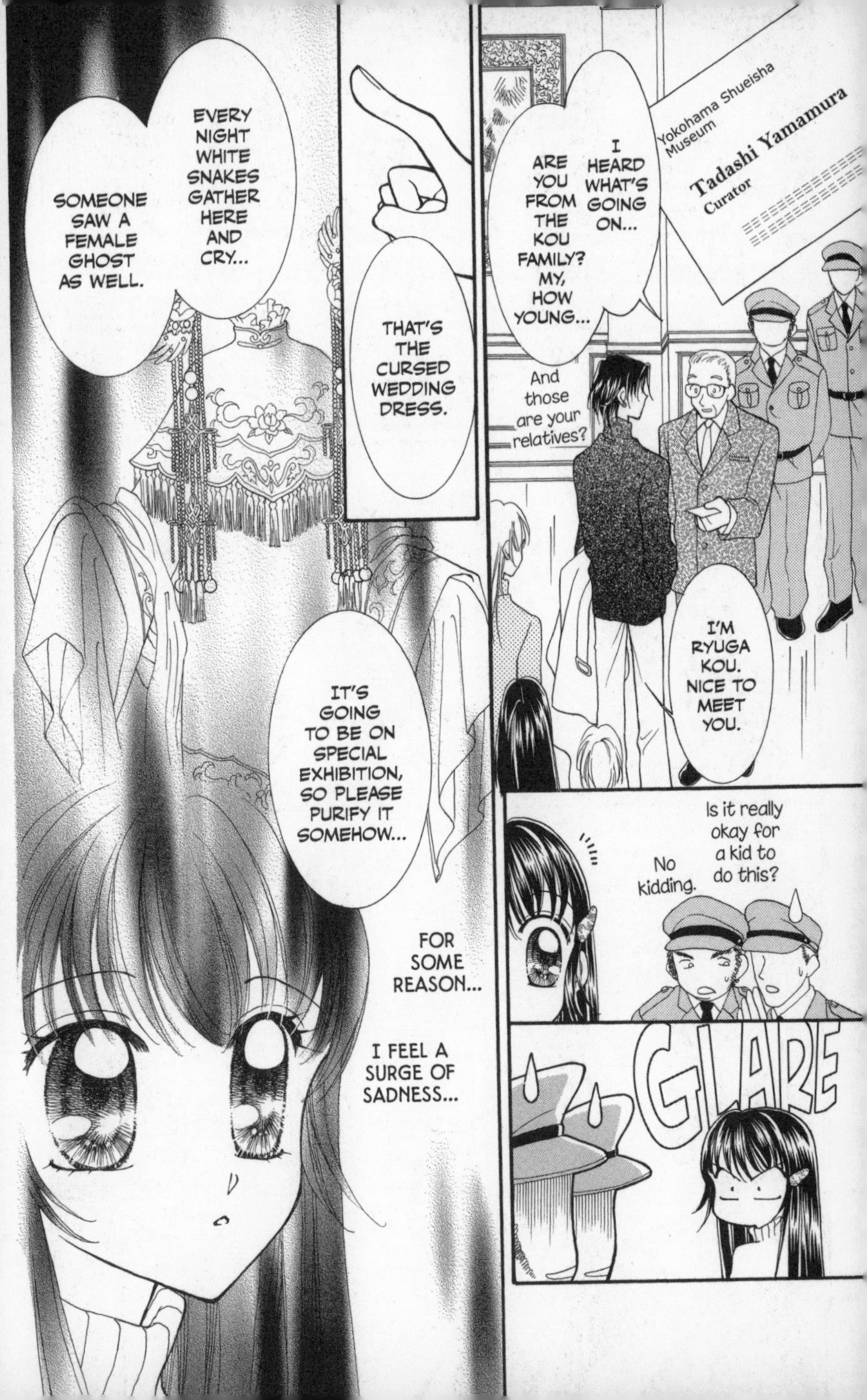
Yokohama Shueisha Museum
Tadashi Yamamura
Curator
I HEARD WHAT'S GOING ON...
ARE YOU FROM THE KOU FAMILY? MY, HOW YOUNG...
And those are your relatives?
I'M RYUGA KOU. NICE TO MEET YOU.
Is it really okay for a kid to do this?
No kidding.
GLARE
THAT'S THE CURSED WEDDING DRESS.
EVERY NIGHT WHITE SNAKES GATHER HERE AND CRY...
SOMEONE SAW A FEMALE GHOST AS WELL.
IT'S GOING TO BE ON SPECIAL EXHIBITION, SO PLEASE PURIFY IT SOMEHOW...
FOR SOME REASON...
I FEEL A SURGE OF SADNESS...

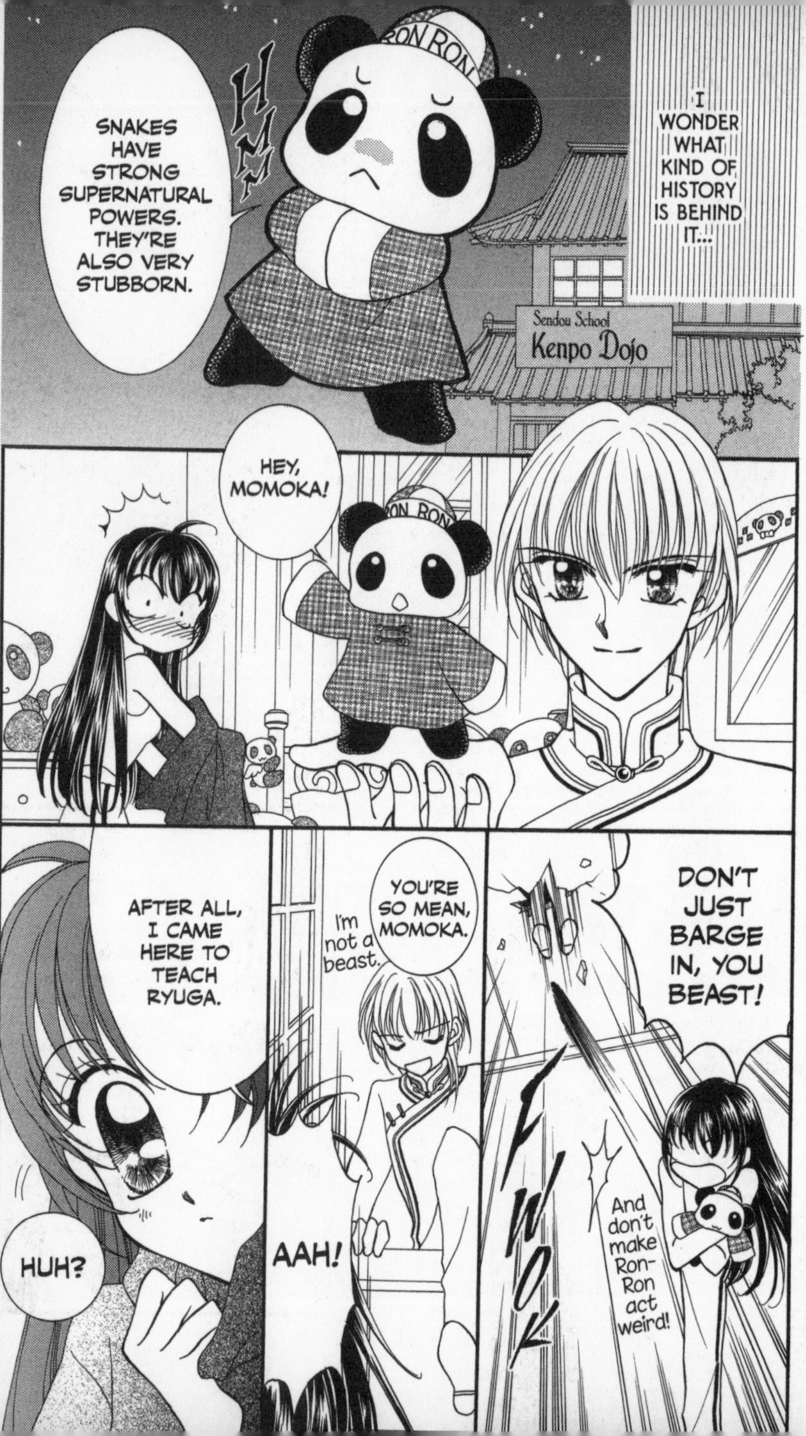
I WONDER WHAT KIND OF HISTORY IS BEHIND IT...
HMM
SNAKES HAVE STRONG SUPERNATURAL POWERS. THEY'RE ALSO VERY STUBBORN.
RON RON
Sendou School
Kenpo Dojo
HEY, MOMOKA!
RON RON
DON'T JUST BARGE IN, YOU BEAST!
And don't make Ron-Ron act weird!
YOU'RE SO MEAN, MOMOKA.
I'm not a beast.
AAH!
AFTER ALL, I CAME HERE TO TEACH RYUGA.
HUH?

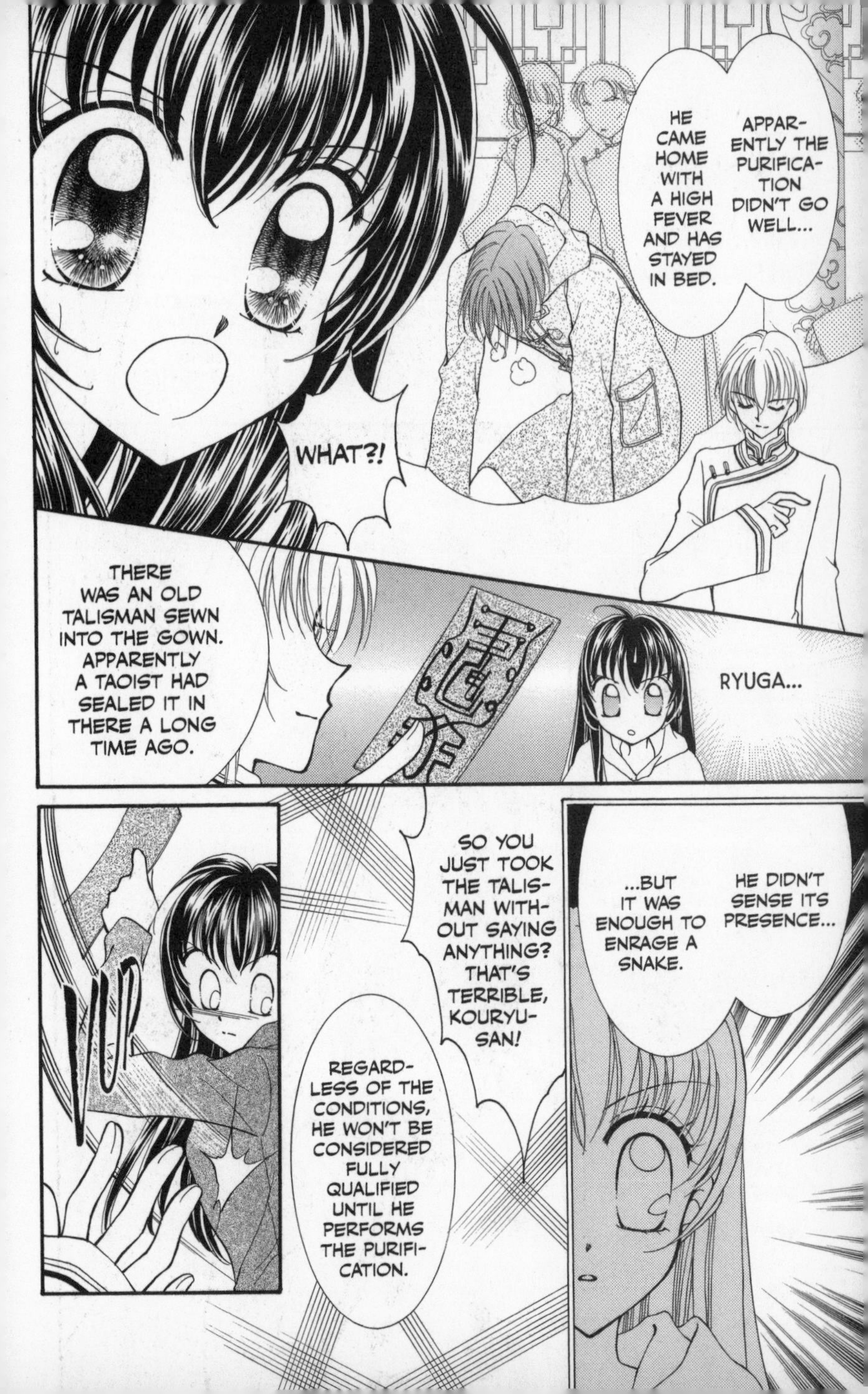
APPARENTLY THE PURIFICATION DIDN'T GO WELL...
HE CAME HOME WITH A HIGH FEVER AND HAS STAYED IN BED.
WHAT?!
RYUGA...
THERE WAS AN OLD TALISMAN SEWN INTO THE GOWN. APPARENTLY A TAOIST HAD SEALED IT IN THERE A LONG TIME AGO.
HE DIDN'T SENSE ITS PRESENCE...
...BUT IT WAS ENOUGH TO ENRAGE A SNAKE.
SO YOU JUST TOOK THE TALISMAN WITHOUT SAYING ANYTHING? THAT'S TERRIBLE, KOURYU-SAN!
REGARDLESS OF THE CONDITIONS, HE WON'T BE CONSIDERED FULLY QUALIFIED UNTIL HE PERFORMS THE PURIFICATION.

6

Every time I show an outline to my editor, I write a subtitle for it. This time I wrote "The Cursed Wedding Dress," and my editor loved it. The Hong Kong one was called "Crying Dragon in Hong Kong," I think. It's like, "What kind of manga is this?"

This time, drawing the wedding dress was even harder than drawing Suzaku.

The hair ornaments were very detailed, and there's a lot of action too. Queen, who was in charge of the wedding dress, said she felt like crying right in the middle of working on it!

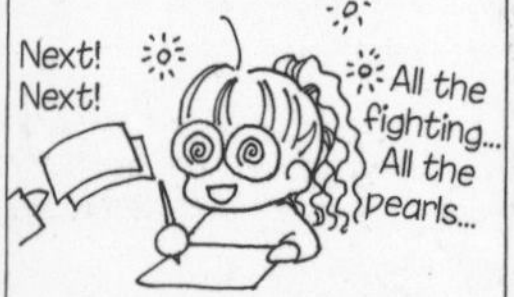
Next! Next!
All the fighting... All the pearls...

I did the last part of the inking for the hair ornaments myself...and I felt like my nose was going to bleed! But this chapter is very gorgeous, and I love it.

I worked on it while I watched the first dawn of the 21st century.

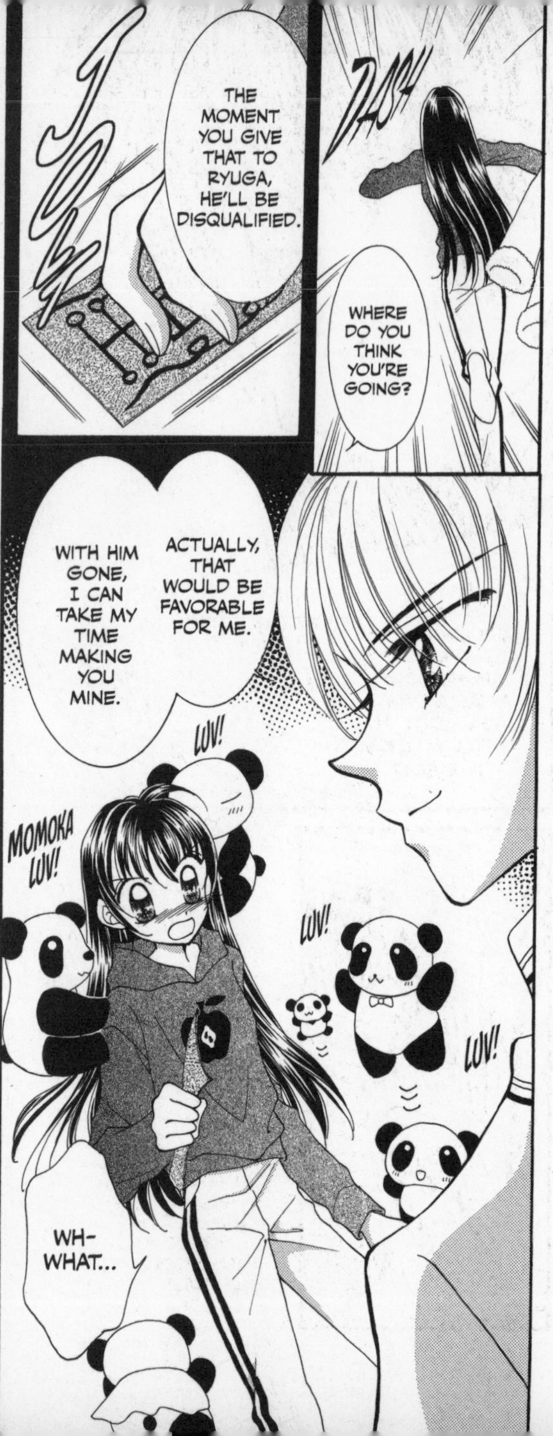
DASH
WHERE DO YOU THINK YOU'RE GOING?
THE MOMENT YOU GIVE THAT TO RYUGA, HE'LL BE DISQUALIFIED.
ACTUALLY, THAT WOULD BE FAVORABLE FOR ME.
WITH HIM GONE, I CAN TAKE MY TIME MAKING YOU MINE.
LUV!
MOMOKA LUV!
LUV!
LUV!
WH-WHAT...

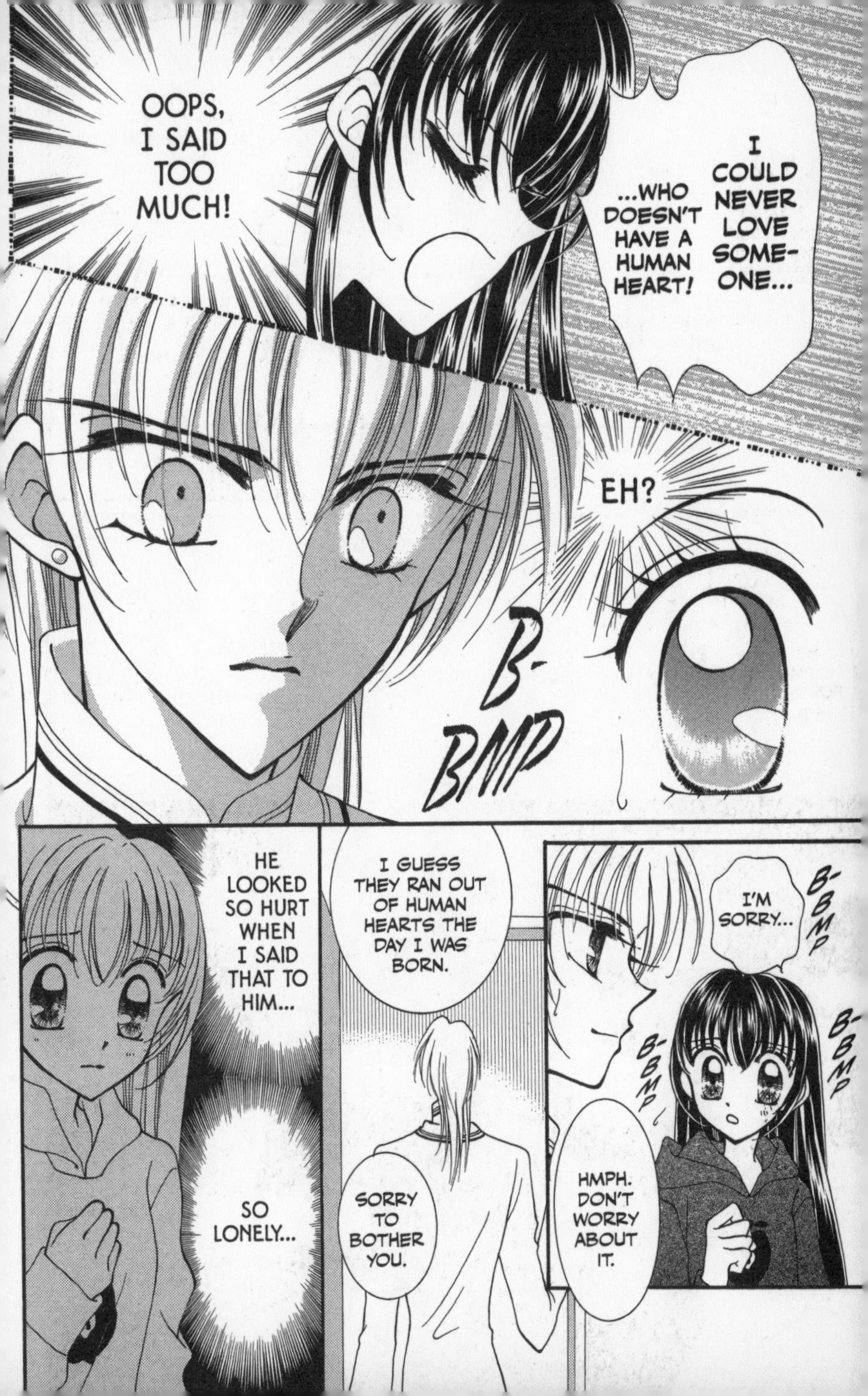
I COULD NEVER LOVE SOME-ONE...
...WHO DOESN'T HAVE A HUMAN HEART!
OOPS, I SAID TOO MUCH!
EH?
B-BMP
I'M SORRY...
B-BMP
B-BMP
B-BMP
HMPH. DON'T WORRY ABOUT IT.
I GUESS THEY RAN OUT OF HUMAN HEARTS THE DAY I WAS BORN.
SORRY TO BOTHER YOU.
HE LOOKED SO HURT WHEN I SAID THAT TO HIM...
SO LONELY...

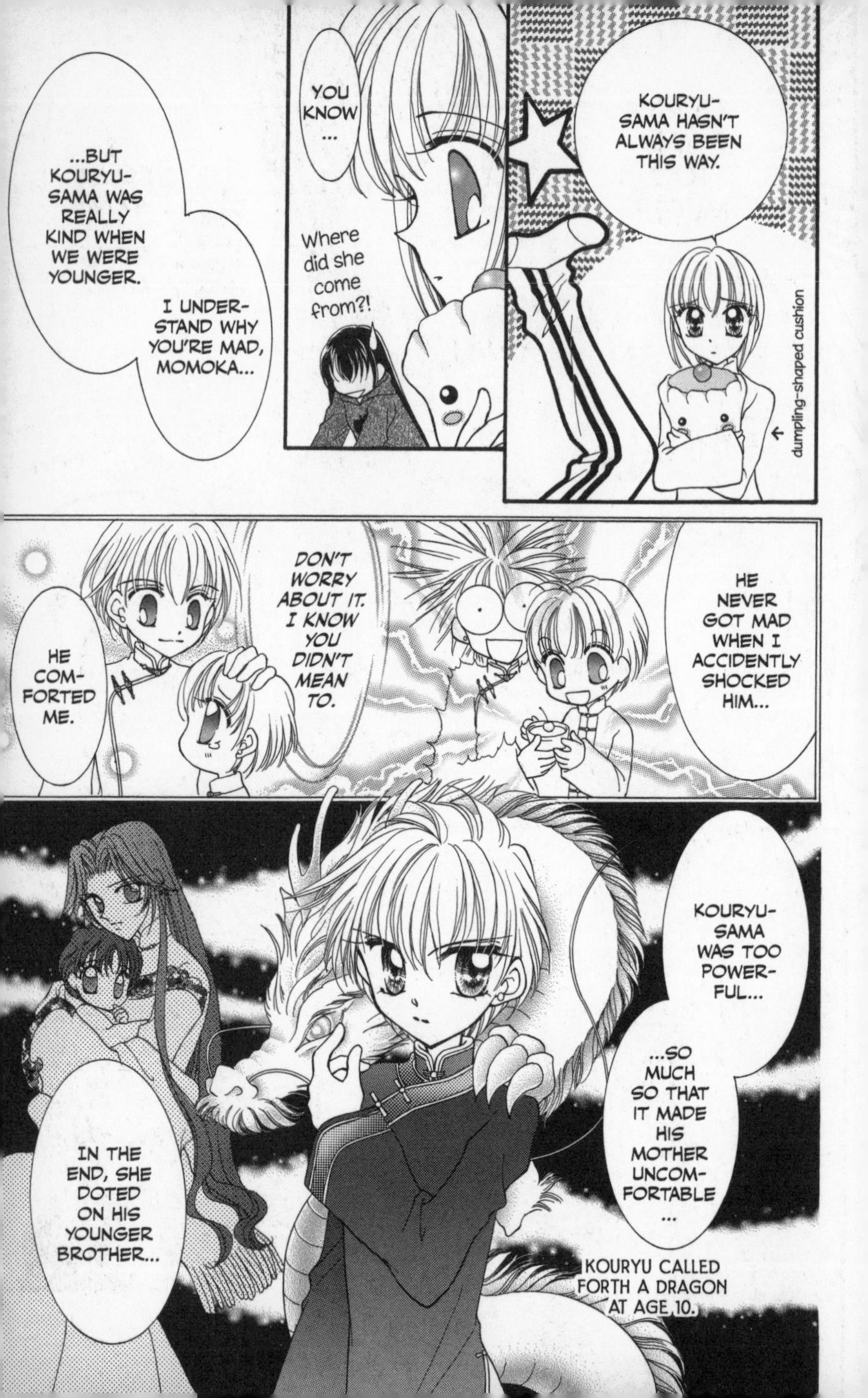
KOURYU-SAMA HASN'T ALWAYS BEEN THIS WAY.
dumpling-shaped cushion
YOU KNOW...
Where did she come from?!
...BUT KOURYU-SAMA WAS REALLY KIND WHEN WE WERE YOUNGER.
I UNDERSTAND WHY YOU'RE MAD, MOMOKA...
HE NEVER GOT MAD WHEN I ACCIDENTLY SHOCKED HIM...
DON'T WORRY ABOUT IT. I KNOW YOU DIDN'T MEAN TO.
HE COMFORTED ME.
KOURYU-SAMA WAS TOO POWERFUL...
...SO MUCH SO THAT IT MADE HIS MOTHER UNCOMFORTABLE...
KOURYU CALLED FORTH A DRAGON AT AGE 10.
IN THE END, SHE DOTED ON HIS YOUNGER BROTHER...

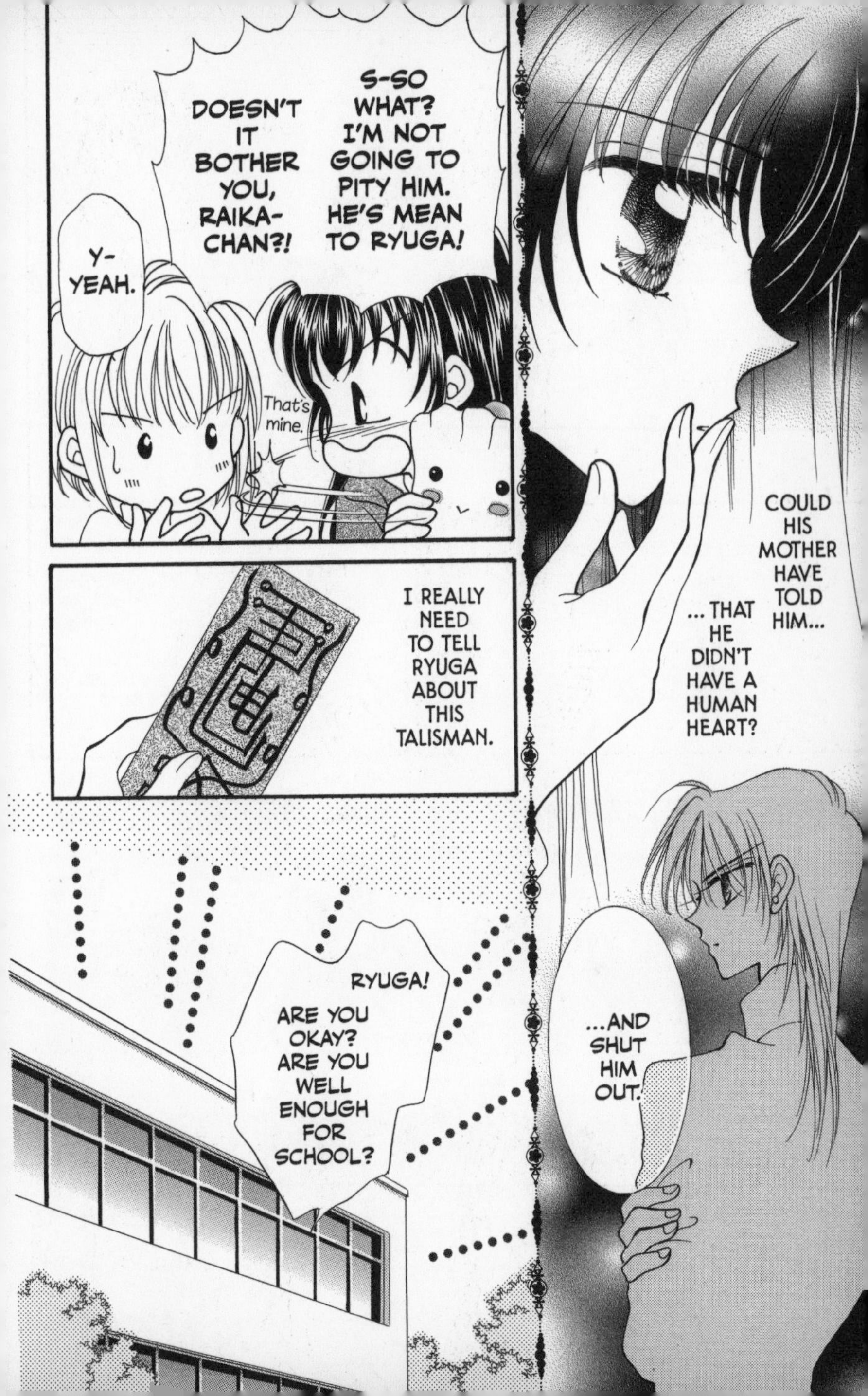
COULD HIS MOTHER HAVE TOLD HIM...
...THAT HE DIDN'T HAVE A HUMAN HEART?
...AND SHUT HIM OUT.
DOESN'T IT BOTHER YOU, RAIKA-CHAN?!
S-SO WHAT? I'M NOT GOING TO PITY HIM. HE'S MEAN TO RYUGA!
Y-YEAH.
That's mine.
I REALLY NEED TO TELL RYUGA ABOUT THIS TALISMAN.
RYUGA!
ARE YOU OKAY? ARE YOU WELL ENOUGH FOR SCHOOL?

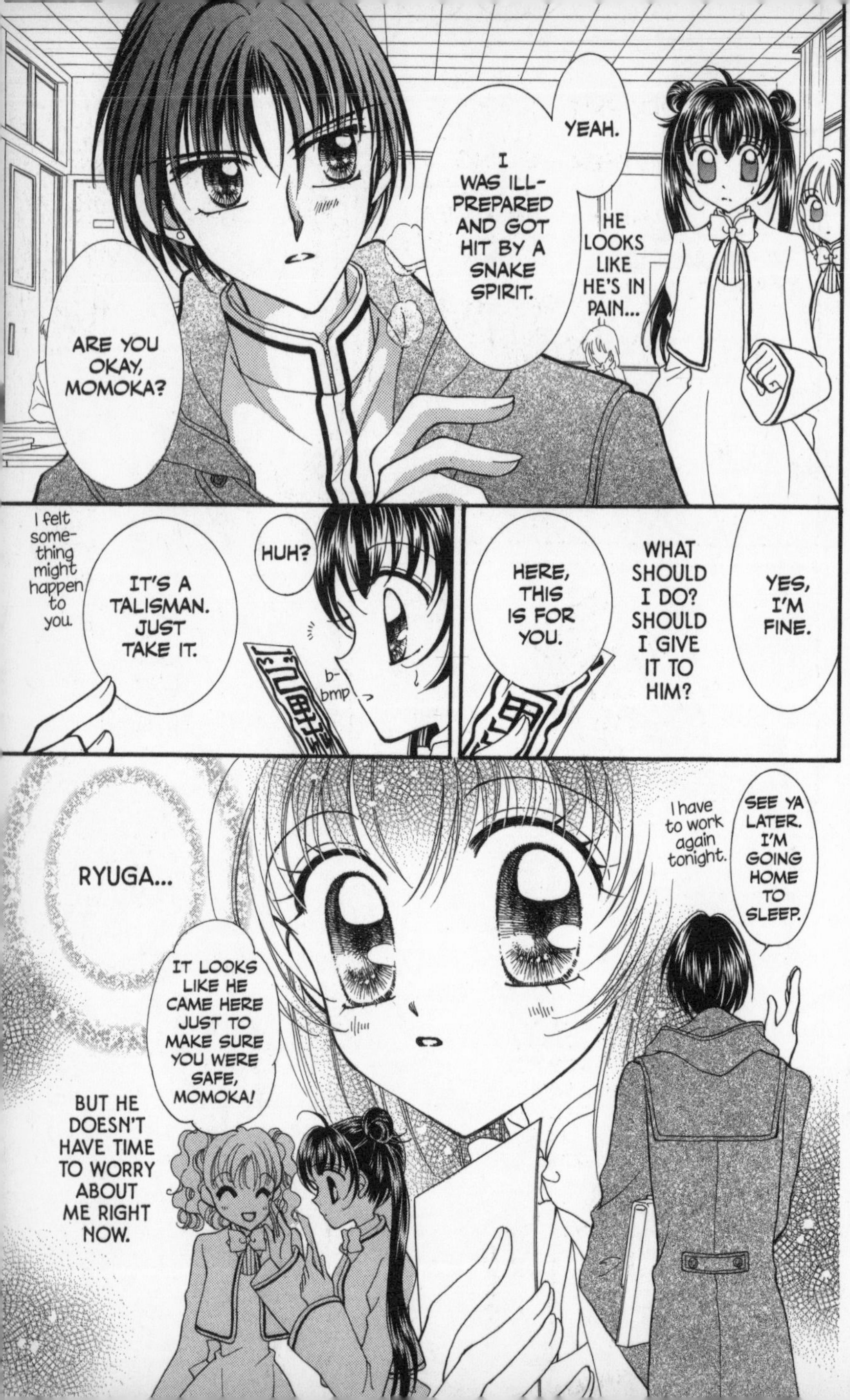
YEAH.
I WAS ILL-PREPARED AND GOT HIT BY A SNAKE SPIRIT.
HE LOOKS LIKE HE'S IN PAIN...
ARE YOU OKAY, MOMOKA?
YES, I'M FINE.
WHAT SHOULD I DO? SHOULD I GIVE IT TO HIM?
HERE, THIS IS FOR YOU.
b-bmp
HUH?
IT'S A TALISMAN. JUST TAKE IT.
I felt something might happen to you.
SEE YA LATER. I'M GOING HOME TO SLEEP.
I have to work again tonight.
RYUGA...
IT LOOKS LIKE HE CAME HERE JUST TO MAKE SURE YOU WERE SAFE, MOMOKA!
BUT HE DOESN'T HAVE TIME TO WORRY ABOUT ME RIGHT NOW.

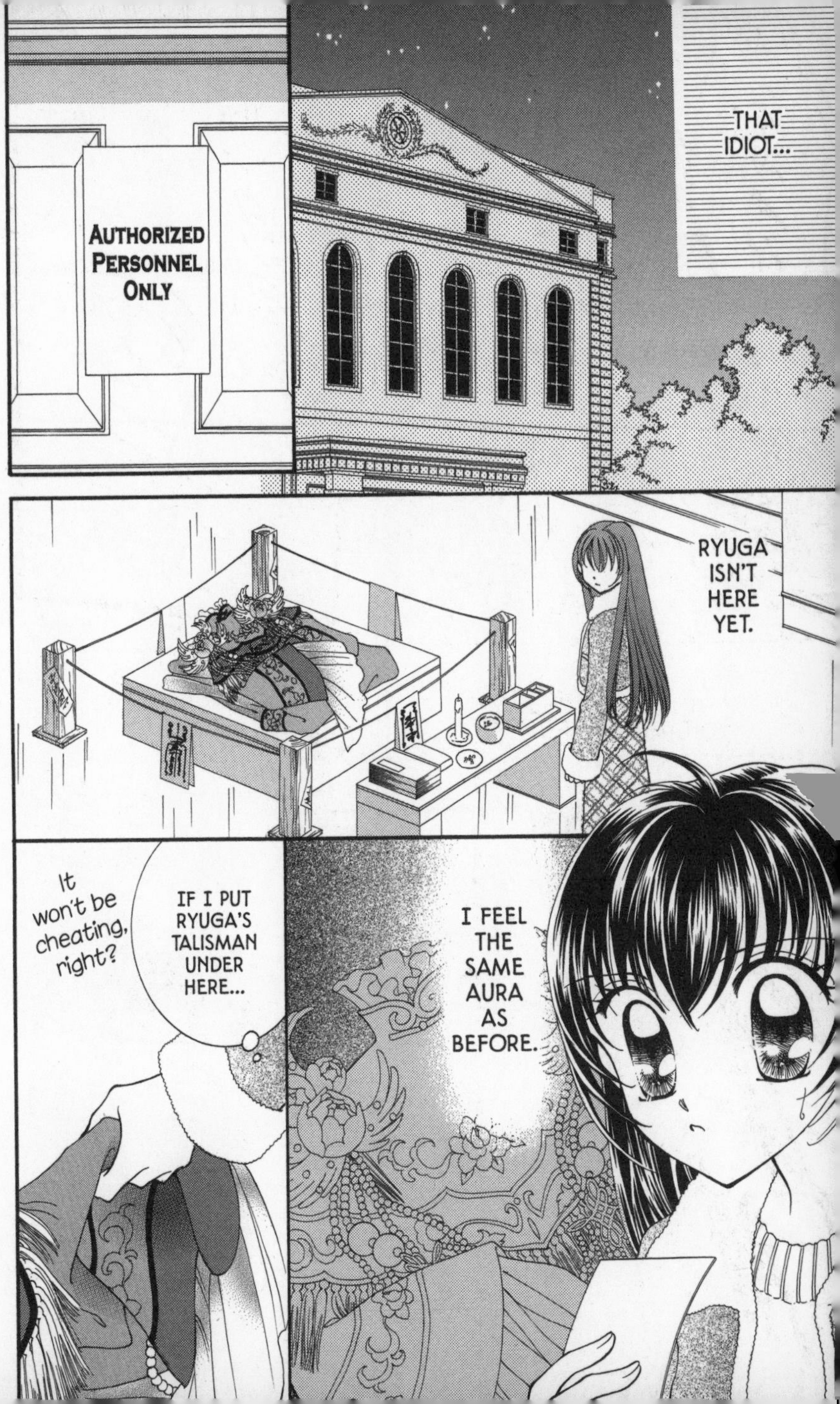
THAT IDIOT...
AUTHORIZED PERSONNEL ONLY
RYUGA ISN'T HERE YET.
I FEEL THE SAME AURA AS BEFORE.
IF I PUT RYUGA'S TALISMAN UNDER HERE...
It won't be cheating, right?

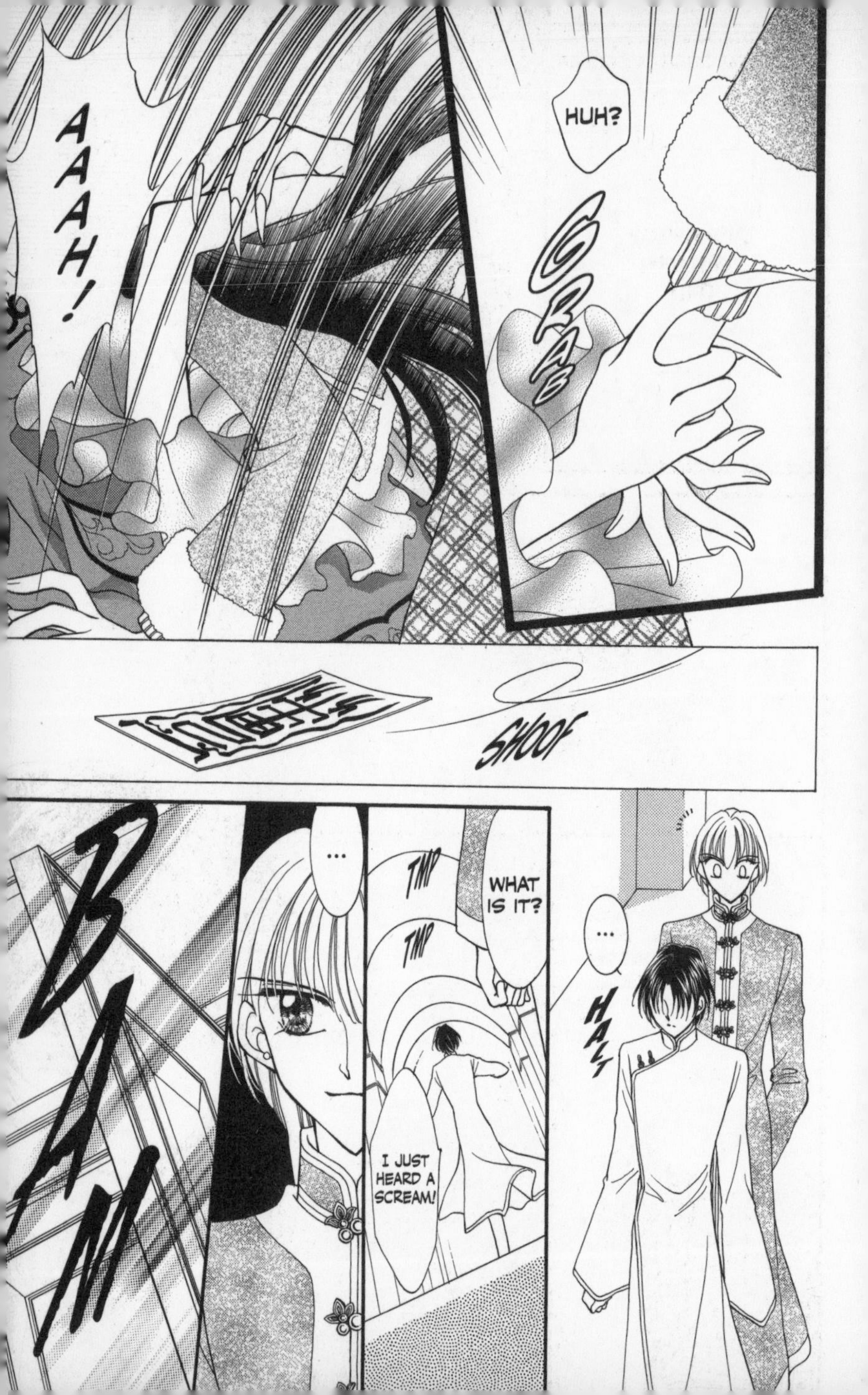
HUH?
GRAB
AAAAH!
SHOOF
...
HALT
WHAT IS IT?
TMP
TMP
I JUST HEARD A SCREAM!
...
BLAM

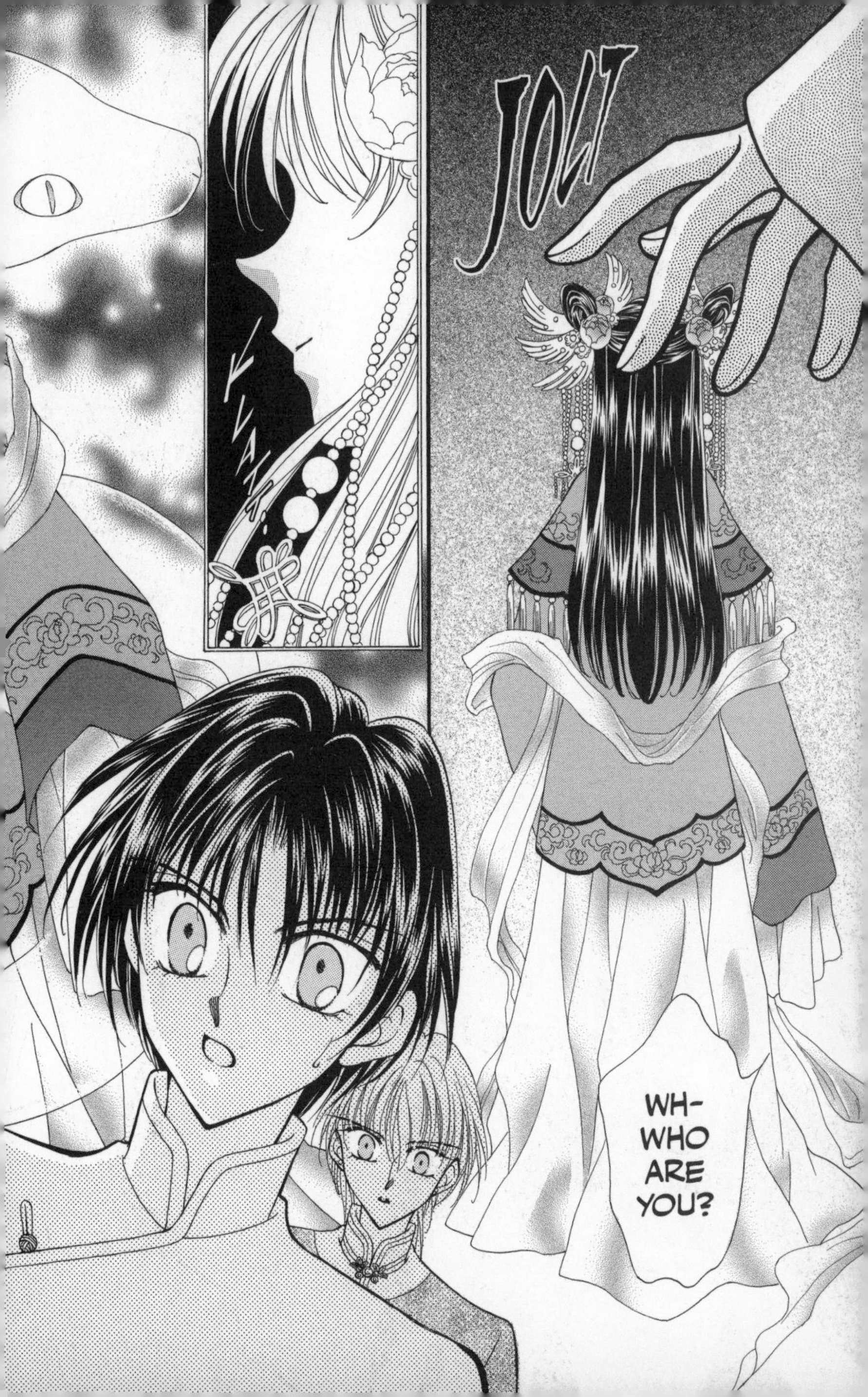
JOLT
KVAK
WH-
WHO
ARE
YOU?

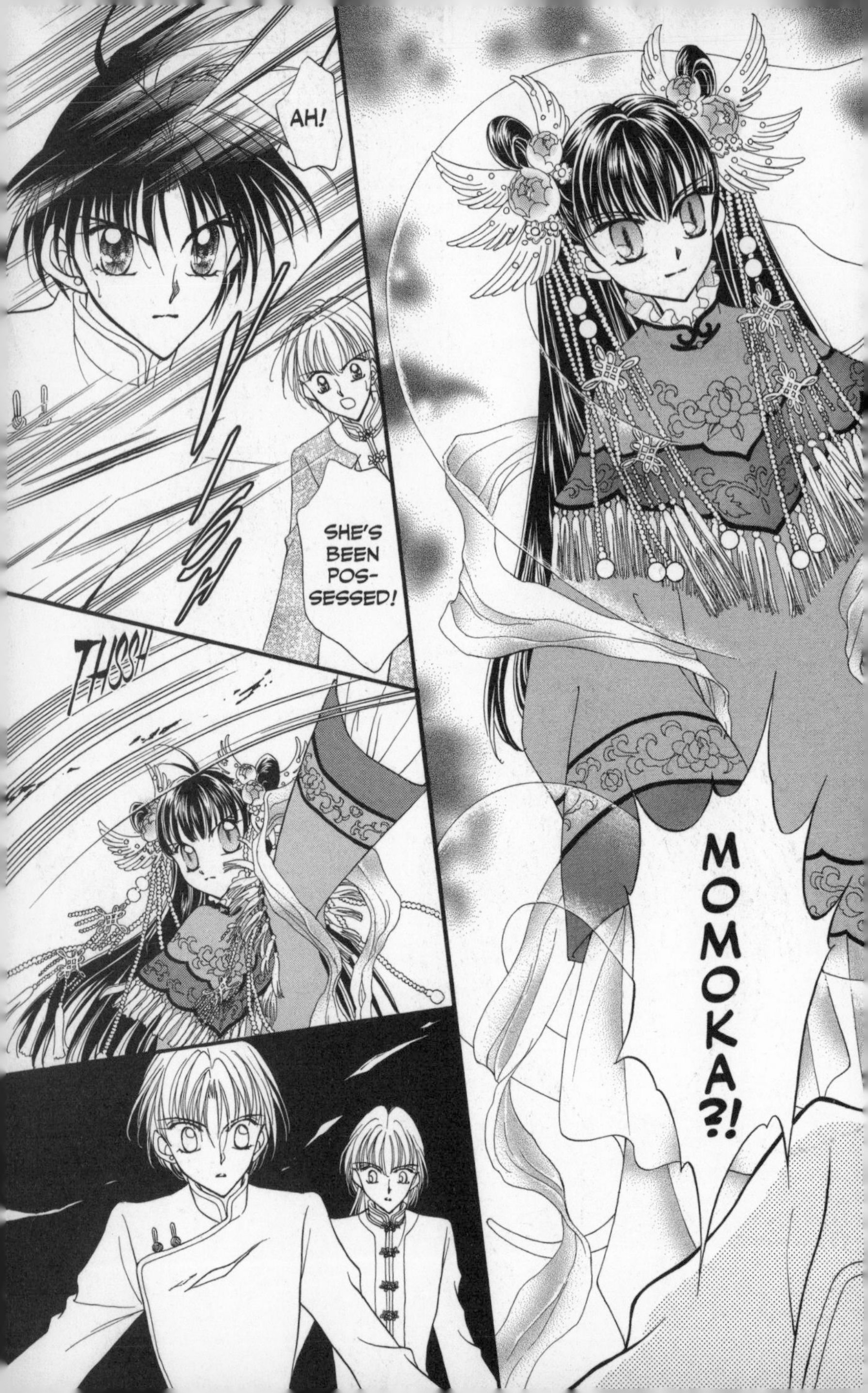
MOMOKA?!
AH!
SHE'S BEEN POS-SESSED!
THSSH

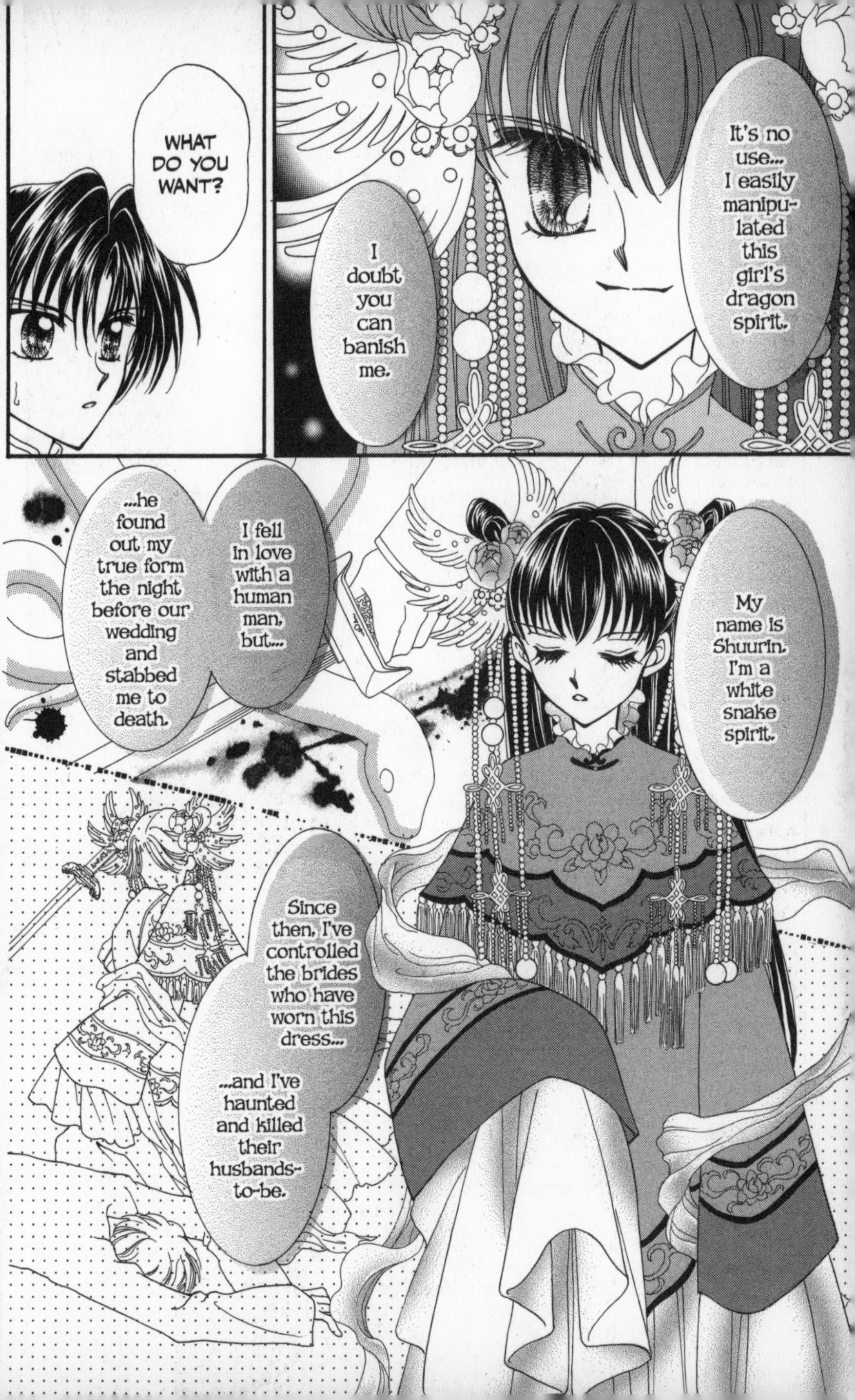
It's no use... I easily manipulated this girl's dragon spirit.
I doubt you can banish me.
WHAT DO YOU WANT?
My name is Shuurin. I'm a white snake spirit.
I fell in love with a human man, but...
...he found out my true form the night before our wedding and stabbed me to death.
Since then, I've controlled the brides who have worn this dress...
...and I've haunted and killed their husbands-to-be.

7

I'll go off a bit on a tangent in this column. Actually I had intended to divide the Hong Kong story into two parts. However, right in the middle, SDG was chosen to be a regular series.

I was limited to 45 pages but it still turned out to be a good story, so I was satisfied.

Kouryu's little brother Houryu was quite popular—I was surprised.

"Houryu-kun is so adorable!!" and "It's a crime to be so cute!" were comments I got a lot. (laugh)

Actually, I'm secretly fond of him too! He's like a little puppy dog!!

In the second half, the two girls eating inside the building are actually me and Queen! (laugh)

Apparently everyone noticed, and I received a lot of responses!

Aahh, now I want to go to Hong Kong again! This time I'd like to go during Obon.

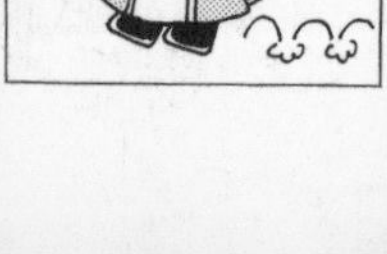
Kyonshi panda

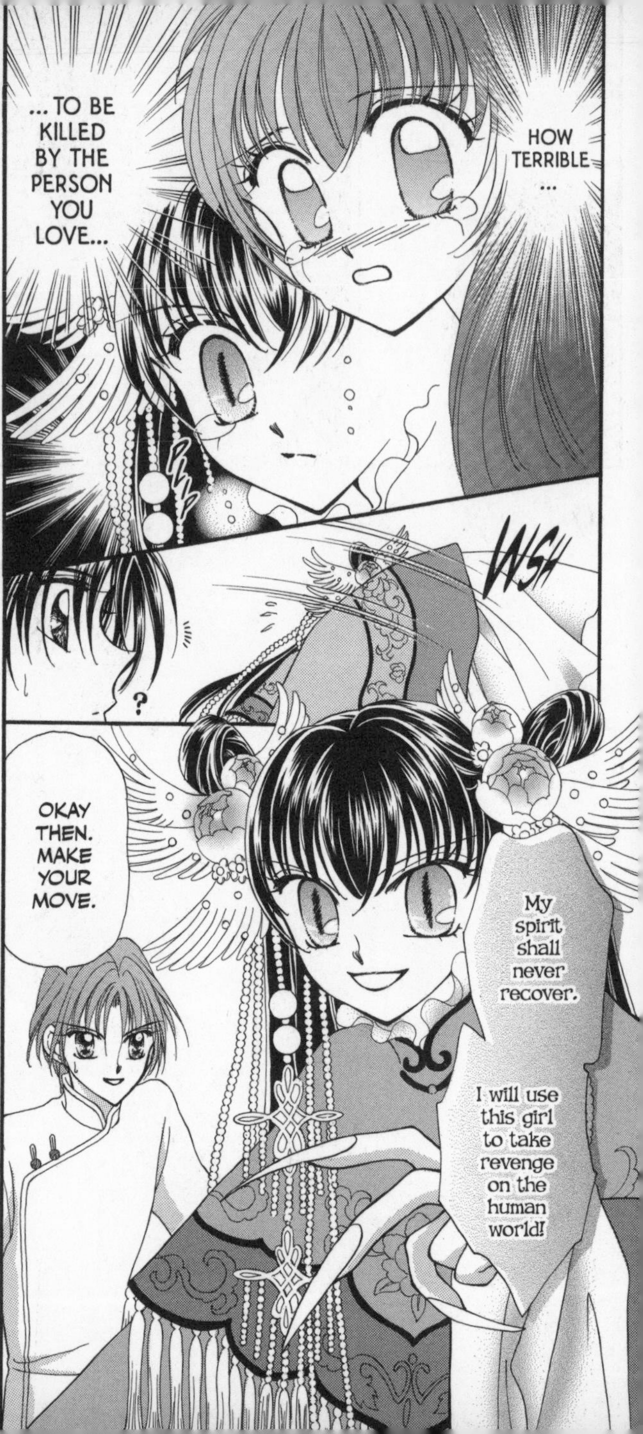
HOW TERRIBLE...
...TO BE KILLED BY THE PERSON YOU LOVE...
WSH
?
My spirit shall never recover.
I will use this girl to take revenge on the human world!
OKAY THEN. MAKE YOUR MOVE.

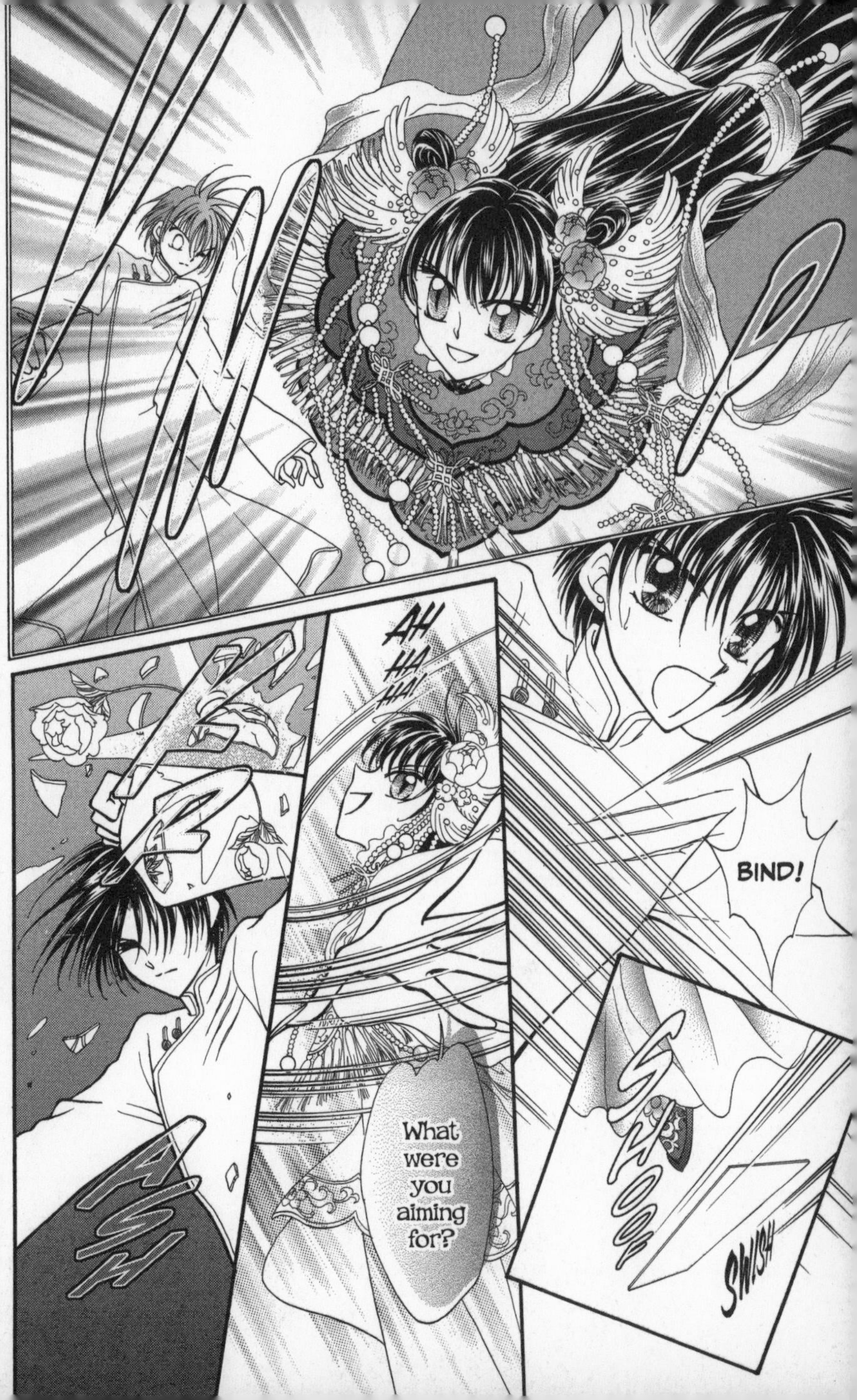
BIND!
SWISH
AH HA HA!
What were you aiming for?

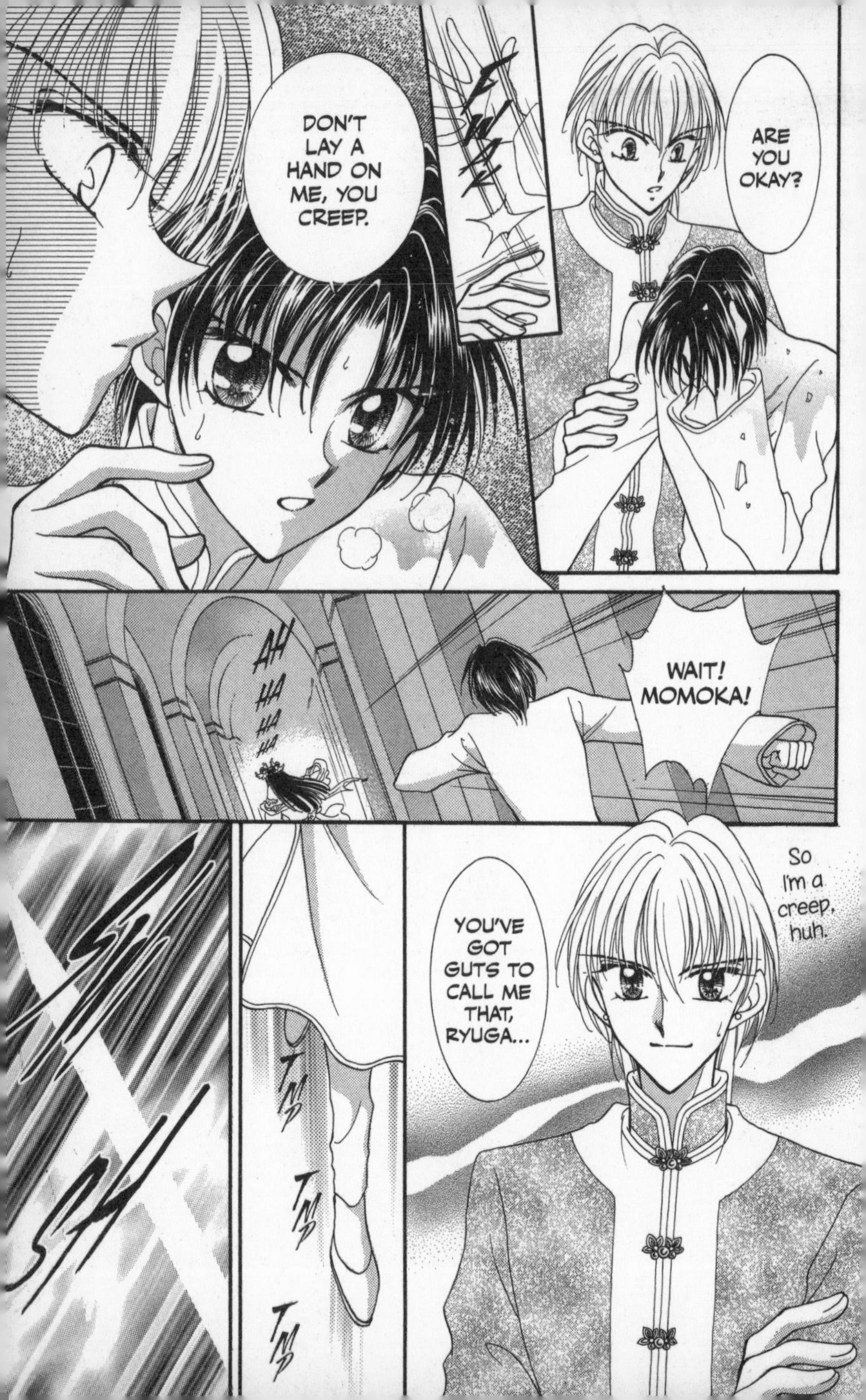
ARE YOU OKAY?
DON'T LAY A HAND ON ME, YOU CREEP.
WAIT! MOMOKA!
AH HA HA HA HA
So I'm a creep, huh.
YOU'VE GOT GUTS TO CALL ME THAT, RYUGA...
TMP
TMP
TMP

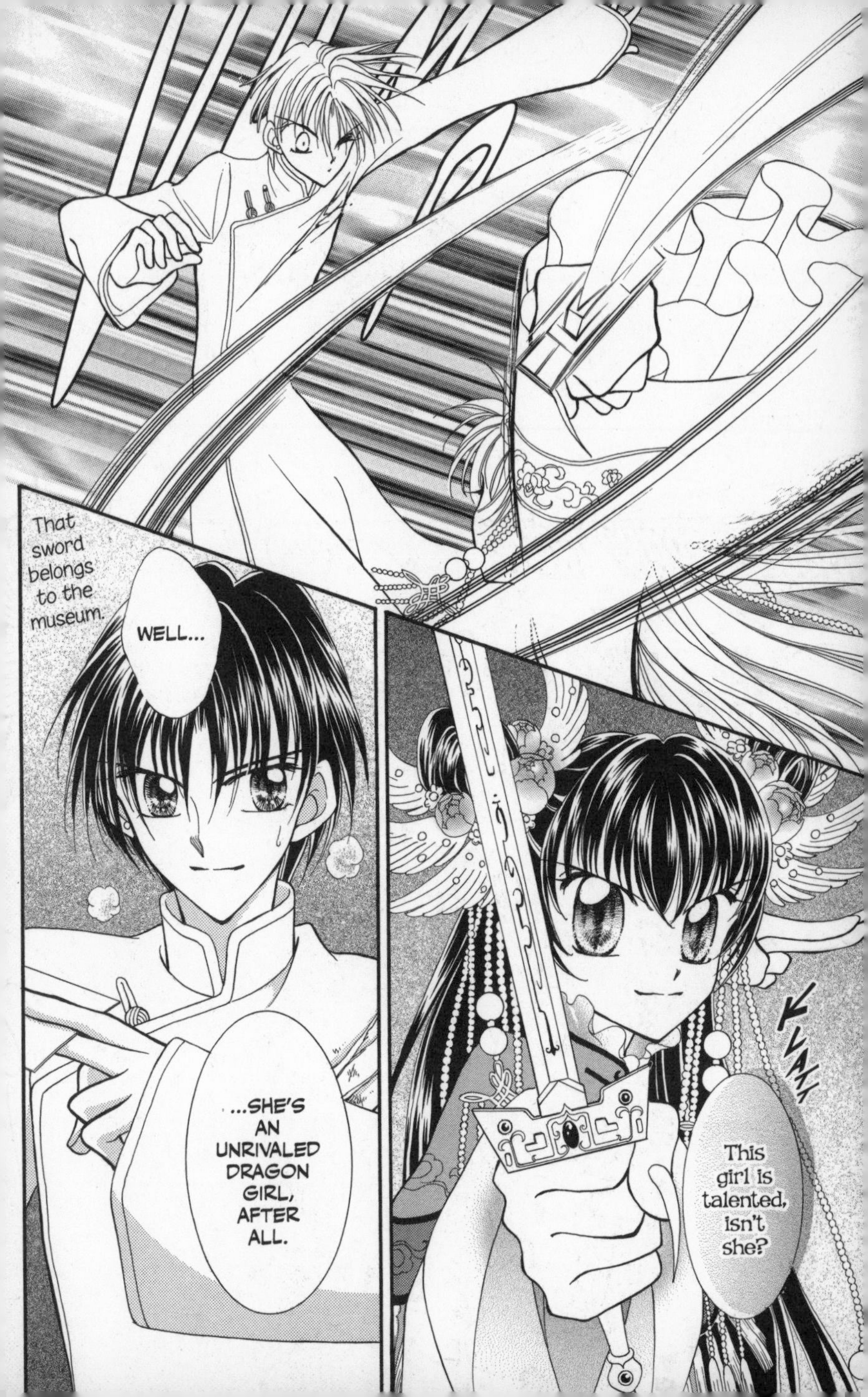
KVAKK
This girl is talented, isn't she?
That sword belongs to the museum.
WELL...
...SHE'S AN UNRIVALED DRAGON GIRL, AFTER ALL.

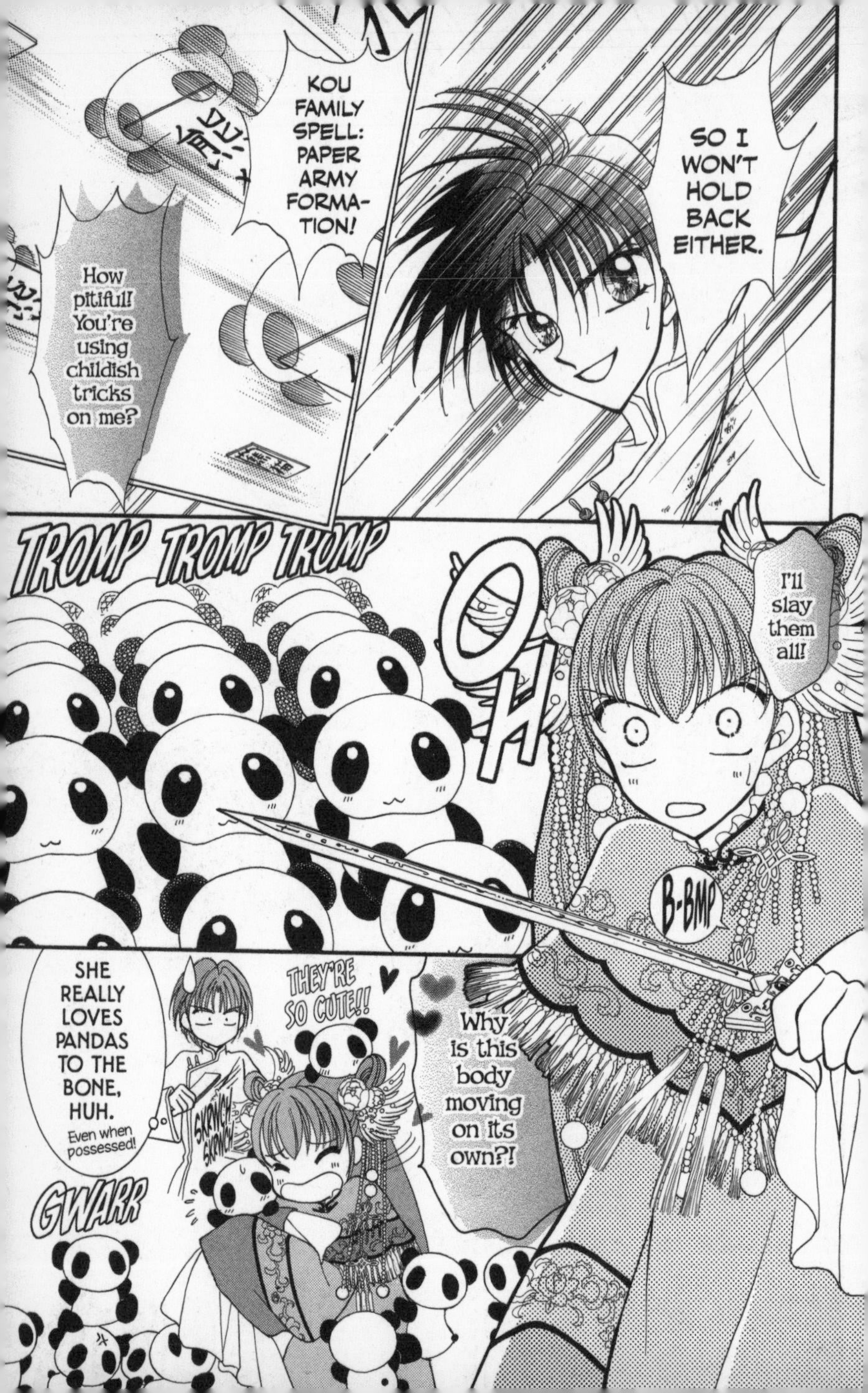
SO I WON'T HOLD BACK EITHER.
KOU FAMILY SPELL: PAPER ARMY FORMATION!
How pitiful! You're using childish tricks on me?
I'll slay them all!
OH
TROMP TROMP TROMP
B-BMP
Why is this body moving on its own?!
THEY'RE SO CUTE!!
SKRWCH SKRWCH
SHE REALLY LOVES PANDAS TO THE BONE, HUH.
Even when possessed!
GWARR

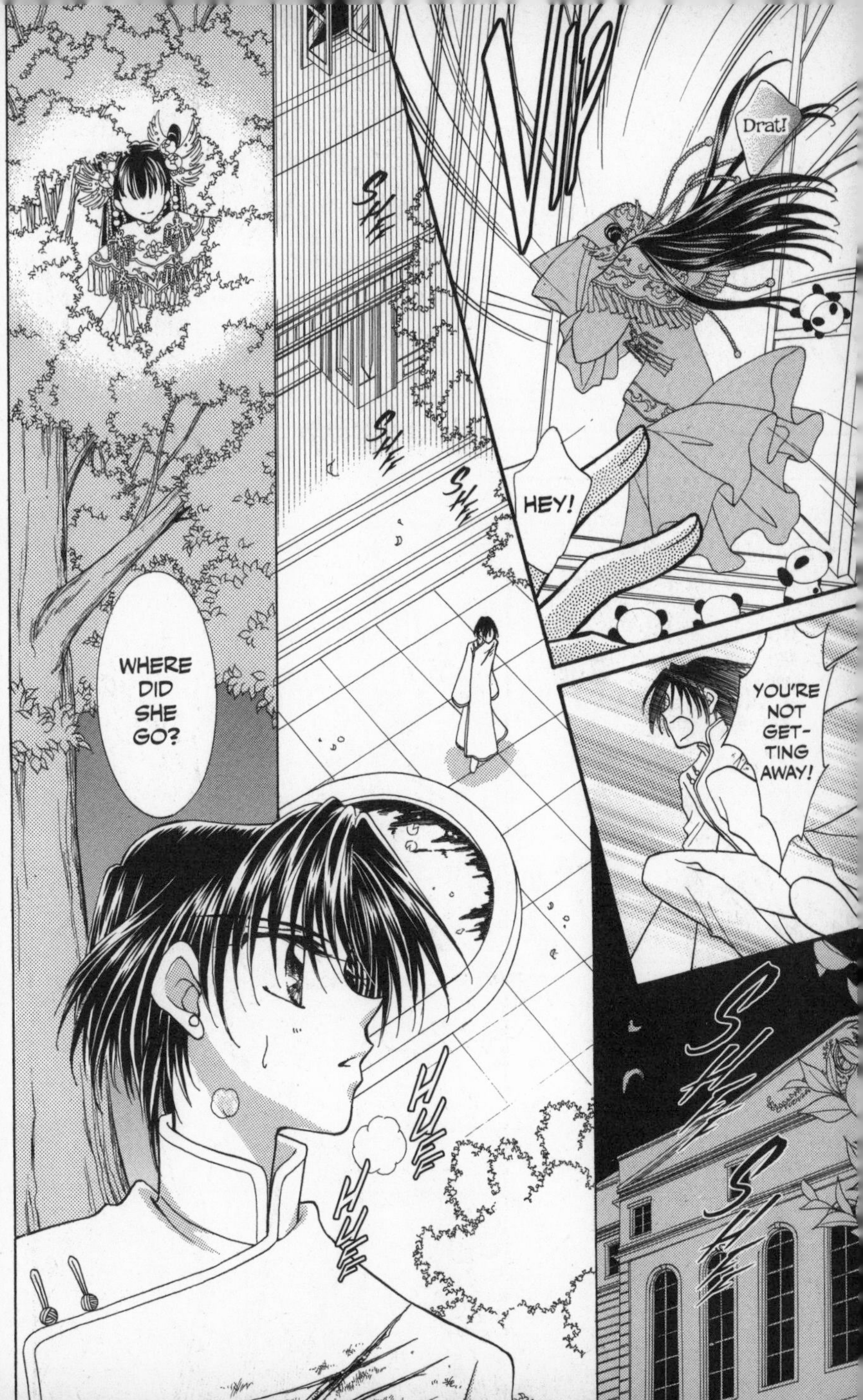
Drat!
HEY!
YOU'RE NOT GET-TING AWAY!
WHERE DID SHE GO?

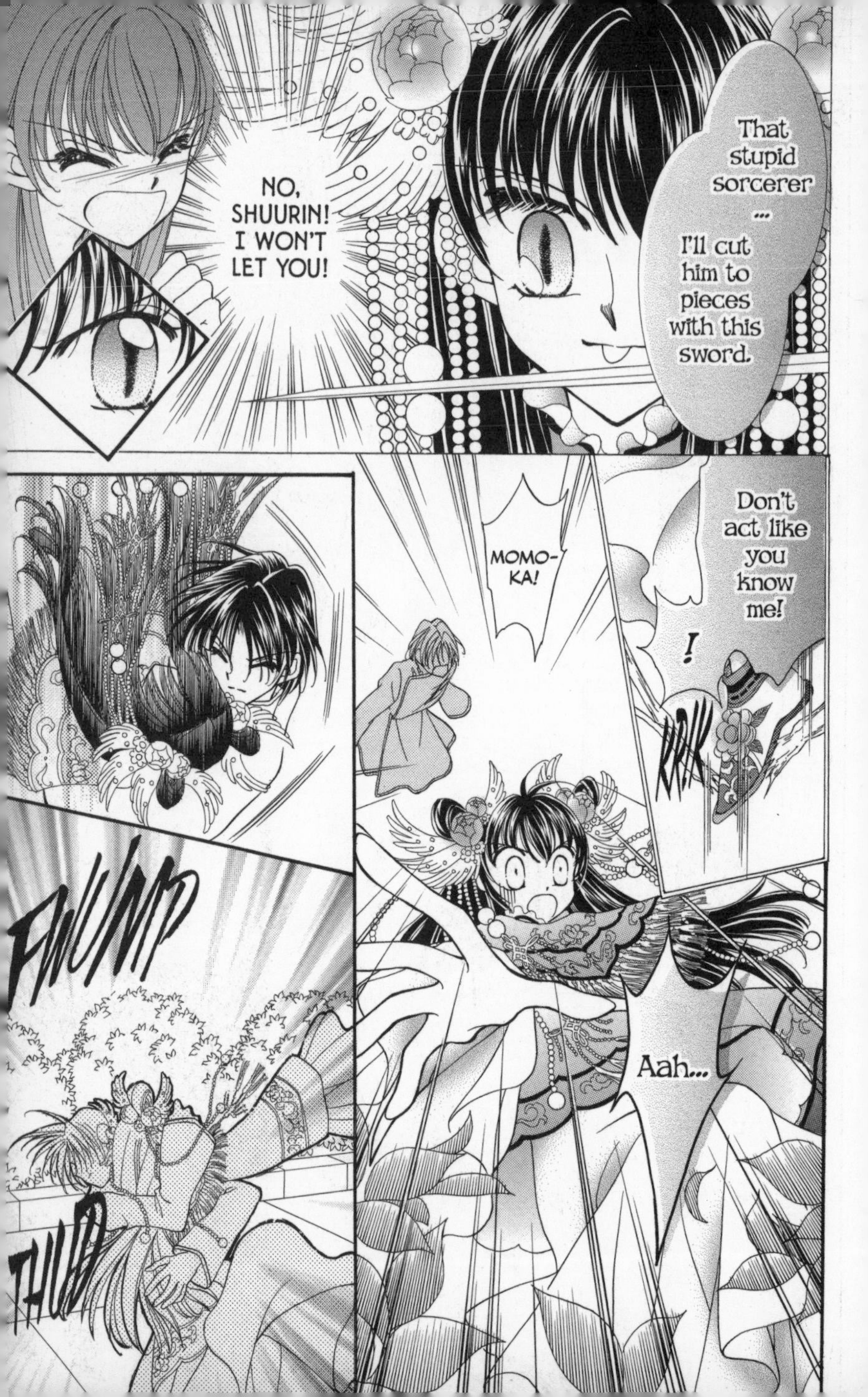

That stupid sorcerer ... I'll cut him to pieces with this sword.
NO, SHUURIN! I WON'T LET YOU!
Don't act like you know me!
!
KRIK
MOMO-KA!
Aah...
FWUMP
THUD

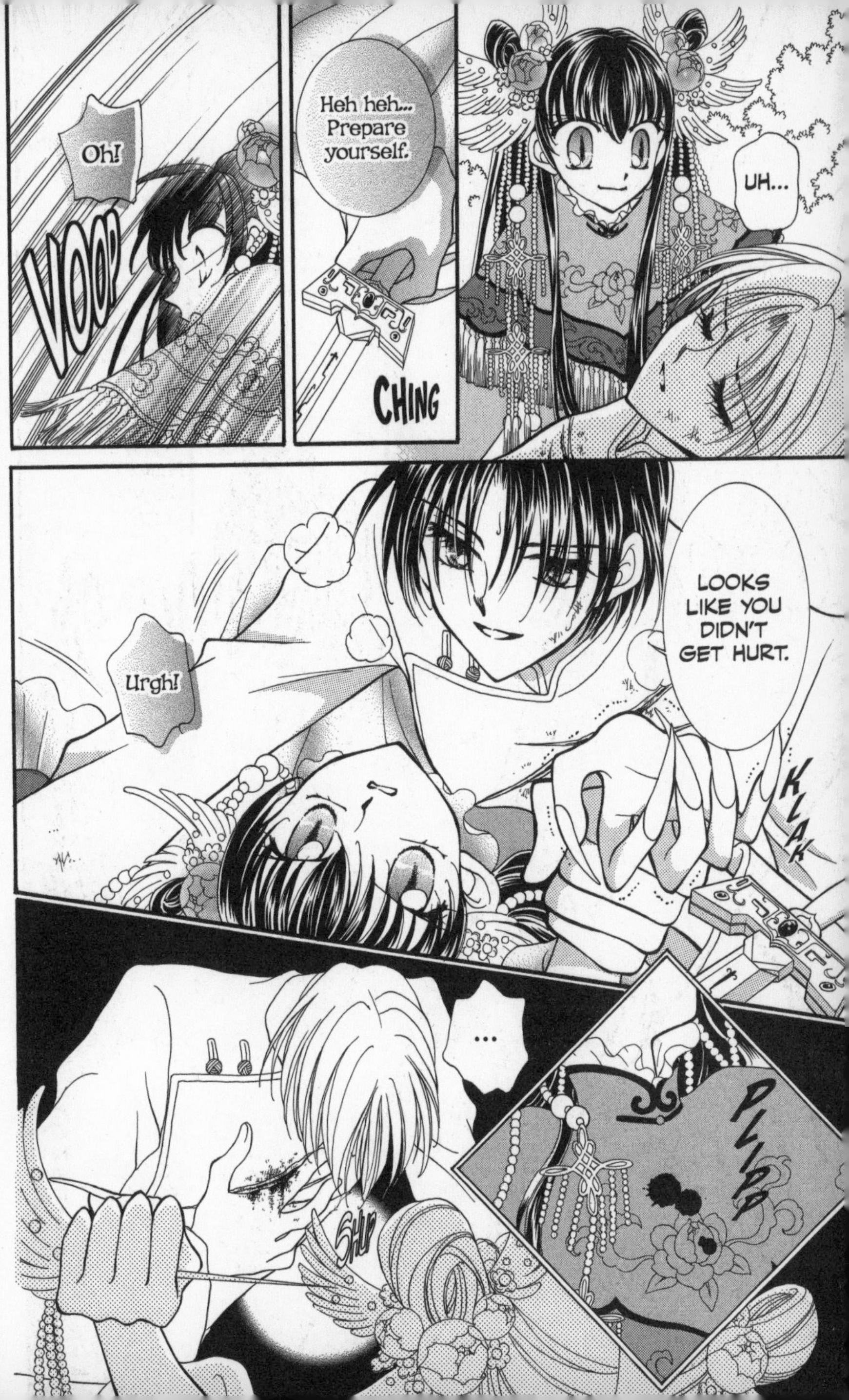
UH...
Heh heh... Prepare yourself.
CHING
Oh!
VOOP
LOOKS LIKE YOU DIDN'T GET HURT.
KLAK
Urgh!
...
PLIP
SHUP

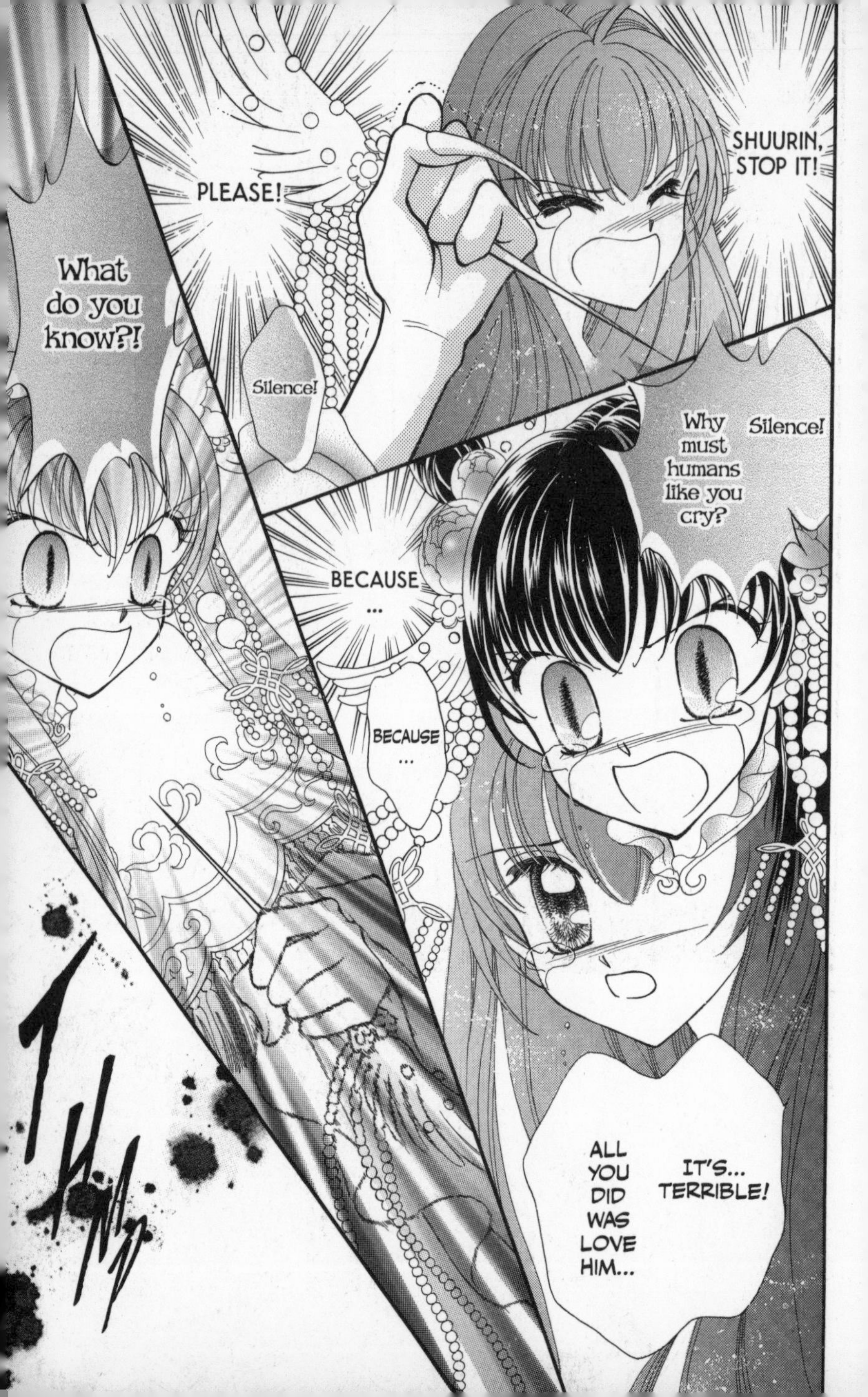
SHUURIN, STOP IT!
PLEASE!
Silence!
Silence!
Why must humans like you cry?
BECAUSE...
BECAUSE...
IT'S... TERRIBLE!
ALL YOU DID WAS LOVE HIM...
What do you know?!

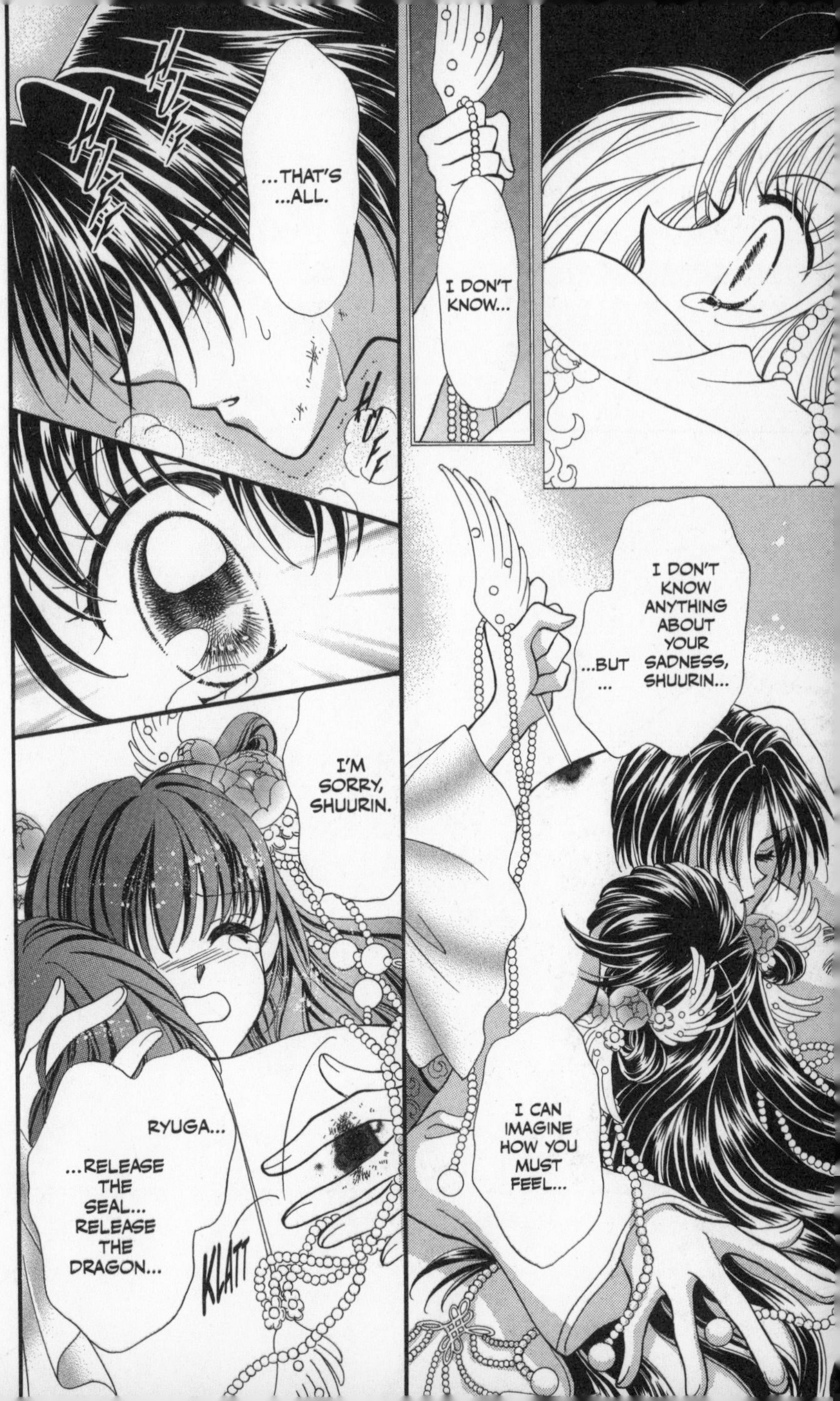
I DON'T KNOW...
...THAT'S ...ALL.
I DON'T KNOW ANYTHING ABOUT YOUR SADNESS, SHUURIN...
...BUT ...
I CAN IMAGINE HOW YOU MUST FEEL...
I'M SORRY, SHUURIN.
RYUGA...
...RELEASE THE SEAL... RELEASE THE DRAGON...
KLATT

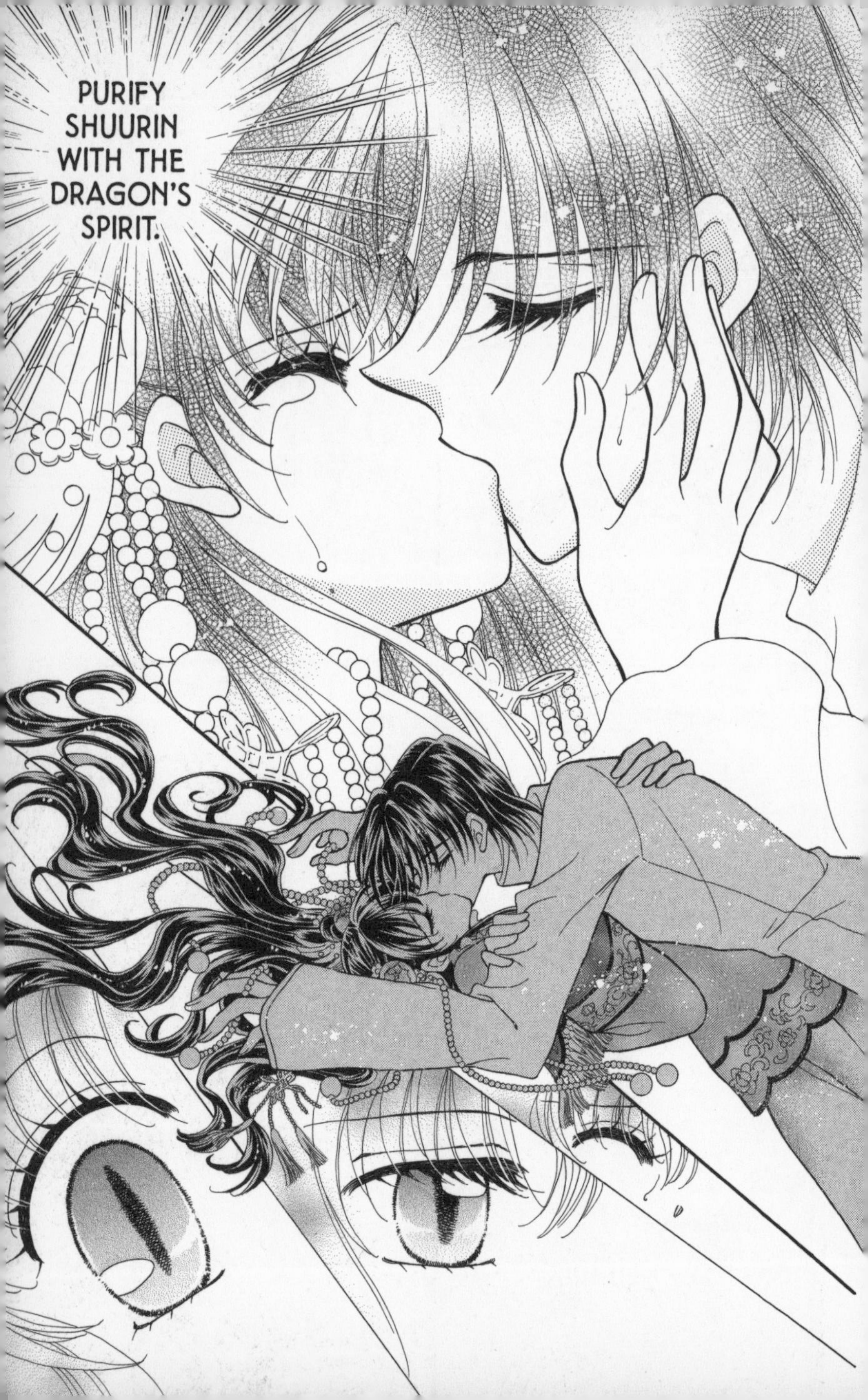
PURIFY SHUURIN WITH THE DRAGON'S SPIRIT.

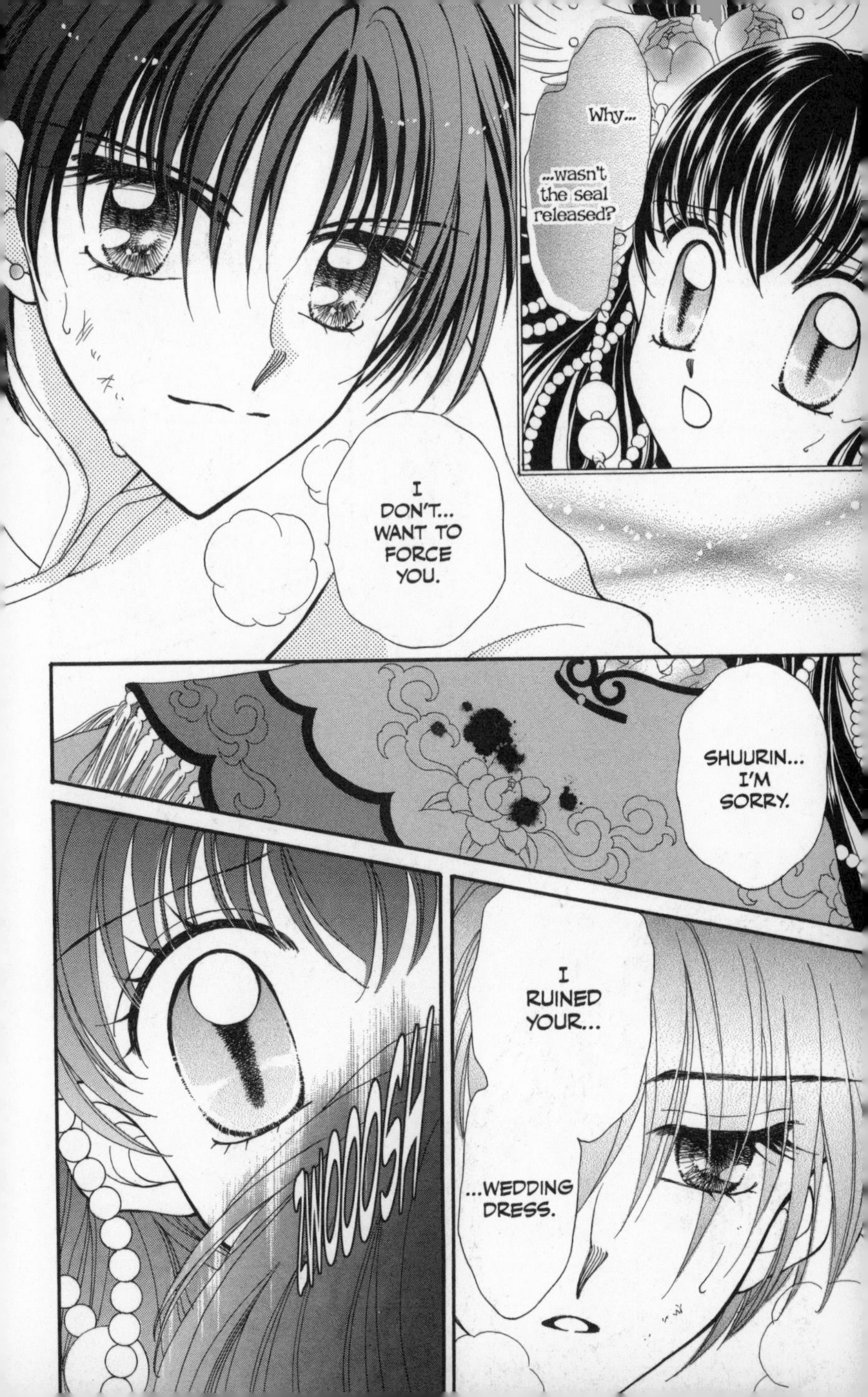
Why...
...wasn't the seal released?
I DON'T... WANT TO FORCE YOU.
SHUURIN... I'M SORRY.
I RUINED YOUR...
...WEDDING DRESS.
ZWOOOSH

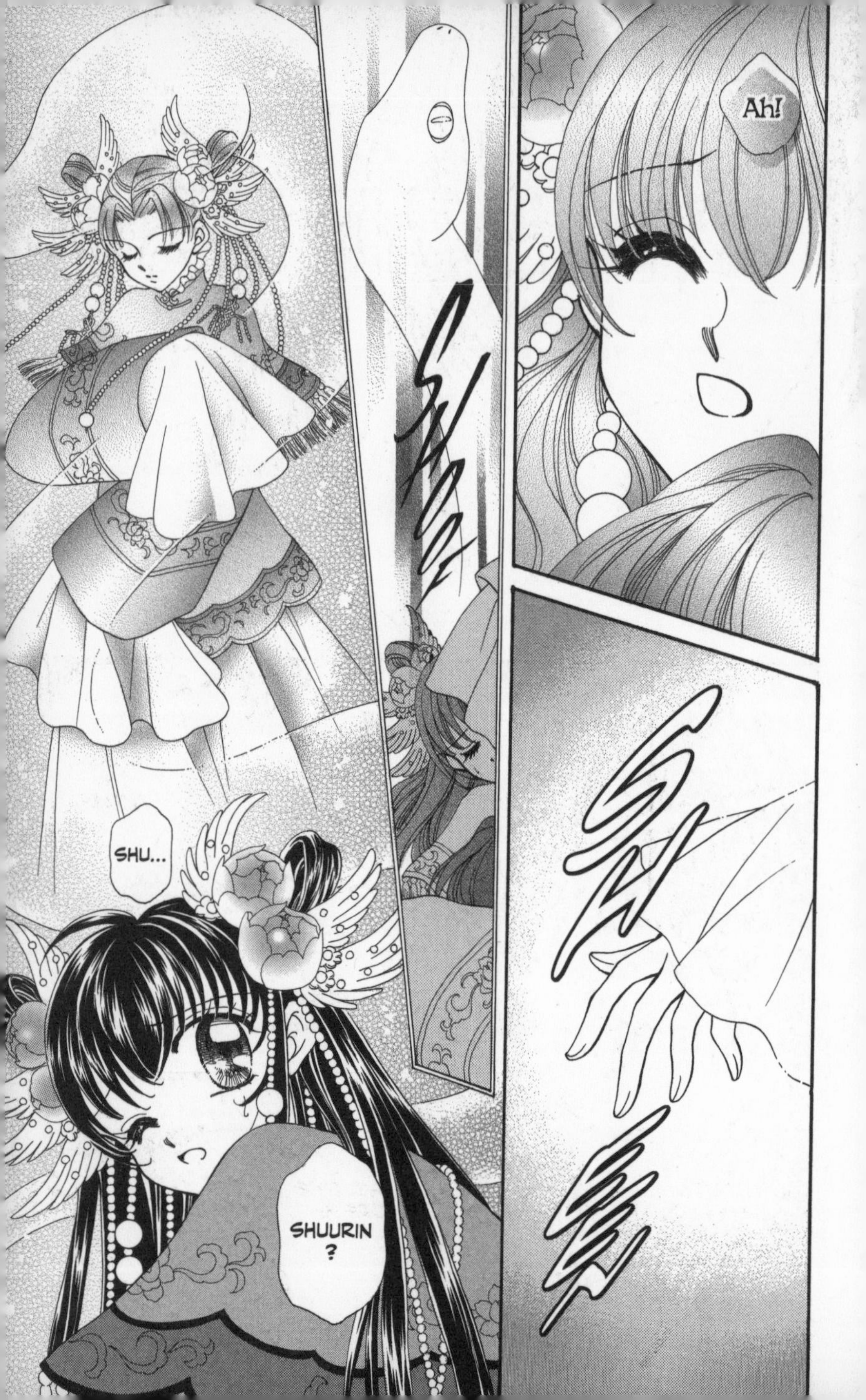
Ah!
SHU...
SHUURIN ?

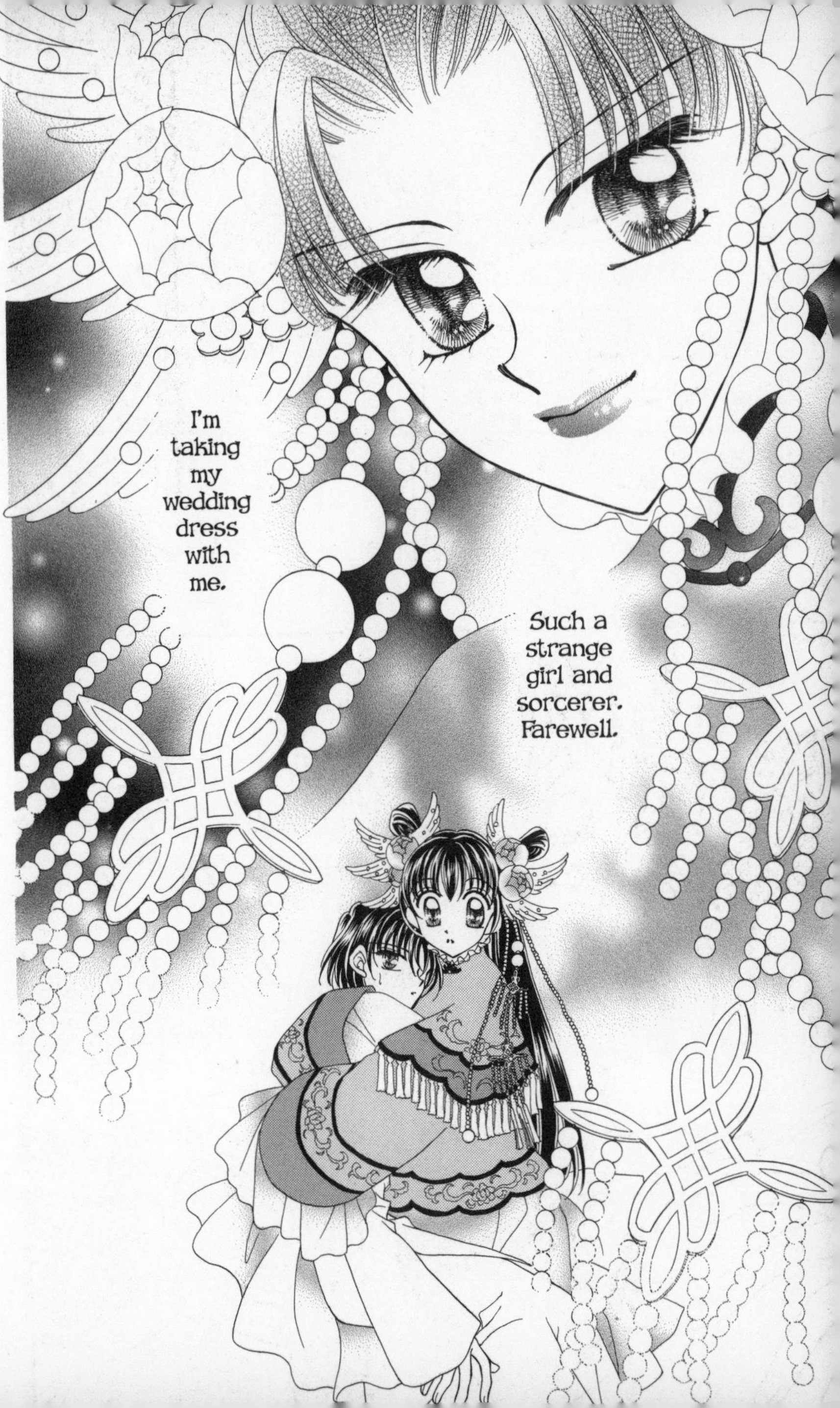
Such a strange girl and sorcerer. Farewell.
I'm taking my wedding dress with me.

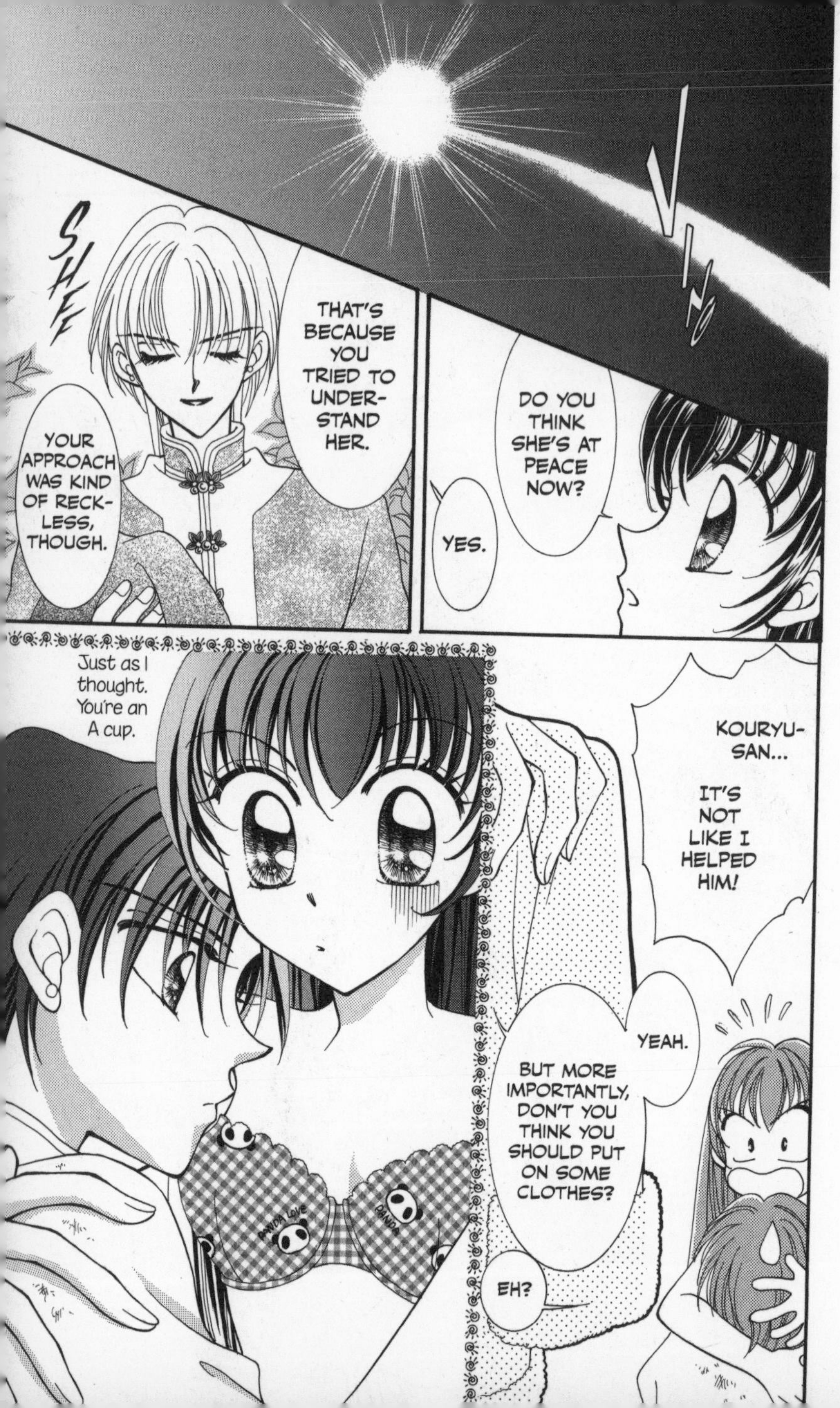
DO YOU THINK SHE'S AT PEACE NOW?
YES.
THAT'S BECAUSE YOU TRIED TO UNDER-STAND HER.
SHFF
YOUR APPROACH WAS KIND OF RECK-LESS, THOUGH.
KOURYU-SAN...
IT'S NOT LIKE I HELPED HIM!
YEAH.
BUT MORE IMPORTANTLY, DON'T YOU THINK YOU SHOULD PUT ON SOME CLOTHES?
EH?
Just as I thought. You're an A cup.
PANDA LOVE
PANDA

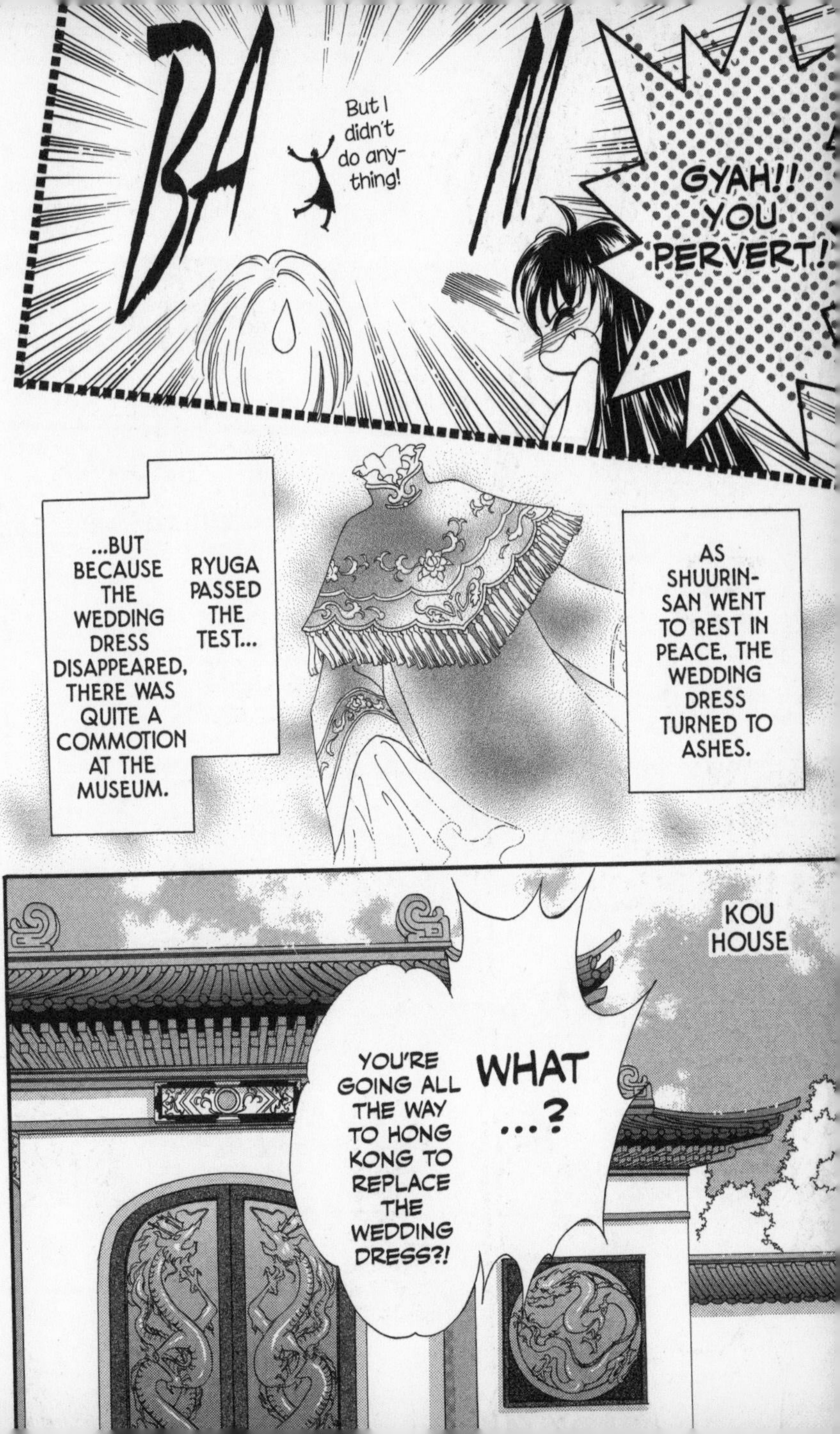
GYAH!! YOU PERVERT!
BAM
But I didn't do any-thing!
AS SHUURIN-SAN WENT TO REST IN PEACE, THE WEDDING DRESS TURNED TO ASHES.
RYUGA PASSED THE TEST...
...BUT BECAUSE THE WEDDING DRESS DISAPPEARED, THERE WAS QUITE A COMMOTION AT THE MUSEUM.
KOU HOUSE
WHAT ...?
YOU'RE GOING ALL THE WAY TO HONG KONG TO REPLACE THE WEDDING DRESS?!

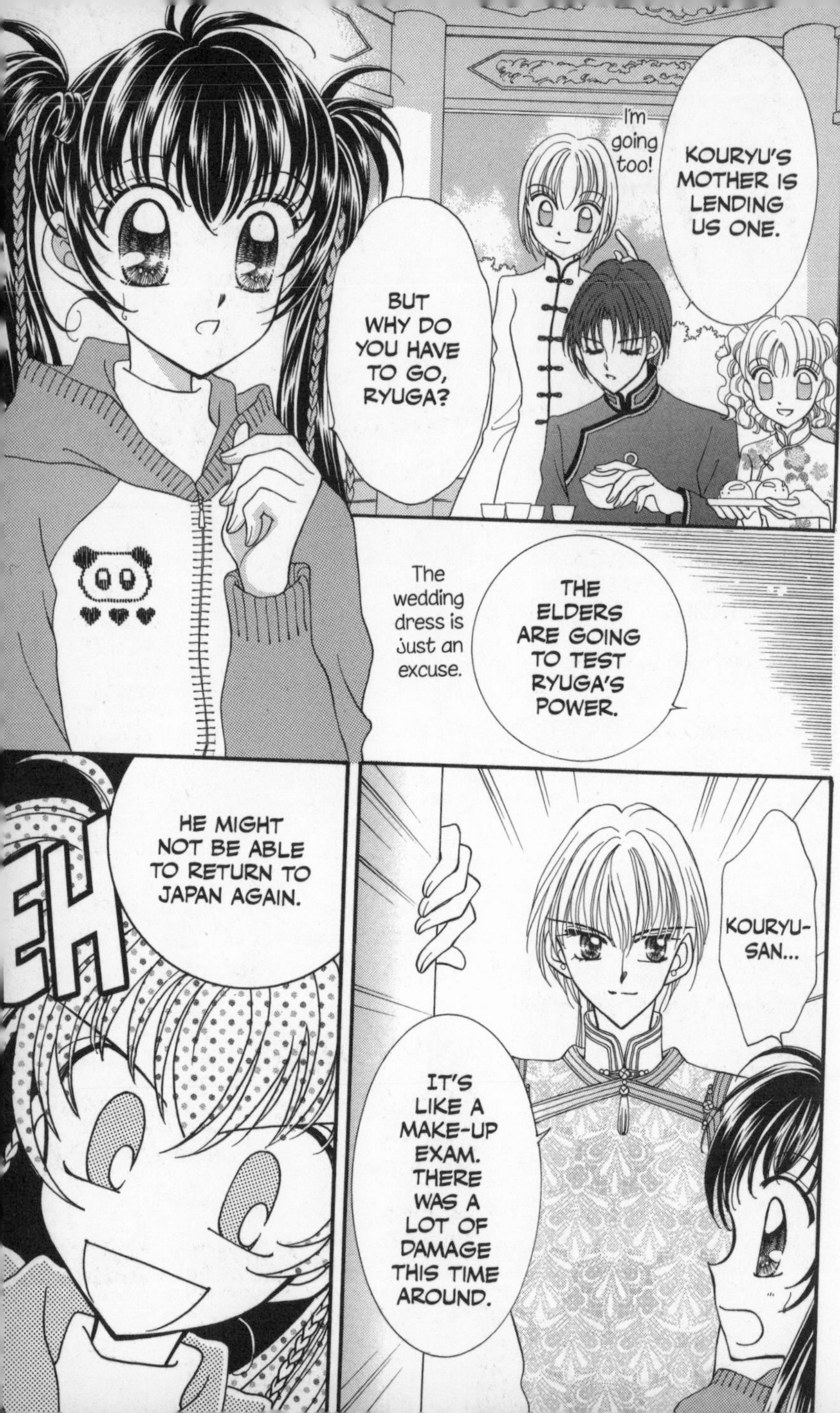
KOURYU'S MOTHER IS LENDING US ONE.
I'm going too!
THE ELDERS ARE GOING TO TEST RYUGA'S POWER.
The wedding dress is just an excuse.
BUT WHY DO YOU HAVE TO GO, RYUGA?
KOURYU-SAN...
IT'S LIKE A MAKE-UP EXAM. THERE WAS A LOT OF DAMAGE THIS TIME AROUND.
HE MIGHT NOT BE ABLE TO RETURN TO JAPAN AGAIN.
EH

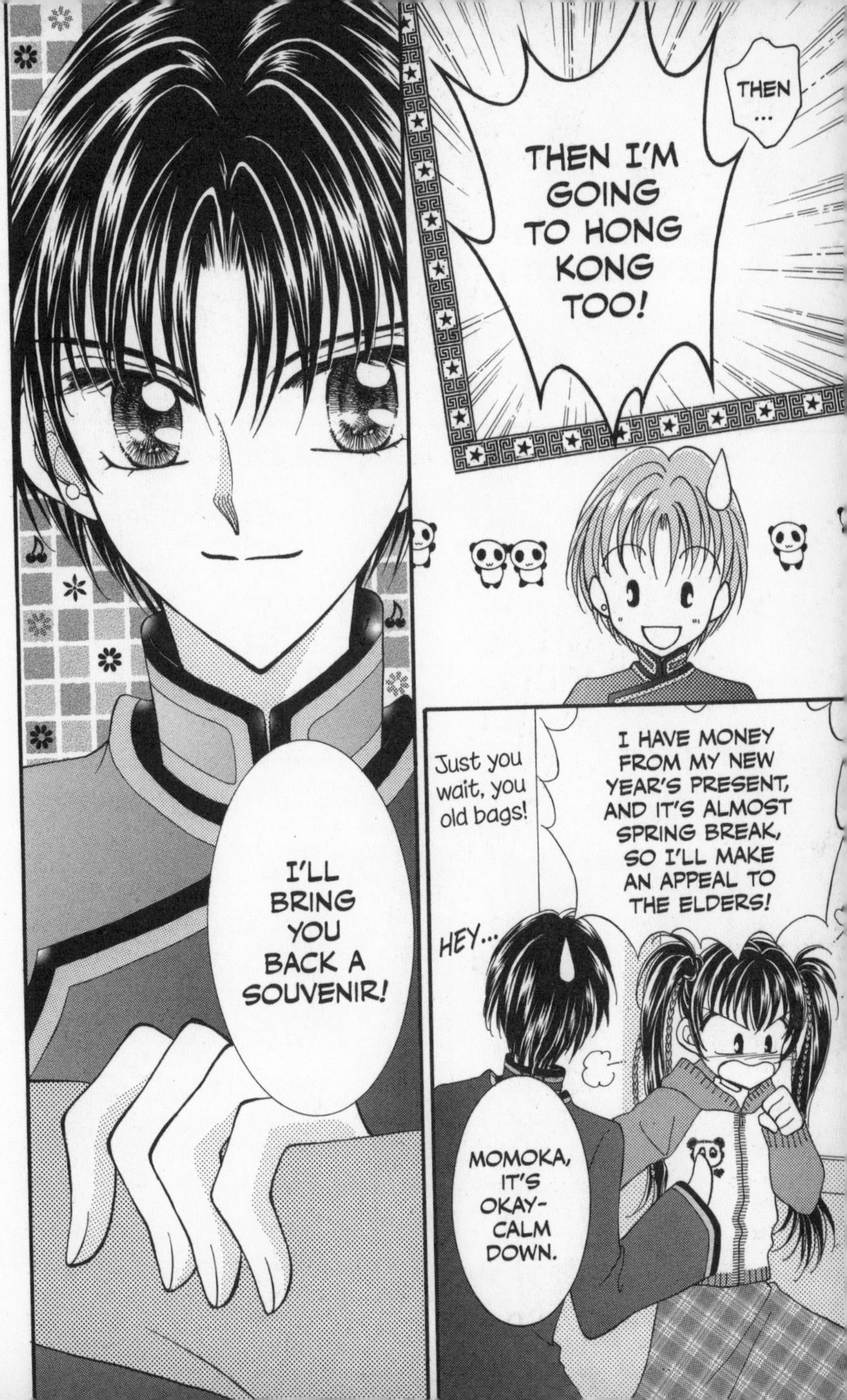
THEN ...
THEN I'M GOING TO HONG KONG TOO!
I HAVE MONEY FROM MY NEW YEAR'S PRESENT, AND IT'S ALMOST SPRING BREAK, SO I'LL MAKE AN APPEAL TO THE ELDERS!
Just you wait, you old bags!
HEY...
MOMOKA, IT'S OKAY- CALM DOWN.
I'LL BRING YOU BACK A SOUVENIR!

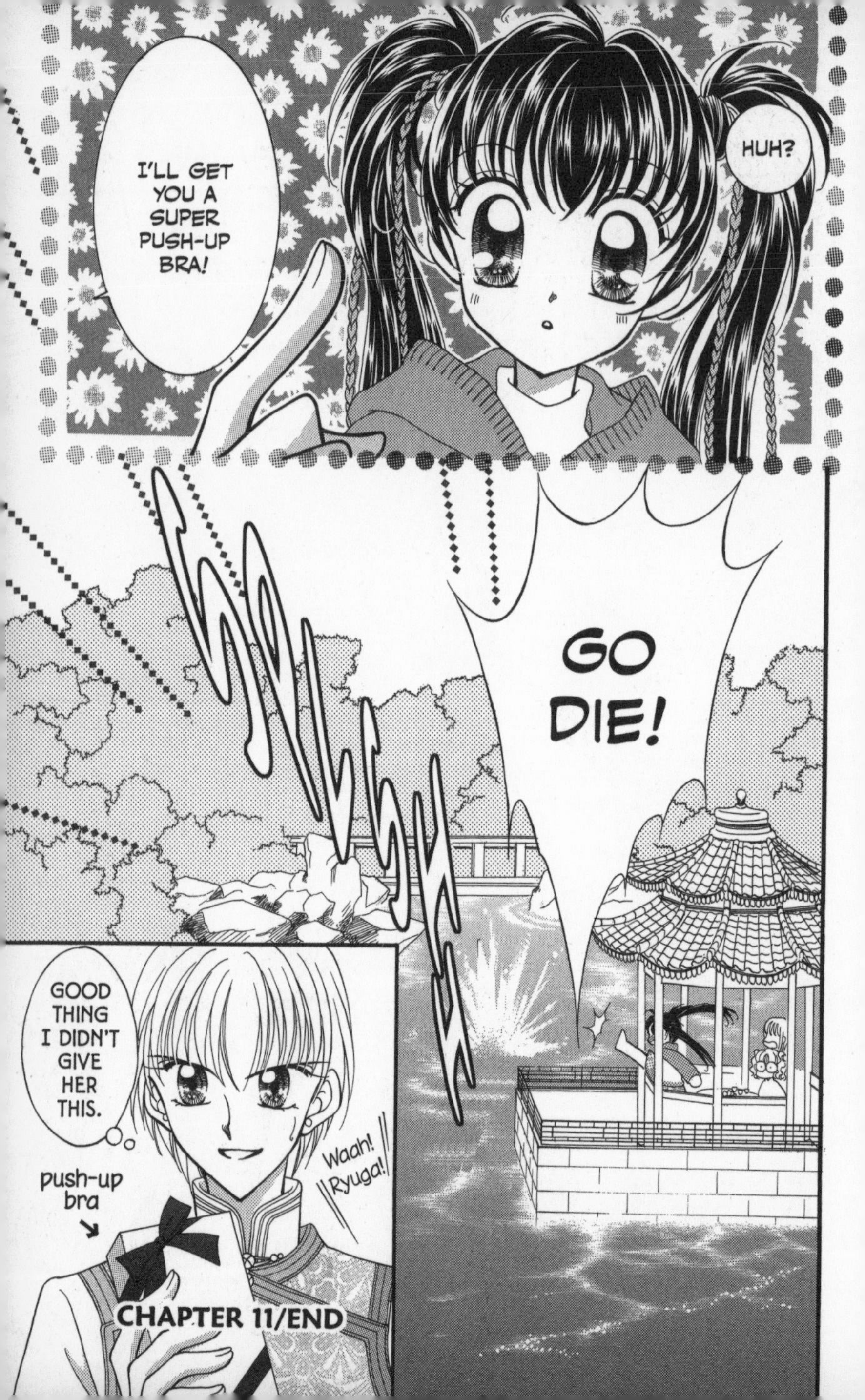
I'LL GET YOU A SUPER PUSH-UP BRA!
HUH?
GO DIE!
Waah! Ryuga!
GOOD THING I DIDN'T GIVE HER THIS.
push-up bra
CHAPTER 11/END

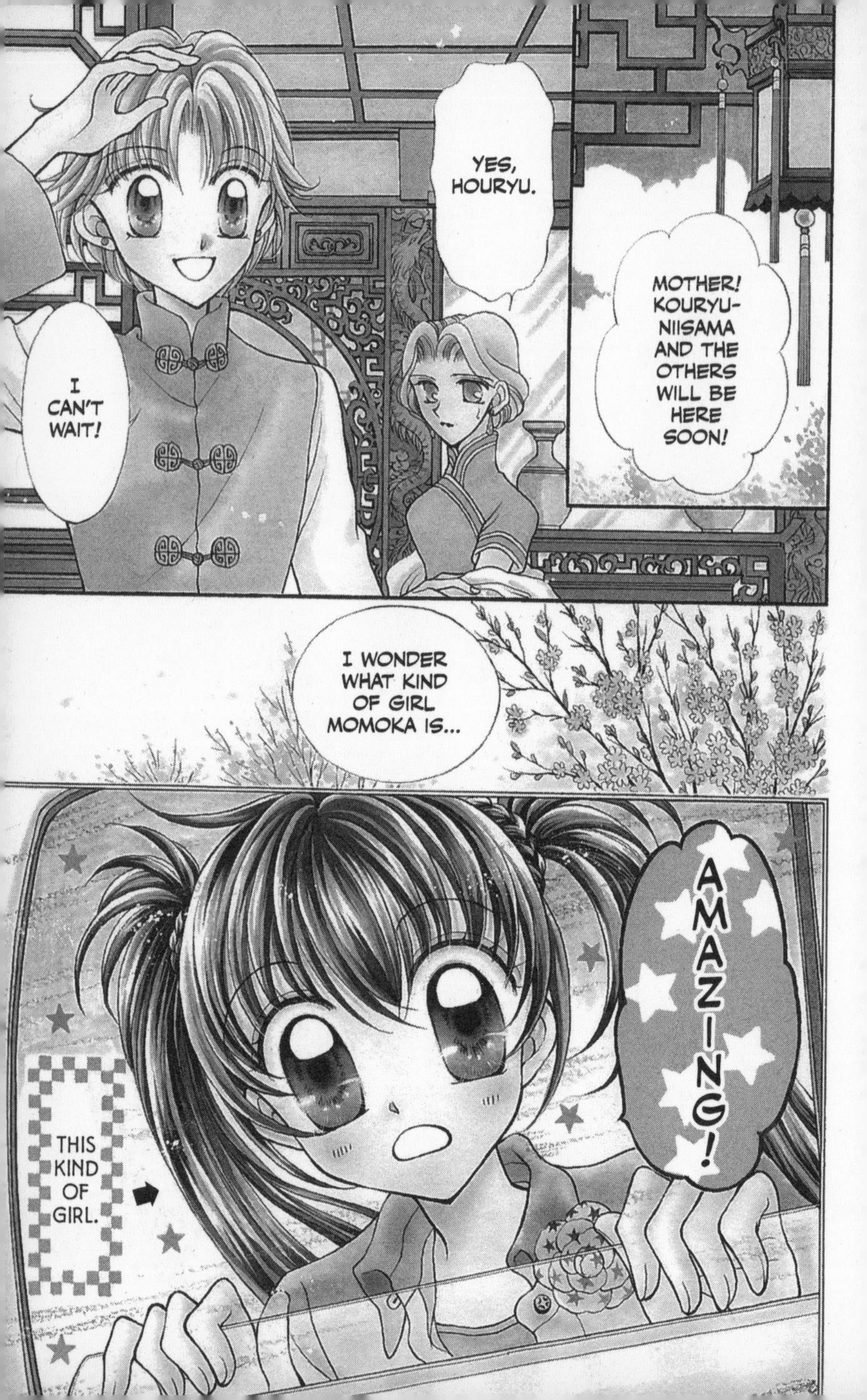
MOTHER! KOURYU-NIISAMA AND THE OTHERS WILL BE HERE SOON!
YES, HOURYU.
I CAN'T WAIT!
I WONDER WHAT KIND OF GIRL MOMOKA IS...
AMAZING!
THIS KIND OF GIRL.

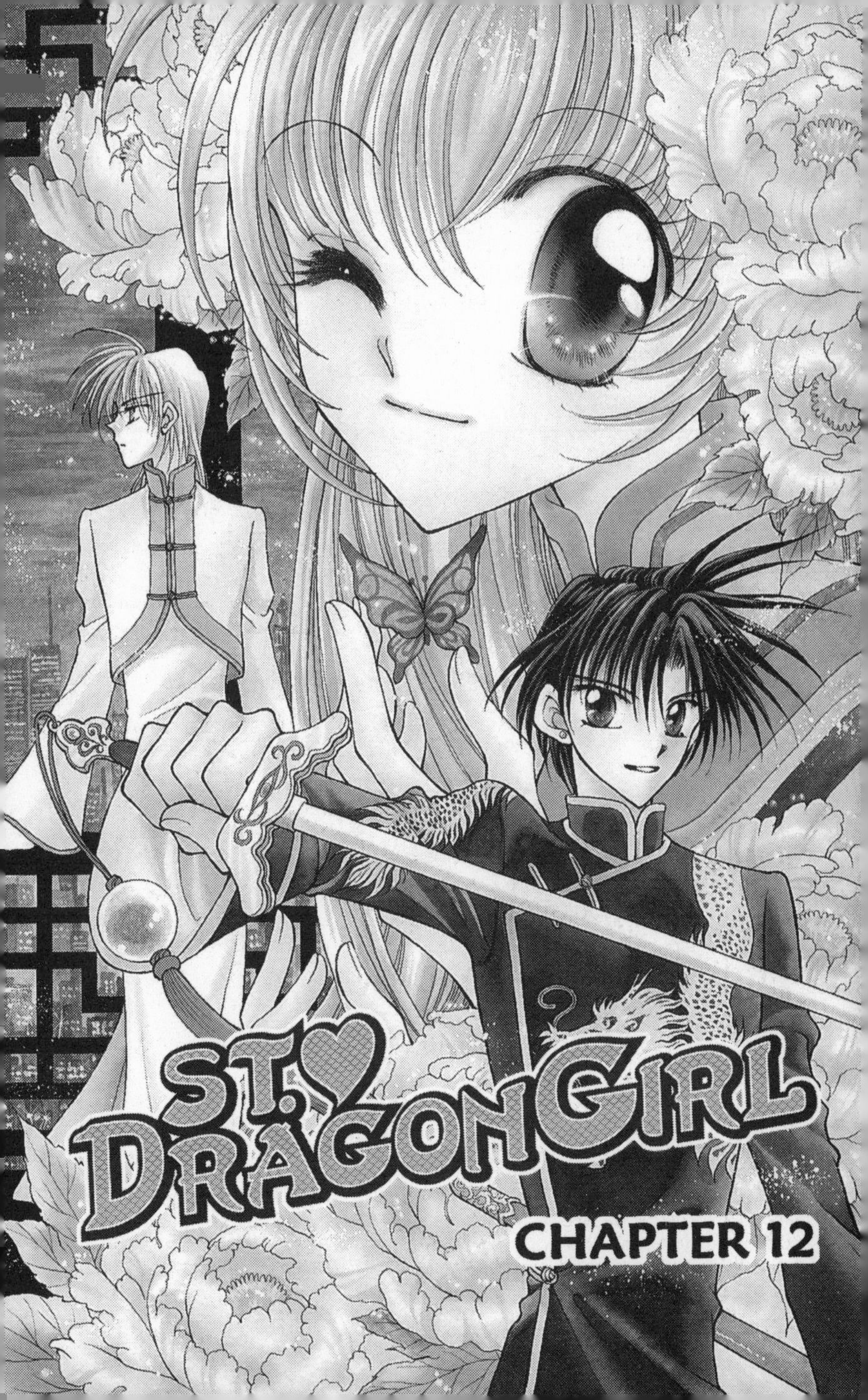
ST.♥DRAGON GIRL
CHAPTER 12

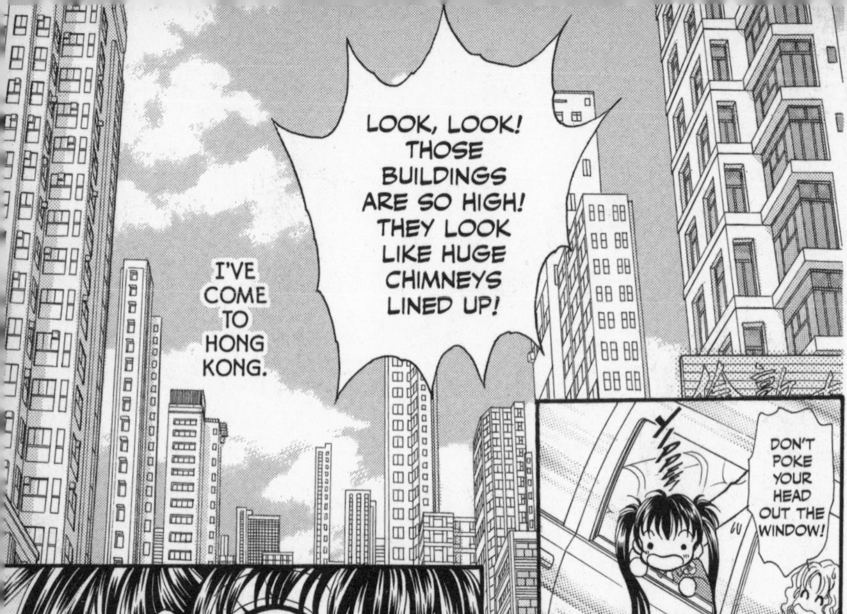
LOOK, LOOK! THOSE BUILDINGS ARE SO HIGH! THEY LOOK LIKE HUGE CHIMNEYS LINED UP!
I'VE COME TO HONG KONG.
DON'T POKE YOUR HEAD OUT THE WINDOW!
I WANTED TO SEE THE BIRTHPLACE OF THE ONE I LOVE.
TUNG YUEN
RYUGA.
IS IT REALLY OKAY THAT I CAME ALONG TOO?
VROOM
HONK HONK

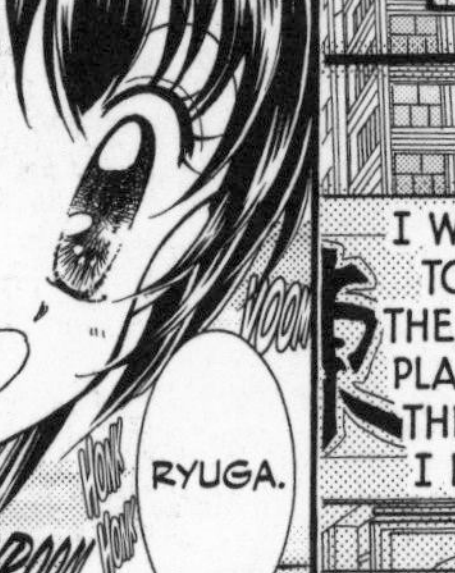
RON RON

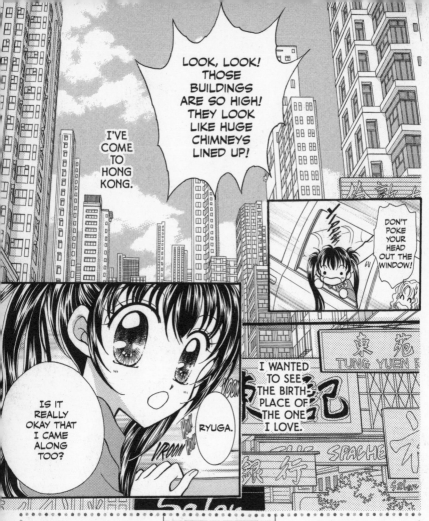

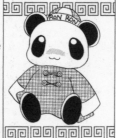

Ron-Ron

Birthday: Unknown.
Stuffed animal.
Made in Hong Kong.

This is a souvenir that Ryuga got in Hong Kong. In fourth grade he gave it away during a present exchange, and Momoka got it.

Momoka loves pandas, but this is her favorite. He's also popular among readers, and some fans even say they love him more than Ryuga. Sometimes spells are cast to make him move and talk, but I wonder what kind of voice he has? For a period of time, I couldn't get the look of his clothes right, and I panicked.

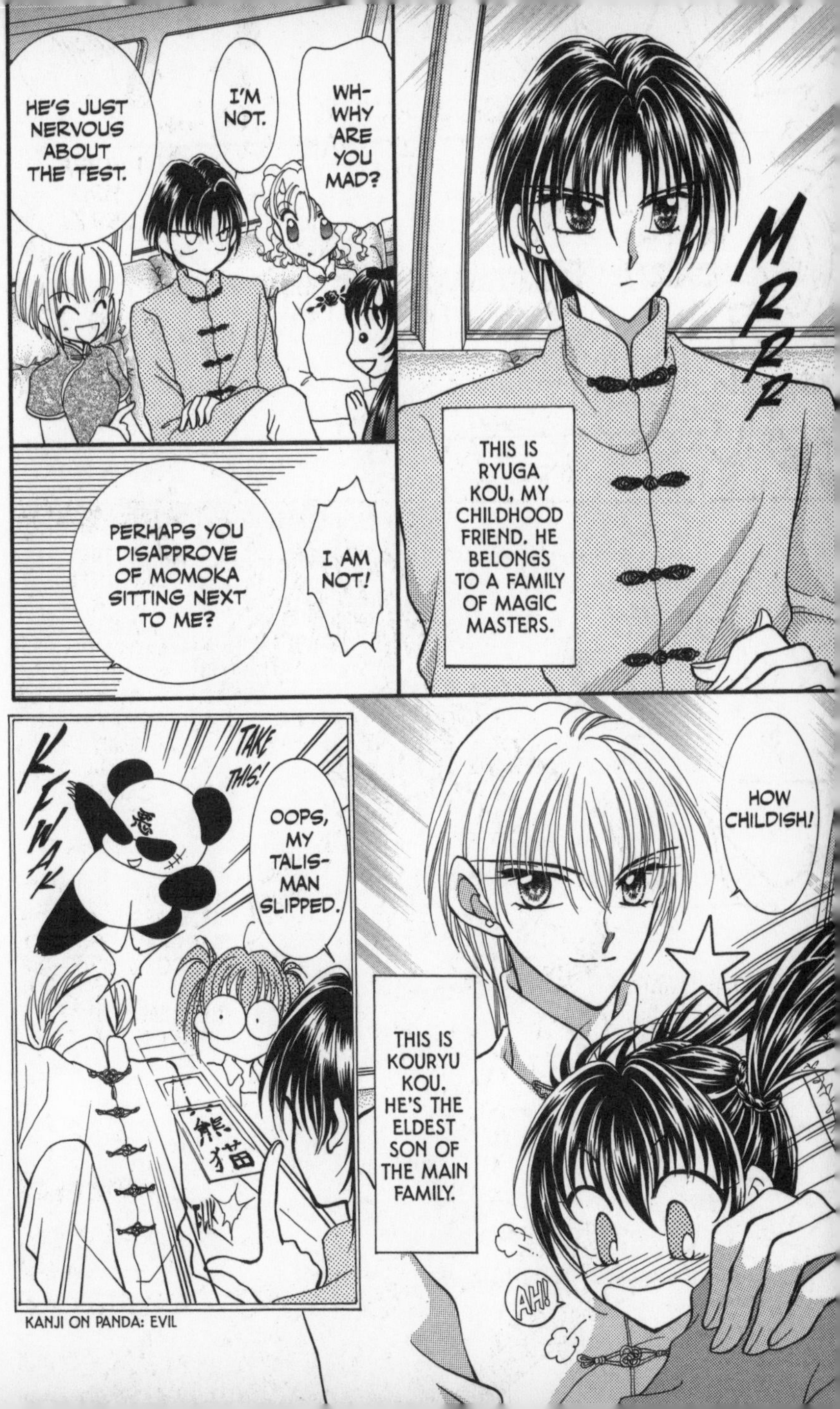
MRRR
THIS IS RYUGA KOU, MY CHILDHOOD FRIEND. HE BELONGS TO A FAMILY OF MAGIC MASTERS.
WH-WHY ARE YOU MAD?
I'M NOT.
HE'S JUST NERVOUS ABOUT THE TEST.
PERHAPS YOU DISAPPROVE OF MOMOKA SITTING NEXT TO ME?
I AM NOT!
HOW CHILDISH!
THIS IS KOURYU KOU. HE'S THE ELDEST SON OF THE MAIN FAMILY.
AH!
TAKE THIS!
OOPS, MY TALIS-MAN SLIPPED.
KFWAK

KANJI ON PANDA: EVIL

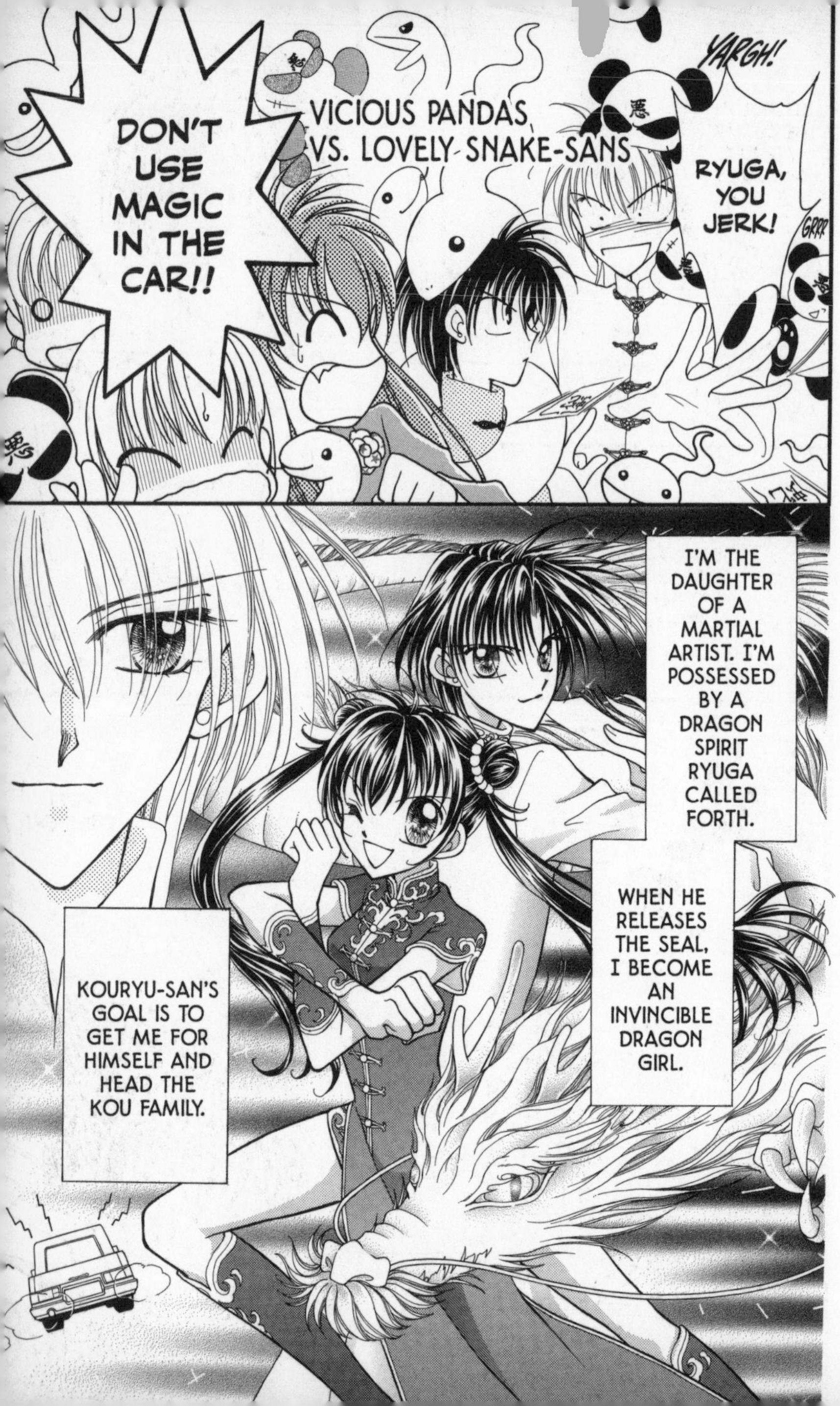
YARGH!
RYUGA, YOU JERK!
GRRR
VICIOUS PANDAS VS. LOVELY SNAKE-SANS
DON'T USE MAGIC IN THE CAR!!
I'M THE DAUGHTER OF A MARTIAL ARTIST. I'M POSSESSED BY A DRAGON SPIRIT RYUGA CALLED FORTH.
WHEN HE RELEASES THE SEAL, I BECOME AN INVINCIBLE DRAGON GIRL.
KOURYU-SAN'S GOAL IS TO GET ME FOR HIMSELF AND HEAD THE KOU FAMILY.

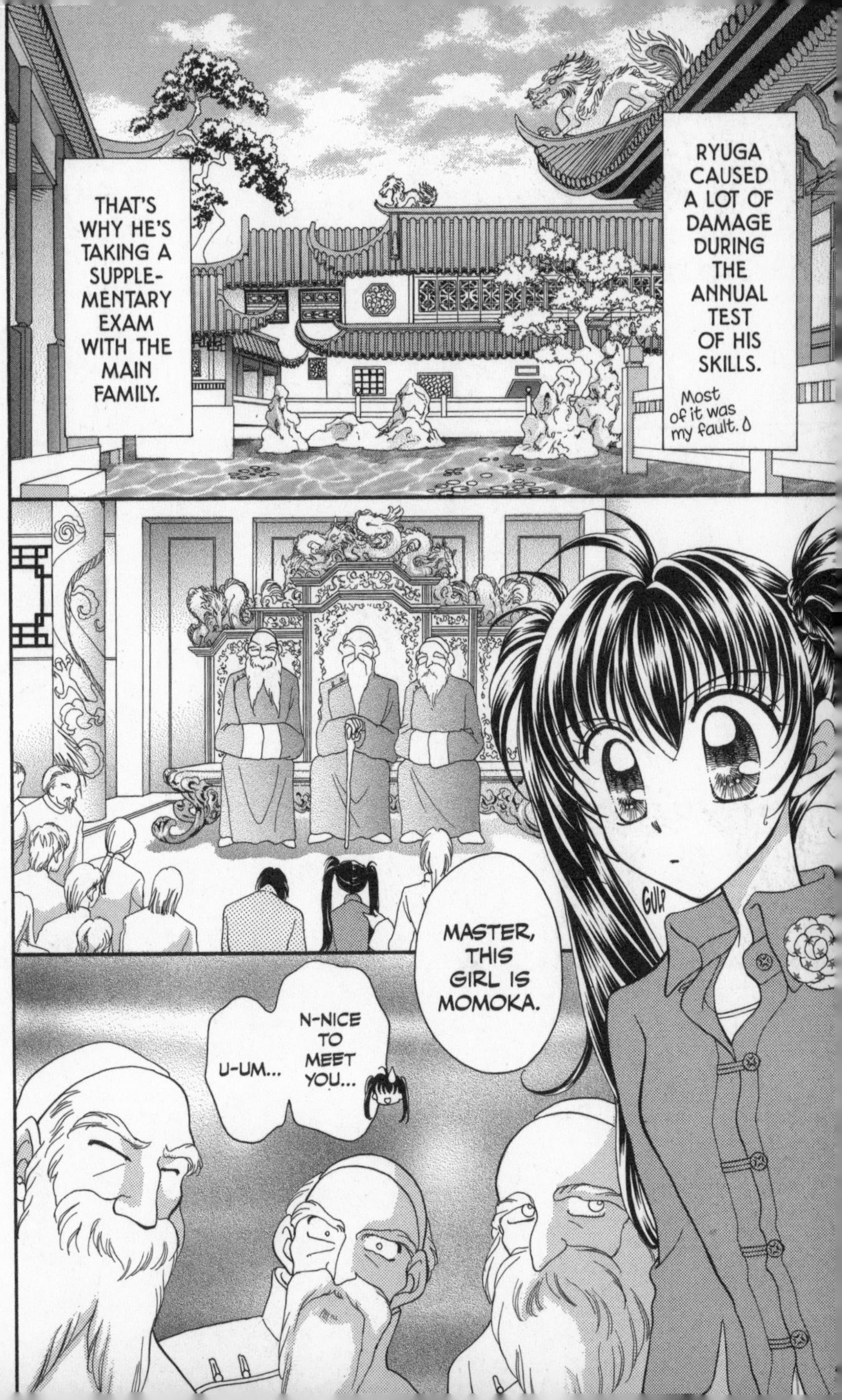
RYUGA CAUSED A LOT OF DAMAGE DURING THE ANNUAL TEST OF HIS SKILLS.
Most of it was my fault.
THAT'S WHY HE'S TAKING A SUPPLE-MENTARY EXAM WITH THE MAIN FAMILY.
GULP
MASTER, THIS GIRL IS MOMOKA.
N-NICE TO MEET YOU...
U-UM...

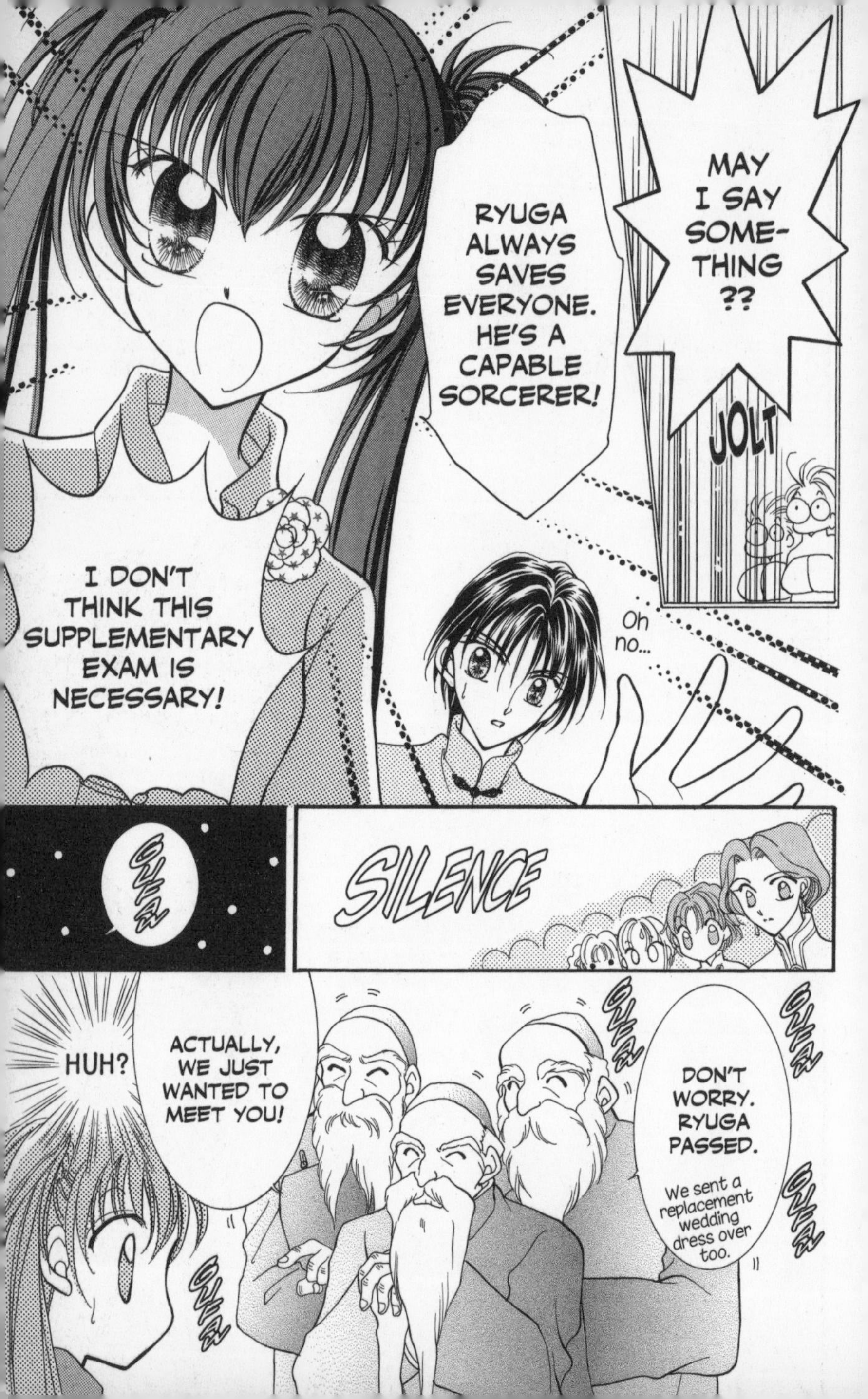

MAY I SAY SOME-THING??
JOLT
RYUGA ALWAYS SAVES EVERYONE. HE'S A CAPABLE SORCERER!
Oh no...
I DON'T THINK THIS SUPPLEMENTARY EXAM IS NECESSARY!
SILENCE
DON'T WORRY. RYUGA PASSED.
We sent a replacement wedding dress over too.
ACTUALLY, WE JUST WANTED TO MEET YOU!
HUH?

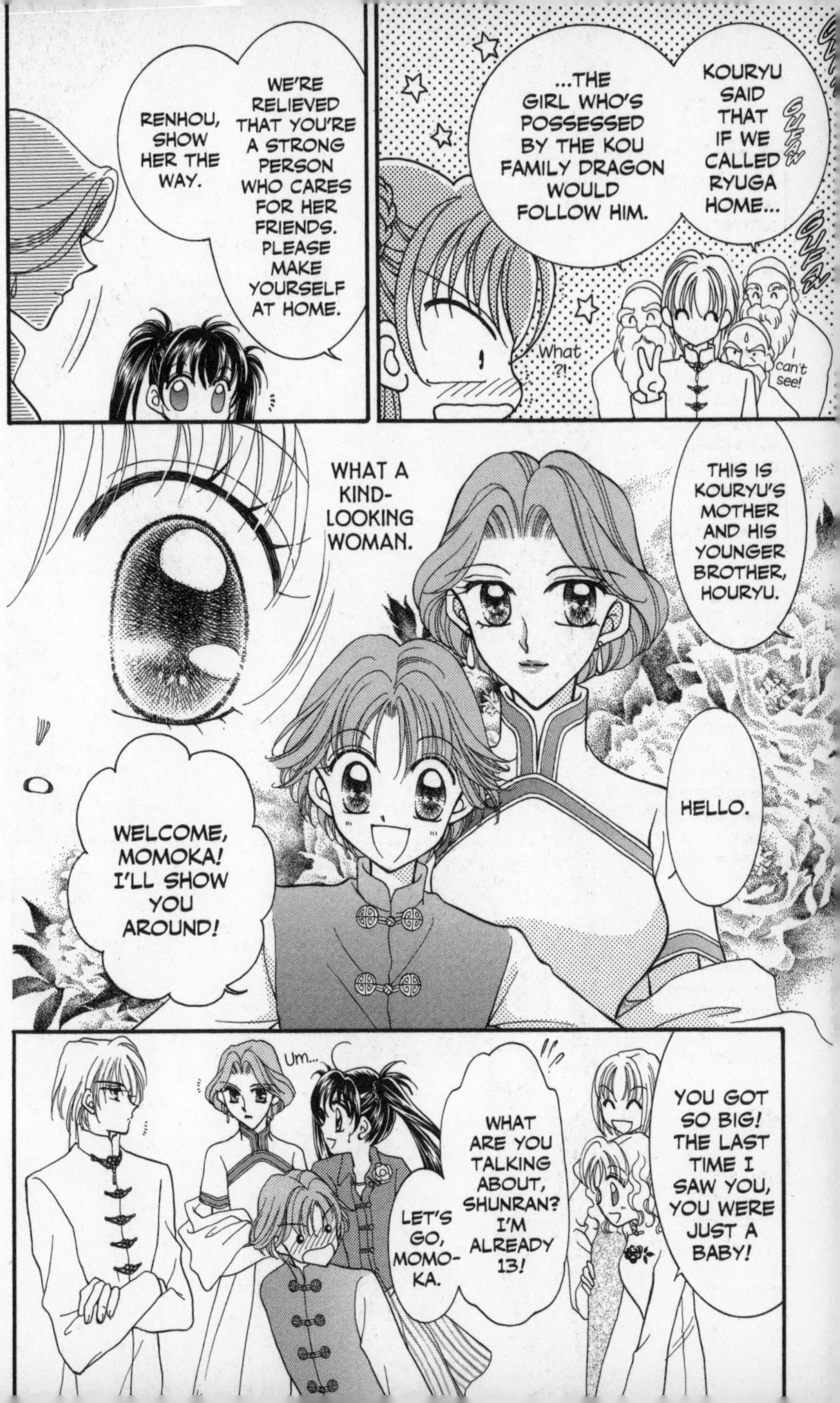
KOURYU SAID THAT IF WE CALLED RYUGA HOME...
...THE GIRL WHO'S POSSESSED BY THE KOU FAMILY DRAGON WOULD FOLLOW HIM.
I can't see!
What?!
WE'RE RELIEVED THAT YOU'RE A STRONG PERSON WHO CARES FOR HER FRIENDS. PLEASE MAKE YOURSELF AT HOME.
RENHOU, SHOW HER THE WAY.
THIS IS KOURYU'S MOTHER AND HIS YOUNGER BROTHER, HOURYU.
HELLO.
WHAT A KIND-LOOKING WOMAN.
WELCOME, MOMOKA! I'LL SHOW YOU AROUND!
YOU GOT SO BIG! THE LAST TIME I SAW YOU, YOU WERE JUST A BABY!
WHAT ARE YOU TALKING ABOUT, SHUNRAN? I'M ALREADY 13!
LET'S GO, MOMOKA.
Um...

8

"Little Dragon" appeared in the summer special edition. At that time, I had just returned from a trip to Hong Kong and was exhausted. However, my engine just wouldn't shut off! But I'm really happy I was able to write about Momoka and her friends when they were small. Next time I want to write about the first time they met.

The final bonus story, "Trouble on a Snowy Night," was in the winter special edition. Around this time I was nearing the deadline for the regular series, so I was really busy. I asked for just eight pages, but it still took a lot of time! I wonder why...

I got to draw Lin-Lin and Len-Len for the first time in a while, so I was really happy. I am also fond of Momoka's father. I hope I can draw her mom soon too!

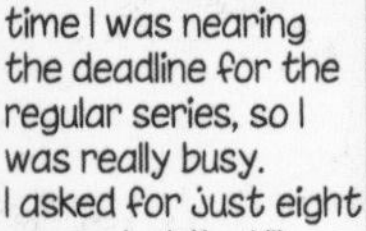
LIN² & LEN²

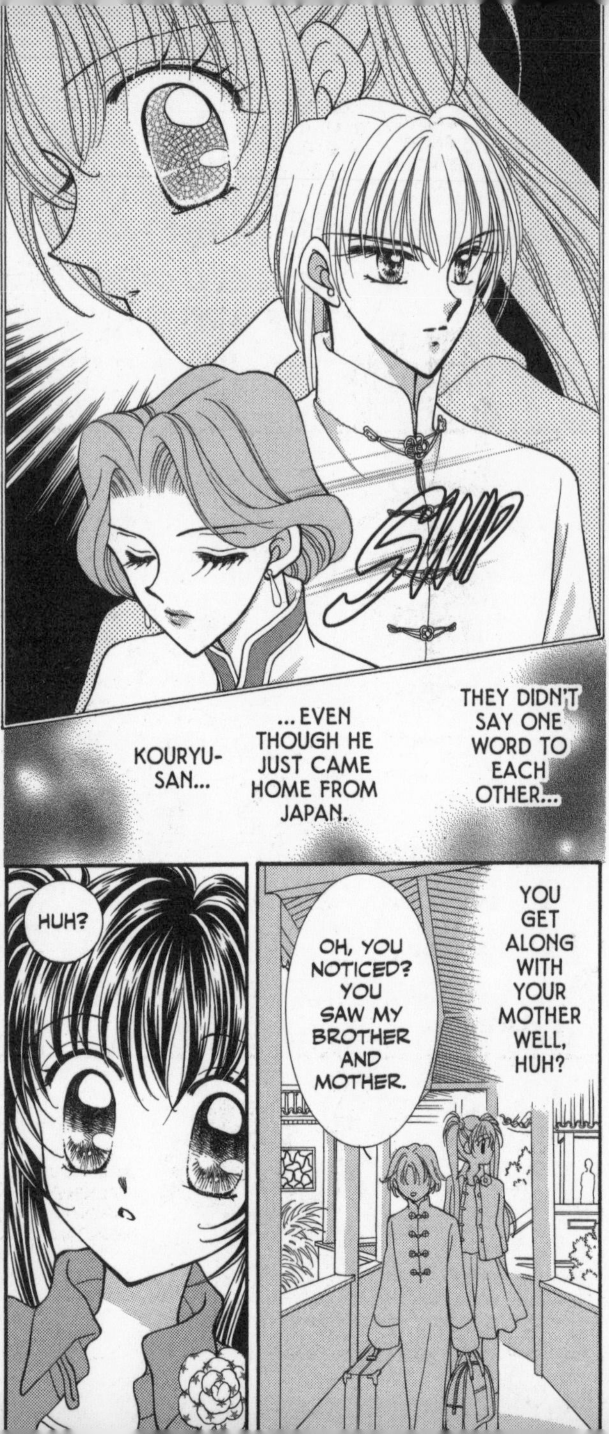
THEY DIDN'T SAY ONE WORD TO EACH OTHER...
...EVEN THOUGH HE JUST CAME HOME FROM JAPAN.
KOURYU-SAN...
YOU GET ALONG WITH YOUR MOTHER WELL, HUH?
OH, YOU NOTICED? YOU SAW MY BROTHER AND MOTHER.
HUH?

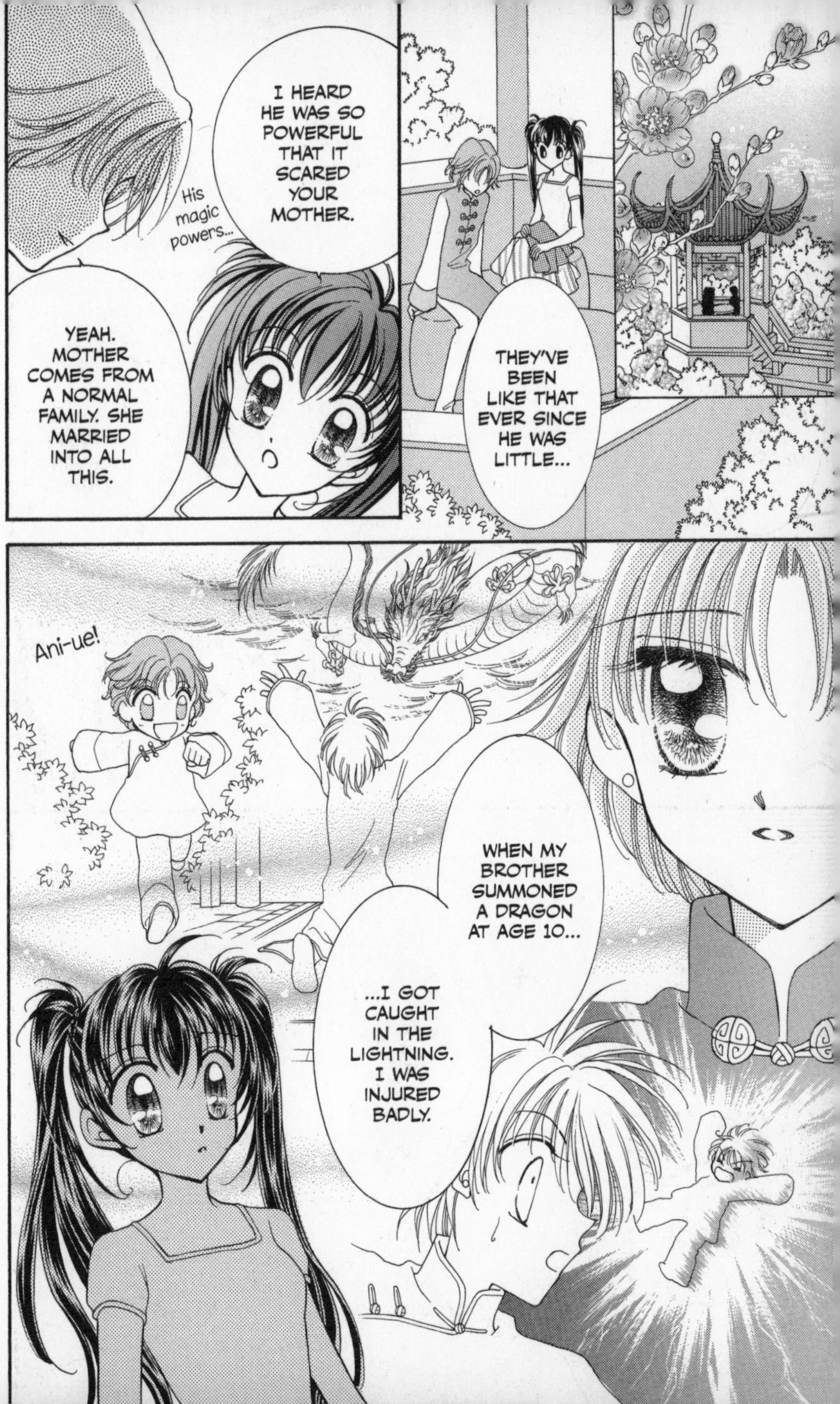
THEY'VE BEEN LIKE THAT EVER SINCE HE WAS LITTLE...
I HEARD HE WAS SO POWERFUL THAT IT SCARED YOUR MOTHER.
His magic powers...
YEAH. MOTHER COMES FROM A NORMAL FAMILY. SHE MARRIED INTO ALL THIS.
WHEN MY BROTHER SUMMONED A DRAGON AT AGE 10...
...I GOT CAUGHT IN THE LIGHTNING. I WAS INJURED BADLY.
Ani-ue!

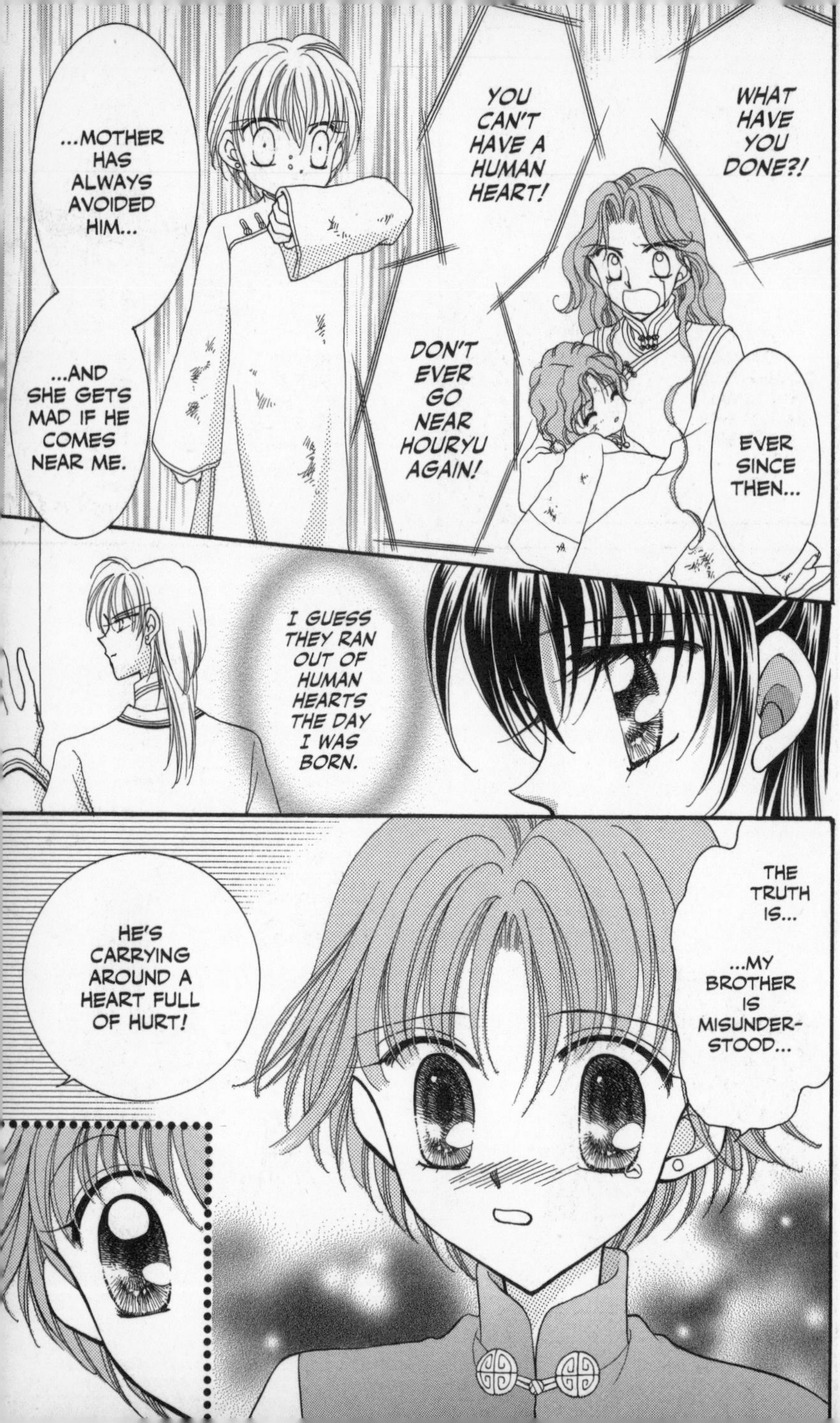
WHAT HAVE YOU DONE?!
YOU CAN'T HAVE A HUMAN HEART!
DON'T EVER GO NEAR HOURYU AGAIN!
EVER SINCE THEN...
...MOTHER HAS ALWAYS AVOIDED HIM...
...AND SHE GETS MAD IF HE COMES NEAR ME.
I GUESS THEY RAN OUT OF HUMAN HEARTS THE DAY I WAS BORN.
THE TRUTH IS...
...MY BROTHER IS MISUNDER-STOOD...
HE'S CARRYING AROUND A HEART FULL OF HURT!

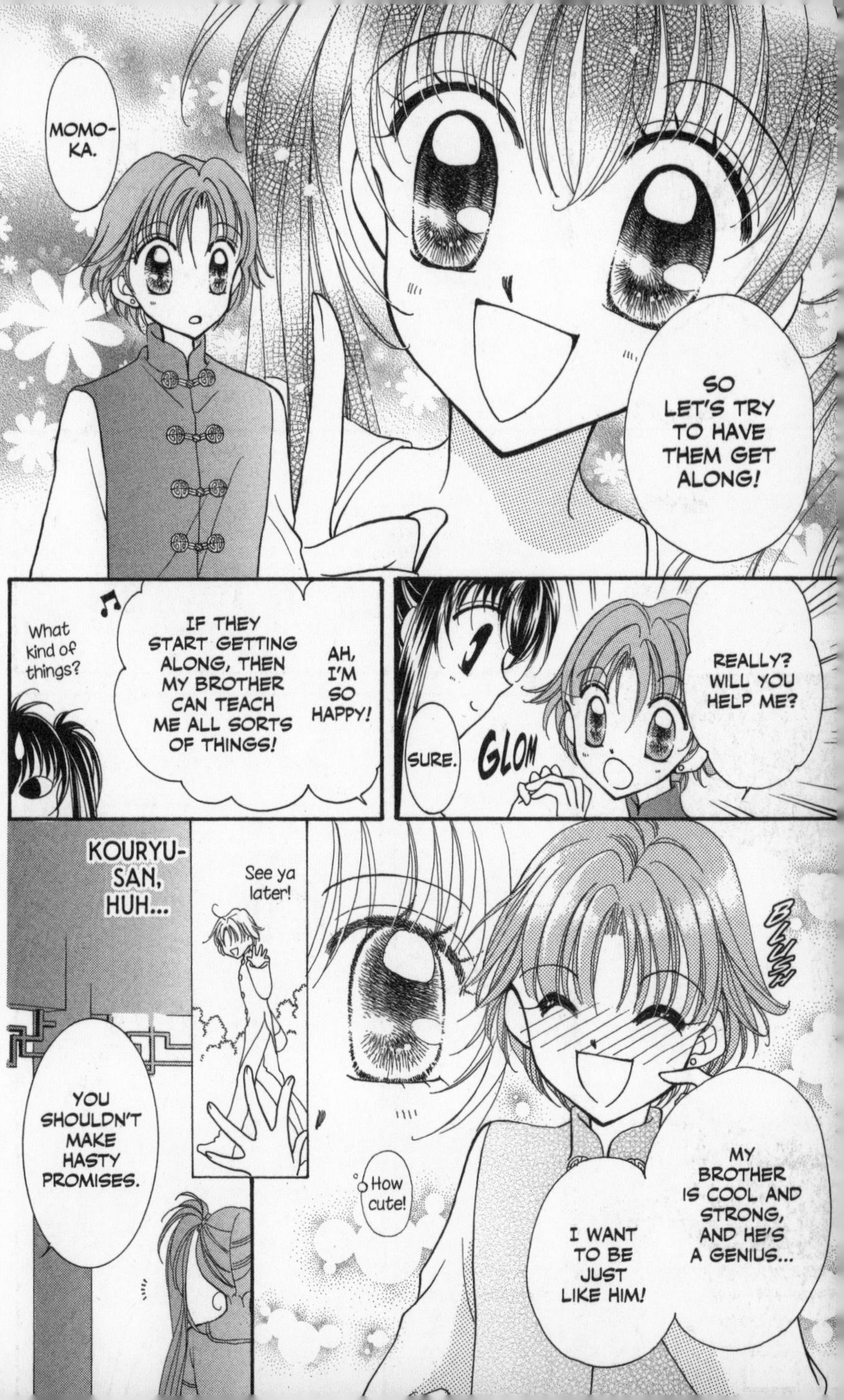
SO LET'S TRY TO HAVE THEM GET ALONG!
MOMO-KA.
REALLY? WILL YOU HELP ME?
SURE.
GLOM
AH, I'M SO HAPPY!
IF THEY START GETTING ALONG, THEN MY BROTHER CAN TEACH ME ALL SORTS OF THINGS!
What kind of things?
MY BROTHER IS COOL AND STRONG, AND HE'S A GENIUS...
I WANT TO BE JUST LIKE HIM!
How cute!
See ya later!
KOURYU-SAN, HUH...
YOU SHOULDN'T MAKE HASTY PROMISES.

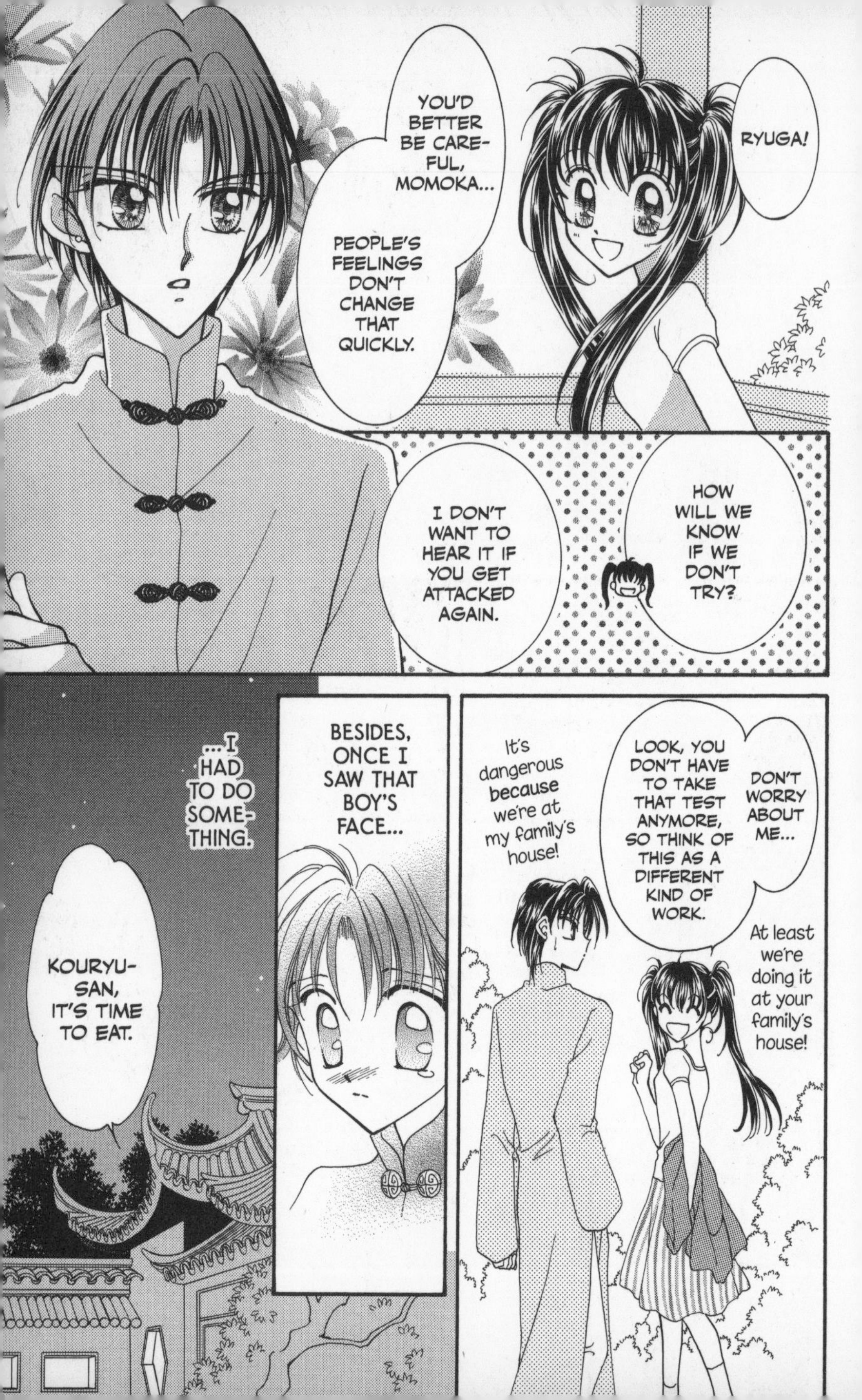
RYUGA!
YOU'D BETTER BE CARE-FUL, MOMOKA...
PEOPLE'S FEELINGS DON'T CHANGE THAT QUICKLY.
HOW WILL WE KNOW IF WE DON'T TRY?
I DON'T WANT TO HEAR IT IF YOU GET ATTACKED AGAIN.
DON'T WORRY ABOUT ME...
LOOK, YOU DON'T HAVE TO TAKE THAT TEST ANYMORE, SO THINK OF THIS AS A DIFFERENT KIND OF WORK.
At least we're doing it at your family's house!
It's dangerous because we're at my family's house!
BESIDES, ONCE I SAW THAT BOY'S FACE...
...I HAD TO DO SOME-THING.
KOURYU-SAN, IT'S TIME TO EAT.

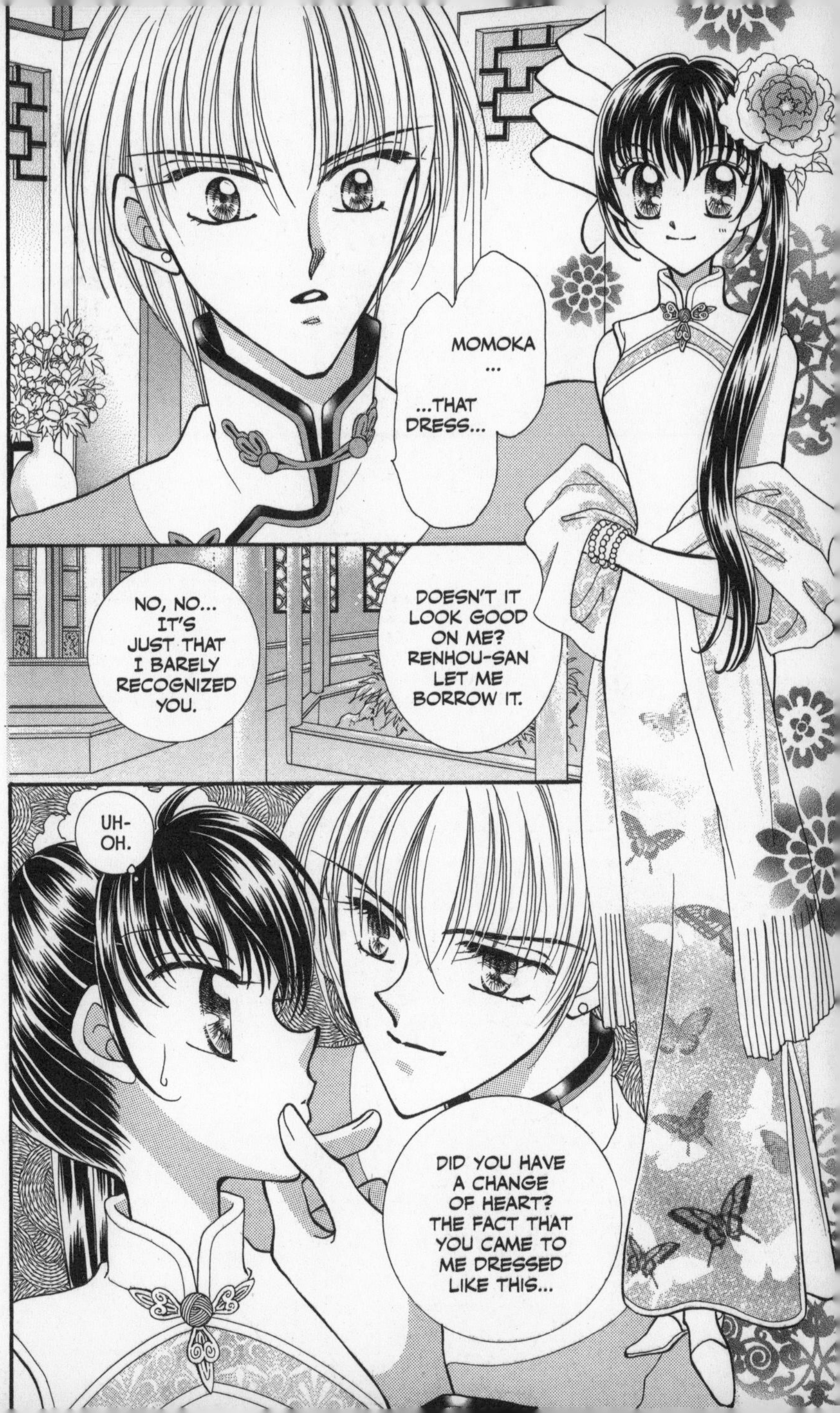
MOMOKA ... ...THAT DRESS...
DOESN'T IT LOOK GOOD ON ME? RENHOU-SAN LET ME BORROW IT.
NO, NO... IT'S JUST THAT I BARELY RECOGNIZED YOU.
UH-OH.
DID YOU HAVE A CHANGE OF HEART? THE FACT THAT YOU CAME TO ME DRESSED LIKE THIS...

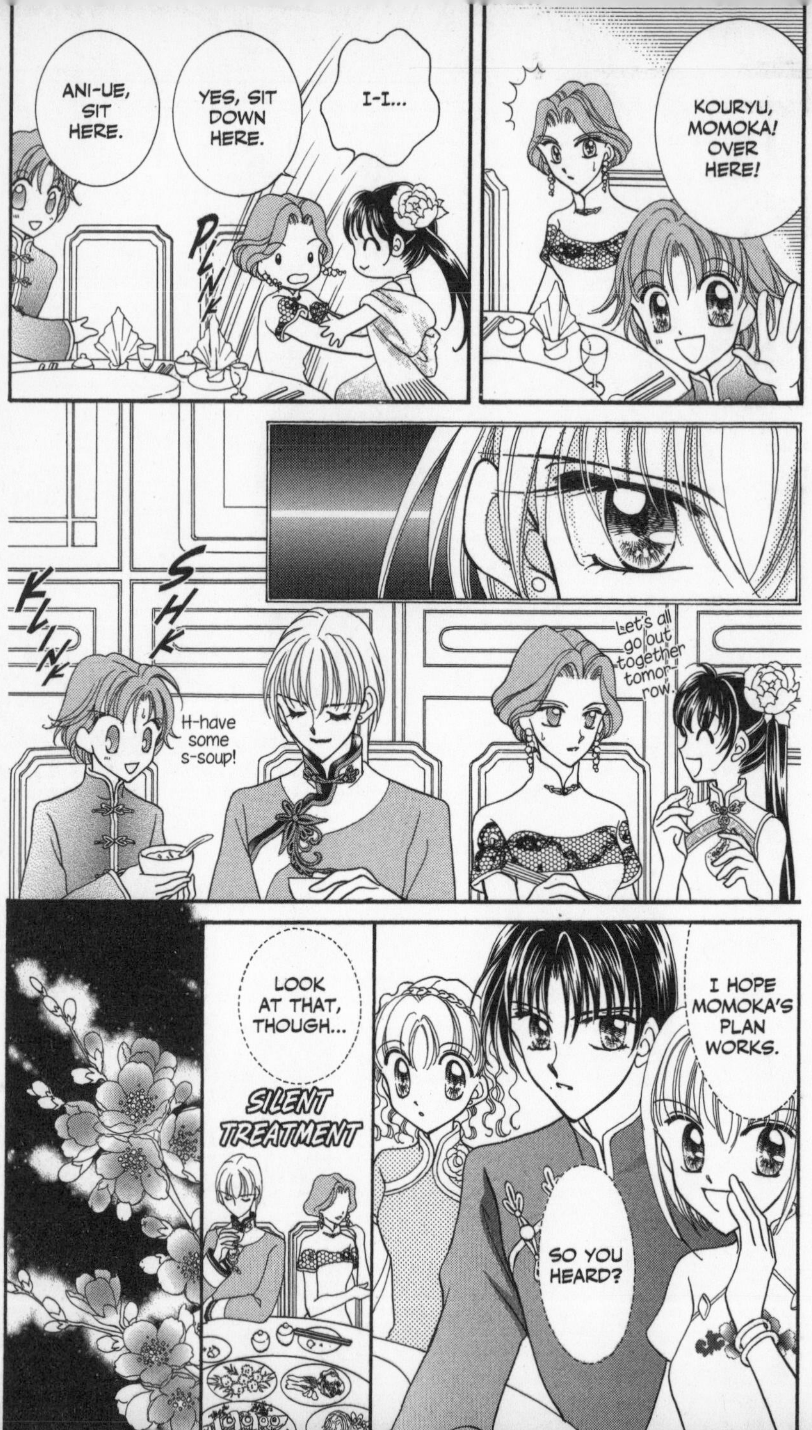
KOURYU, MOMOKA! OVER HERE!
I-I...
YES, SIT DOWN HERE.
ANI-UE, SIT HERE.
PLNK
Let's all go out together tomorrow.
SHK
H-have some s-soup!
KLINK
I HOPE MOMOKA'S PLAN WORKS.
SO YOU HEARD?
LOOK AT THAT, THOUGH...
SILENT TREATMENT

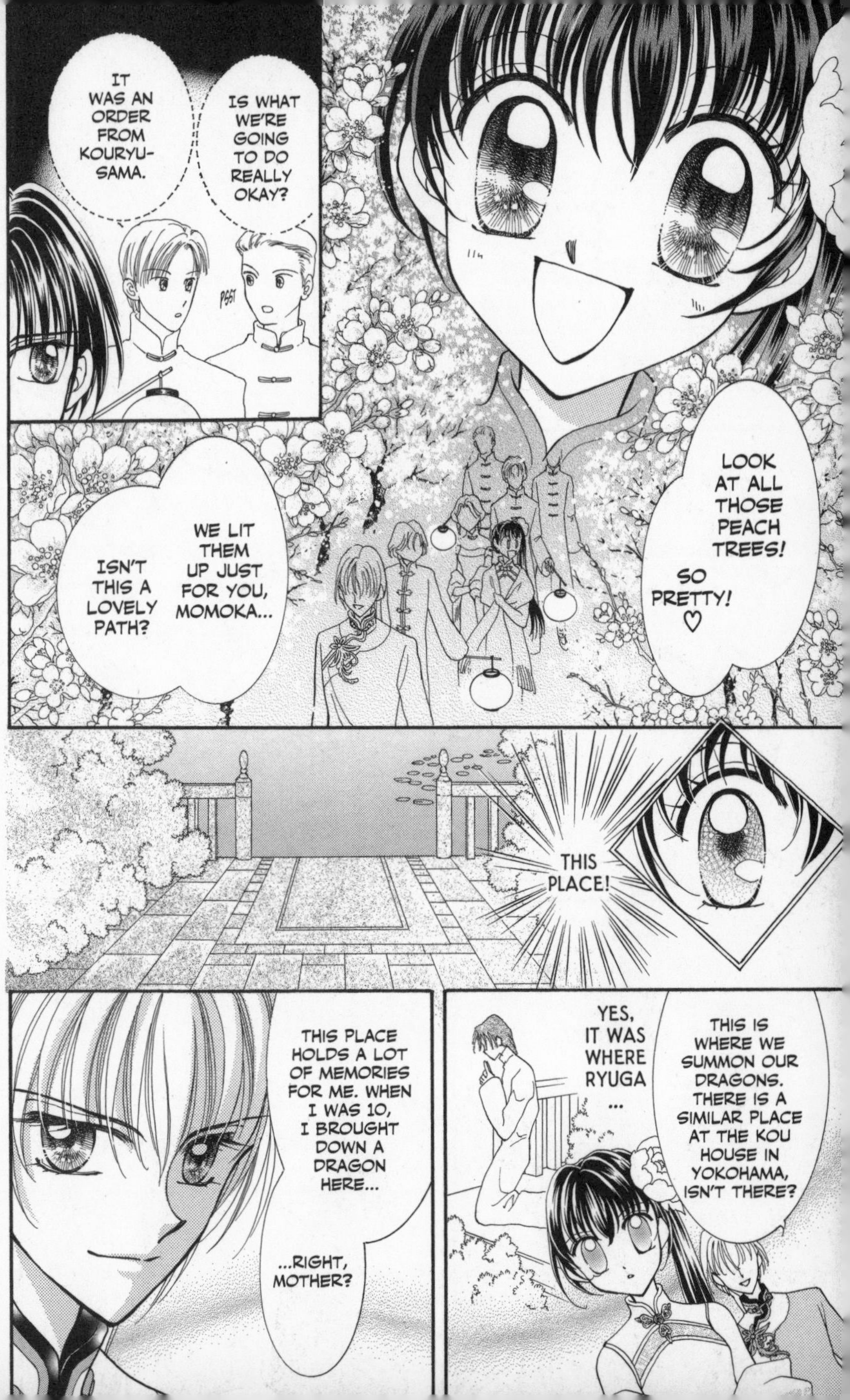
LOOK AT ALL THOSE PEACH TREES!
SO PRETTY! ♡
WE LIT THEM UP JUST FOR YOU, MOMOKA...
ISN'T THIS A LOVELY PATH?
IS WHAT WE'RE GOING TO DO REALLY OKAY?
PSST
IT WAS AN ORDER FROM KOURYU-SAMA.
THIS PLACE!
THIS IS WHERE WE SUMMON OUR DRAGONS. THERE IS A SIMILAR PLACE AT THE KOU HOUSE IN YOKOHAMA, ISN'T THERE?
YES, IT WAS WHERE RYUGA ...
THIS PLACE HOLDS A LOT OF MEMORIES FOR ME. WHEN I WAS 10, I BROUGHT DOWN A DRAGON HERE...
...RIGHT, MOTHER?

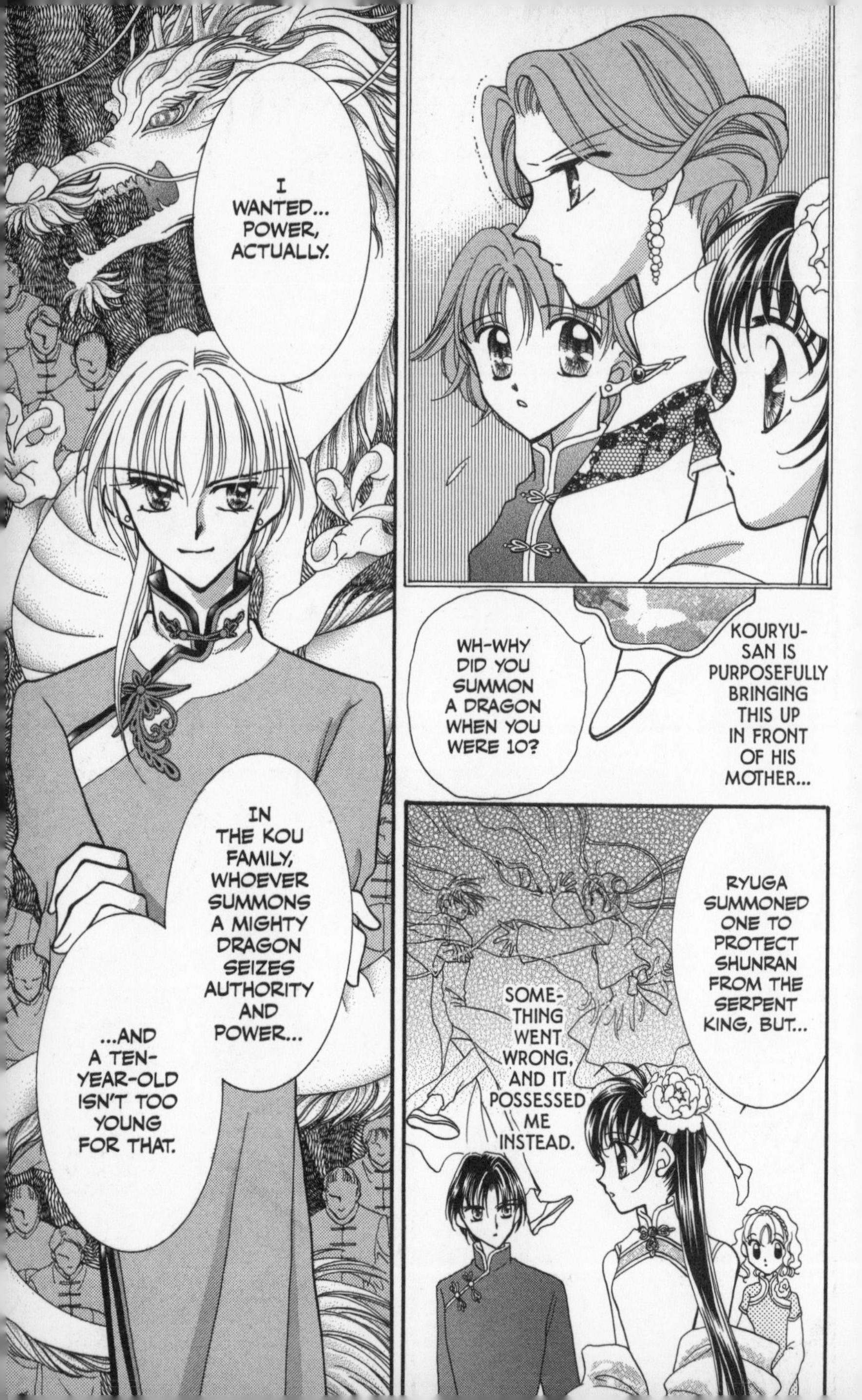
KOURYU-SAN IS PURPOSEFULLY BRINGING THIS UP IN FRONT OF HIS MOTHER...
WH-WHY DID YOU SUMMON A DRAGON WHEN YOU WERE 10?
RYUGA SUMMONED ONE TO PROTECT SHUNRAN FROM THE SERPENT KING, BUT...
SOME-THING WENT WRONG, AND IT POSSESSED ME INSTEAD.
I WANTED... POWER, ACTUALLY.
IN THE KOU FAMILY, WHOEVER SUMMONS A MIGHTY DRAGON SEIZES AUTHORITY AND POWER...
...AND A TEN-YEAR-OLD ISN'T TOO YOUNG FOR THAT.

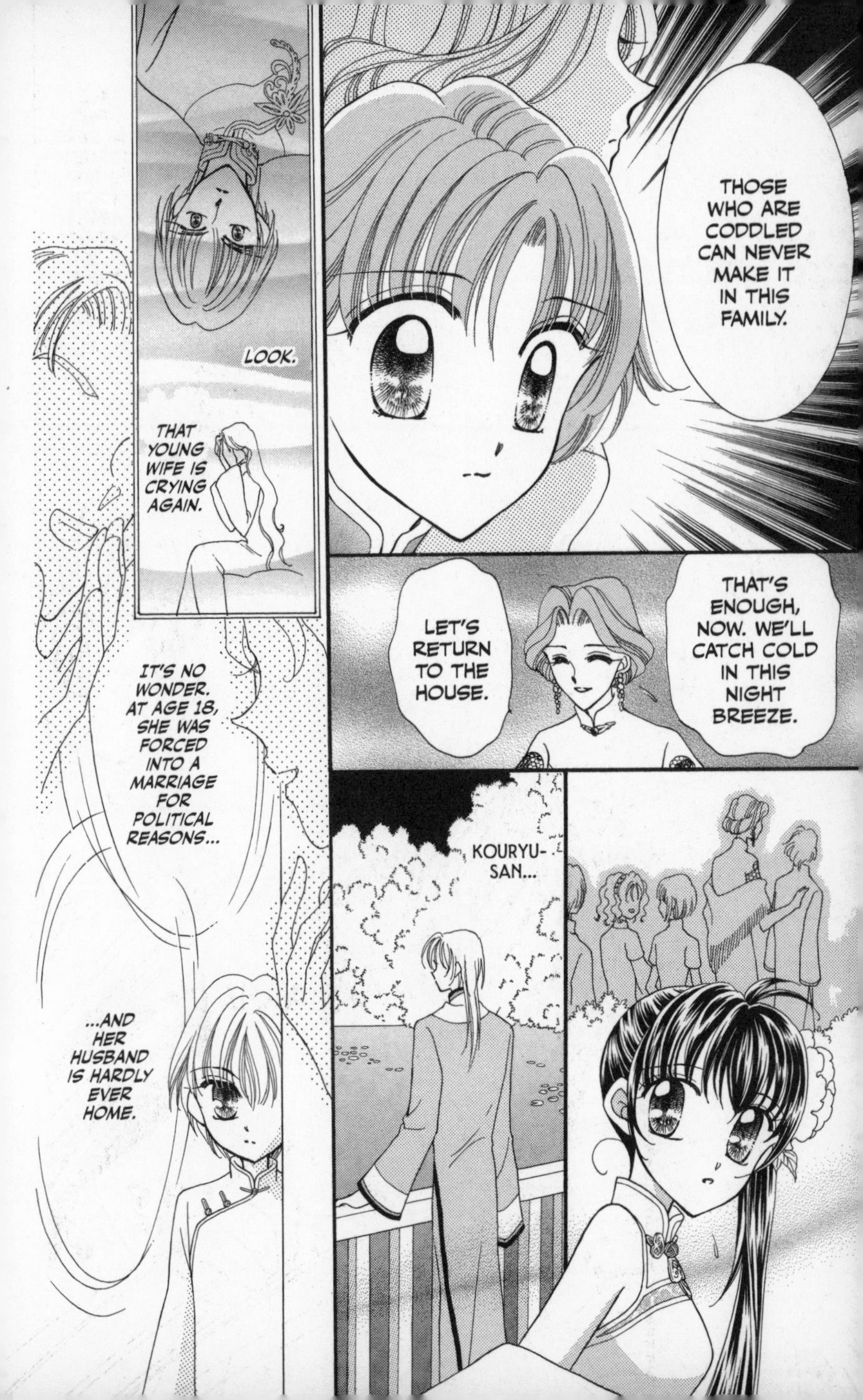
THOSE WHO ARE CODDLED CAN NEVER MAKE IT IN THIS FAMILY.
THAT'S ENOUGH, NOW. WE'LL CATCH COLD IN THIS NIGHT BREEZE.
LET'S RETURN TO THE HOUSE.
KOURYU-SAN...
LOOK.
THAT YOUNG WIFE IS CRYING AGAIN.
IT'S NO WONDER. AT AGE 18, SHE WAS FORCED INTO A MARRIAGE FOR POLITICAL REASONS...
...AND HER HUSBAND IS HARDLY EVER HOME.

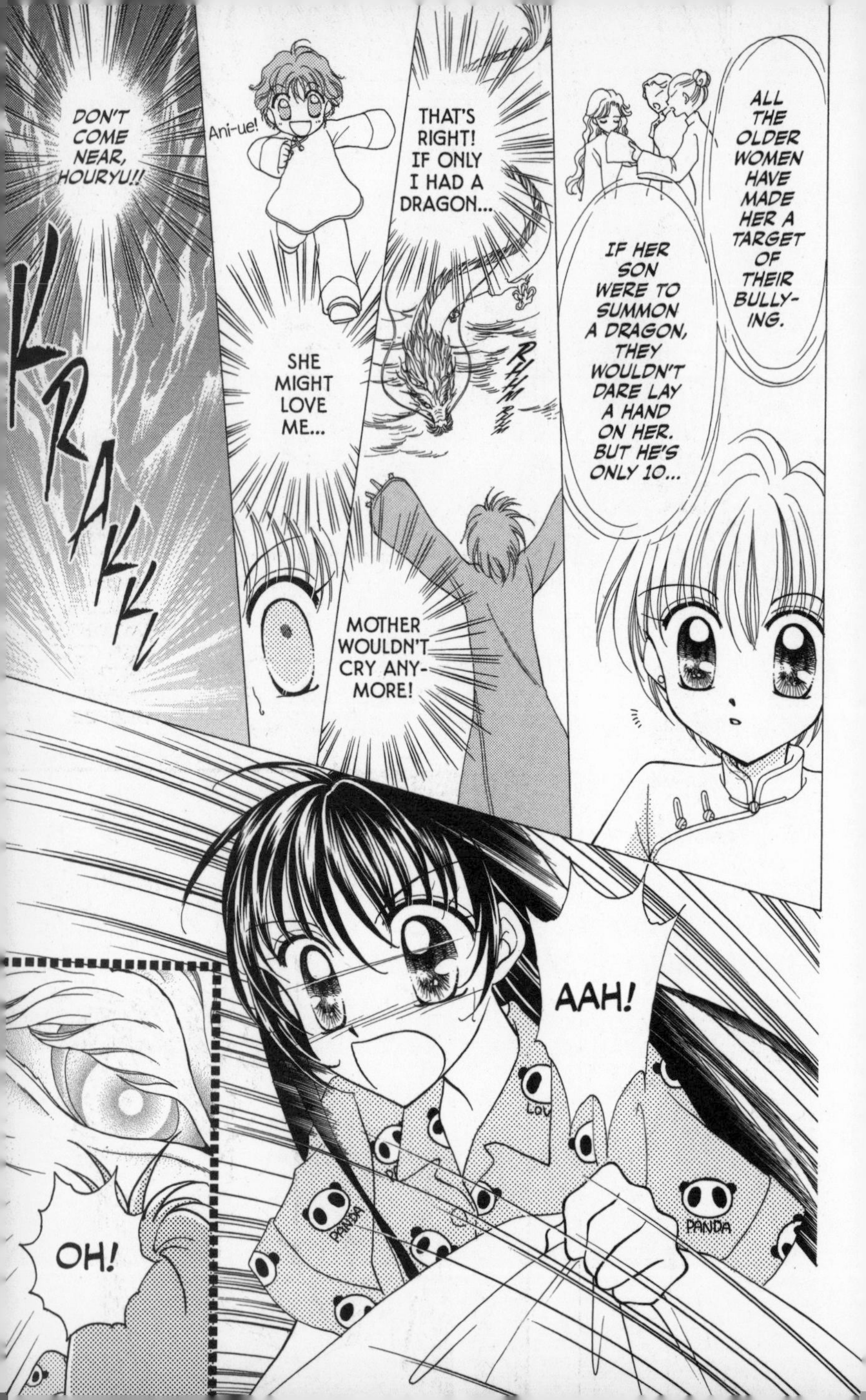
ALL THE OLDER WOMEN HAVE MADE HER A TARGET OF THEIR BULLYING.
IF HER SON WERE TO SUMMON A DRAGON, THEY WOULDN'T DARE LAY A HAND ON HER. BUT HE'S ONLY 10...
THAT'S RIGHT! IF ONLY I HAD A DRAGON...
MOTHER WOULDN'T CRY ANYMORE!
Ani-ue!
SHE MIGHT LOVE ME...
DON'T COME NEAR, HOURYU!!
KRAKKK
AAH!
OH!

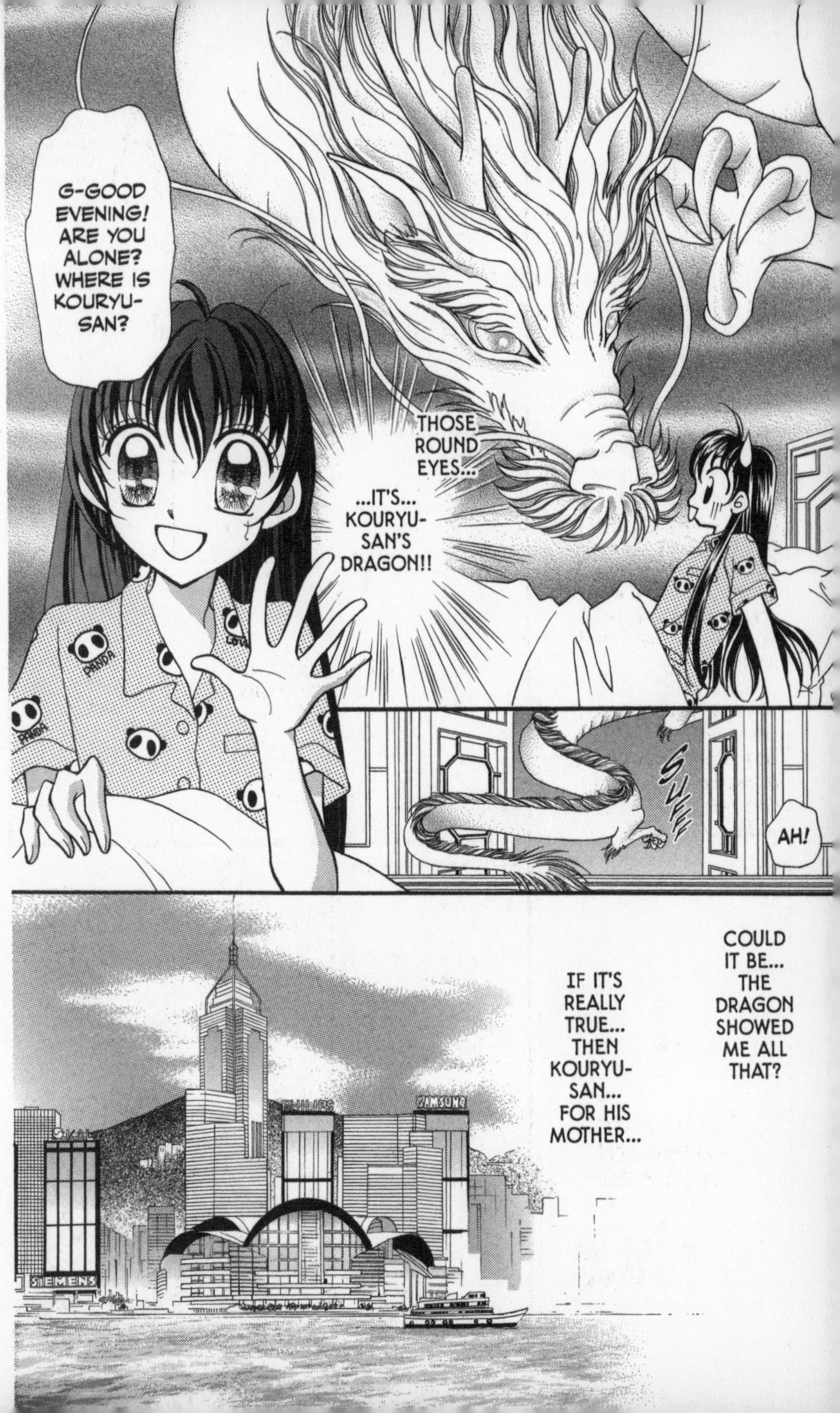
THOSE ROUND EYES...
...IT'S... KOURYU-SAN'S DRAGON!!
G-GOOD EVENING! ARE YOU ALONE? WHERE IS KOURYU-SAN?
AH!
COULD IT BE... THE DRAGON SHOWED ME ALL THAT?
IF IT'S REALLY TRUE... THEN KOURYU-SAN... FOR HIS MOTHER...
SAMSUNG
PHILIPS
SIEMENS

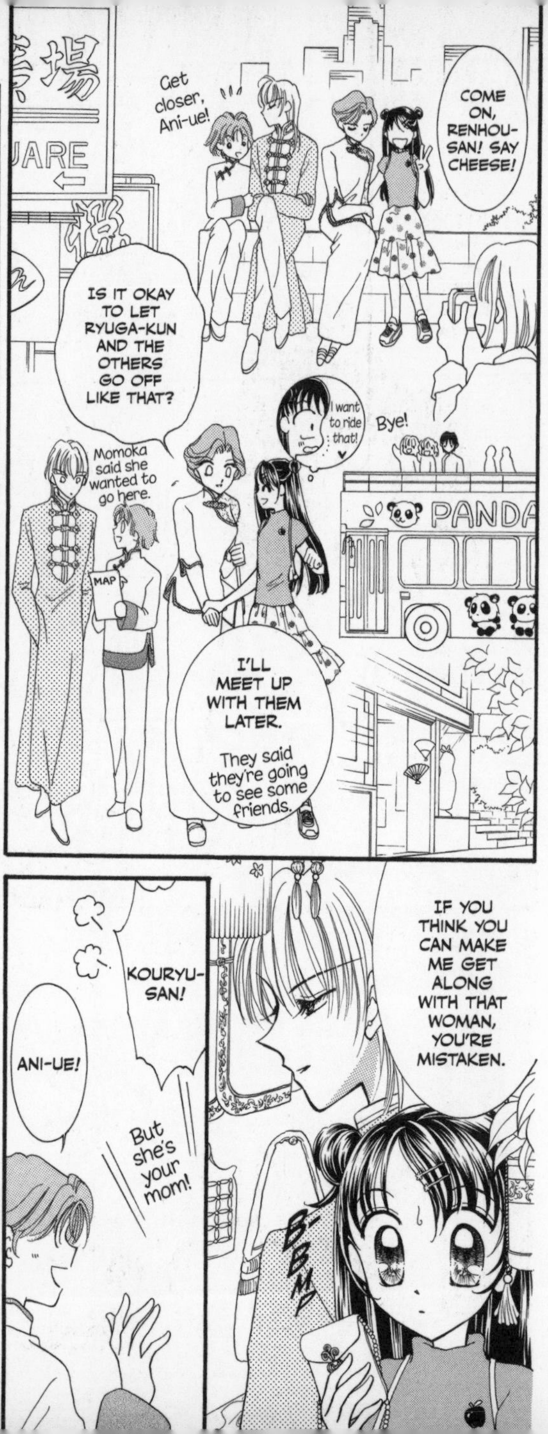
UARE
COME ON, RENHOU-SAN! SAY CHEESE!
Get closer, Ani-ue!
IS IT OKAY TO LET RYUGA-KUN AND THE OTHERS GO OFF LIKE THAT?
Bye!
I want to ride that!
PANDA
Momoka said she wanted to go here.
MAP
I'LL MEET UP WITH THEM LATER.
They said they're going to see some friends.
IF YOU THINK YOU CAN MAKE ME GET ALONG WITH THAT WOMAN, YOU'RE MISTAKEN.
B-BMP
KOURYU-SAN!
ANI-UE!
But she's your mom!

9

This is the last sidebar for this volume. This is kind of random, but in China, the number 9 is considered lucky. The next luckiest number is 8. I can understand 8, but 9 is kind of a surprise...

In vol. 3, we didn't have many pages left over, so there's no creator's pages at the end... but there are two bonus stories in this, so that'll make this volume complete, right? Should I be saying that myself?

Anyway, your letters are the source of my energy! No matter what they are, please send me your comments! Well, I'll see you in vol. 4!

Please send in your fan art! See page 198.

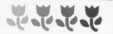

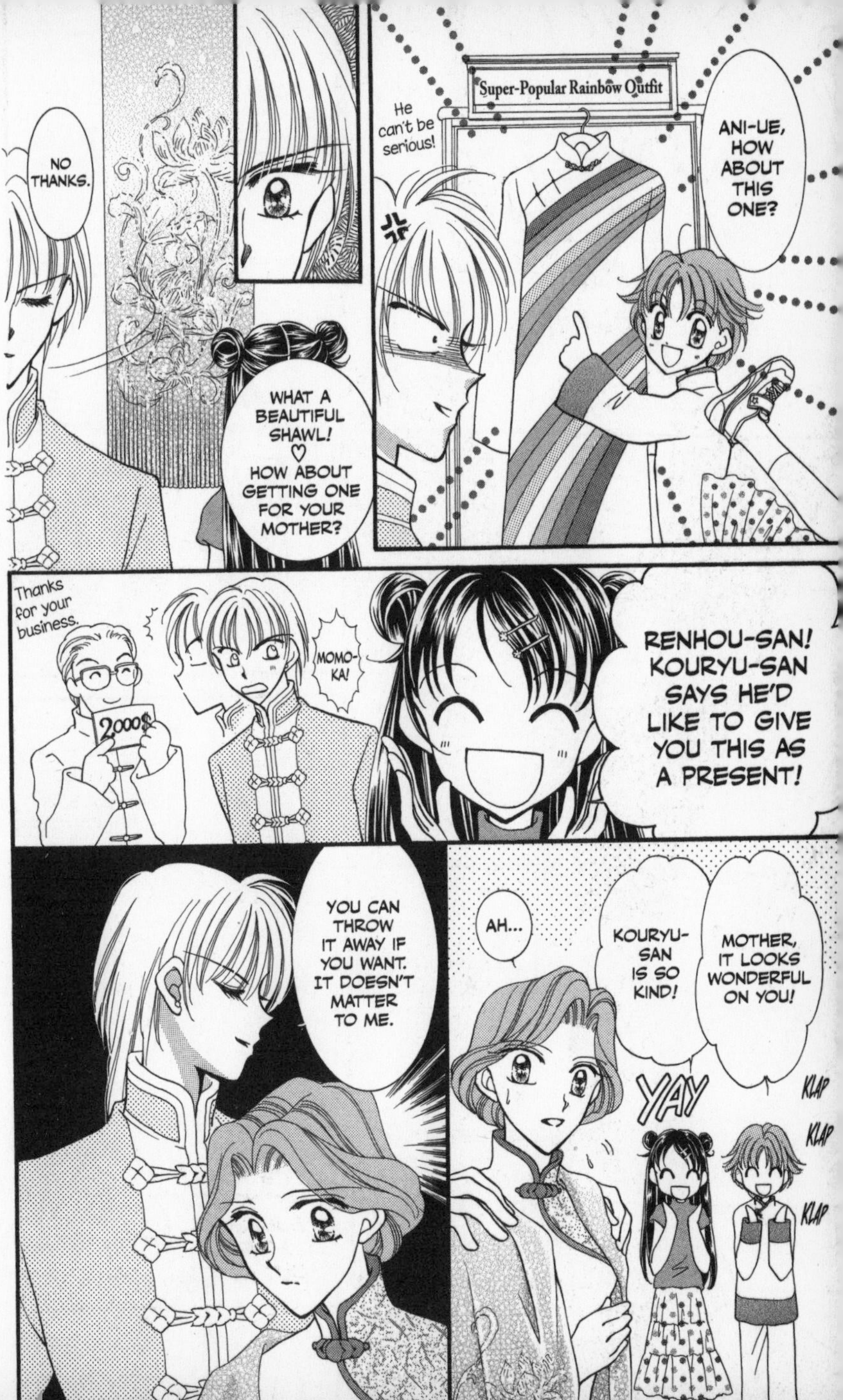
Super-Popular Rainbow Outfit
ANI-UE, HOW ABOUT THIS ONE?
He can't be serious!
WHAT A BEAUTIFUL SHAWL! ♡ HOW ABOUT GETTING ONE FOR YOUR MOTHER?
NO THANKS.
RENHOU-SAN! KOURYU-SAN SAYS HE'D LIKE TO GIVE YOU THIS AS A PRESENT!
MOMO-KA!
2000$
Thanks for your business.
MOTHER, IT LOOKS WONDERFUL ON YOU!
KOURYU-SAN IS SO KIND!
AH...
YAY
KLAP
KLAP
KLAP
YOU CAN THROW IT AWAY IF YOU WANT. IT DOESN'T MATTER TO ME.

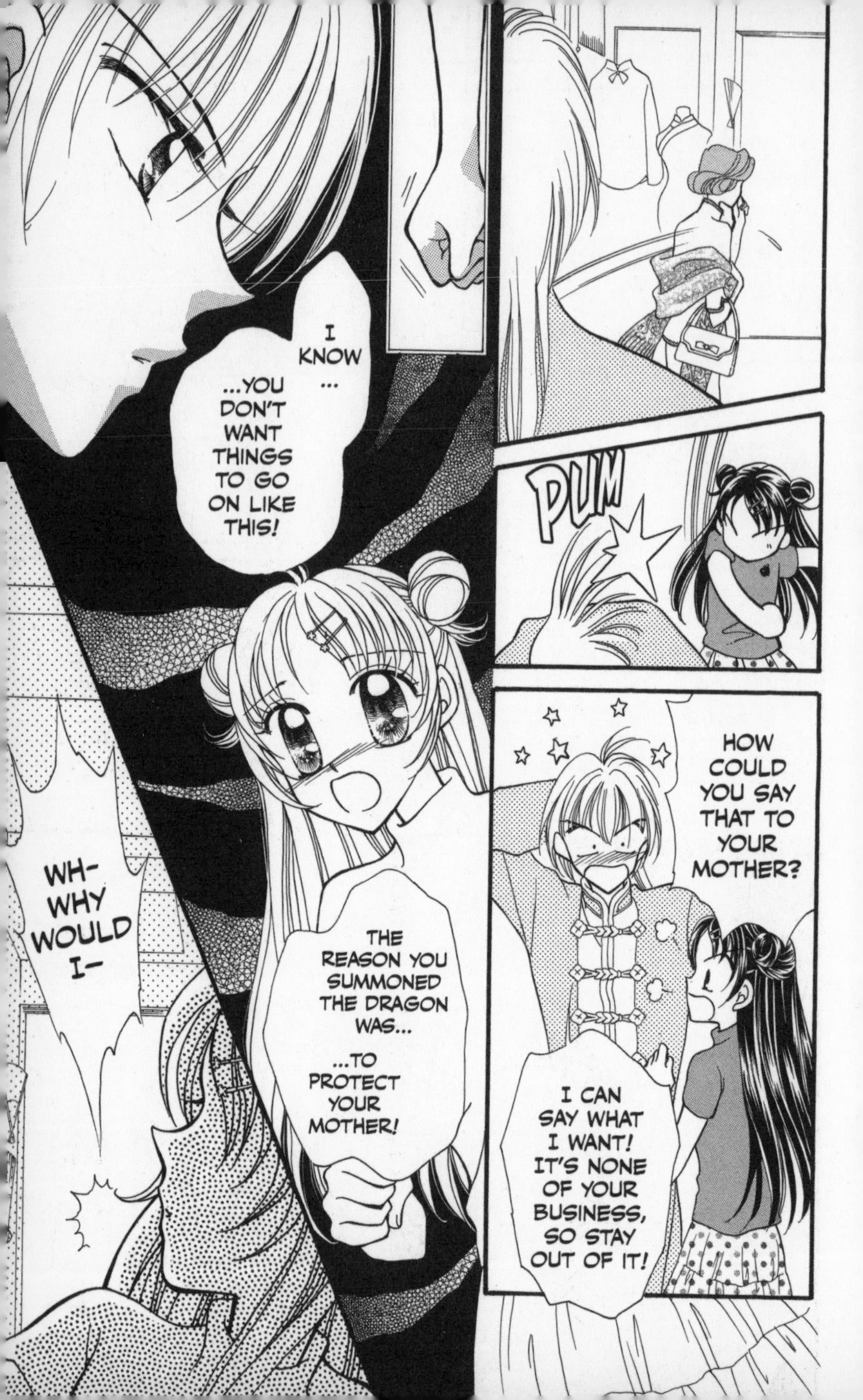
PUM
HOW COULD YOU SAY THAT TO YOUR MOTHER?
I CAN SAY WHAT I WANT! IT'S NONE OF YOUR BUSINESS, SO STAY OUT OF IT!
I KNOW ...
...YOU DON'T WANT THINGS TO GO ON LIKE THIS!
THE REASON YOU SUMMONED THE DRAGON WAS...
...TO PROTECT YOUR MOTHER!
WH-WHY WOULD I-

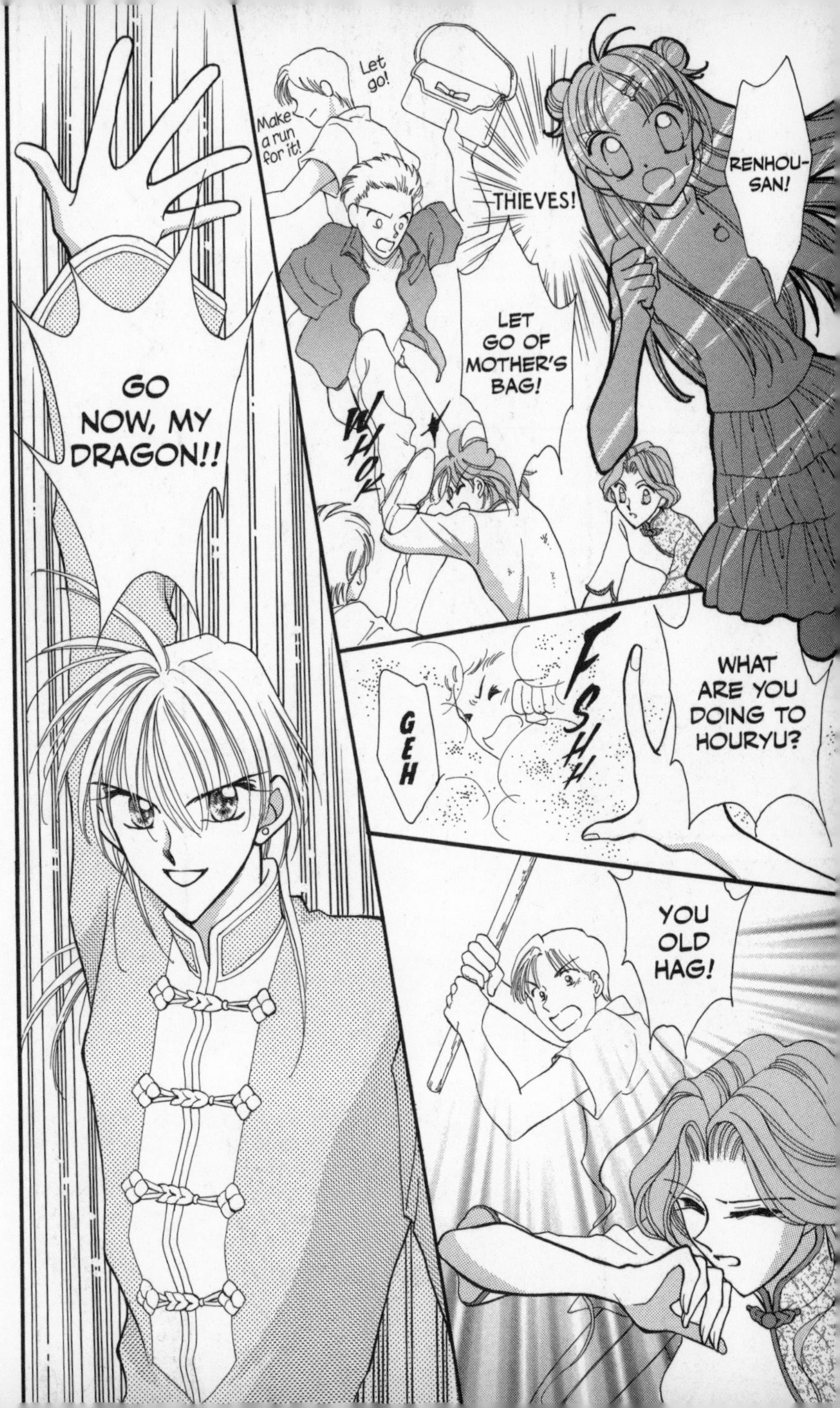
RENHOU-SAN!
THIEVES!
Let go!
Make a run for it!
LET GO OF MOTHER'S BAG!
WHOY
WHAT ARE YOU DOING TO HOURYU?
FSHH
GEH
YOU OLD HAG!
GO NOW, MY DRAGON!!

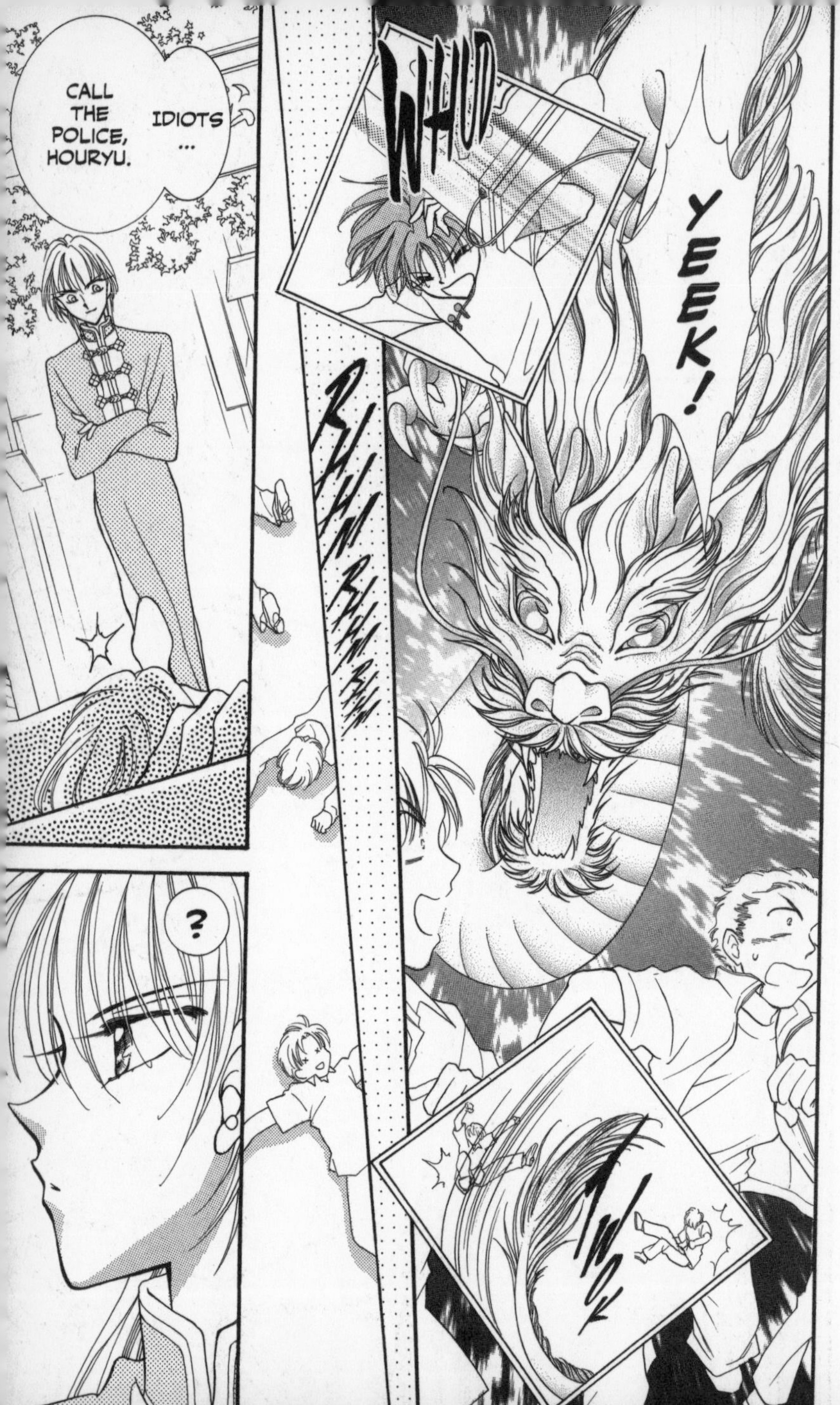
WHUD
YEEK!
IDIOTS ...
CALL THE POLICE, HOURYU.
?

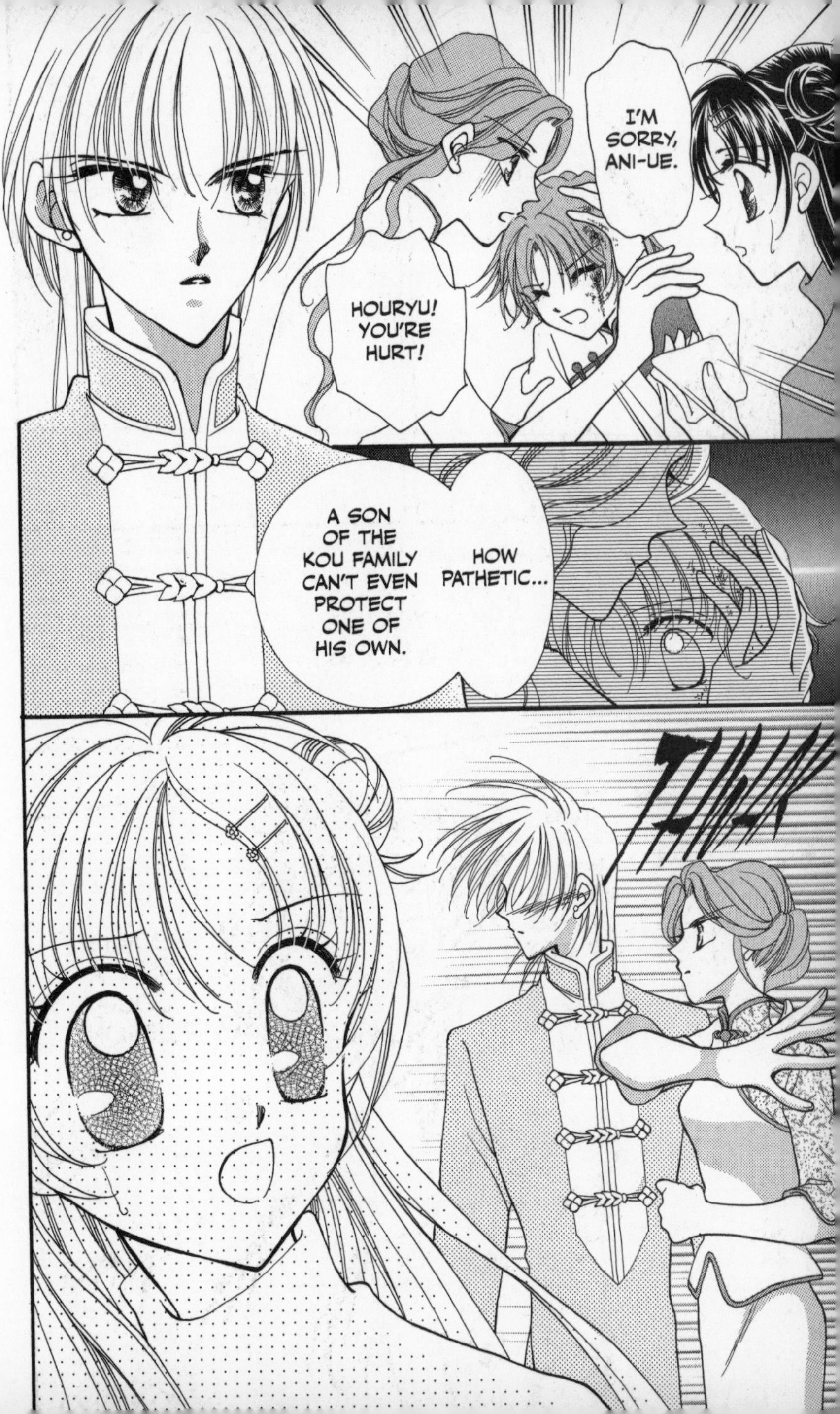
I'M SORRY, ANI-UE.
HOURYU! YOU'RE HURT!
HOW PATHETIC...
A SON OF THE KOU FAMILY CAN'T EVEN PROTECT ONE OF HIS OWN.

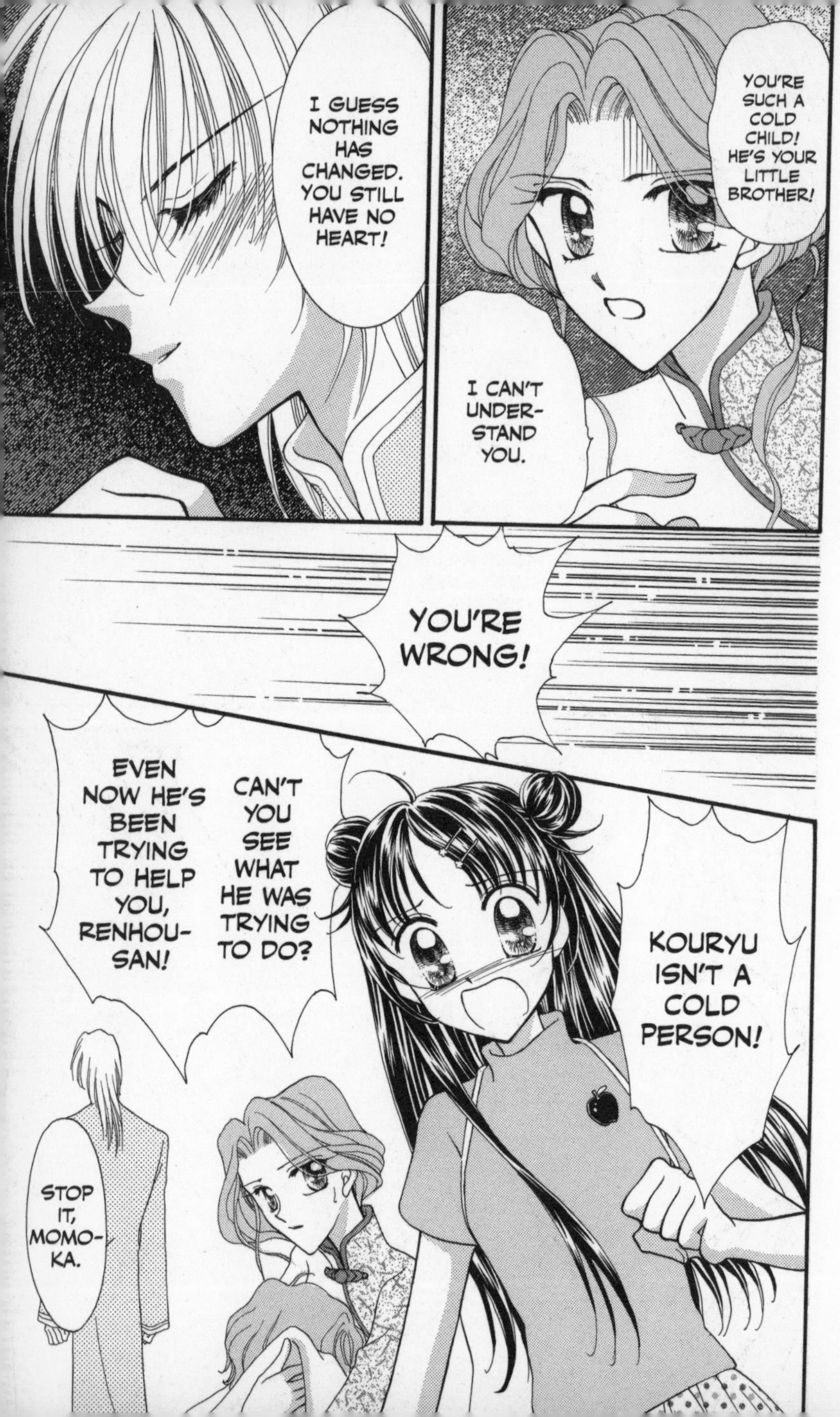
YOU'RE SUCH A COLD CHILD! HE'S YOUR LITTLE BROTHER!
I CAN'T UNDER-STAND YOU.
I GUESS NOTHING HAS CHANGED. YOU STILL HAVE NO HEART!
YOU'RE WRONG!
KOURYU ISN'T A COLD PERSON!
CAN'T YOU SEE WHAT HE WAS TRYING TO DO?
EVEN NOW HE'S BEEN TRYING TO HELP YOU, RENHOU-SAN!
STOP IT, MOMO-KA.

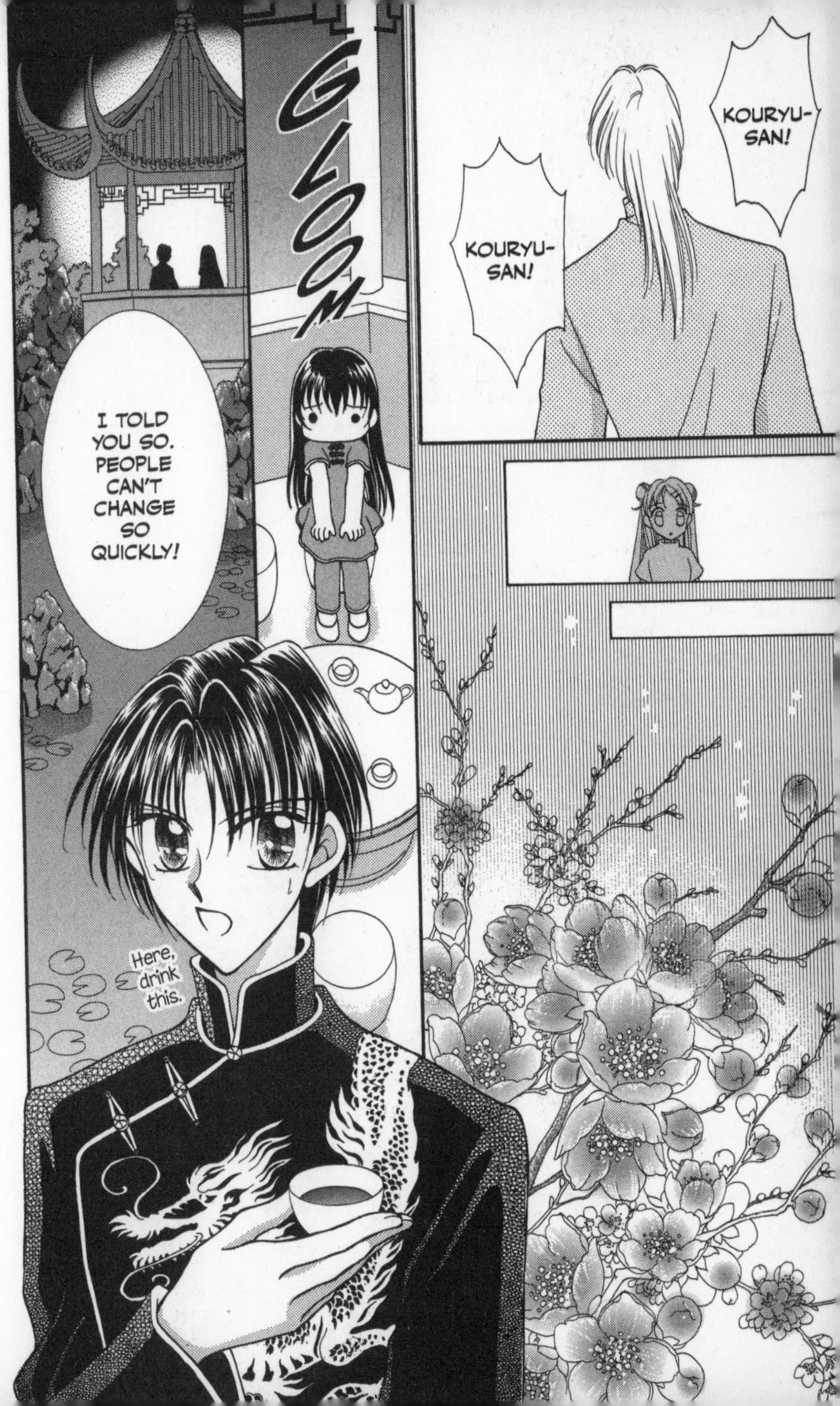
KOURYU-SAN!
KOURYU-SAN!
GLOOM
I TOLD YOU SO. PEOPLE CAN'T CHANGE SO QUICKLY!
Here, drink this.

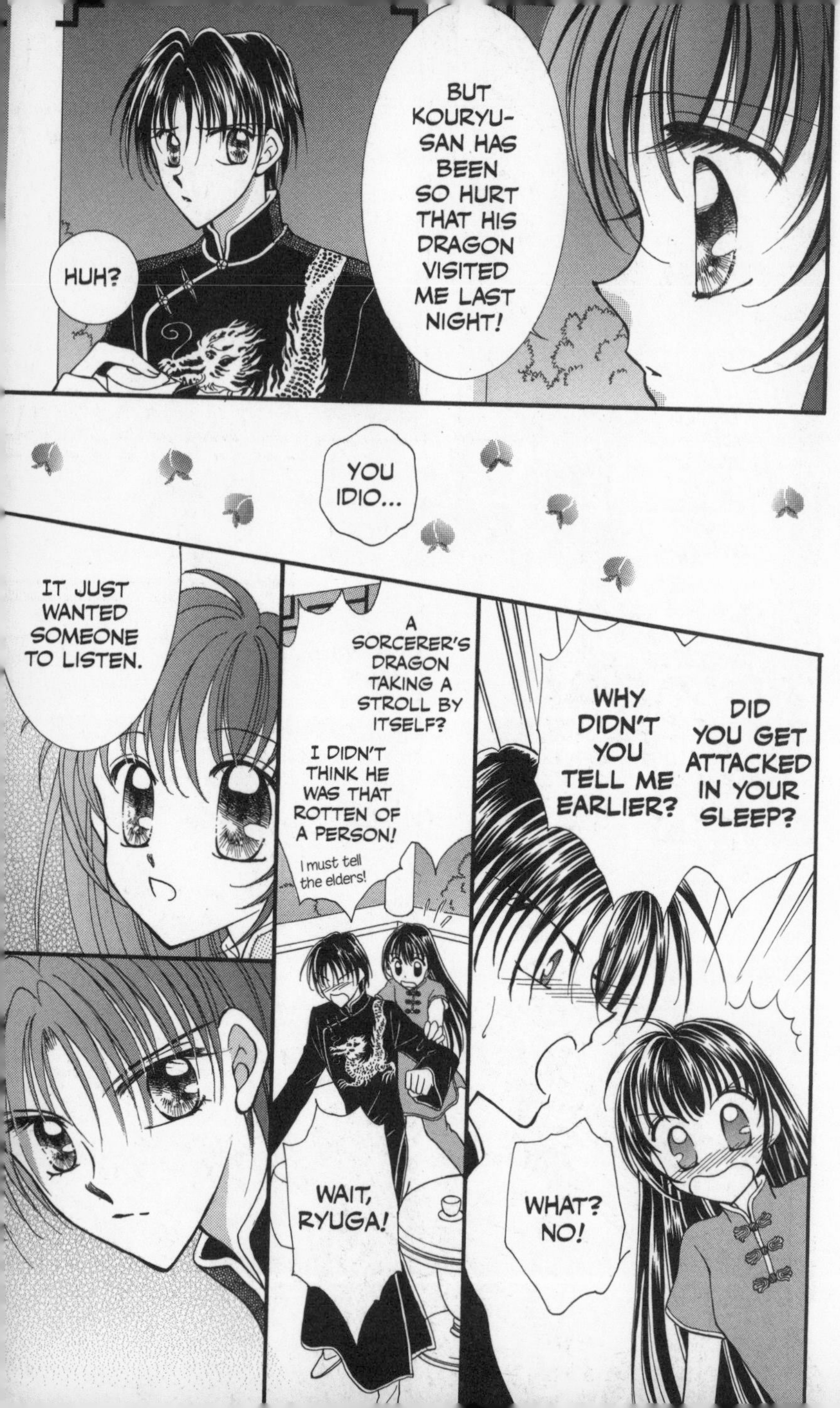
BUT KOURYU-SAN HAS BEEN SO HURT THAT HIS DRAGON VISITED ME LAST NIGHT!
HUH?
YOU IDIO...
DID YOU GET ATTACKED IN YOUR SLEEP?
WHY DIDN'T YOU TELL ME EARLIER?
WHAT? NO!
A SORCERER'S DRAGON TAKING A STROLL BY ITSELF?
I DIDN'T THINK HE WAS THAT ROTTEN OF A PERSON!
I must tell the elders!
WAIT, RYUGA!
IT JUST WANTED SOMEONE TO LISTEN.

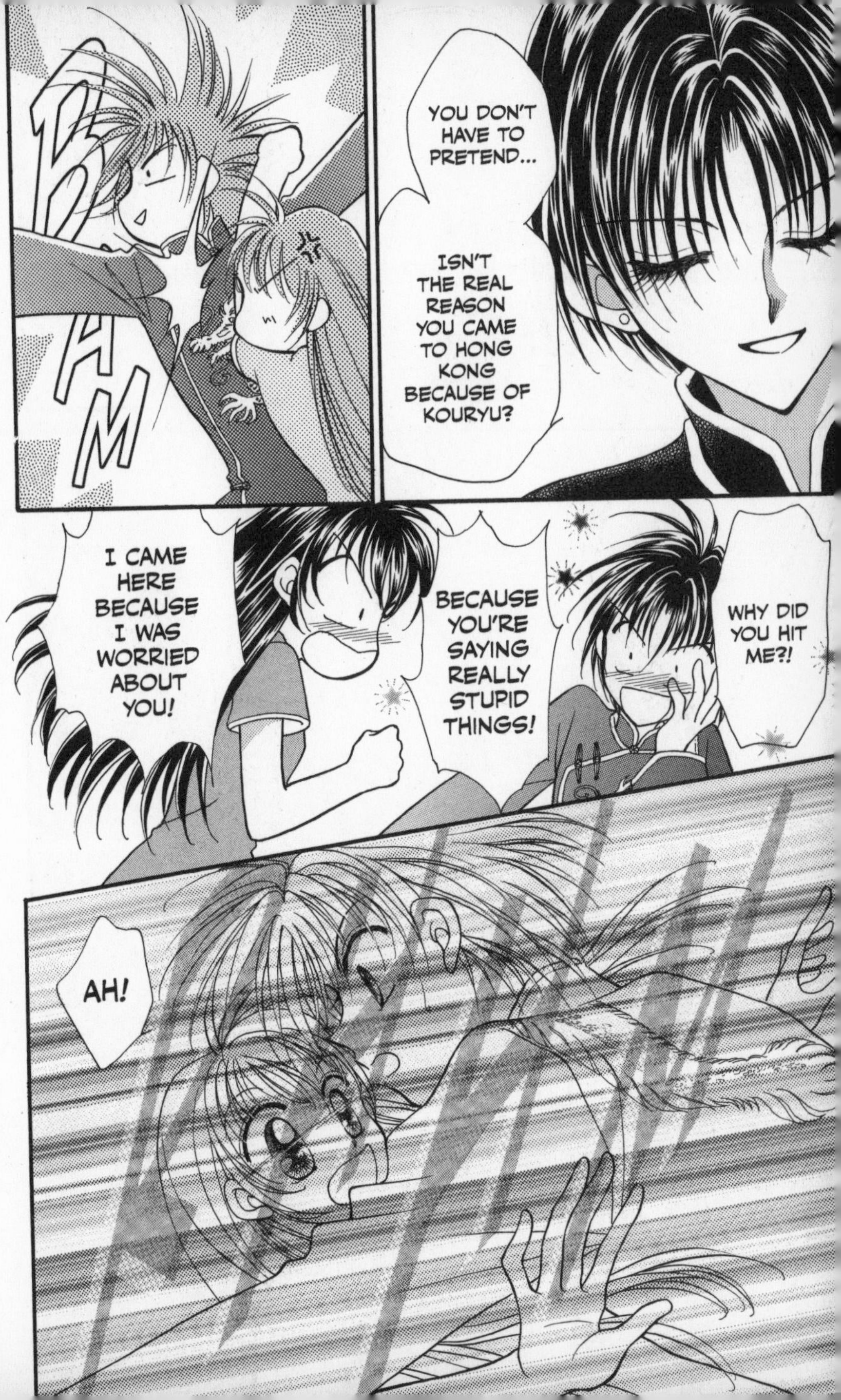
YOU DON'T HAVE TO PRETEND...
ISN'T THE REAL REASON YOU CAME TO HONG KONG BECAUSE OF KOURYU?
BAM
WHY DID YOU HIT ME?!
BECAUSE YOU'RE SAYING REALLY STUPID THINGS!
I CAME HERE BECAUSE I WAS WORRIED ABOUT YOU!
AH!

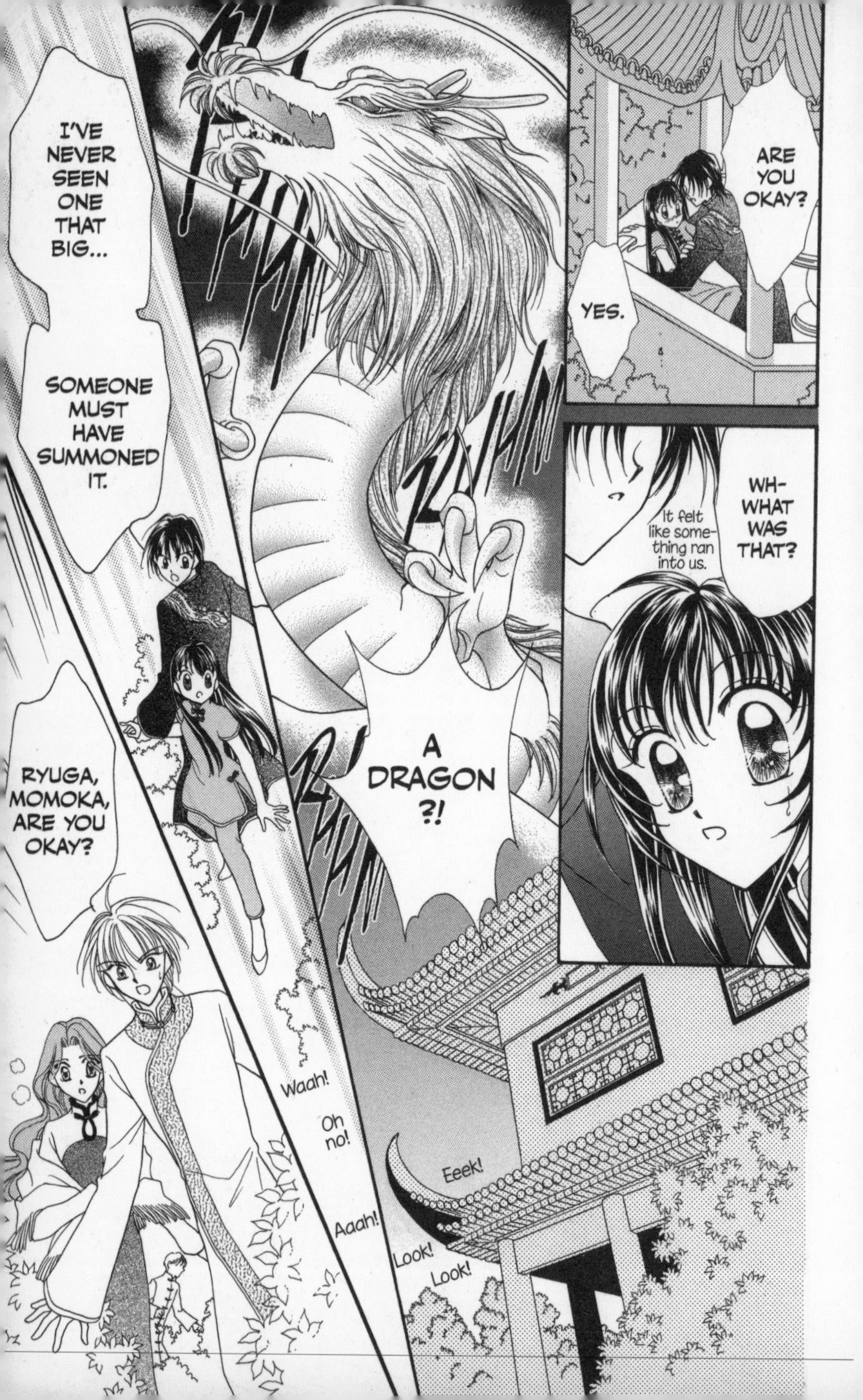
ARE YOU OKAY?
YES.
WH-WHAT WAS THAT?
It felt like something ran into us.
A DRAGON?!
Eeek!
Look!
Look!
Aaah!
Oh no!
Waah!
I'VE NEVER SEEN ONE THAT BIG...
SOMEONE MUST HAVE SUMMONED IT.
RYUGA, MOMOKA, ARE YOU OKAY?

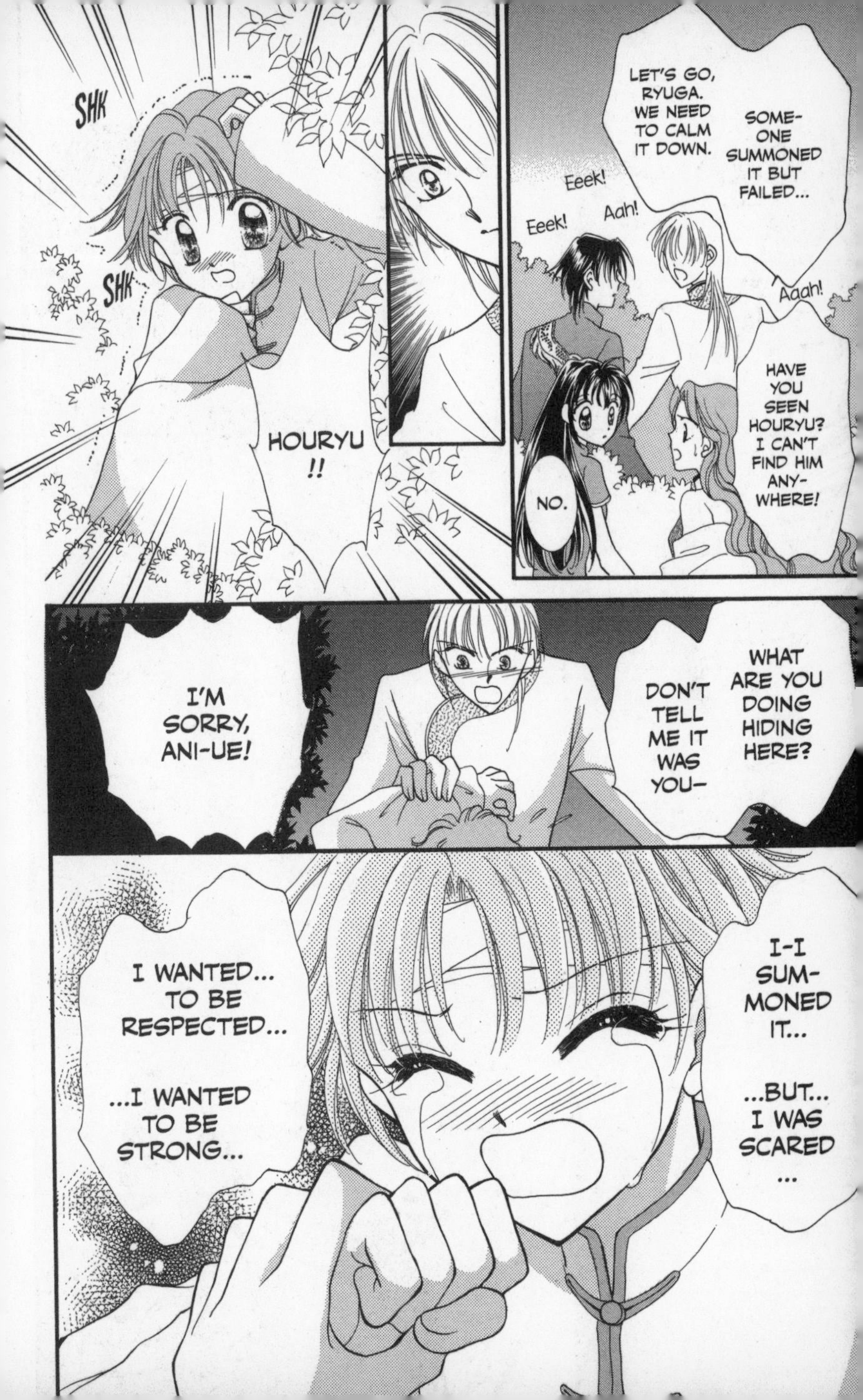
SOME-ONE SUMMONED IT BUT FAILED...
LET'S GO, RYUGA. WE NEED TO CALM IT DOWN.
Eeek!
Aah!
Eeek!
Aaah!
HAVE YOU SEEN HOURYU? I CAN'T FIND HIM ANY-WHERE!
NO.
SHK
SHK
HOURYU !!
WHAT ARE YOU DOING HIDING HERE?
DON'T TELL ME IT WAS YOU—
I'M SORRY, ANI-UE!
I-I SUM-MONED IT...
...BUT... I WAS SCARED ...
I WANTED... TO BE RESPECTED...
...I WANTED TO BE STRONG...

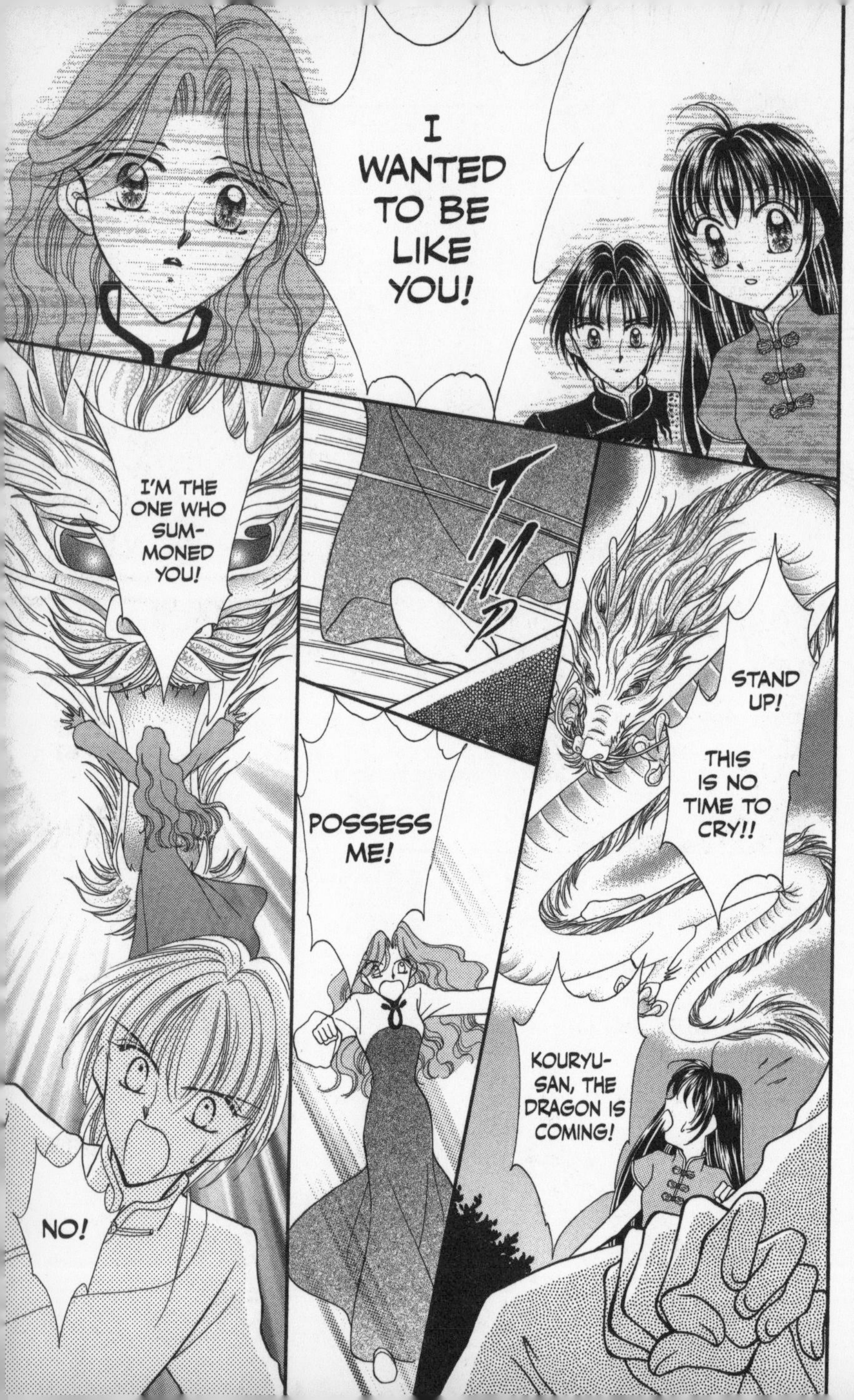
I WANTED TO BE LIKE YOU!
STAND UP!
THIS IS NO TIME TO CRY!!
KOURYU-SAN, THE DRAGON IS COMING!
POSSESS ME!
I'M THE ONE WHO SUM-MONED YOU!
NO!

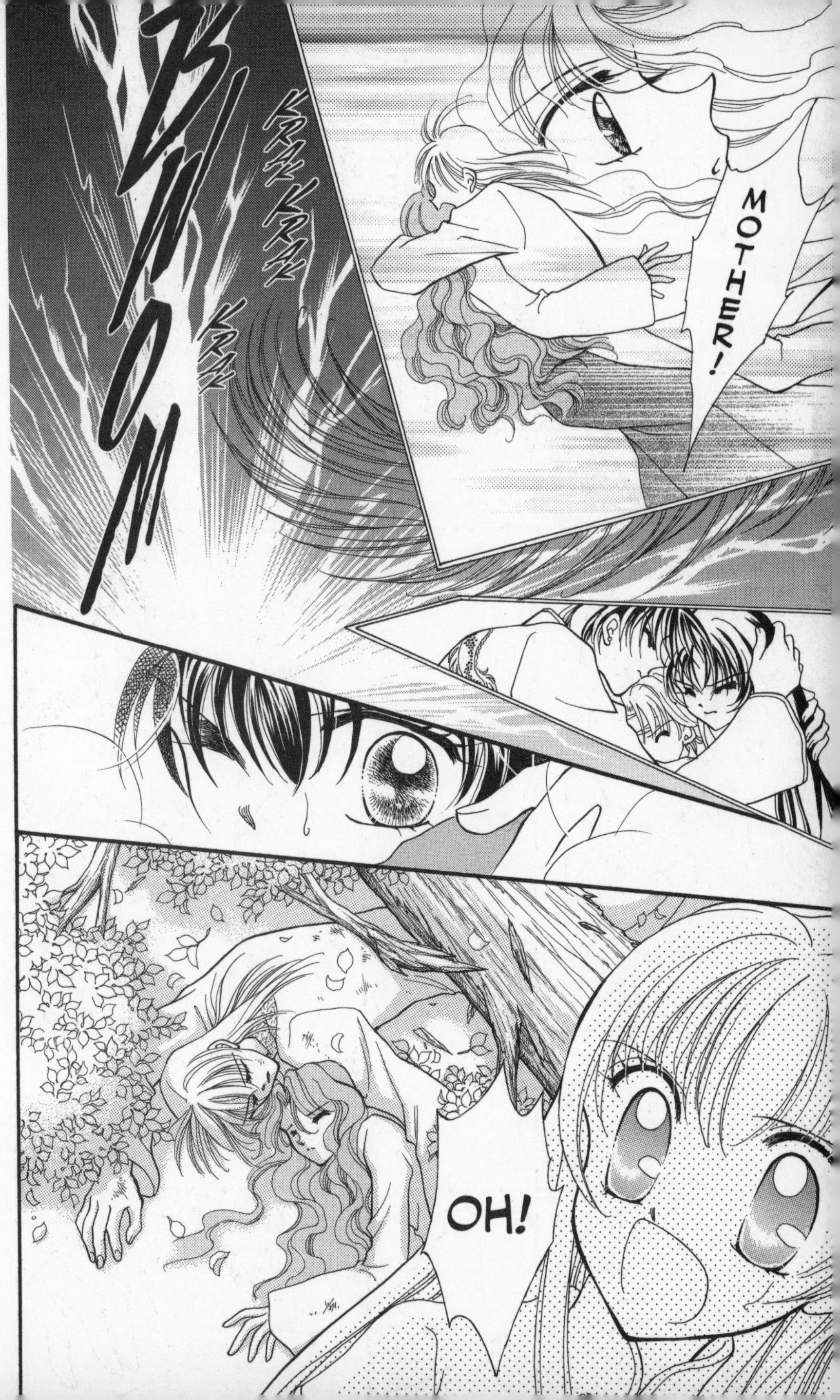
MOTHER!
KRAK KRAK KRAK
OH!

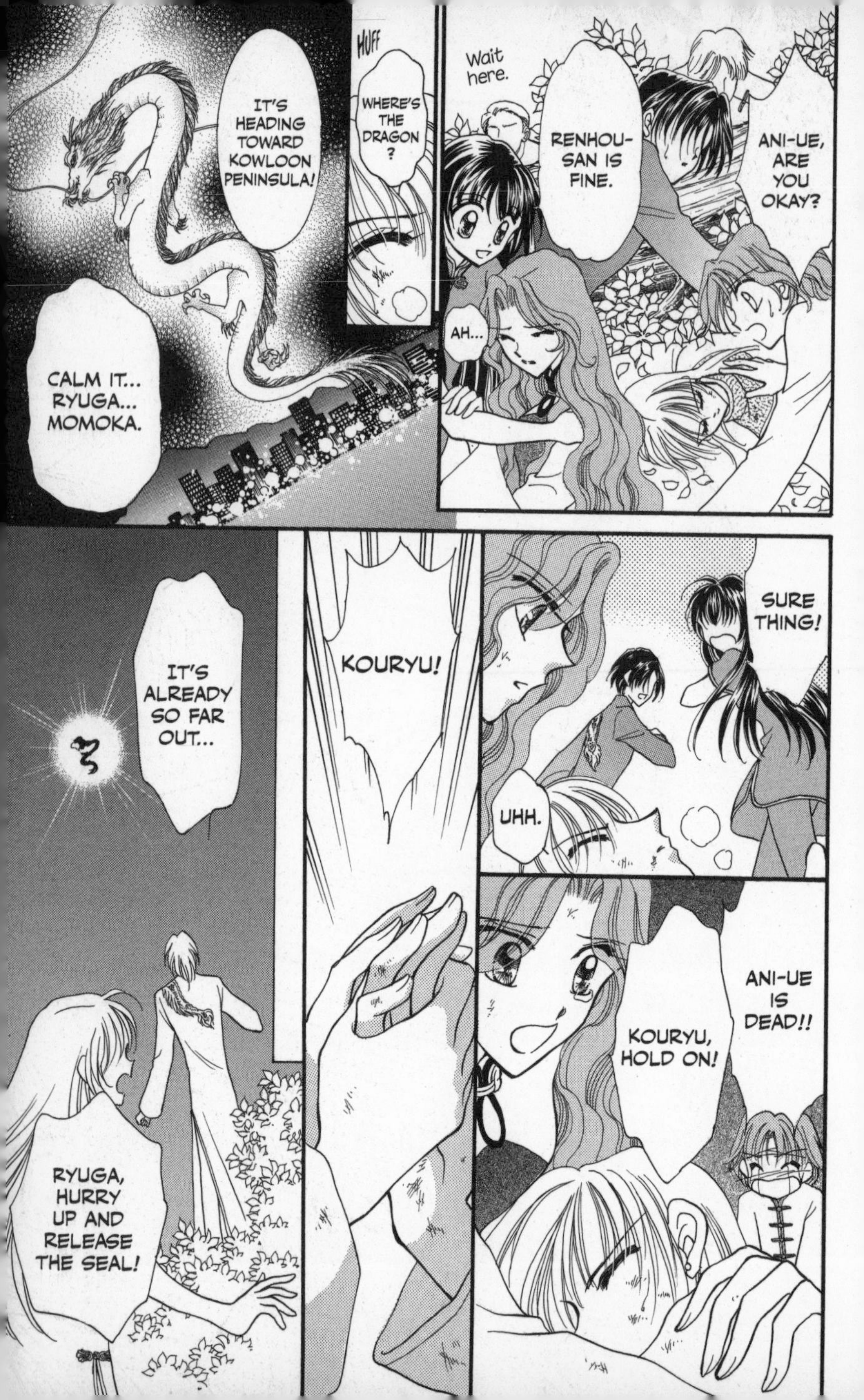
ANI-UE, ARE YOU OKAY?
RENHOU-SAN IS FINE.
Wait here.
AH...
HUFF
WHERE'S THE DRAGON?
IT'S HEADING TOWARD KOWLOON PENINSULA!
CALM IT... RYUGA... MOMOKA.
SURE THING!
UHH.
ANI-UE IS DEAD!!
KOURYU, HOLD ON!
KOURYU!
IT'S ALREADY SO FAR OUT...
RYUGA, HURRY UP AND RELEASE THE SEAL!

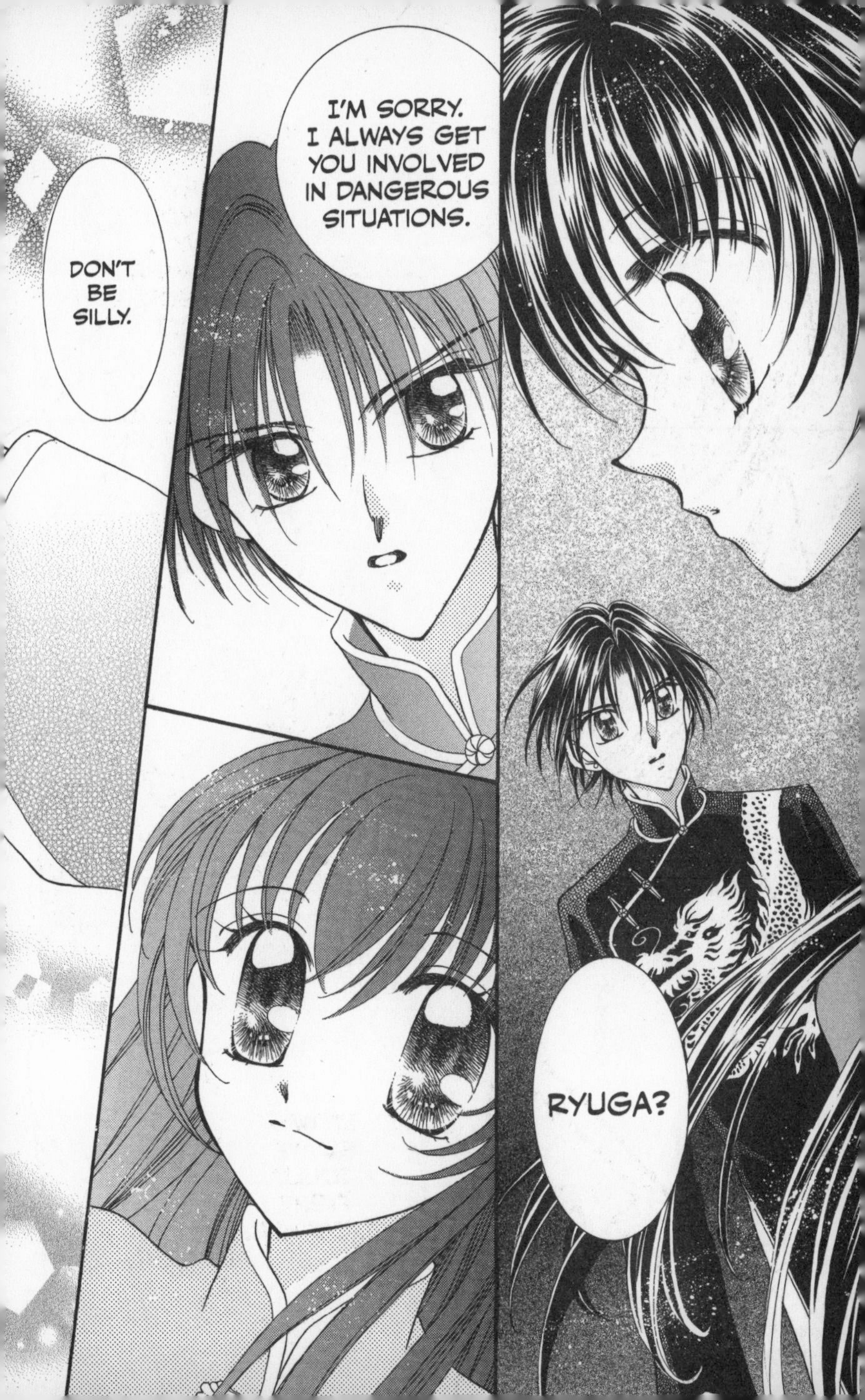
RYUGA?
I'M SORRY. I ALWAYS GET YOU INVOLVED IN DANGEROUS SITUATIONS.
DON'T BE SILLY.

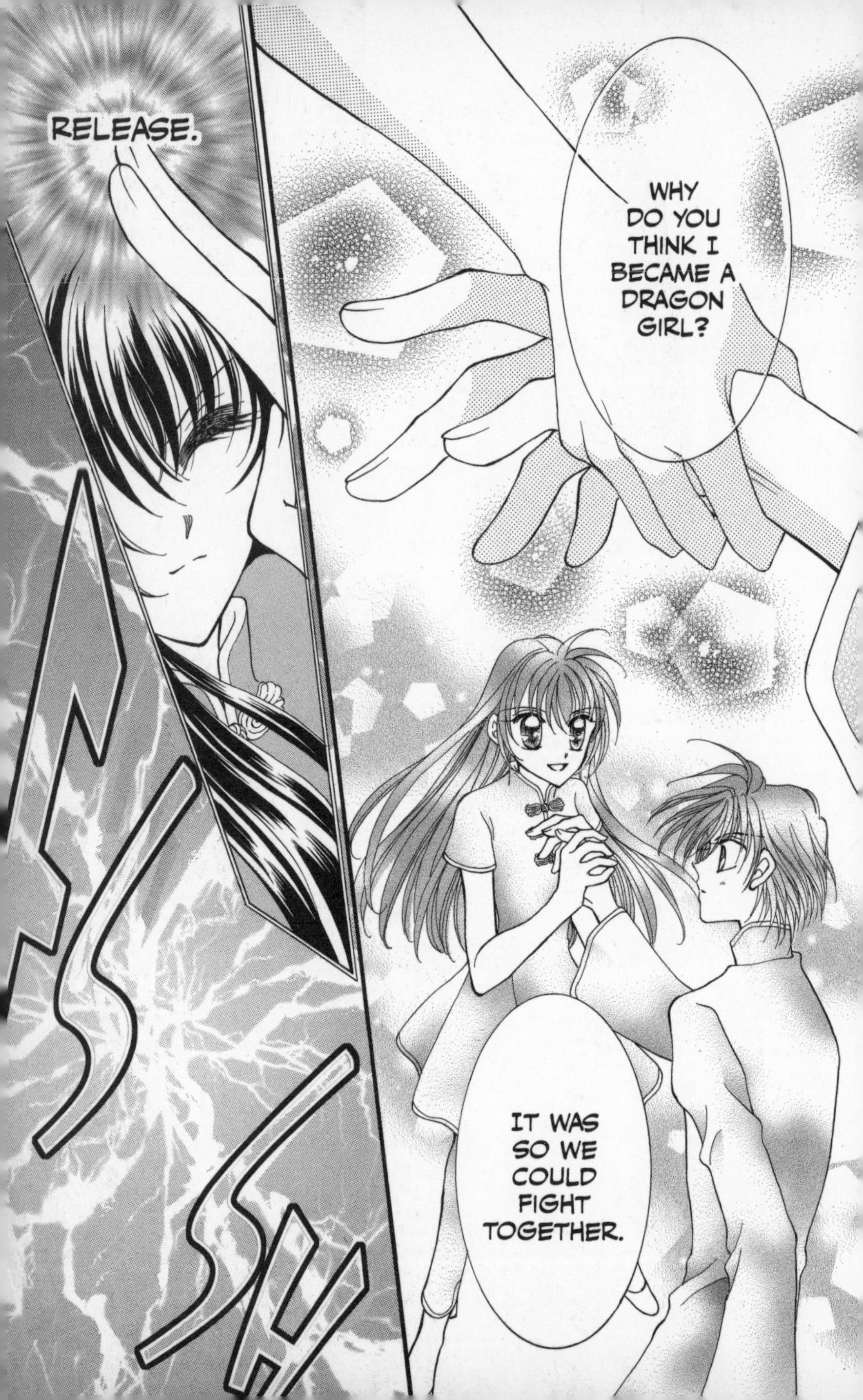
WHY DO YOU THINK I BECAME A DRAGON GIRL?
IT WAS SO WE COULD FIGHT TOGETHER.
RELEASE.

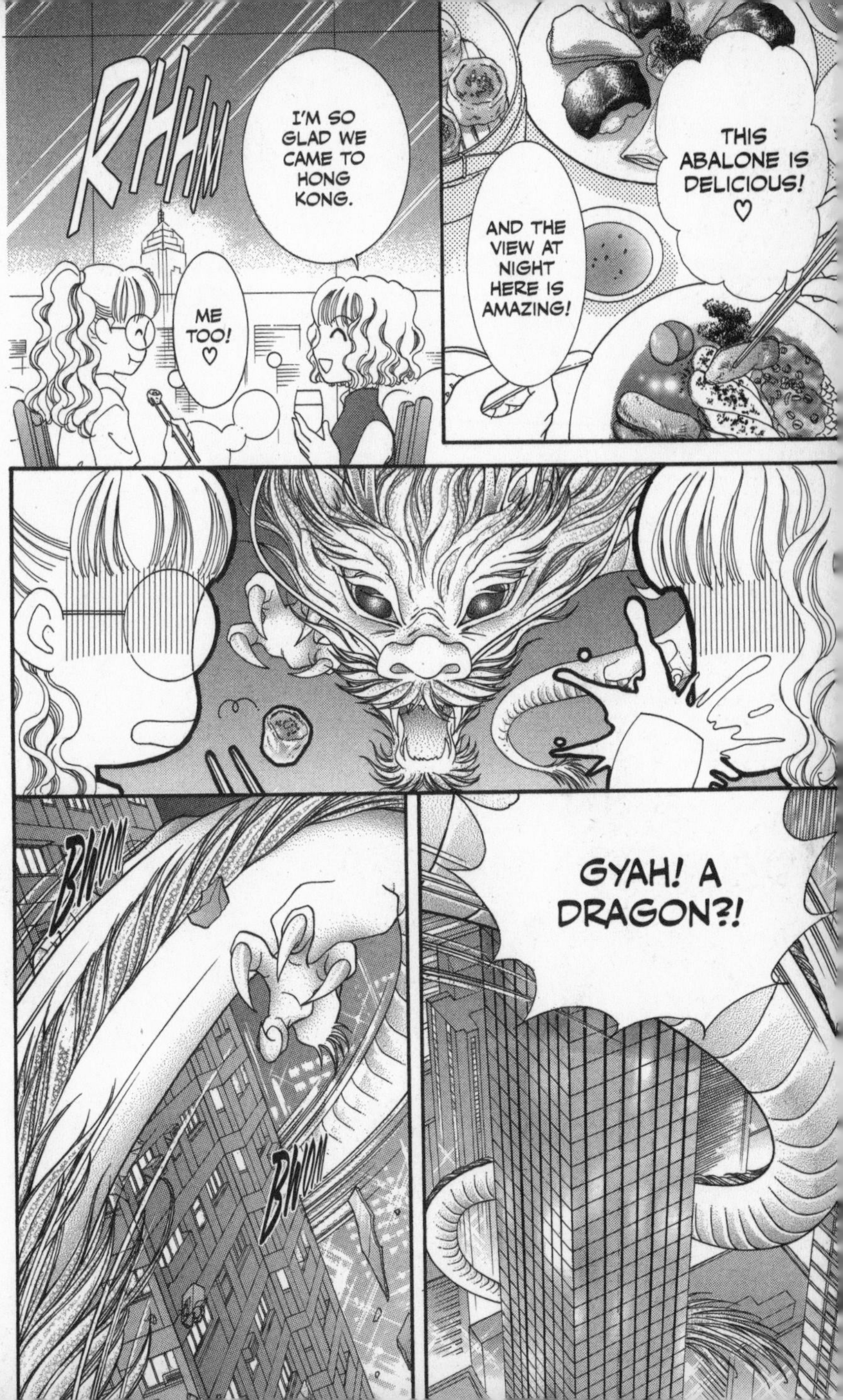
THIS ABALONE IS DELICIOUS! ♡
AND THE VIEW AT NIGHT HERE IS AMAZING!
I'M SO GLAD WE CAME TO HONG KONG.
RHHM
ME TOO! ♡
GYAH! A DRAGON?!
BWOM
BWOM

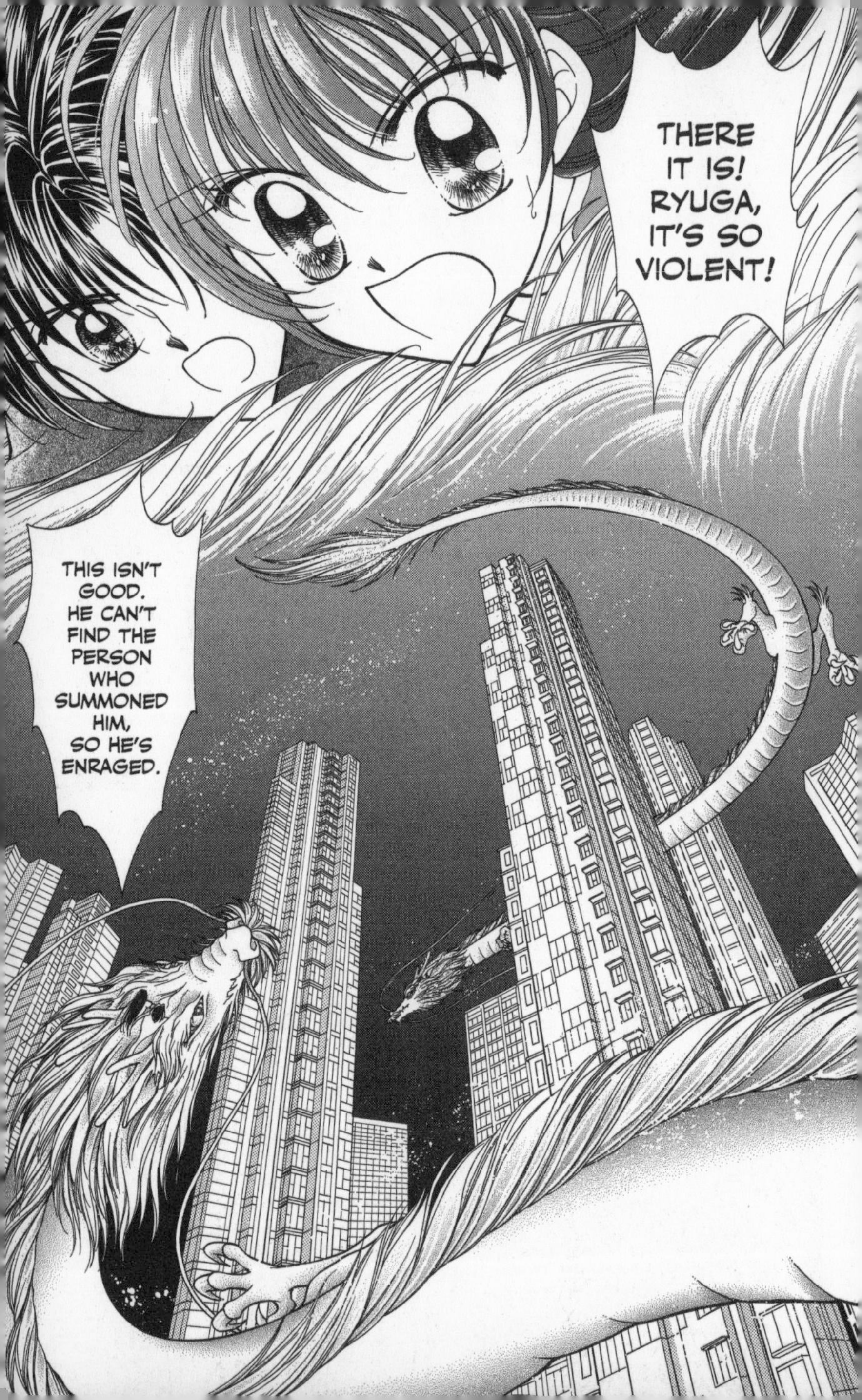
THERE IT IS! RYUGA, IT'S SO VIOLENT!
THIS ISN'T GOOD. HE CAN'T FIND THE PERSON WHO SUMMONED HIM, SO HE'S ENRAGED.

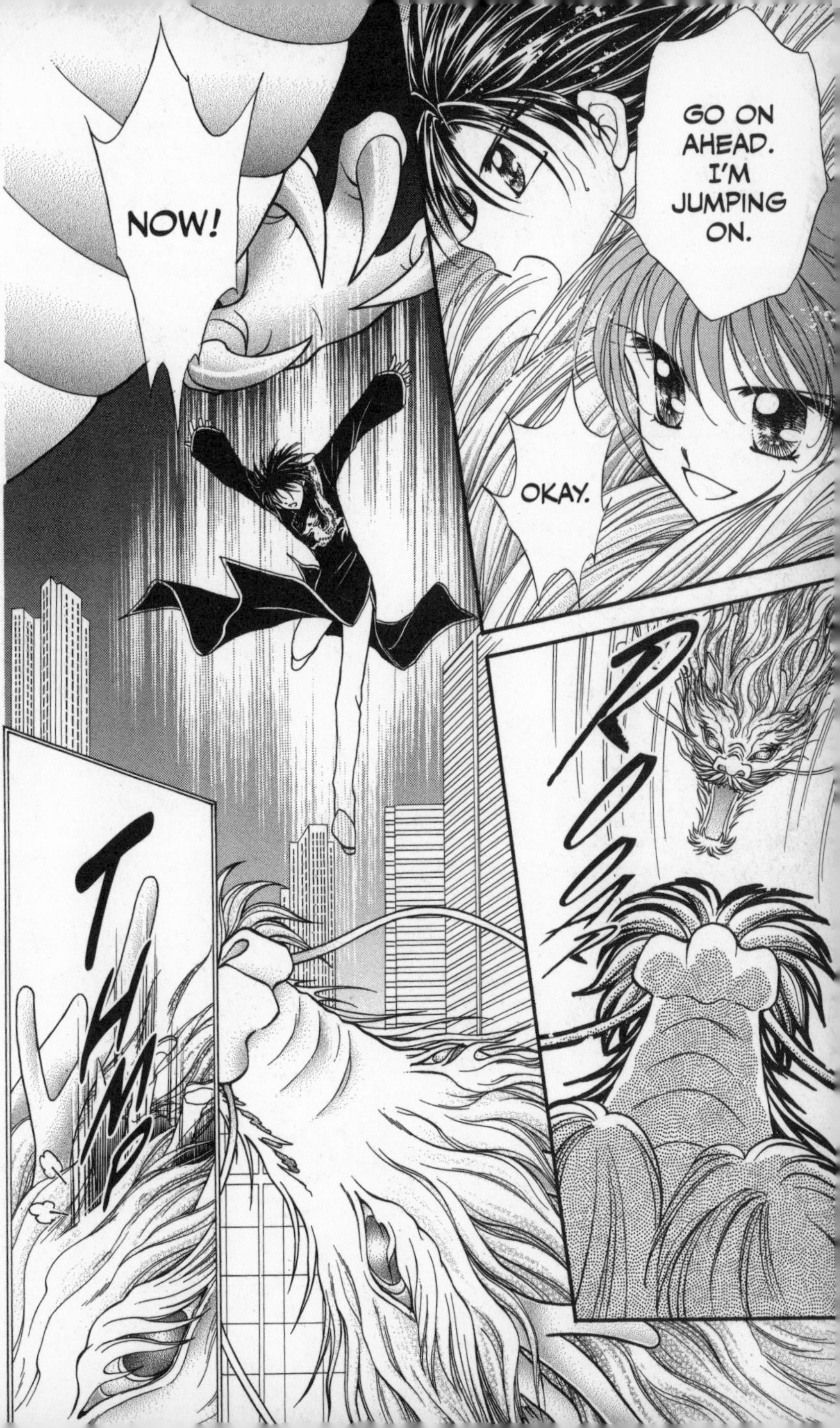
GO ON AHEAD. I'M JUMPING ON.
OKAY.
NOW!

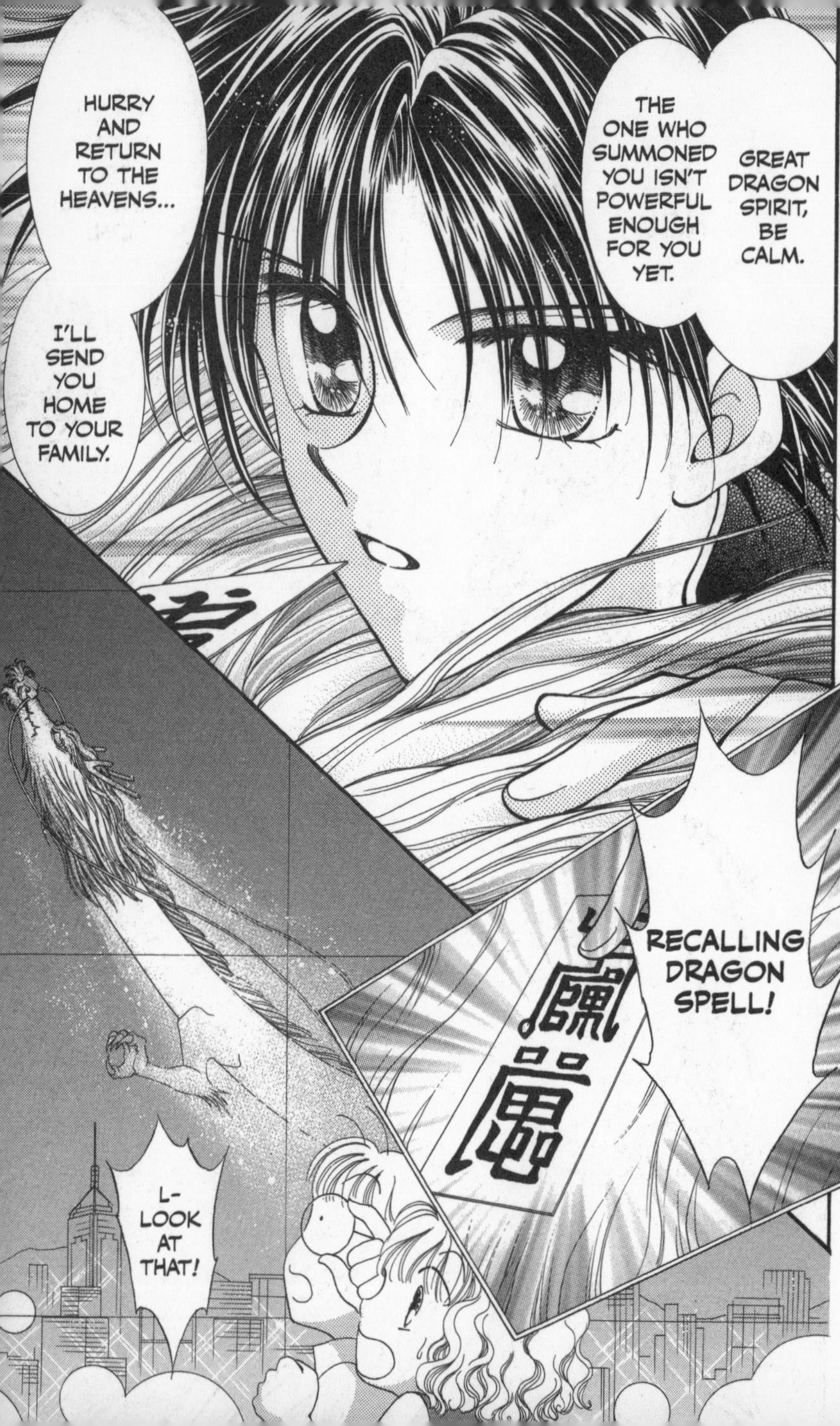
GREAT DRAGON SPIRIT, BE CALM.
THE ONE WHO SUMMONED YOU ISN'T POWERFUL ENOUGH FOR YOU YET.
HURRY AND RETURN TO THE HEAVENS...
I'LL SEND YOU HOME TO YOUR FAMILY.
RECALLING DRAGON SPELL!
L-LOOK AT THAT!

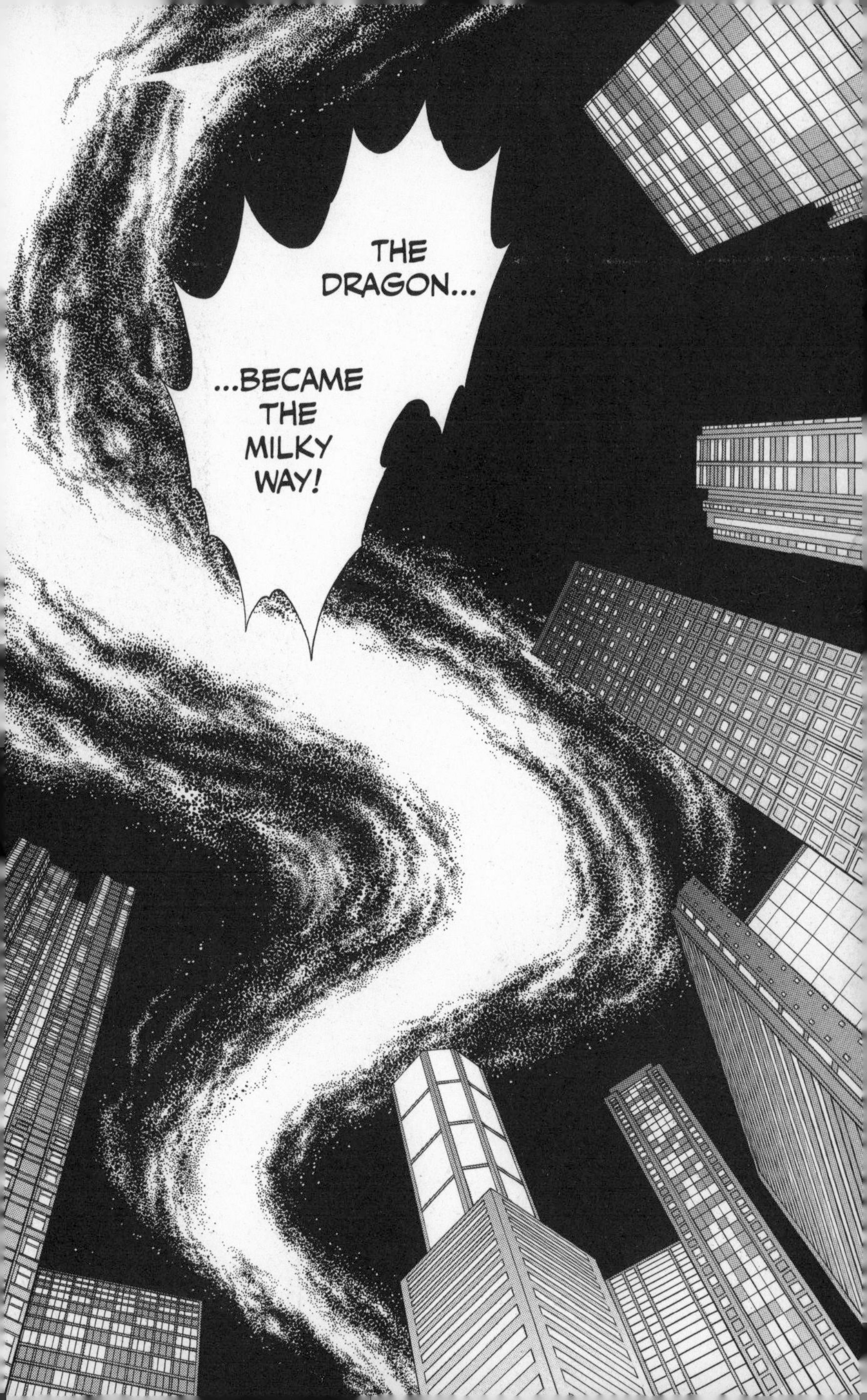
THE DRAGON...
...BECAME THE MILKY WAY!

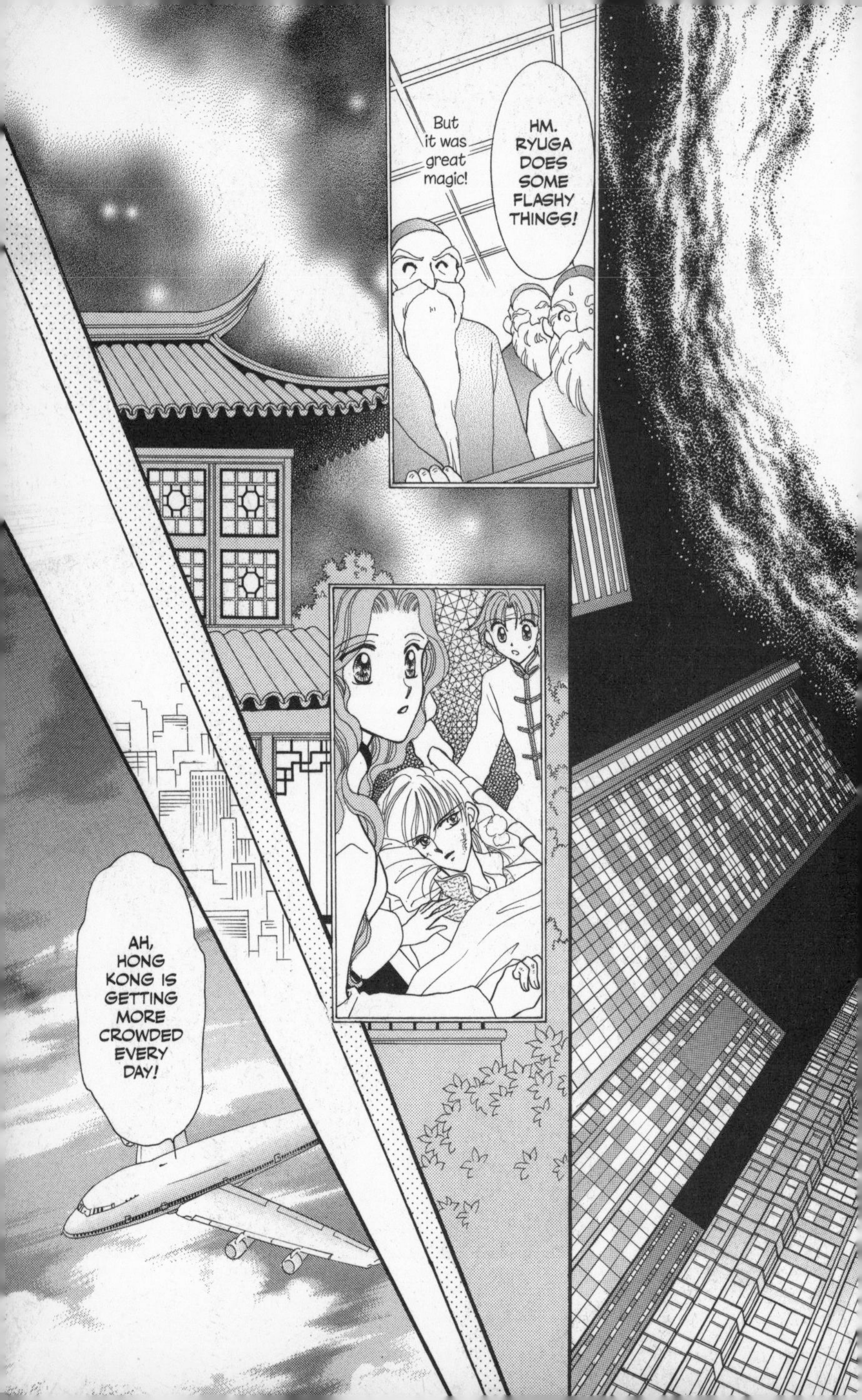
HM. RYUGA DOES SOME FLASHY THINGS!
But it was great magic!
AH, HONG KONG IS GETTING MORE CROWDED EVERY DAY!

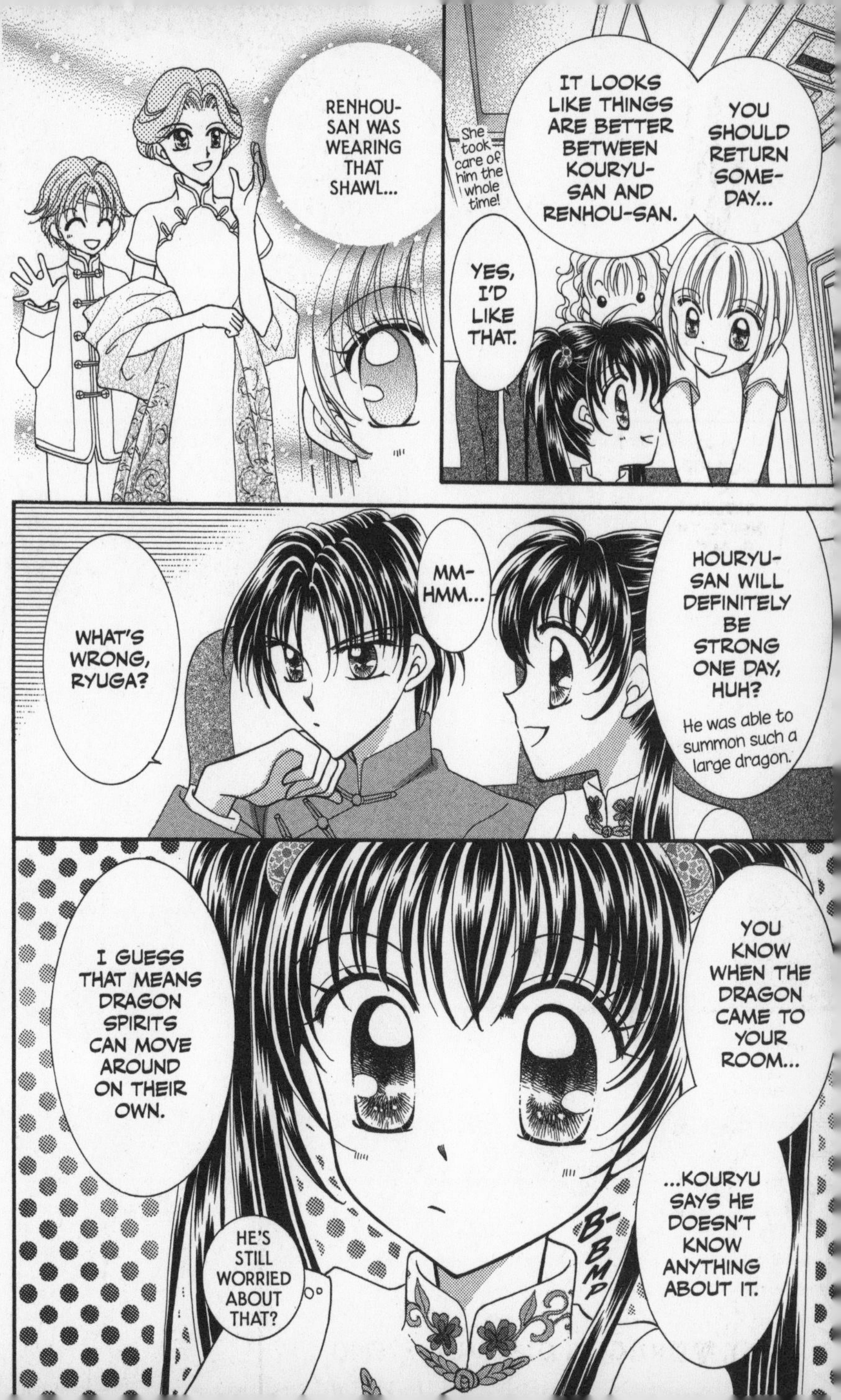
IT LOOKS LIKE THINGS ARE BETTER BETWEEN KOURYU-SAN AND RENHOU-SAN.
She took care of him the whole time!
YOU SHOULD RETURN SOME-DAY...
YES, I'D LIKE THAT.
RENHOU-SAN WAS WEARING THAT SHAWL...
HOURYU-SAN WILL DEFINITELY BE STRONG ONE DAY, HUH?
He was able to summon such a large dragon.
MM-HMM...
WHAT'S WRONG, RYUGA?
YOU KNOW WHEN THE DRAGON CAME TO YOUR ROOM...
...KOURYU SAYS HE DOESN'T KNOW ANYTHING ABOUT IT.
B-BMP
I GUESS THAT MEANS DRAGON SPIRITS CAN MOVE AROUND ON THEIR OWN.
HE'S STILL WORRIED ABOUT THAT?

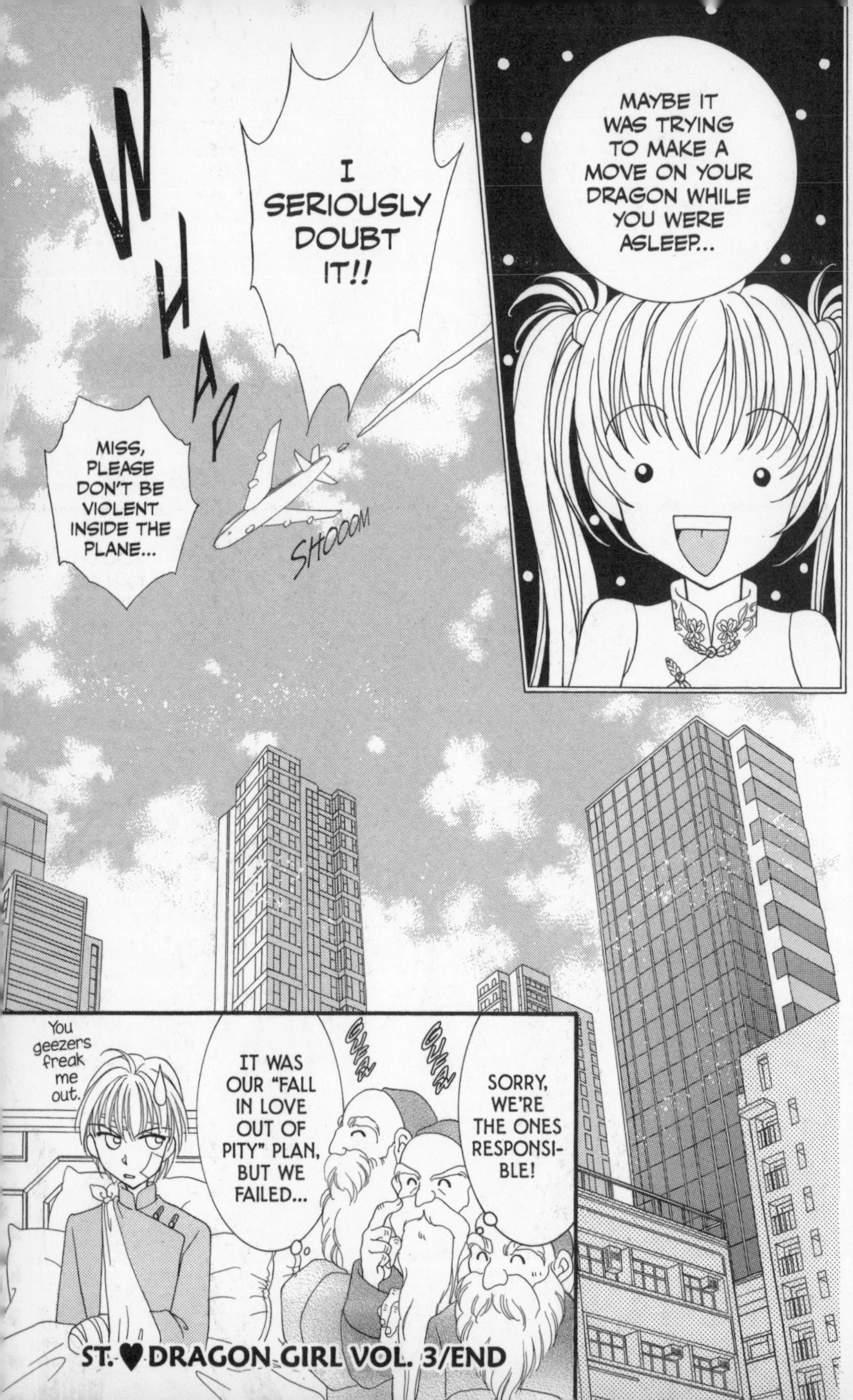
MAYBE IT WAS TRYING TO MAKE A MOVE ON YOUR DRAGON WHILE YOU WERE ASLEEP...
I SERIOUSLY DOUBT IT!!
WHAP
MISS, PLEASE DON'T BE VIOLENT INSIDE THE PLANE...
SHOOOM
SORRY, WE'RE THE ONES RESPONSI-BLE!
IT WAS OUR "FALL IN LOVE OUT OF PITY" PLAN, BUT WE FAILED...
You geezers freak me out.
ST. ♥ DRAGON GIRL VOL. 3/END

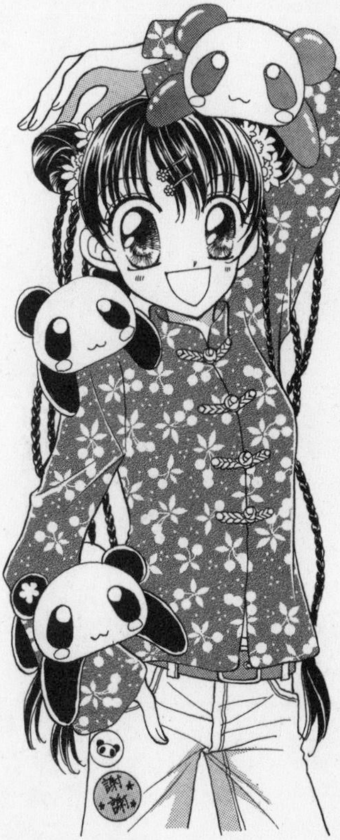
謝謝

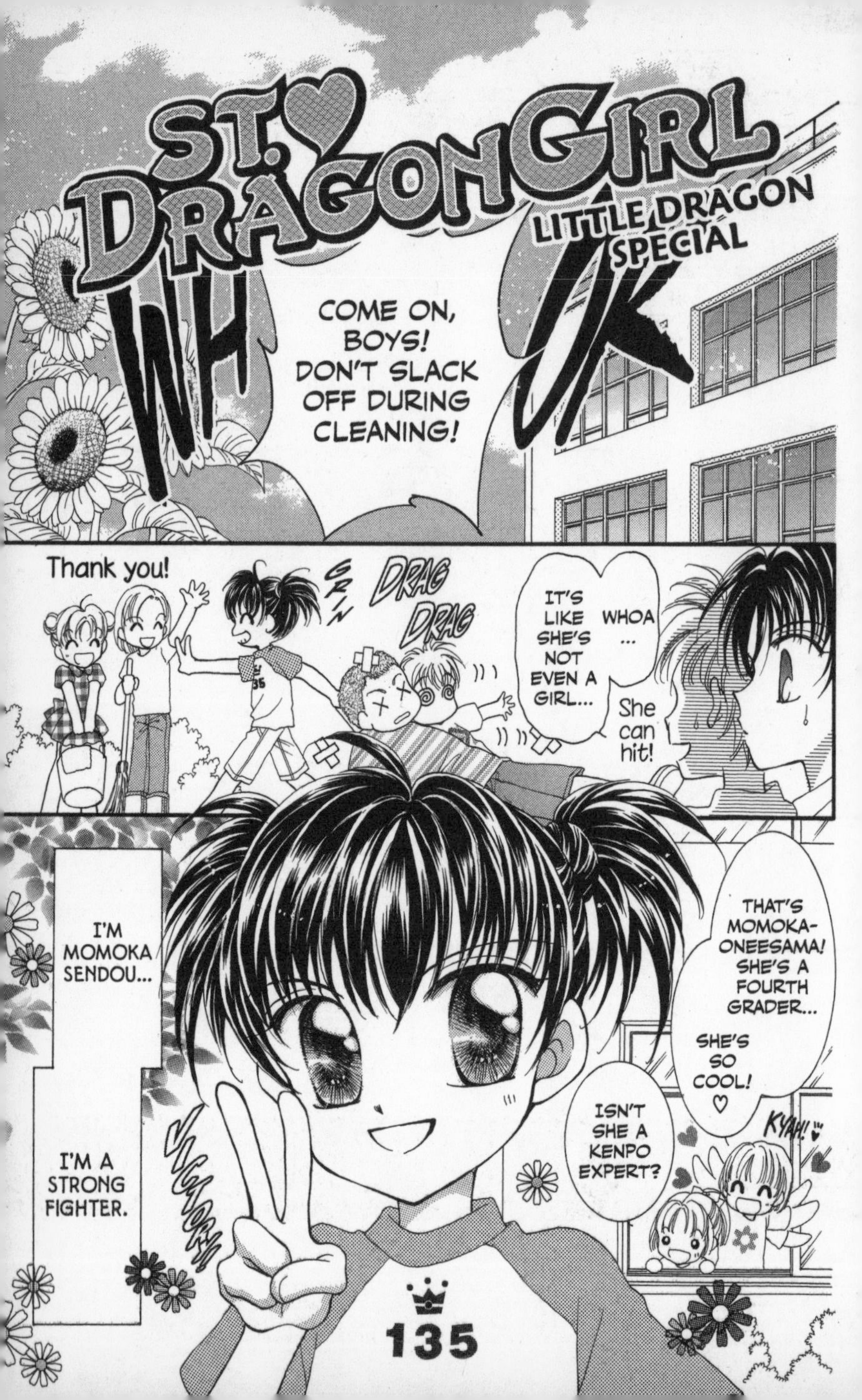
ST. ♥ DRAGON GIRL
LITTLE DRAGON SPECIAL
WHK
COME ON, BOYS! DON'T SLACK OFF DURING CLEANING!
WHOA...
IT'S LIKE SHE'S NOT EVEN A GIRL...
She can hit!
DRAG DRAG
GRIN
Thank you!
THAT'S MOMOKA-ONEESAMA! SHE'S A FOURTH GRADER...
SHE'S SO COOL! ♡
KYAH!
ISN'T SHE A KENPO EXPERT?
I'M MOMOKA SENDOU...
I'M A STRONG FIGHTER.

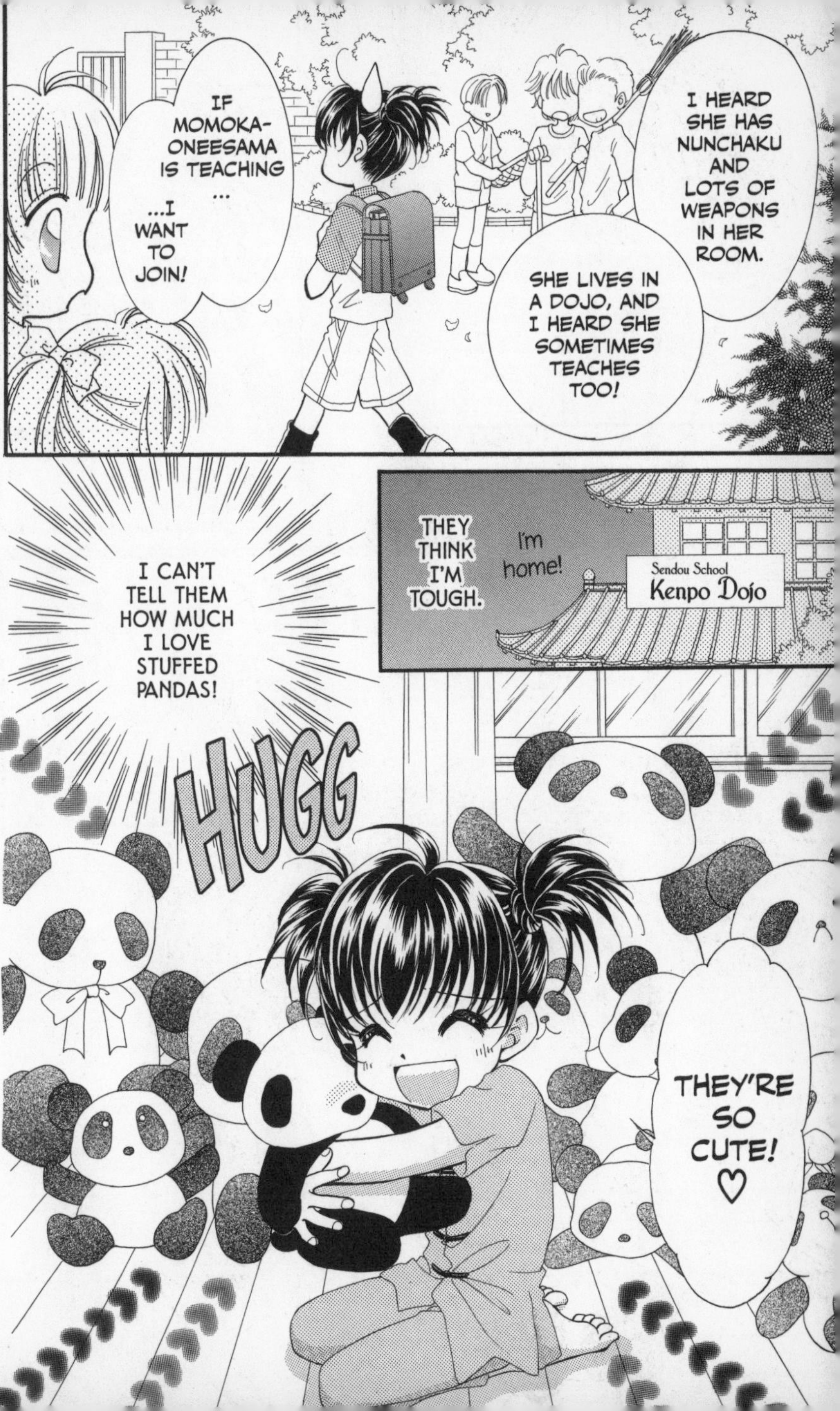
I HEARD SHE HAS NUNCHAKU AND LOTS OF WEAPONS IN HER ROOM.
SHE LIVES IN A DOJO, AND I HEARD SHE SOMETIMES TEACHES TOO!
IF MOMOKA-ONEESAMA IS TEACHING...
...I WANT TO JOIN!
Sendou School Kenpo Dojo
I'm home!
THEY THINK I'M TOUGH.
I CAN'T TELL THEM HOW MUCH I LOVE STUFFED PANDAS!
HUGG
THEY'RE SO CUTE! ♡

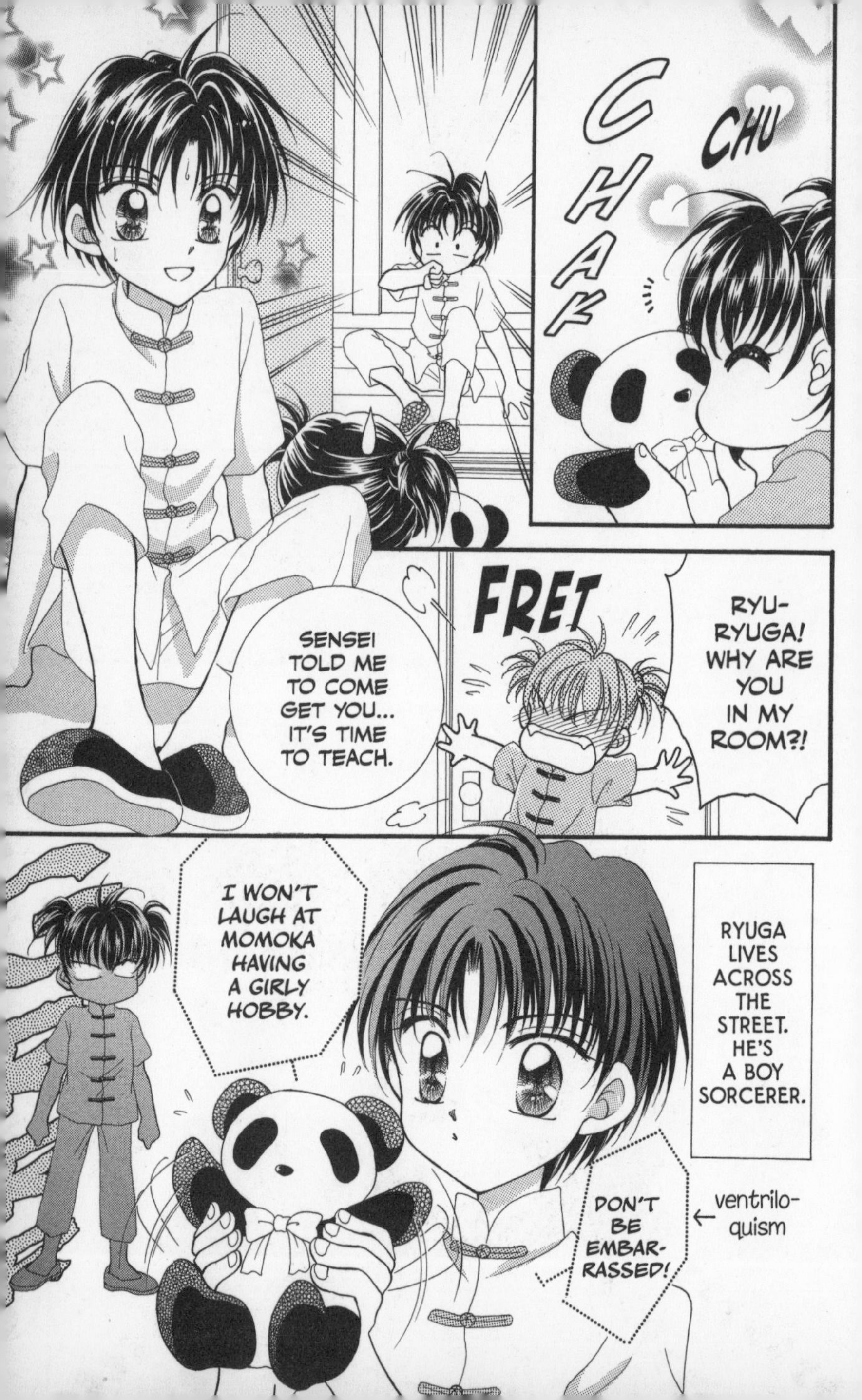
CHU
CHAK
RYU-RYUGA! WHY ARE YOU IN MY ROOM?!
FRET
SENSEI TOLD ME TO COME GET YOU... IT'S TIME TO TEACH.
RYUGA LIVES ACROSS THE STREET. HE'S A BOY SORCERER.
I WON'T LAUGH AT MOMOKA HAVING A GIRLY HOBBY.
ventrilo-quism
DON'T BE EMBAR-RASSED!

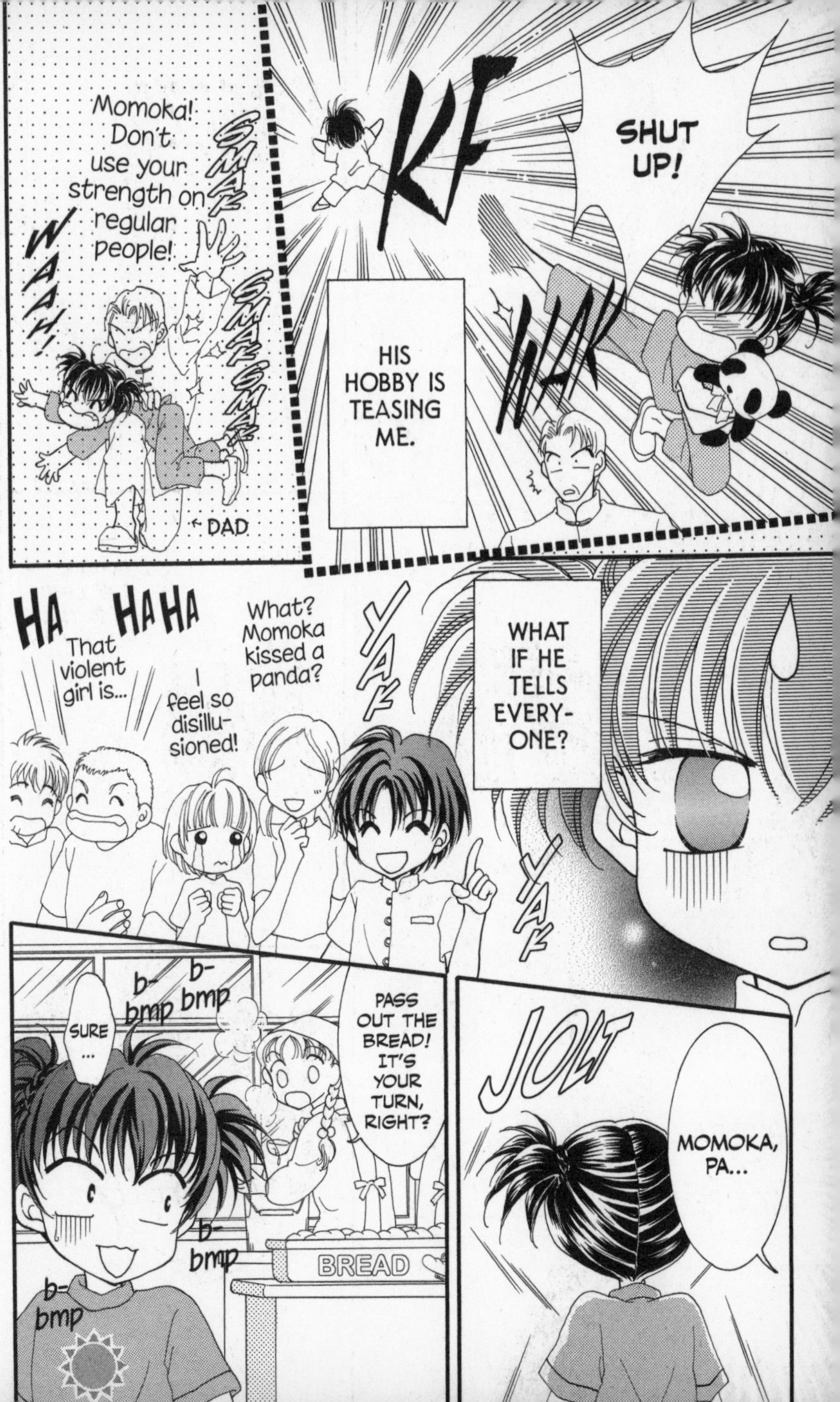
SHUT UP!
HIS HOBBY IS TEASING ME.
Momoka! Don't use your strength on regular people!
WAAH!
← DAD
WHAT IF HE TELLS EVERY-ONE?
YAK
YAK
What? Momoka kissed a panda?
I feel so disillu-sioned!
That violent girl is...
HA HAHA
JOLT
MOMOKA, PA...
PASS OUT THE BREAD! IT'S YOUR TURN, RIGHT?
SURE...
b-bmp
b-bmp
b-bmp
b-bmp
BREAD

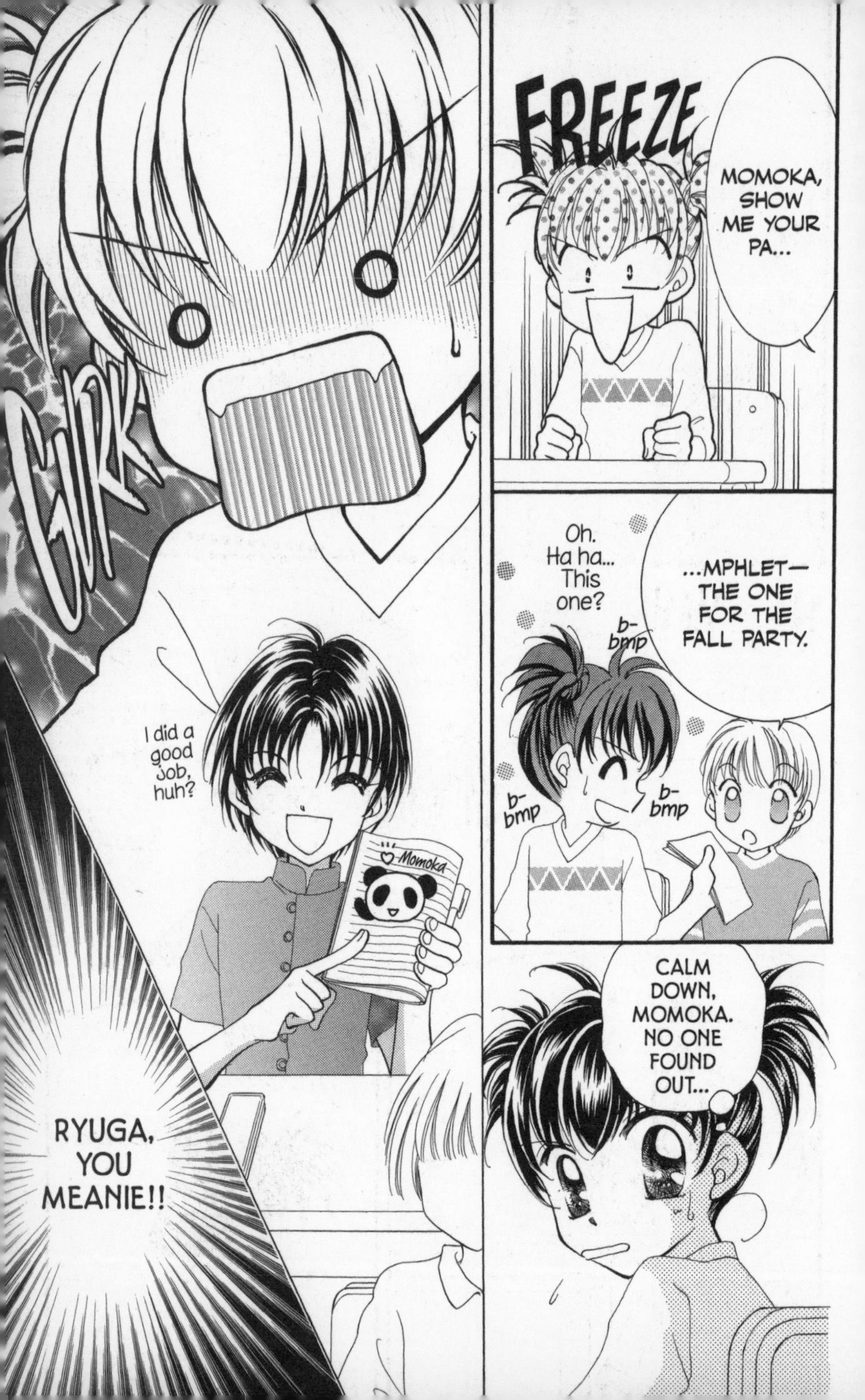
FREEZE
MOMOKA, SHOW ME YOUR PA...
...MPHLET— THE ONE FOR THE FALL PARTY.
Oh. Ha ha... This one?
b-bmp
b-bmp
b-bmp
CALM DOWN, MOMOKA. NO ONE FOUND OUT...
I did a good job, huh?
Momoka
RYUGA, YOU MEANIE!!

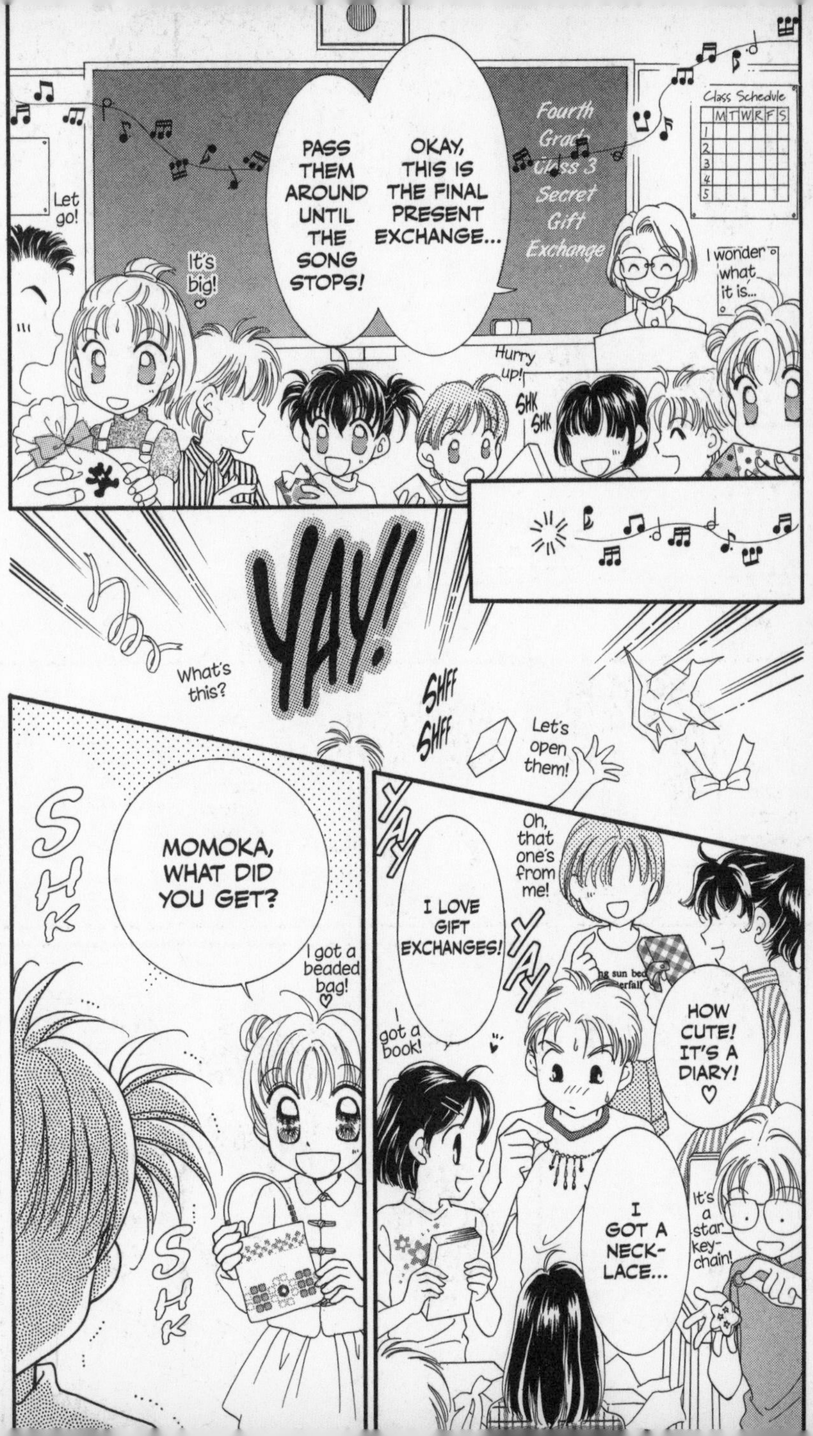
Class Schedule
M T W R F S
1 2 3 4 5
Fourth Grade Class 3 Secret Gift Exchange
I wonder what it is...
Hurry up!
SHK SHK
OKAY, THIS IS THE FINAL PRESENT EXCHANGE...
PASS THEM AROUND UNTIL THE SONG STOPS!
It's big!
Let go!
YAY!
SHFF SHFF
Let's open them!
What's this?
Oh, that one's from me!
HOW CUTE! IT'S A DIARY!
It's a star key-chain!
I GOT A NECKLACE...
YAY
YAY
I LOVE GIFT EXCHANGES!
I got a book!
MOMOKA, WHAT DID YOU GET?
I got a beaded bag!
SHK
SHK

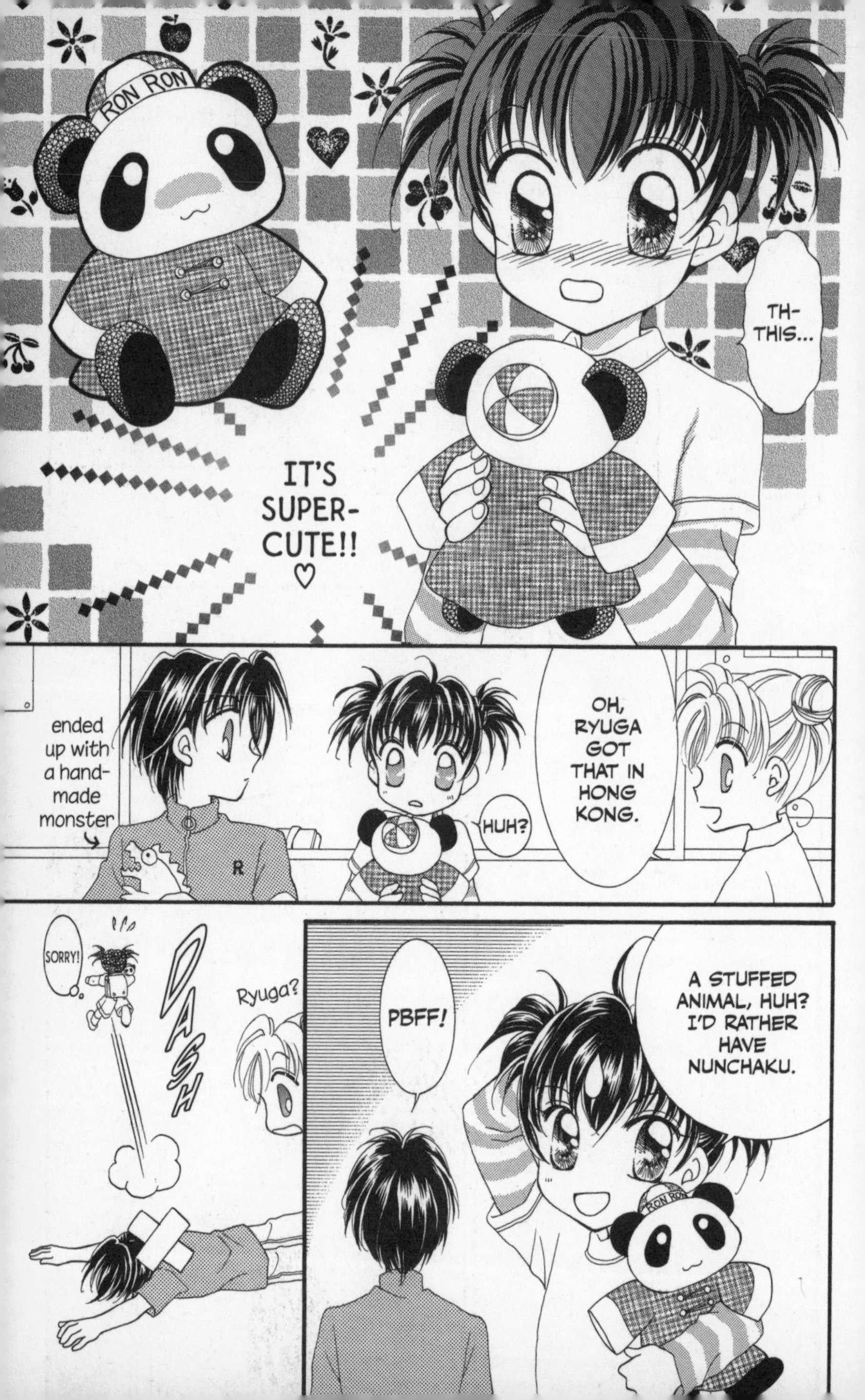
RON RON
TH-THIS...
IT'S SUPER-CUTE!! ♡
OH, RYUGA GOT THAT IN HONG KONG.
HUH?
ended up with a hand-made monster
A STUFFED ANIMAL, HUH? I'D RATHER HAVE NUNCHAKU.
PBFF!
Ryuga?
DASH
SORRY!

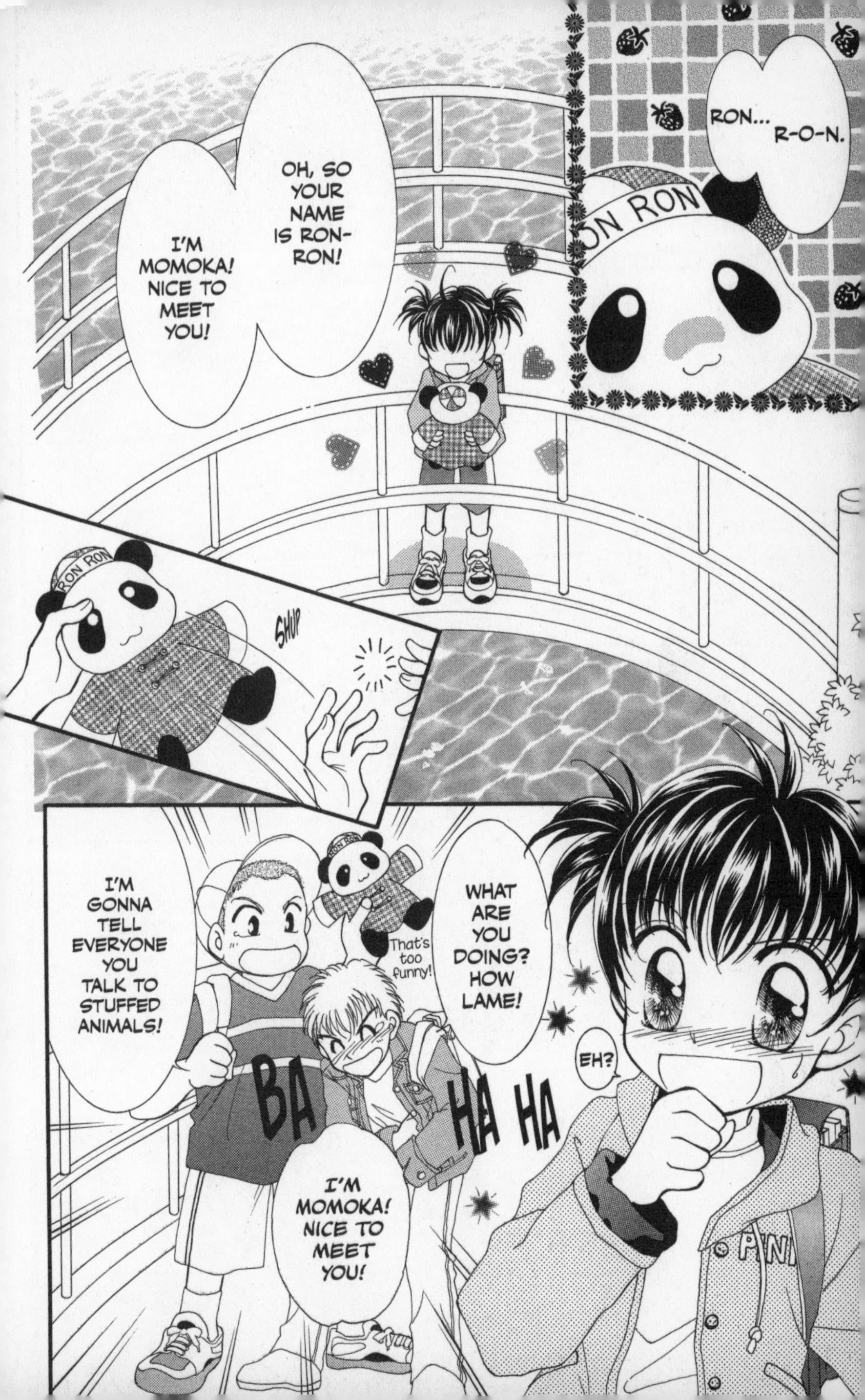
RON... R-O-N.
OH, SO YOUR NAME IS RON-RON!
I'M MOMOKA! NICE TO MEET YOU!
RON RON
SHUP
EH?
WHAT ARE YOU DOING? HOW LAME!
That's too funny!
I'M GONNA TELL EVERYONE YOU TALK TO STUFFED ANIMALS!
BA HA HA
I'M MOMOKA! NICE TO MEET YOU!

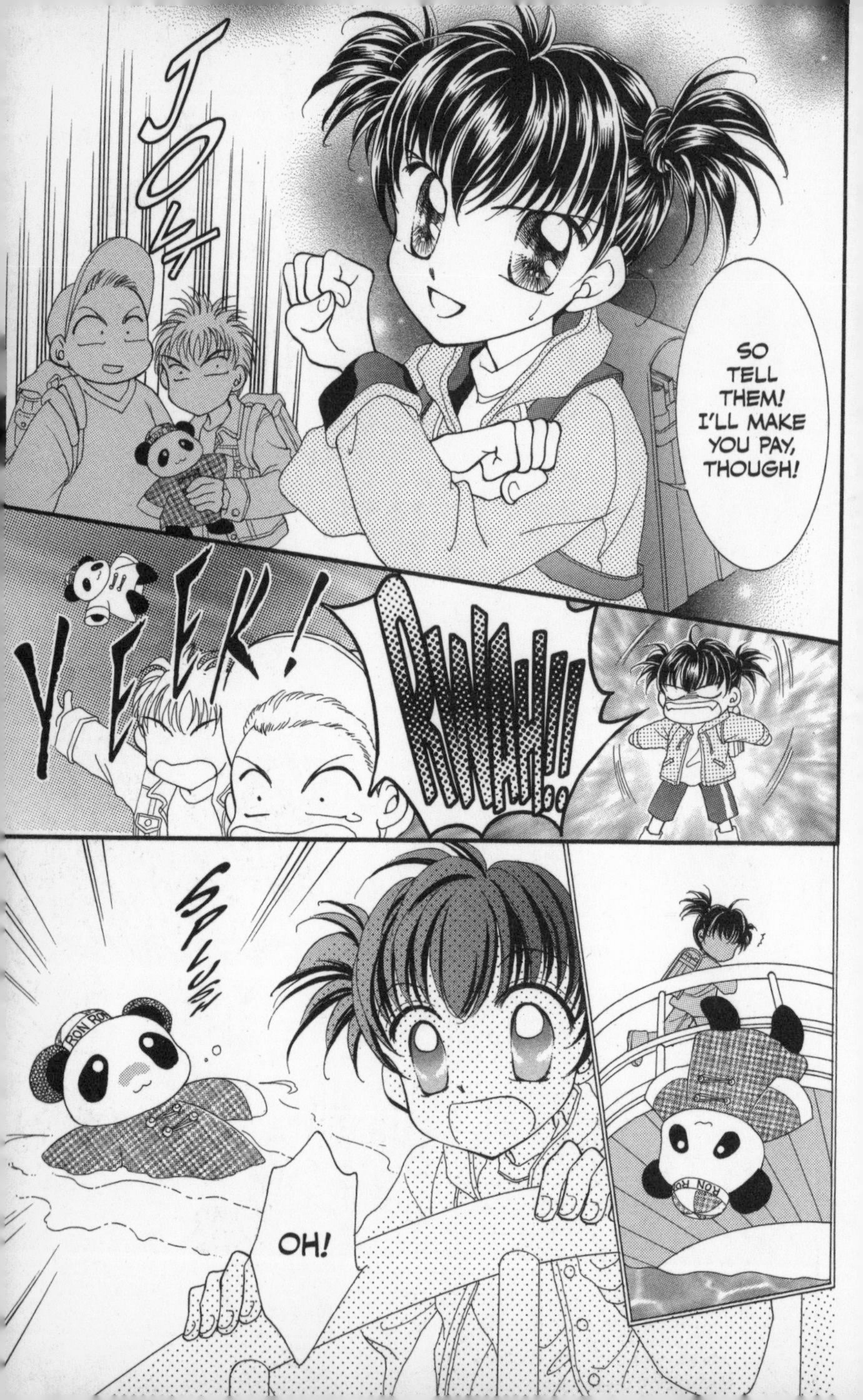
SO TELL THEM! I'LL MAKE YOU PAY, THOUGH!
JOLT
YEEK!
OH!

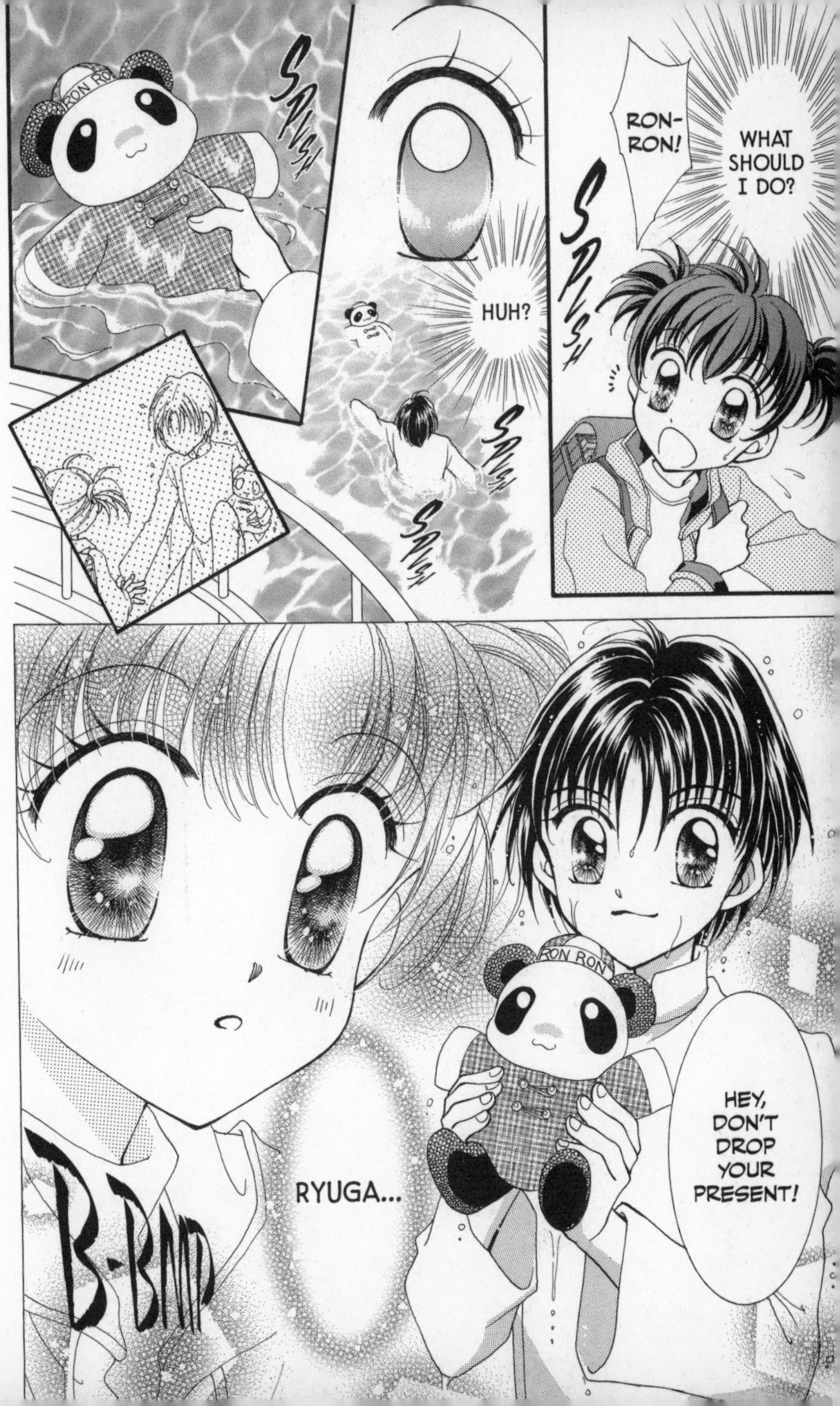
WHAT SHOULD I DO?
RON-RON!
SPLISH
HUH?
SPLISH
SPLISH
SPLISH
HEY, DON'T DROP YOUR PRESENT!
RYUGA...
B-BMP

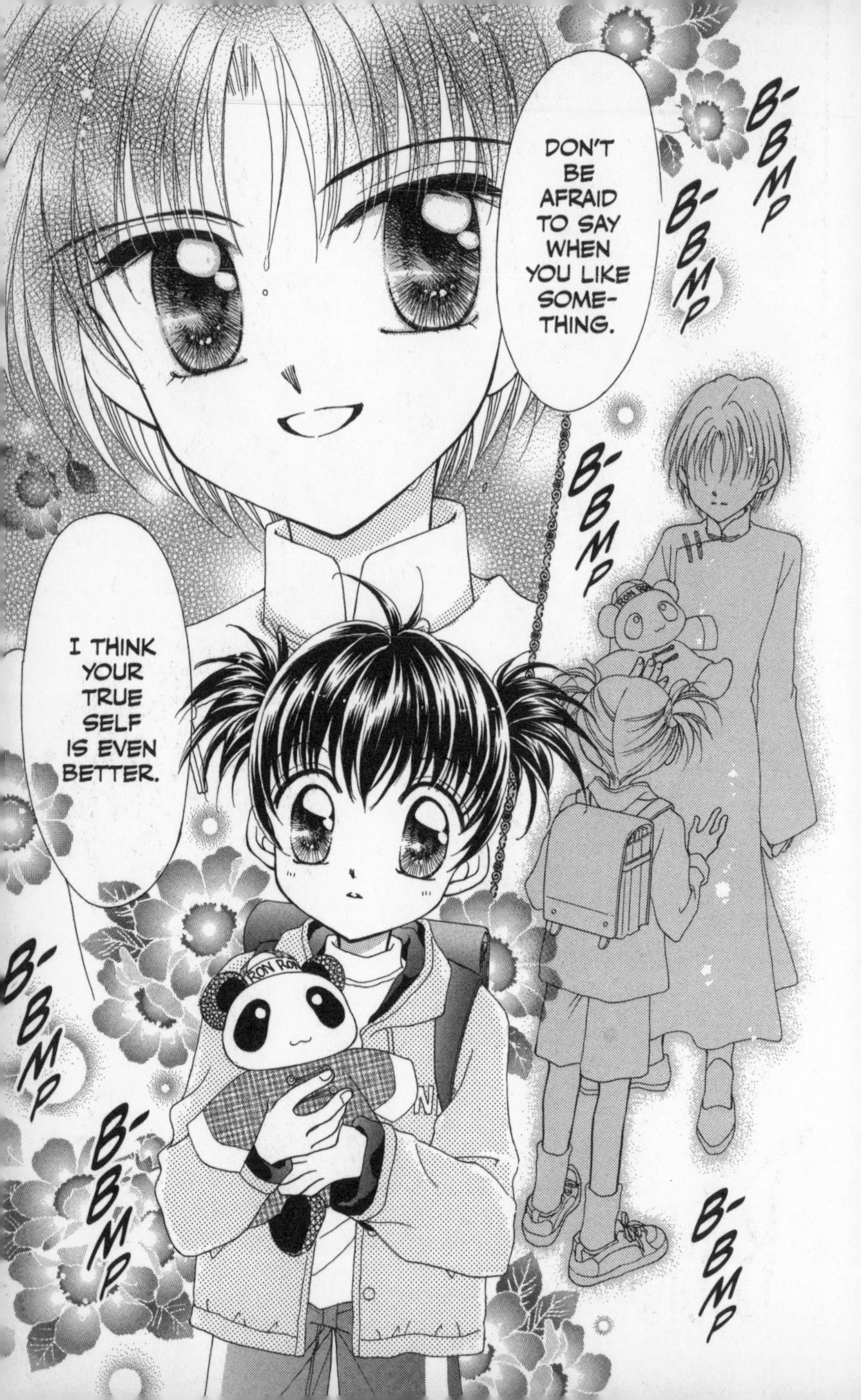
B-BMP
B-BMP
DON'T BE AFRAID TO SAY WHEN YOU LIKE SOME-THING.
B-BMP
I THINK YOUR TRUE SELF IS EVEN BETTER.
B-BMP
B-BMP
B-BMP

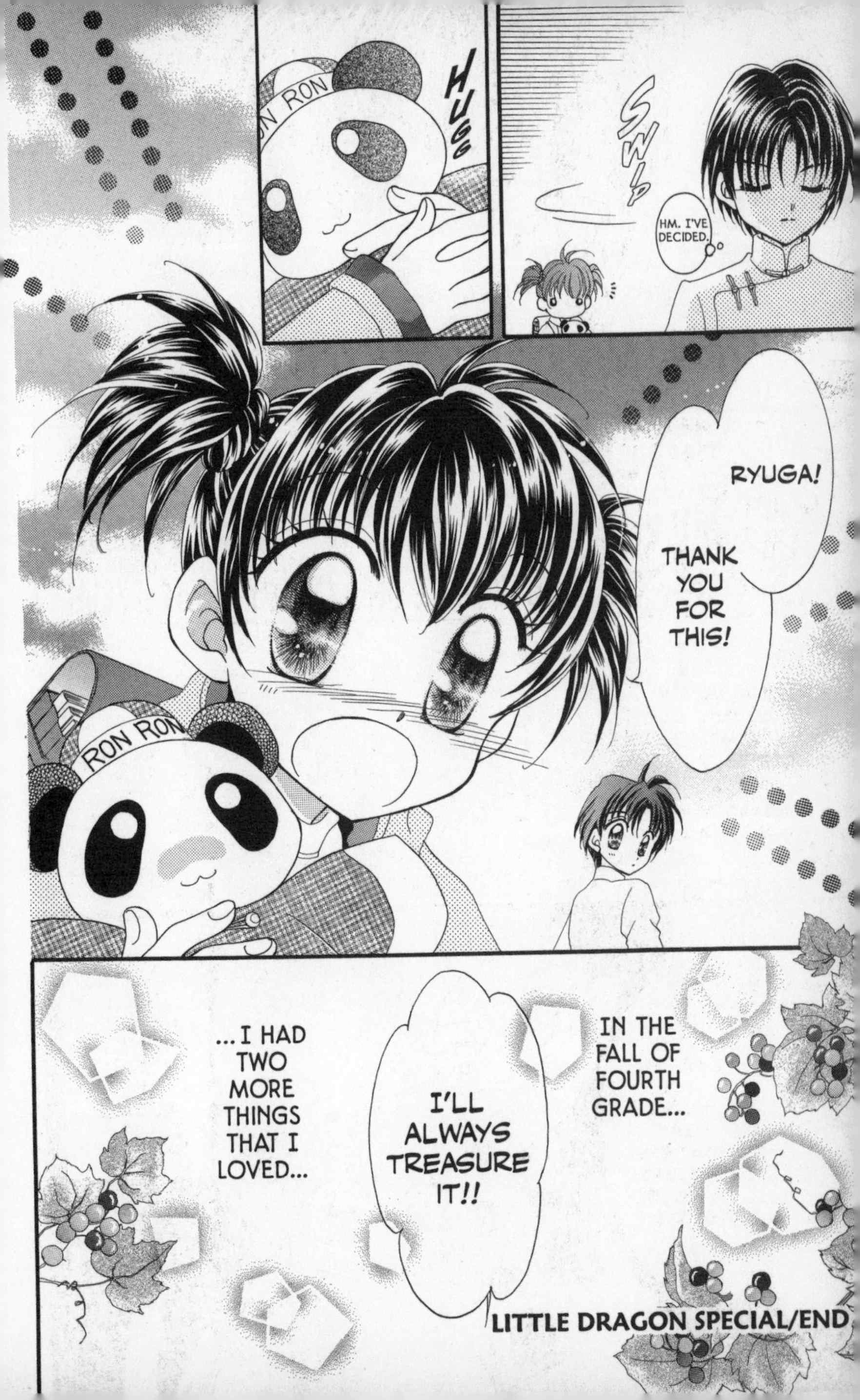
SWIP
HM. I'VE DECIDED.
HUGG
RON RON
RYUGA!
THANK YOU FOR THIS!
RON RON
IN THE FALL OF FOURTH GRADE...
I'LL ALWAYS TREASURE IT!!
...I HAD TWO MORE THINGS THAT I LOVED...
LITTLE DRAGON SPECIAL/END

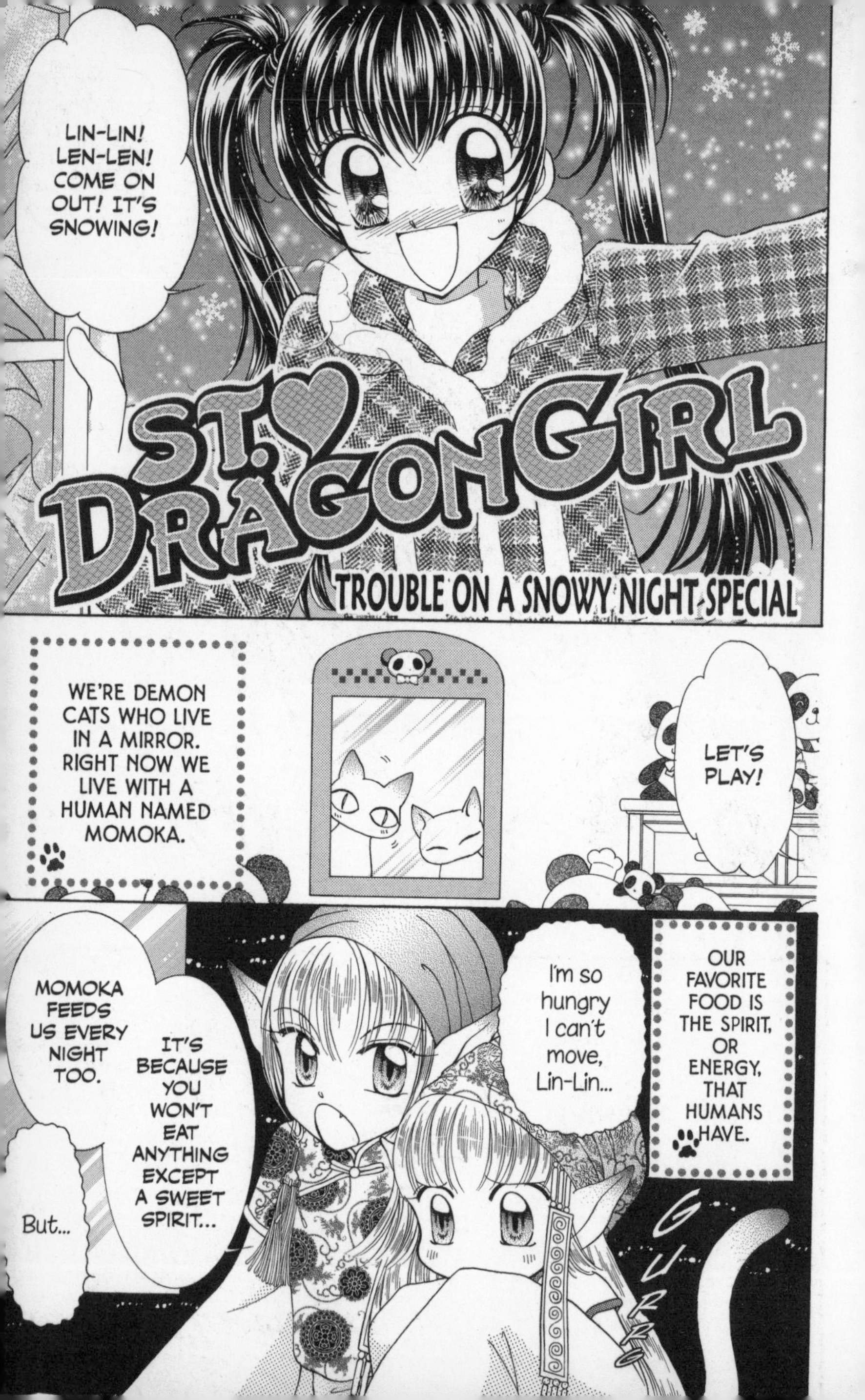
LIN-LIN! LEN-LEN! COME ON OUT! IT'S SNOWING!
ST. DRAGON GIRL
TROUBLE ON A SNOWY NIGHT SPECIAL
LET'S PLAY!
WE'RE DEMON CATS WHO LIVE IN A MIRROR. RIGHT NOW WE LIVE WITH A HUMAN NAMED MOMOKA.
OUR FAVORITE FOOD IS THE SPIRIT, OR ENERGY, THAT HUMANS HAVE.
I'm so hungry I can't move, Lin-Lin...
IT'S BECAUSE YOU WON'T EAT ANYTHING EXCEPT A SWEET SPIRIT...
MOMOKA FEEDS US EVERY NIGHT TOO.
But...
GURR

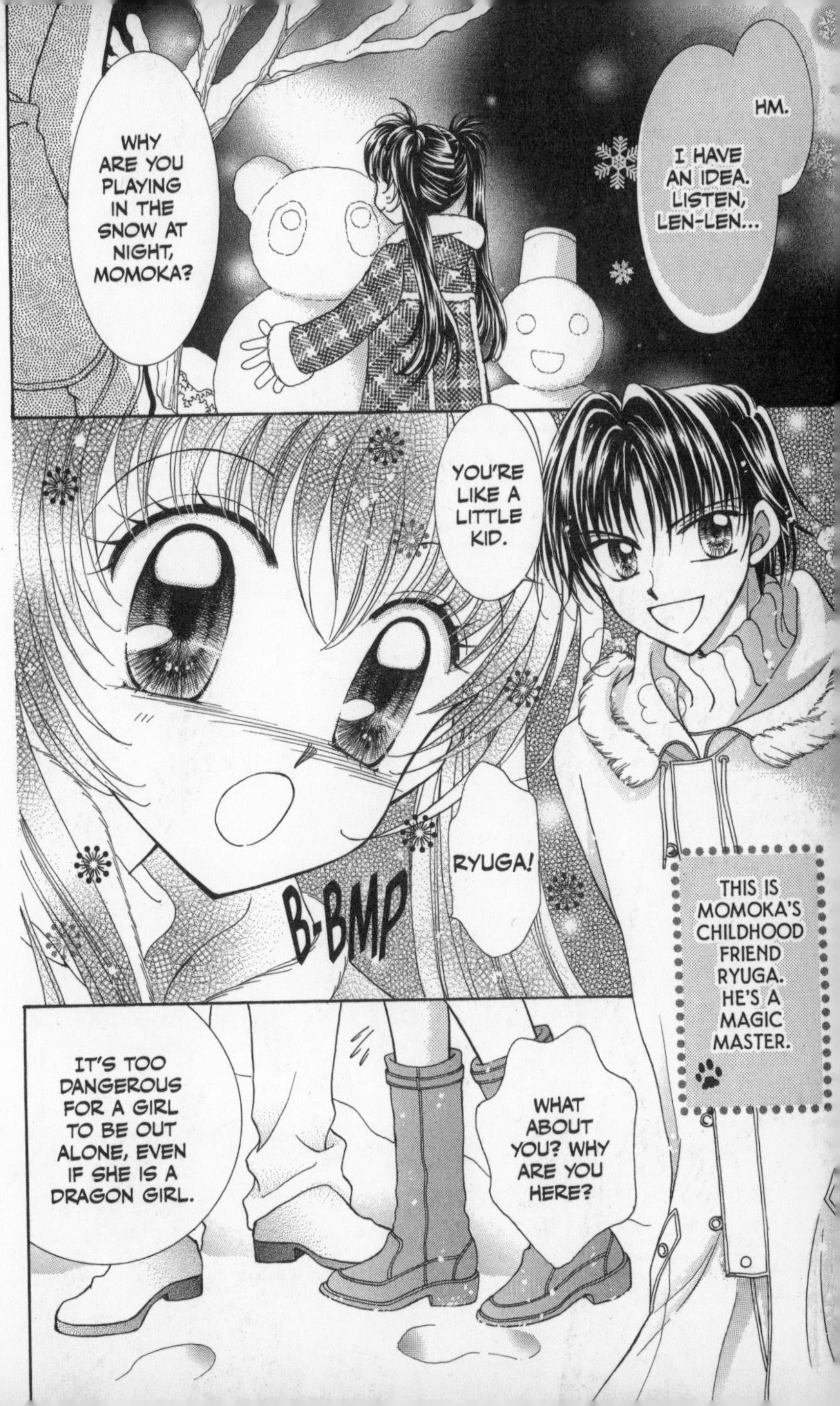
HM.
I HAVE AN IDEA. LISTEN, LEN-LEN...
WHY ARE YOU PLAYING IN THE SNOW AT NIGHT, MOMOKA?
YOU'RE LIKE A LITTLE KID.
THIS IS MOMOKA'S CHILDHOOD FRIEND RYUGA. HE'S A MAGIC MASTER.
RYUGA!
B-BMP
WHAT ABOUT YOU? WHY ARE YOU HERE?
IT'S TOO DANGEROUS FOR A GIRL TO BE OUT ALONE, EVEN IF SHE IS A DRAGON GIRL.

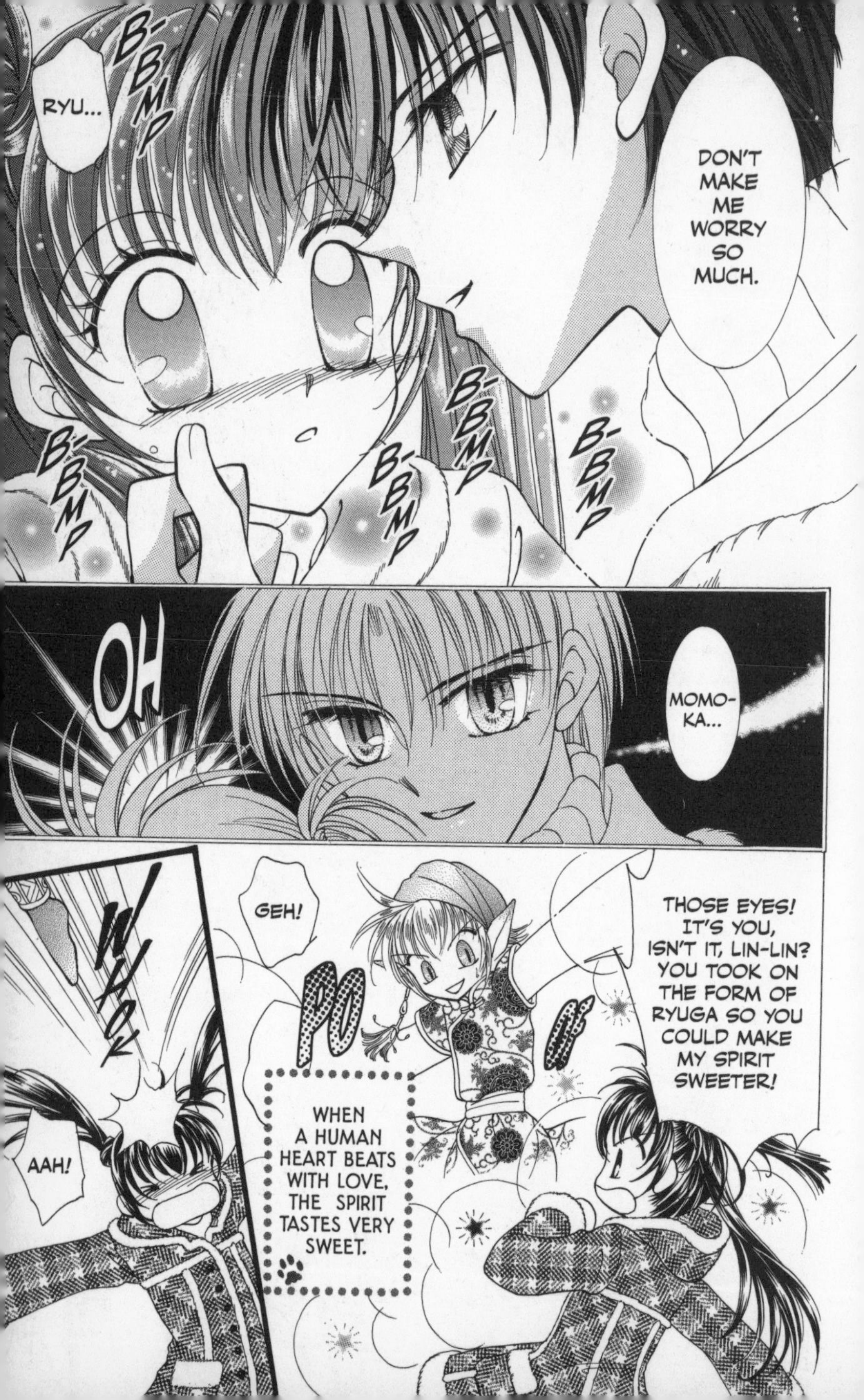
DON'T MAKE ME WORRY SO MUCH.
RYU...
B-BMP
B-BMP
B-BMP
B-BMP
B-BMP
MOMO-KA...
OH
THOSE EYES! IT'S YOU, ISN'T IT, LIN-LIN? YOU TOOK ON THE FORM OF RYUGA SO YOU COULD MAKE MY SPIRIT SWEETER!
GEH!
PO
WHEN A HUMAN HEART BEATS WITH LOVE, THE SPIRIT TASTES VERY SWEET.
WHACK
AAH!

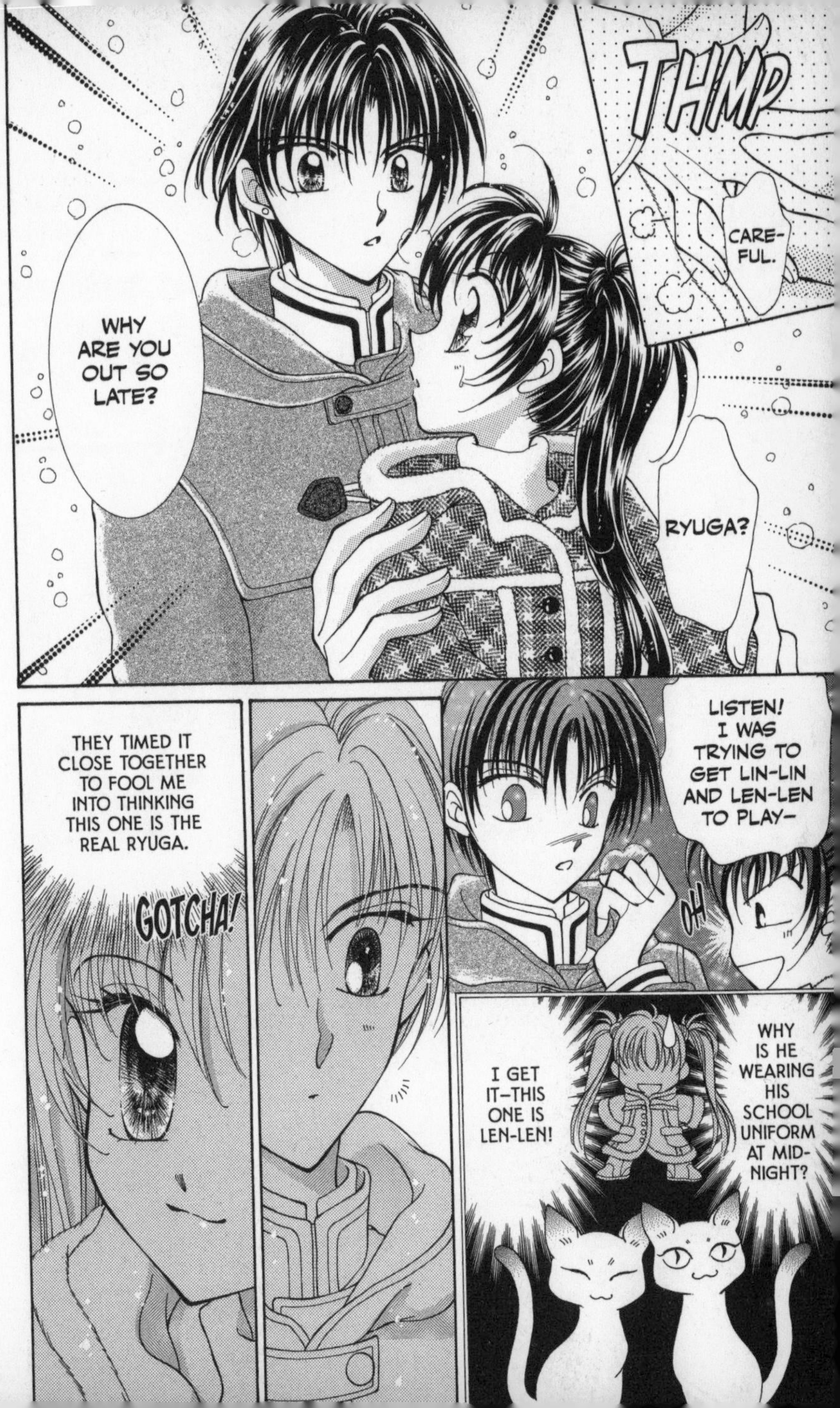
THMP
CARE-FUL.
RYUGA?
WHY ARE YOU OUT SO LATE?
LISTEN! I WAS TRYING TO GET LIN-LIN AND LEN-LEN TO PLAY—
OH
WHY IS HE WEARING HIS SCHOOL UNIFORM AT MID-NIGHT?
I GET IT—THIS ONE IS LEN-LEN!
THEY TIMED IT CLOSE TOGETHER TO FOOL ME INTO THINKING THIS ONE IS THE REAL RYUGA.
GOTCHA!

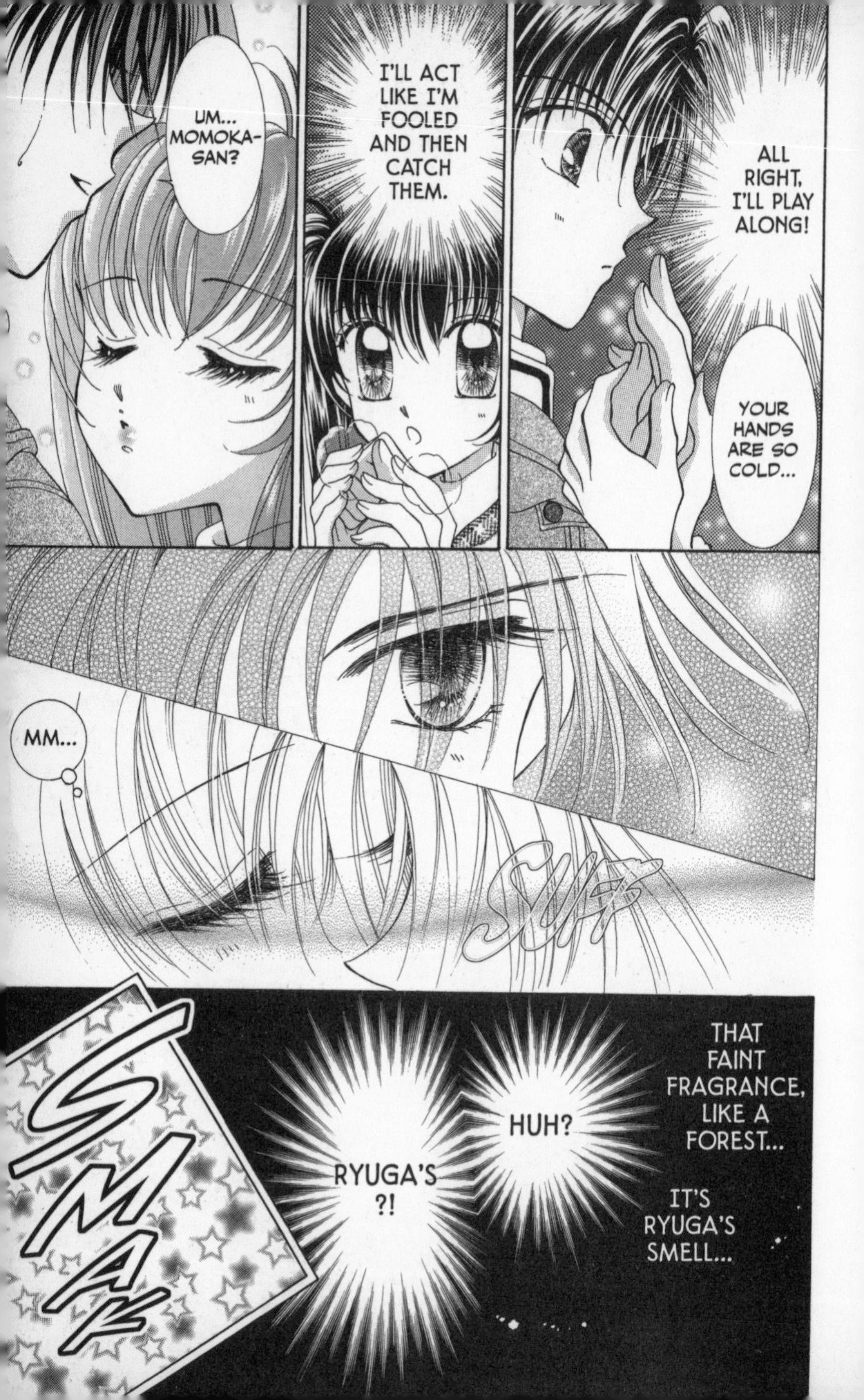
ALL RIGHT, I'LL PLAY ALONG!
YOUR HANDS ARE SO COLD...
I'LL ACT LIKE I'M FOOLED AND THEN CATCH THEM.
UM... MOMOKA-SAN?
MM...
SNIFF
THAT FAINT FRAGRANCE, LIKE A FOREST...
IT'S RYUGA'S SMELL...
HUH?
RYUGA'S ?!

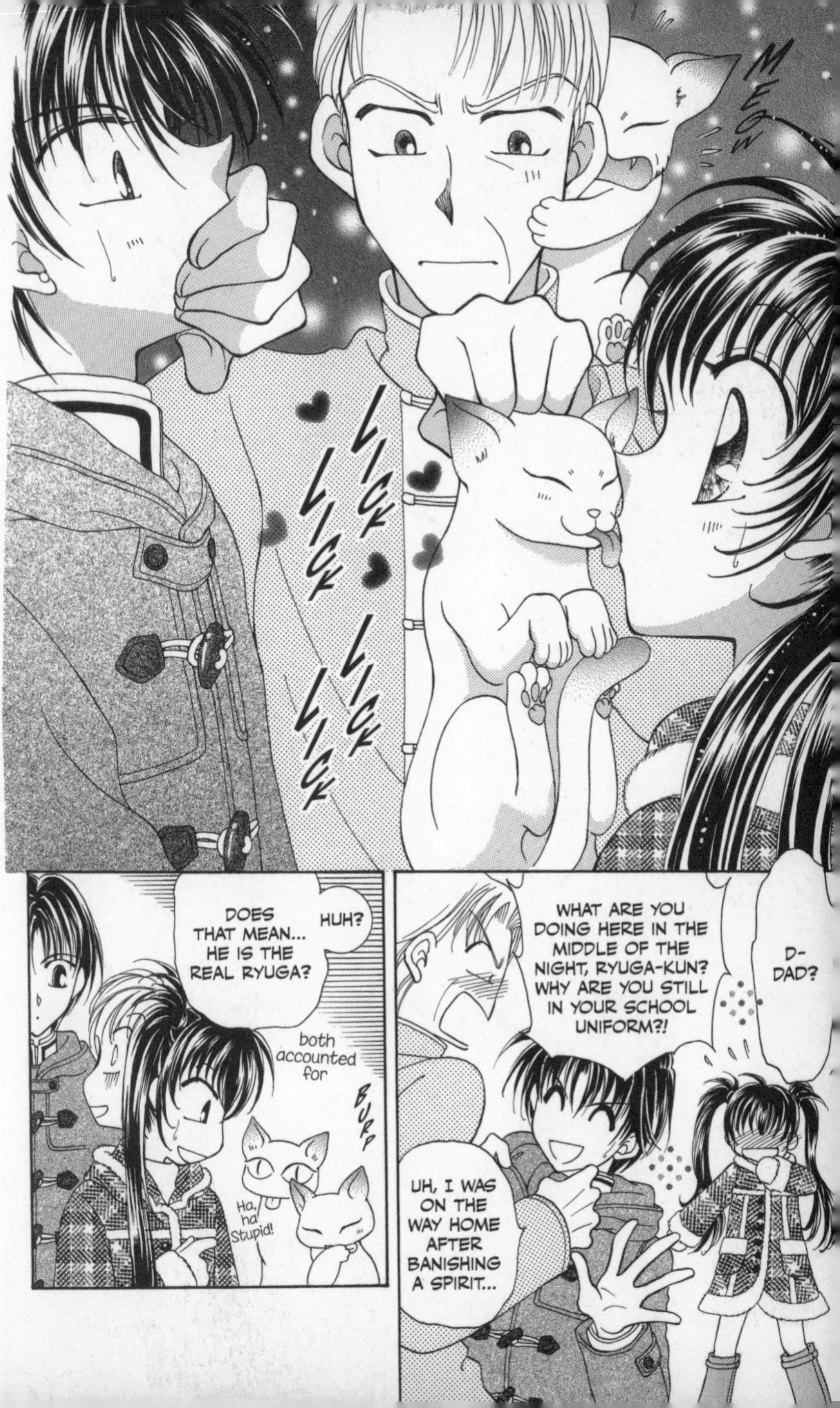
MEOW
LICK LICK LICK LICK LICK
D-DAD?
WHAT ARE YOU DOING HERE IN THE MIDDLE OF THE NIGHT, RYUGA-KUN? WHY ARE YOU STILL IN YOUR SCHOOL UNIFORM?!
UH, I WAS ON THE WAY HOME AFTER BANISHING A SPIRIT...
HUH?
DOES THAT MEAN... HE IS THE REAL RYUGA?
both accounted for
BURP
Ha, ha Stupid!

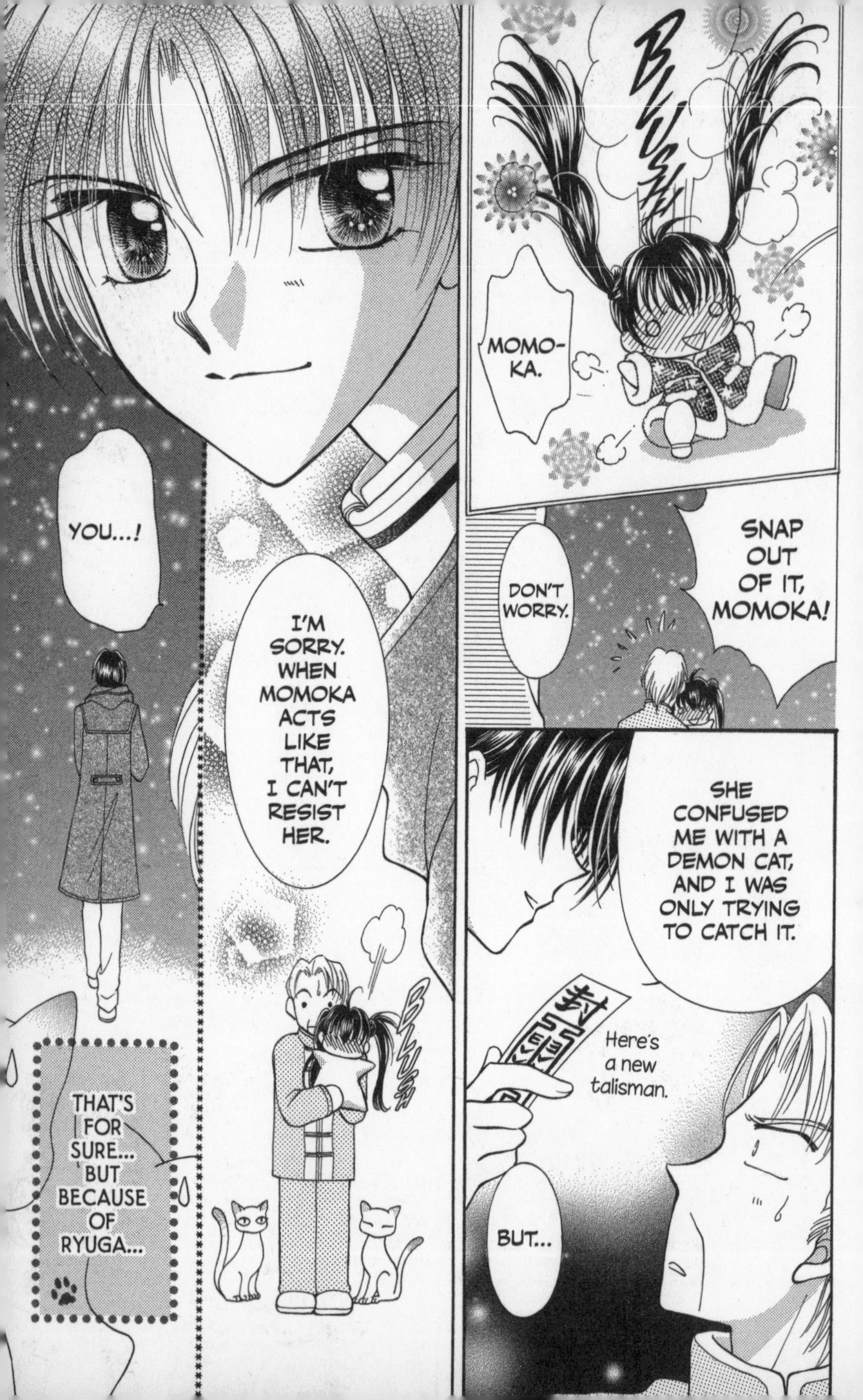
BWUSH!
MOMO-KA.
SNAP OUT OF IT, MOMOKA!
DON'T WORRY.
SHE CONFUSED ME WITH A DEMON CAT, AND I WAS ONLY TRYING TO CATCH IT.
Here's a new talisman.
BUT...
I'M SORRY. WHEN MOMOKA ACTS LIKE THAT, I CAN'T RESIST HER.
BWUSH
YOU...!
THAT'S FOR SURE... BUT BECAUSE OF RYUGA...

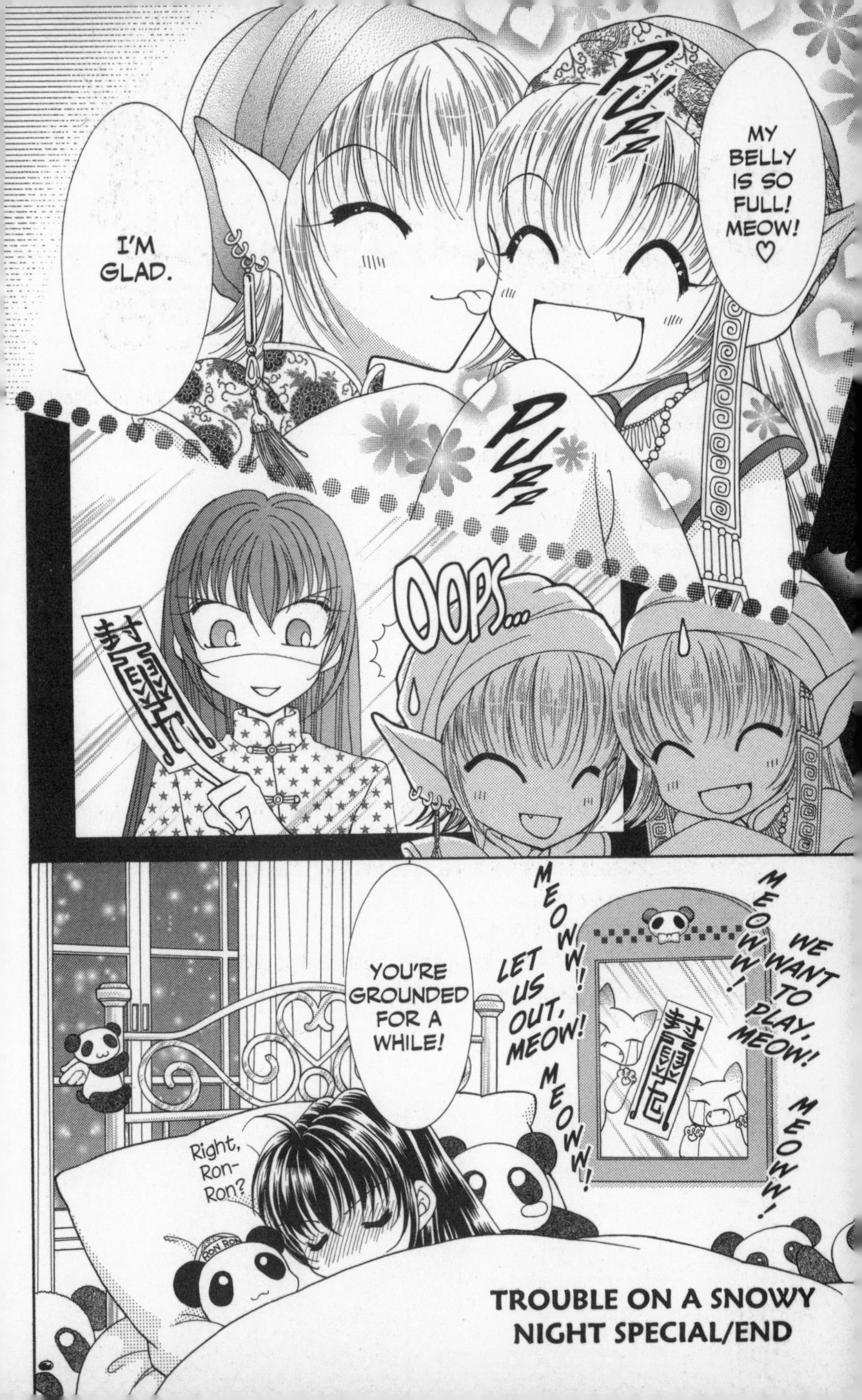
MY BELLY IS SO FULL! MEOW! ♡
PUFF
I'M GLAD.
PUFF
OOPS...
WE WANT TO PLAY, MEOW!
MEOWW!
MEOWW!
MEOWW!
LET US OUT, MEOW!
MEOWW!
YOU'RE GROUNDED FOR A WHILE!
Right, Ron-Ron?
RON RON

TROUBLE ON A SNOWY NIGHT SPECIAL/END

ST. DRAGON GIRL NOTES

HONORIFICS
In Japan, people are usually addressed by their name followed by a suffix. The suffix shows familiarity or respect, depending on the relationship.

Male (familiar): first or last name + kun
Female (familiar): first or last name + chan
Adult (polite): last name + san
Upperclassman (polite): last name + senpai
Teacher or professional: last name + sensei
Close friends or lovers: first name only, no suffix

TERMS
Oneechan means "older sister," but is also used to address a female who is older than the speaker.

Momoka teases Yuki by calling him "ghosty" names: Yuu-chan (from *yuurei*, or "ghost") and Reitarou (*rei* means "spirit").

When Yuki possesses Momoka, he uses the term *ore* to refer to himself. This pronoun is used by men.

Torii is a Shinto archway or gate.

Kyonshi, or *jiāngshī* in Chinese, means "reanimated corpse."

Ani-ue is a very respectful way of saying "older brother."

FAN ART SUBMISSIONS!

I'm looking for fan art to include in future volumes of the *St.♥ Dragon Girl* manga.
Please fill out the form on the next page and send it in with your fan art to:

> Nancy Thistlethwaite, Editor
> VIZ Media, LLC
> P.O. Box 77010
> San Francisco, CA 94107

Guidelines:
- All fan art will be presented in black and white, but you can send color art if you want.
- Submissions should be no bigger than 8 1/2" by 11".
- All submissions must have a completed release form (see next page) for consideration.

Please be sure to include the following with your fan art.

FAN ART RELEASE

In exchange for allowing the artwork I submitted with this Fan Art Release ("Fan Art") to be considered for inclusion in the *St. ♥ Dragon Girl* manga series and/or other publications, I hereby irrevocably authorize and grant a non-exclusive, transferable, worldwide, perpetual license to VIZ Media, LLC and others authorized by it, to use, copy, print, publicly display, broadcast and edit the Fan Art and my name, in whole or in part, with or without my name identification, in any and all media now known or hereinafter developed without time, territory or other restrictions and to refrain from doing any or all of the foregoing. I release them all from any claims, liability, costs, losses or damages of any kind in connection therewith, including but not limited to copyright infringement, right of publicity/privacy, blurring or optical distortion. I agree that I have no right to approve any use of the Fan Art or my name as licensed above or the content thereof.

I represent and warrant that I am of the age of majority in my state or province of residence (or, if not, that a parent or legal guardian will sign on my behalf) and that this release does not in any way conflict with any existing commitments on my part. I represent that no other person, firm or entity claiming or deriving rights through me is entitled to grant the rights in the Fan Art I've granted to you (or granted by my parent or legal guardian on my behalf) and that I have the right to license it as outlined herein. I further represent and warrant that I have the full right to enter into this agreement without violating the legal or equitable rights of any third party and that no payments shall be due to me or any third party in conjunction with the use of the Fan Art or my name as outlined herein.

ACCEPTED AND AGREED TO:

Print Name: _____

Signature: _____

(Sign or have your Parent or Legal Guardian do so, if you are a minor)

Address: _____

Date: _____

Wow! This is the tenth manga volume I've had published! (cry) I'd like to take this opportunity to thank the publishers, all the readers, and my friends and family. Thanks for always helping and supporting me. I'm going to continue doing my best, so please continue to take care of me in the future! ♥

—Natsumi Matsumoto

Natsumi Matsumoto debuted with the manga *Guuzen Janai Yo!* (No Coincidence!) in *Ribon Original* magazine. *St. ♥ Dragon Girl* was such a hit that it spawned a sequel, *St. ♥ Dragon Girl Miracle*. Her other series include *Angel Time* and *Alice kara Magic*. In her free time, Natsumi studies Chinese and practices tai chi. She also likes visiting aquariums and collecting the toy prizes that come with snack food in Japan.

St.♥ Dragon Girl
Vol. 3
The Shojo Beat Manga Edition

STORY AND ART BY | **Natsumi Matsumoto**

English Adaptation | **Heidi Vivolo**
Translation | **Andria Cheng**
Touch-up Art & Lettering | **Gia Cam Luc**
Design | **Fawn Lau**
Editor | **Nancy Thistlethwaite**

Editor in Chief, Books | **Alvin Lu**
Editor in Chief, Magazines | **Marc Weidenbaum**
VP, Publishing Licensing | **Rika Inouye**
VP, Sales & Product Marketing | **Gonzalo Ferreyra**
VP, Creative | **Linda Espinosa**
Publisher | **Hyoe Narita**

Printed in Canada

Published by VIZ Media, LLC
P.O. Box 77010
San Francisco, CA 94107

Shojo Beat Manga Edition
10 9 8 7 6 5 4 3 2 1
First printing, June 2009

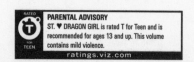

store.viz.com

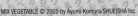

I·O·N

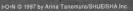

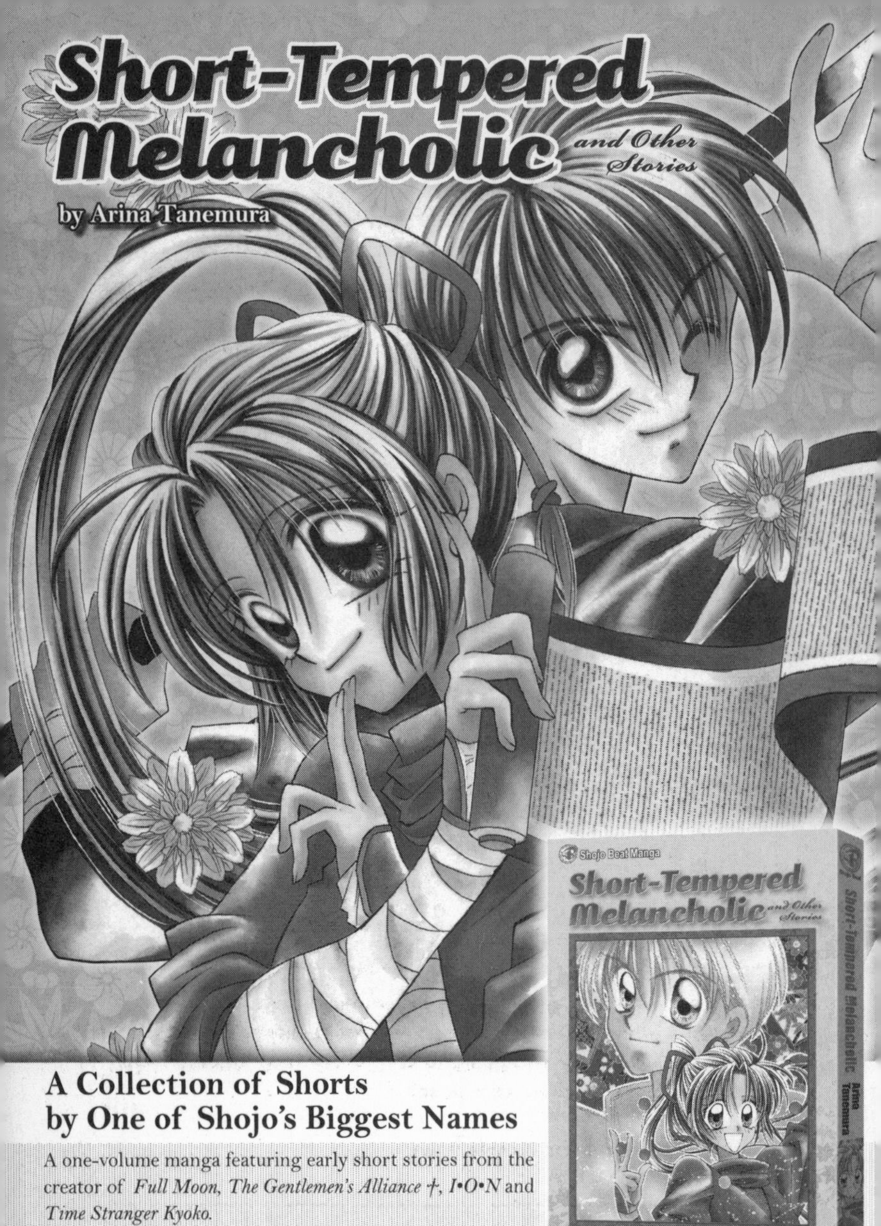
Short-Tempered Melancholic
and Other Stories
by Arina Tanemura
Shojo Beat Manga
Short-Tempered Melancholic and Other Stories
Short-Tempered Melancholic
Arina Tanemura
Story & Art by
Arina Tanemura
VIZ

Tell us what you think about Shojo Beat Manga!

W9-AFG-438

Our survey is now available online. Go to:

shojobeat.com/mangasurvey

Help us make our product offerings better!